"The first textbook in more than ten years to offer a solidly linguistic account of second language acquisition, this book clearly asserts that the 'L' of 'SLA' is for 'Language' and it is an excellent alternative to textbooks that increasingly focus less on language and more on nonlinguistic variables. Every chapter ends with a series of exercises that use authentic language and data from published articles. This book is a must-read for linguists interested in SLA and second language acquisition researchers interested in language."

Kathleen Bardovi-Harlig, Indiana University

"A welcome addition to the field of second language acquisition. It is a must read for students and scholars who want to understand generative approaches to SLA."   *Susan Gass*, Michigan State University

"Slabakova guides the reader systematically through a rich array of observations and hypotheses, leading up to her 'bottleneck hypothesis': a proposal about where learning difficulty lies for second language learners. This thought-provoking overview will be required reading for anyone seriously interested in understanding the complex business of how people learn second languages."   *Roger Hawkins*, University of Essex

"An up-to-date, lively and accessible account of the generative approach to second language acquisition research. Readers across the field will find it an extremely useful introduction to key theoretical ideas and current debates in generativist SLA, illustrated with discussion of an impressive range of empirical studies. Students will enjoy the regular thought-provoking questions and activities, as well as the links to classroom instruction."

Rosamond Mitchell, University of Southampton

"A thought-provoking perspective on generative linguistic approaches to second language acquisition, as well as an up-to-date overview of current issues and research. The main focus is on adult second language acquisition, placed in the broader context of linguistic theory, first language acquisition, and bilingualism. The book will be of considerable interest to researchers and students in fields such as second language acquisition, linguistics, and applied linguistics."   *Lydia White*, McGill University

"The time is right for an update of generative perspectives on second language acquisition and Slabakova's *Second Language Acquisition* does the trick. In this book, the author brings together linguistic and psycholinguistic (processing) aspects of language acquisition in a variety of contexts, with eventual implications for and ties with instructional matters. The result is an up-to-date and readable text suitable for classroom and non-classroom use that will both inform and provoke. Highly recommended."

Bill VanPatten, Michigan State University

D1597383

OXFORD CORE LINGUISTICS
GENERAL EDITOR

David Adger

PUBLISHED

Core Syntax

David Adger

I-Language: An Introduction to Linguistics as Cognitive Science
Second edition

Daniela Isac and Charles Reiss

Second Language Acquisition

Roumyana Slabakova

IN PREPARATION

Theoretical Morphology

Edited by Karlos Arregui-Urbina and Andrew Nevins

Introduction to Acoustic Phonetics

Charles Reiss

Introduction to Linguistic Theory

Peter Svenonius

Second Language Acquisition

Roumyana Slabakova

OXFORD
UNIVERSITY PRESS

OXFORD
UNIVERSITY PRESS

Great Clarendon Street, Oxford, OX2 6DP,
United Kingdom

Oxford University Press is a department of the University of Oxford.
It furthers the University's objective of excellence in research, scholarship,
and education by publishing worldwide. Oxford is a registered trade mark of
Oxford University Press in the UK and in certain other countries

Published in the United States of America by Oxford University Press
198 Madison Avenue, New York, NY 10016, United States of America

British Library Cataloguing in Publication Data
Data available

Library of Congress Control Number: 2015948877

ISBN 978–0–19–968726–8 (hbk)
978–0–19–968727–5 (pbk)

Printed in Great Britain by
Clays Ltd, St Ives plc

Links to third party websites are provided by Oxford in good faith and
for information only. Oxford disclaims any responsibility for the materials
contained in any third party website referenced in this work.

To Lydia White

Contents

Preface

This book is going to ask a lot of important questions about how adults acquire second (L2) and subsequent (Ln) languages, and will provide answers arising from the last thirty years of generative second language acquisition research (GenSLA for short). In the quest to elucidate the cognitive processes involved in second language acquisition and how second language knowledge is represented in the mind, we will progress from the general to the more specific. The book is structured in three parts, where the names of the parts play with the three words: *second, language,* and *acquisition* in various combinations. The first part is called *Language*. It introduces key concepts and contemporary views of the language architecture. It also discusses the most important issue of linguistic theory from the point of L2 acquisition: how languages vary and how we can describe and explain language variation. Also in this part of the book, psycholinguistic and neurocognitive underpinnings of language processing add to the account of linguistic architecture to provide a comprehensive picture of language in the mind. As White (1989, 2003) has convinced us, a fundamental theory of what is being acquired, what Gregg (1989) calls a property theory of language, is essential for understanding the process of second language acquisition (SLA).

The second part is called *Language Acquisition*, addressing issues of a transition theory (Gregg 1989, 2003), namely, how do language learners move from one state of (incomplete) knowledge to another, and eventually to complete knowledge of the linguistic system? This part of the book situates SLA in the big picture of language acquisition in general and demonstrates how comparisons between the different language acquisition contexts and conditions (first language (L1) acquisition, the acquisition of two first languages (2L1), child L2 acquisition, adult L2 acquisition, heritage language acquisition, and language attrition) are relevant to understanding SLA. All acquisition conditions will be treated from the perspective of two seminal issues, which are the main focus of this book: the Critical Period Hypothesis and the importance of linguistic input for language acquisition. The position I will defend in the book is that continued high-quality comprehensible linguistic input emerges as the indispensable condition for successful language acquisition, overriding potential critical periods (at least in some modules of the grammar).

The third and main part of the book is called *Second Language Acquisition*, and it examines the broad topic of L2 acquisition, focusing predominantly on adult L2 acquisition. It communicates the findings of the generative approach with respect to the modular properties of language that have to be acquired: functional morphology, syntax, the mental lexicon, the interface of morphosyntax and meaning, discourse and pragmatic properties, and language processing. Each chapter comprises recent discoveries obtained through behavioral, psycholinguistic, and neurolinguistic measures. The key research techniques for obtaining such measures (for example, judgment tests, self-paced reading, eye tracking, event-related brain potentials, etc.) are introduced. The themes of critical periods and the seminal importance of linguistic input continue to be developed throughout the third part, as well. This part culminates with a chapter on language teaching and the implications of the generative research findings for the language classroom.

Throughout the book, I have tried to make explicit the teaching relevance of the findings, and you will find these thoughts specially marked in their own boxes. Where appropriate, I have also tried to foster active reading by asking the readers to answer some questions related to the material, before reading further. These are of course not obligatory, and I have not provided answers to them, but I do hope you will find them fun to do, and helpful. In the glossary, you will find definitions of the most important terms that are introduced.

Who is this book for? It is intended for students who have already been exposed to linguistic analysis, having taken courses such as an introduction to linguistics, syntax, and phonology. They will typically be advanced undergraduate students or graduate students in linguistics, modern languages, psychology, cognitive science, computer science, and education departments or programs, who are interested in second language acquisition. Although I introduce the main concepts and ideas that I discuss, space considerations prevent me from doing so at great length. Thus, the reader who is familiar with generative linguistics concepts will have an easier time following and learning. However, everyone who is interested in language and language acquisition will benefit from the book, particularly if you decide that you do not have to understand every last detail of the analyses, but get the gist and the main ideas of the chapters. The exercises after each chapter are fairly open-ended, apply the main concepts to new material or data, and aim to make you think like a linguist doing SLA research.

Finally, I would like to express my deepest gratitude to several groups of people. First, to my family, the rock of my life, a constant source of love and pride and joy. Second, to my students through the years, who have been persuaded by generative SLA ideas, but have also asked tough questions and thus have pushed the boundaries of scientific inquiry. Third, to my wonderful colleagues in the field of SLA, too numerous to mention but certainly hugely influential on my thinking, every one of them. Special thanks go to Silvina Montrul, Sharon Unsworth, Heather Marsden, Terje Lohndal and an anonymous reviewer for reading and commenting on the manuscript. Their comments improved it significantly. All remaining errors are mine alone. I do hope that the views expressed here stimulate constructive further inquiries in the cognitive processes of second language acquisition.

List of abbreviations

2L1	simultaneous acquisition of two languages (i.e., two first languages)
A-P	articulatory-perceptual
ANOVA	analysis of variance
AoA	age of arrival, age of acquisition
AP	adjective phrase
BIA+	Bilingual Interactive Activation Plus
BSM	Bilingual Syntax Measure
C-I	conceptual-intentional
cl	classifier
cL2, cL2A	child second language (acquisition)
CP	complementizer phrase
CPH	Critical Period Hypothesis
EPP	External Projection Principle
ERP	event-related brain potential
ESL	English as a second language
fMRI	functional Magnetic Resonance Imaging
FTFA	Full Transfer Full Access hypothesis
GenSLA	generative second language acquisition
GJT	grammaticality judgment task
HAS	high-amplitude sucking paradigm
IP	inflectional phrase
JSL	Japanese as a second language
L1, L2, Ln	first language, second language, n-th language
L2A	second language acquisition
LI	lexical item

LoR	length of residence
MLU	mean length of utterance
MSIH	Missing Surface Inflection Hypothesis
MT	Minimal Trees hypothesis
NP	noun phrase
NS	nuclear stress
NSP	Null Subject Parameter
P&P	Principles and Parameters
perf	perfective
PP	preposition phrase
POS	Poverty of the Stimulus
PTH	Prosodic Transfer Hypothesis
PPh	phonological phrase
PWd	prosodic word
S	sentence (the top node of a clause, later replaced with the term CP)
SD	standard deviation
SLA	second language acquisition
TP	tense phrase
TVJT	Truth Value Judgment Task
UG	Universal Grammar
V2	Verb-Second
VOT	voice onset time
VP	verb phrase

List of figures

PART I

Language

1

Language architecture

1.1 What is language? What is knowledge of language?

Pose the question of "What defines us as human beings?" to people around you, and most likely, among the first answers that you get, they will mention "language" or "languages." The ability to produce and understand language in order to satisfy our communication needs is our most prized human ability. It is a fundamentally human capacity that relies on unique brain circuitry. It has probably played a decisive role in our evolving as a species. Man has been called *Homo loquens*, as the only animal capable of language.[1] The Harvard psychologist Elizabeth Spelke, interviewed by the actor Alan Alda for a PBS series called *The Human Spark*,[2] considers the question of what makes us uniquely human and distinguishes us from other species. Professor Spelke has looked for the answer to this question in

---

[1] This term is attributed to the eighteenth-century German philosophers J. G. Herder and J. F. Blumenbach.

[2] Available to view at http://www.pbs.org/wnet/humanspark/episodes/program-three-brain-matters/video-full-episode/418/. The quote is at around minute 7.

studying human babies. Although she argues that human infants and the infants and adults of other species have highly similar capacities early on, she suggests that it is language that ignites the uniquely human spark. It is when children start acquiring words at 9 or 10 months of age, and when they start to put these words together a few months later, that the uniquely human capacities emerge.

Also unique (and very useful) is the human ability to learn a second (and a third and a fourth, etc.) language, other than the mother tongue that we grew up speaking. Of course, many people around the world grow up with two or more native languages; the majority start out with one mother tongue but add other languages while they are still children, or learn them as adults. Not just "lingualism," the ability to acquire and use a language, but *multilingualism*, being able to learn and use many languages throughout the lifetime, is another fundamental dimension of the human condition.

Indeed, available data indicate that there are many more bilingual or multilingual individuals in the world than there are monolinguals. In addition, a majority of children in the world have been educated at least partially through the medium of their non-native language. According to Grosjean (2012: 6), the extent of bilingualism is significant.[3] For example, European Union documents report that 56% of the population of the 25 EU countries is bilingual, to the extent that they can have a conversation in a non-native language. In North America, 35% of Canadians and 18–20% of Americans are considered to be bilingual. These numbers are only slated to go up in our increasingly global world.

The emphasis in this book, however, is going to be on two or more language systems as represented in the mind/brain when we speak, write, sign, hear, and comprehend language. Contemporary linguistics is a cognitive science animated by the following fundamental questions:

What is knowledge of language?
How is that knowledge acquired?
How is that knowledge put to use?

---

[3] See the amusing discussion on what scientists really know about those numbers at Grosjean's blog: https://www.psychologytoday.com/blog/life-bilingual/201411/chasing-down-those-65.

How is that knowledge implemented in the brain?
How did that knowledge emerge in the species?[4]

Not all the answers to the fundamental questions are equally developed in our current understanding of language. Furthermore, the last question will remain largely outside our purview in this text. However, the other four questions are fundamental for the understanding of how humans acquire a second language, so we will start with the basics.

A central characteristic of language is that we have to account for the *infinite* number of sentences that any one of us can produce in the languages we know, but at the same time this infinite capacity is based on a *finite* amount of language experience (the number of sentences we encounter while learning a language), and a finite set of rules for what constitutes an acceptable sentence in that language. By the way, I use "sentence" to exemplify a unit of language. The same is largely true of smaller or bigger units of language, such as phrases or discourse.

Since the seminal work of Noam Chomsky in the 1950s, these five questions have constituted the focus of inquiry of generative linguistics. These research questions have come to signify that the human language faculty should be studied as another regular attribute of our species, and that the capacity for language is a function of the mind/brain like many other biological functions such as vision, hearing, etc. For Chomsky and his followers in science, language is a "natural object." Such a view of the language faculty has been reflected in a new term currently in circulation, "biolinguistics."[5]

In 2005, Chomsky published a programmatic article called "Three factors in language design." In this article, he identified the elements essential to the growth of language within an individual, as follows:

a. Genetic endowment
b. Experience
c. Principles not specific to the faculty of language.

---

[4] Cited from Boeckx and Grohmann 2007: 1; see Chomsky 1986: 3, 1988: 3.
[5] Not all generative linguists agree that the innate knowledge is to be understood entirely within the framework of evolutionary biology. For example, Mark Baker has argued for a nonbiological nativism (Baker 2007).

Knowledge of language is represented in the mind/brain. It critically relies on an innate biological endowment for language known as Universal Grammar. At a first approximation, it could be thought of as the information pertaining to language that we do not need to learn because it is universal, common to all languages and it comes to us as part of being human. This is the first factor of language design, which Chomsky called "the genetic endowment." The second factor is the environment: language acquisition depends on abundant comprehensible input available to the language learner. Without comprehensible input, no specific language can be learned. The third factor subsumes generic principles of good design that are not specific to the language faculty, such as principles of data analysis and principles of efficient computation. We will be making frequent mention of the three factors in this textbook, as all of them are crucial in considering second language acquisition (abbreviated as either L2A or SLA).

The importance of the second factor for the growth of language is indisputable. Linguistic *input* is the language that we hear around us, for example, infant-directed speech. *Comprehensible input* is language that we can understand by linking the linguistic form with an extralinguistic situation, for example, hearing the sentence *The dog wants to go out* in the presence of a familiar dog, maybe the family dog, who is lingering by the door and looking at the speaker, begging. The mapping of linguistic form (in this case, the sentence) and meaning (the extralinguistic situation) is absolutely crucial for language acquisition, as neither of these two sides of language on its own constitutes knowledge of language, without the other side.

Children learn the language or languages of their surroundings, provided by parents, siblings, peers, and the whole linguistic community. For example, a child born to American parents and adopted at infancy by Brazilian adoptive parents, will be surrounded by Brazilian Portuguese and may grow up speaking only that language. A child born to a French-speaking mother and an English-speaking father in Quebec is likely to grow up with two first languages. A child born to Polish-speaking parents in the UK may learn to speak Polish at first, as long as she has no exposure to English. Chances are that this child will learn English later when she goes to preschool and become a child bilingual. Later on, that child may or may not forget how to speak Polish, or as linguists say, her Polish may *attrite*, depending on how much input and what quality of linguistic input she gets. She will then be a *heritage speaker* of Polish, bilingual in Polish and English, and possibly English-dominant.

Although it is indisputable that the language we learn is based on our linguistic experience, the necessity of Universal Grammar for language acquisition (Chomsky's first factor) is debated. In what is known as the *innatist* (*nativist*) view, the innate biological endowment, or language faculty, prepares us for the acquisition of whatever language we encounter at birth. Is there such a faculty? And if it exists, what does it consist of? Some generative linguists suggest that this is an innate ability that is also language-specific (aka domain-specific), that is, independent of other cognitive faculties. An alternative suggestion is that we are equipped with learning mechanisms, such as being able to pick out statistical regularities in the input, which can be applied to many types of learning, only one of which is language learning. The second approach is referred to as *emergentist* or *usage-based,* since according to it, linguistic representation in the mind/brain emerges solely based on the linguistic experience and is in a sense created by that usage.

In this book, we will entertain arguments for the former, generative approach, because this approach has uncovered more facts about SLA than other approaches. But first, a short aside. Why do we call it "generative?" Because it is a description of language with the purpose of listing the explicit rules that (ideally) *generate* all the grammatical sentences of that language, but only the grammatical sentences. It all started in the late 1950s. Linguists before Chomsky assumed that almost everything in linguistics was known, and that describing all languages adequately was a finite task that would be accomplished sooner rather than later. They also assumed that languages were so different from each other that it would be difficult to establish any common ground among them. Chomsky turned those two assumptions on their head, showing that there are many more commonalities across languages of the world than there are differences. As a result of that, it became obvious that almost nothing about this linguistic common ground, Universal Grammar, was known, and so in a sense contemporary linguistics had to start from scratch.

The 1970s and 80s were characterized by the tension between describing all possible natural languages and explaining the ease and speed of language acquisition: the fact that children seem to generate their native grammar without being taught it by their caregivers, relatively fast and effortlessly. In order to accommodate the ease and speed of language acquisition, Universal Grammar (what we are born with) had to be quite complex, detailed, and highly specific. Acquisition according to the Principles and Parameters approach, which took shape in the early 80s, was a matter of putting to good use the universal principles, the properties common to all languages, and picking out the parameter values that were relevant to the language being acquired. In order for this process to be easy and productive, the parametric values, or options, were considered to be predetermined by Universal Grammar. Following a suggestion of the linguist Hagit Borer, these parametric options were thought to be grammatical choices that every language makes; they are fixed in our lexicon of functional morphemes. And without a doubt, lexical properties, including idiosyncratic words such as nouns and verbs, but also functional morphemes such as past tense and plural endings, are acquired based on experience.

How does Universal Grammar prepare us, or allow us, to acquire the language we encounter? First of all, it supplies a number of universal rules and properties that come to the language learner for free. As the linguist Mark Baker likes to say, the more languages differ, the more we discover that they are the same. Such language universals may include grammatical functions such as subject and object, the rule that every sentence must have a subject, be it pronounced or not, as well as a subject–object asymmetry: the verb and object combine to make a unit first, to the exclusion of the subject. The child does not need to learn those linguistic facts from experience, although they will be confirmed by her experience.

How about the properties that differ across languages? Universal Grammar restricts and defines the options that we entertain when we encounter the comprehensible input of the language we are learning. Generative linguists demonstrate that language variation is tightly controlled, both across grammars and in acquisition. A light switch that can be turned On or Off provided an apt metaphor to illustrate the idea. To take an example, let us consider the Null Subject Parameter proposed by Nina Hyams, one of the first parameters to be studied in child language acquisition (Hyams 1986). In English every sentence must have an overt subject, see example in (1) where the variant without a subject pronoun is unacceptable. In some languages, notably Italian and Spanish, the subject can be null (silent, or not pronounced), because the relevant information (who is doing the eating) is already encoded on the verb in the form of agreement morphology, as in (2). Importantly, the context, not the verb ending, points to the actual person who consumed the pizza, but that is true of the English pronoun *she* as well. So the Italian–English contrast can be described as a parameter with an On value (null subjects are possible) and an Off value (null subjects are not possible).

(1) She ate the pizza. / *Ate the pizza.
(2) Ø Ha mangiat-o la pizza
     Ø has eaten-3SG the pizza
     'She/he ate the pizza.'

To recap, Universal Grammar, according to generative linguistics, contains a blueprint of all the rules that a speaker will need to generate all and only acceptable sentences in a language. This blueprint includes universal rules, operating in all human languages, as well as the options for the variable rules, or parametric options.

Note, however, that the number of sentences that can be generated in each human language is infinite, while the rules that generate them, including principles and parameters, is finite. This critical tension in the human language capacity is as valid for the usage of a native language as for all subsequent languages: the distinction between *competence* and *performance*. What is it that we know when we know a language? We know the rules necessary and sufficiently to generate every possible acceptable sentence in this language, along with its words and its functional lexicon. This is our linguistic competence. Do we have to have heard or produced every acceptable sentence? Of course not. Nobody can do that, since there seems to be no obvious limit on what we could say. That would be our linguistic performance. Language is freely compositional and creative. From a finite number of words and rules, we can compose entirely new, unheard-of sentences every time we open our mouths to talk, or write an email, or engage in internal monologue called thinking. Note that those same rules tell us when a sentence is unacceptable, as the sentence marked with a star symbol (*) in (1).

This finite competence–infinite performance dichotomy is extended to language acquisition as well: learners acquire the grammar of a language based on finite input, but once they have even a modest competence in a language, they can produce and interpret sentences they have never heard before. This is true of the first language, as well as of the additional languages a person acquires. To cite a brilliant illustration of this duality of the human linguistic experience from Baker (2001: 51–52), our knowledge of language (our competence) is like a recipe for baking bread. Using that recipe, one can bake a concrete loaf of bread (in performance) as many times as needed. But each and every bread contains the information of its recipe inside, although slight variations are inevitable.

1.2 The language architecture

In the previous section, we mentioned that cognitive scientists in general, and linguists in particular, find language interesting to study because it is a structured and accessible product of the human mind. As such, language offers a means to study the nature of the mind that produces it. Describing how language is structured, or what the "language architecture" is, allows cognitive scientists to work out both how it is acquired and how it is put to use in everyday communication. From the very beginning of generative grammar, linguists have spent a lot of time thinking about what the ingredient parts of a linguistic message are and how these come together to produce a message. From now on, I will use the term "grammar" to refer to the system of rules that underlies our knowledge of language.

The major domains of linguistics mirror the processes involved in encoding and decoding a linguistic message. A sentence pronounced in appropriate discourse is made up of sound waves produced by the speaker and perceived by the hearer. For example, the word *bag* is composed by the sounds [b], [æ], and [g] arranged in a sequence acceptable in the grammar of English. In sign language, the equivalent would be linguistic gestures. The study of the acoustic signal and the articulation of speech sounds is *phonetics*. In hearing an utterance, the speech sounds are translated into mental representations in the mind of the hearer, using the language-specific rules for combining the sounds into syllables. *Phonology* studies the system of relationships among the speech sounds. The phonological system of a language includes an inventory of sounds and their features, as well as rules that specify how sounds interact with each other, such as how one sound might change when it is next to another. While the distinction between phonology and phonetics can often be blurred, it will be useful to understand it properly here. Phonetics analyzes the production and perception of all human speech sounds regardless of the language and is the basis for further phonological analyses. Phonology analyzes the sound patterns of a particular language by determining which phonetic sounds are significant and explaining how these sounds are combined by the speakers.

Once the sound waves are perceived and analyzed, they are assembled into morphemes, the smallest meaningful units of language, and then into words. The word *work-s* as in the example in (3) is made up of two morphemes: the lexical verb *work* and the grammatical morpheme *-s* signaling a present tense verb form agreeing with a third person subject (Josh). The study of this domain of language is called *morphology*. For the assembly of lexical items, a hearer needs access to her *mental lexicon*, where verbs, nouns, adjectives, etc., as well as functional (grammatical) morphemes, are stored.

(3)   Josh works in the library.
(4)   *Josh in library the works.

Next, morphemes and words are arranged together into phrases and sentences, following a language-specific word order. For example, the word arrangement in (4) is not an acceptable word order in English. (The star (*) indicates that a sentence is ungrammatical.) Possible word orders and subsequent displacement of some phrases to other positions in the sentence is the study of *syntax*. It is very common in generative linguistics to talk about *morphosyntax*, simply because the grammatical features that regulate the word order and the displacement of phrases in the syntax reside in the functional morphology. We shall see exactly how that happens in later chapters. The functional morphology encodes the language-specific information, while syntactic operations are considered to be universal. In a sense, morphology provides the blueprint of what is going to happen in the syntax, and that is why these two areas of the grammar are considered indispensable to each other.

The message thus composed in the mind/brain of the hearer needs to be interpreted by the Conceptual-Intentional system. To that aim, another series of compositional operations of interpretation is executed, following the rules of *semantics*. Finally, the sentence meaning is examined in light of the extralinguistic context and the discourse information; the meaning can potentially be amended to take these into account. Both semantics and *pragmatics* have to do with the meaning of language, but semantics refers to the meaning of words (lexical semantics) in a language and the compositional meaning of the whole sentence, while pragmatics brings the context to bear on the message. In each situation, the speaker and the hearer in the conversation define the ultimate meaning of the words, based on other clues that lend subtext to the meaning. Let us take an example to illustrate the semantics–pragmatics distinction.

(5)   Q: Have you seen my gym bag?
      A: No, I haven't.

In example (5), it seems that the questioner is looking for his bag, maybe because he needs it to go to the gym. In this case, he is not really asking whether the hearer has ever seen his bag, but he is talking about *today*. The question is really a masked request for information on the bag's where-abouts. The hearer, of course, is aware of the intended additional meaning, and responds that she does not have that information. However, another discourse situation is also possible. The questioner has just bought a gym bag, maybe because he intends to start going to the gym on a regular basis, and is really asking the hearer's opinion of the new bag. The answer then could be extended in the following way: *No, I haven't. It's very nice.* In both situations, the speaker and the hearer are aware of the contextual circum-stances, how subtly they change the meaning, and the conversational exchange is appropriate. You, as readers of the conversational exchange, have no problem interpreting the meaning in the situations I described, and probably in others, too. These literal and subsequently subtly changed additional interpretations are also part and parcel of the language faculty. In sum, what is said, or the literal meaning of the output of syntax is the realm of semantics; while what is additionally conveyed and understood, depending on the context and other factors, is within the realm of pragmatics.

I mentioned earlier that linguists have been engaged in describing the relationships between these parts of the grammar, technically known as linguistic *modules*, from the earliest days of the generative enterprise. Ever since Aristotle, it has been known that linguistic signs are a pairing, or a mapping, of sound and meaning. In contemporary linguistic terms, they are known as the Articulatory-Perceptual system (A-P), the sound, and the Conceptual-Intentional system (C-I), the thought. It is a truism that the faculty of language interfaces with at least these two systems that human beings have independently of language. Thus, the first generative model of the language architecture illustrated the conception of language as a vehicle to relate sound and meaning. Figure 1.1 illustrates the production of a sentence. Words from the lexicon are combined in the syntax until the

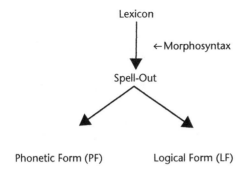

Figure 1.1   A representation of the classic inverted Y model of language architecture

point of spell-out, where they divide into sound (Phonetic Form) and meaning (Logical Form). Since form and meaning are independent of each other, the two are represented as bifurcating from spell-out and not touching after that. PF and LF are the linguistic representations that interface with and instruct the A-P system and the C-I system. This is known as the classic inverted Y model (you can see why).

With the Minimalist Program in the 1990s, there came a realization that the linguistic message can be too long and complicated to process as a whole, and the syntactic derivation had to be divided into more manageable chunks.[6] At least partially, the motivation for this development of the theory was to accommodate processing concerns such as observable cycles in the pronunciation and interpretation of an utterance.[7] Chomsky later developed this intuition into Phase Theory, whose cornerstone is the hypothesis that the syntactic derivation proceeds phase by phase—by building up a smaller chunk of syntactic structure, evaluating it at several steps, and then continuing to successively construct the next relevant chunk(s) until the lexical array of all words to be used in the sentence is depleted. The overriding principle is *Minimizing Computation* (Chomsky 2012), a third-factor principle ensuring maximal simplicity of linguistic operations (see the three factors of language design in Section 1.1). Currently, the verb phrase, the complementizer phrase, and the determiner phrase, to be discussed later on, are proposed to be such phases. Figure 1.2 below illustrates Multiple Spell-Out as a series of inverted Y-s. Once a chunk of a sentence is cyclically

---

[6] This idea, originally due to Joan Bresnan, was developed by Uriagereka (1999).

[7] The primary motivation for multiple spell-out and phases was syntax-internal, (Uriagereka 2012; Chomsky 2012).

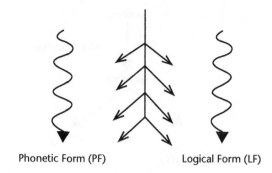

Phonetic Form (PF)   Logical Form (LF)

Figure 1.2   Visual representation of Multiple Spell-Out

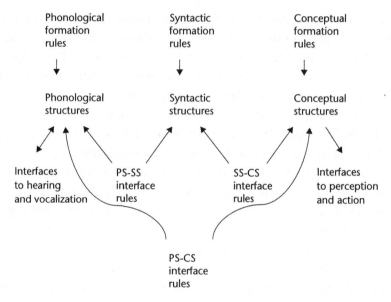

Figure 1.3   Jackendoff's (2002) Parallel Architecture of the language faculty

shipped out to pronunciation and to interpretation, it can no longer be changed.

A different, and dissenting, view of the language faculty has been proposed by Ray Jackendoff, illustrated in Figure 1.3.

Jackendoff's major objection to the classical inverted Y model of language architecture is that it is too "syntactocentric," in the sense that it views the syntax as the only module of the grammar where structure is generated. Jackendoff proposes that structure is generated at all three levels of his model: phonological structures, syntactic structures, and conceptual structures. Note that the modules we discussed earlier (phonetics and

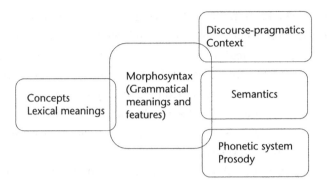

Figure 1.4   Modular design of the language faculty, following Reinhart (2006)

phonology, morphology and syntax, semantics and pragmatics) fit neatly two by two into Jackendoff's phonological, syntactic, and conceptual structures. For example, he places the pragmatic notions topic and focus (to be discussed later) on a separate tier within conceptual structures.

Finally, a model that conceives of semantic and discourse-pragmatic information separately is Reinhart's (2006) model, illustrated in Figure 1.4. In this model, as you can see, the discourse-pragmatics is a separate module from the semantics, having its own box in the graph. The motivation of that representation would be that processes at the semantics level are checked separately and possibly re-interpreted in view of the discourse context, which may very well be the case, as my example (5) illustrated.

> Before going forward, say whether Reinhart's model is syntacto-centric or not. Why?

Next, I shall elaborate on the interfaces between the different modules. To borrow some terminology from Jackendoff, the processes that take place within each module can be considered *integrative* processes, they build up linguistic units (phonemes, morphemes, words, phrases, sentences) on each level. However, the linguistic object already built in one module has to pass for further compositional calculation onto another module. This happens at the *interfaces* between modules and is essentially a matching procedure. Let's take as an example the interface between syntax and semantics. Fairly uncontroversially, syntactic structure needs to be correlated with semantic structure for a form–meaning mapping; however, this correlation is not always trivial (Jackendoff 2002). The syntactic processor works with objects like syntactic trees, their constituents and relations: noun phrases, verb phrases, grammatical features, etc. The semantic processor operates with events and states, agents and patients, individuals and propositions. The operations at the interface are limited precisely to those structures that need to be correlated and they "do not see" other structures and operations (such as the marking of case: Nominative, Accusative, etc) that would have no relevance to the other module.

It has been proposed that grammatical operations that happen at the interfaces between linguistic modules are somehow harder and more demanding, since they have to take information into account at two modules, not just one. Furthermore, when we take a cross-linguistic perspective, we can see that conditions are created for mismatches at the interfaces. To take one example, while the English past progressive tense signifies an ongoing event in the past, Spanish Imperfect can have both an ongoing and a habitual interpretation. The English simple past tense, on the other hand, has a one-time finished event interpretation and a habitual interpretation, while the Spanish preterit has only the former. Thus, the same semantic primitives (ongoing, habitual, and one-time finished event), arguably part of universal conceptual structure, are distributed over different pieces of functional morphology.

Whether linguistic properties at the interfaces are harder than integrative properties is ultimately an empirical question that can be solved through experimental research.

1.3 What exactly has to be acquired?

Why would we be interested in these models of language architecture in a textbook on second language acquisition? How are they relevant to the process of acquiring another language? In this section, I address the teaching relevance of the language architecture and knowledge about language. First of all, students of language acquisition have to have a good grasp of what language is, the complex object that is first being internalized and then externalized. Yes, I am biased in thinking that everyone should know some basic facts about linguistic structure; I am a linguist, after all. However, this is particularly true of language teachers, the people who shape and guide learners' acquisition process.

Secondly, and much more importantly, the language architecture is the foundation of proposals on where the differences among languages lie. Consequently, we are able to formulate concrete proposals on how the differences between language X and language Y will be acquired. If we can be extremely specific on precisely what it is that has to be acquired, we can also be explicit on the specifics of the learning task. For example, as mentioned above, the Minimalist assumption is that language variation is relegated to the functional lexicon, while the syntactic operations are essentially the same across languages. Furthermore, Jackendoff has explicitly argued that conceptual (meaning) structures are universal. Consequently, a child acquiring her native language does not need to learn syntactic operations, but she does have to learn the grammatical features pertinent to her language that are captured in the functional morphology. It makes sense, then, to argue that acquiring the functional lexicon constitutes one of the most important acquisition tasks.

What happens when we learn a second language? Again, we would like the answer to this question to follow logically from the language architecture discussed in the previous section. A second language learner has access to the universal properties of language through Universal Grammar, or through his/her native language, which exemplifies these universal properties. There are several things to acquire. First of all comes the lexicon: all the words of the second language are likely to be new to the learner. Then, all the parametric options that are different between the L1 (native language) and the L2 (second language), such as word order, null subject, etc., have to be acquired, as well. Parametric differences may be encoded in the functional lexicon, but they are manifested through various word dislocations, null versus overt grammatical functions, and grammatical meaning associations. For example, the question words may go to the beginning of the sentence or remain in place (*in situ*), and some languages even allow *wh*-words in intermediate locations: this information is encoded in the complementizer phrase but it is visible in the various dislocations.

Finally, when learning a second language, a speaker may be confronted with different mappings between units of meaning and units of morphosyntactic structure, such as the example mentioned in the previous section between grammatical morphemes and what aspectual meanings they subsume in English and Spanish. We can make concrete hypotheses about the variable degrees of difficulty that learners encounter, but only if we are aware of the matches and mismatches between L1 and L2 grammar structures.

In this and subsequent chapters, I will provide information in boxes like this one. In them, I will try to make explicit the connection between linguistic and language acquisition theory, and teaching practice. In this first case, this whole section is intended to discuss the relevance of the language architecture to language learners and teachers. There is one more such point of relevance, in the box below.

Teaching relevance

In acquiring a second language, some linguistic modules may present more difficulty than others. For example, it is well known that the phonetics/phonology of a second language, if it is acquired after childhood, may never become nativelike. This is not true of the semantics or the morphosyntax, however. In short, different modules may be acquired in different ways. That is why knowledge of the modules is relevant for teachers.

1.4 The scientific method in SLA research

The scientific method is a system of techniques for investigating natural phenomena, acquiring new knowledge, as well as correcting and integrating previous knowledge. To be termed scientific, a method of inquiry must be based on empirical and measurable evidence and subject to specific principles of reasoning. Generative linguistics uses the scientific method in investigating language and language acquisition. The method generally involves scrutinizing some data, making generalizations about patterns in the data, developing hypotheses that account for these generalizations, and testing the hypotheses against more data. Finally, the hypotheses are revised to account for any new findings and then tested again. Of course, there are adjustments one has to expect for the various scientific disciplines, and we will see how the method works in linguistics.

When describing a language that has not been described so far, linguists start by gathering some sentences from informants in the field who speak the language natively. Based on these preliminary data, they form hypotheses. To take an example from word order, one hypothesis can be that the subject in this language must precede the object and the verb. This is the case in many languages, so it is an informed hypothesis. Then linguists check this hypothesis against more data. Linguistic theory allows us to make predictions. Any theory or linguistic model worth its name should be capable of making predictions. For example, if there is a lot of agreement morphology on the verbal forms in a language, a reasonable prediction would be that the subjects could be possibly null, not pronounced. When more data from newly described languages is uncovered, linguistic theories change, sometimes slightly, sometimes more dramatically, in order to be able to accommodate the new data.

In generative second language acquisition (GenSLA), we start with the foundational assumptions and the language architecture we have already discussed in this chapter, as well as the theories of L2 development that we will discuss in the next chapters. We normally choose a linguistic phenomenon that we would like to investigate, such that it addresses the predictions of a certain theory. The next step is to find a description of this phenomenon in the native and in the target language literature (or provide that description ourselves, if we speak these languages natively). It is fairly typical to investigate properties that differ in the L1 and L2, for the common sense reason that if they don't differ, there might be nothing much to acquire.

GenSLA is theoretically motivated. Researchers test a particular theory or model proposing how the L2 development unfolds. There are no (published) studies in the generative literature that are motivated just by noticing that learners make a certain error, or whose purpose is to see how learners acquire a certain construction. The research questions of GenSLA are always informed by hypotheses and predictions based on theory of linguistic behavior and development. At the end of the experimental study, we want to be able to say something about the L2 competence and how it evolves. A common outcome of such studies is support or lack of support for the existing body of theories. That is, these theories are *falsifiable*, a necessary condition of the scientific method. Often researchers who reject a certain theoretical hypothesis come up with an alternative proposal in order to accommodate the new findings. However, that alternative proposal has to be able to explain everything that the rejected proposal explains, plus the new data.

Let's take for example L1 transfer, the theoretical proposal postulating that, in acquiring a second language, learners are influenced by the particular parameter value in their native language. We will encounter other developmental theories and proposals later on. L1 transfer of morphosyntactic parameter values and meanings into the second language is the most fundamental, although self-evident, proposal about L2 acquisition that one can think of. It also obeys Occam's razor[8] because it is a parsimonious and economical hypothesis. For instance, if the learners' L1 is a null-subject language and they are acquiring a non-null-subject language, they might tend not to pronounce subjects, at least at first. That is exactly what the theory of L1 transfer predicts.

> Before continuing, think of what the prediction would be in the opposite direction, that is, if the learners' L1 is a non-null-subject language and they are learning a null-subject language.

Next, in order to test a prediction, we have to obtain quantifiable data, either longitudinally from a small number of learners over the course of their development, or cross-sectionally, from a larger number of experimental participants at one time. A control group of native speakers is obligatorily tested as well, in order to validate the test instrument. In some cases, the control group results also serve to support or refute various theoretical claims in the literature. If we want to be able to make claims about development with a cross-sectional design, we include learners at various levels of proficiency, say, beginner, intermediate, and advanced learners. In order to ascertain proficiency levels, it is customary to offer an independent test of language proficiency.

In fact, one of the earliest studies in generative SLA, White (1985), was designed just as I described above: Lydia White tested the Null Subject Parameter in the English L2 competence of Spanish native speakers.[9] She hypothesized that learners initially apply the Null Subject Parameter value to the target language, English, which does not allow null subjects. Eventually, the *L2 input* (the second language data that learners are exposed to), working together with Universal Grammar, will allow learners to overcome the L1 transfer and start using overt subjects in all English sentences. She tested learners at five proficiency levels from beginning to advanced, as well

---

[8] This is a problem-solving principle attributed to William of Ockam (*c.*1287–1347), an English Franciscan friar, theologian, and scholastic philosopher. The principle states that among competing hypotheses, the one with the fewest assumptions should be selected.

[9] She also had a second important research question, namely, whether all constructions in a cluster of constructions will transfer, which we will discuss in later chapters.

as a comparison group of French native speakers learning English, since French, just as English, does not allow null subjects.

> Think of the predictions for the Spanish and the French learners of English. Do we expect them to behave differently?

The experimental participants evaluated acceptable sentences with a subject and unacceptable sentences without a subject, such as the second sentence in (6). A star in front of a sentence signals that it is unacceptable, at least for most native speakers.

(6)   John is greedy. *Eats like a pig.

The findings suggested that indeed it was difficult for the low proficiency learners to identify the missing subject sentences as unacceptable in English. This difficulty was reflected in lower accuracy for the Spanish learners, as compared to the French learners. However, with increased proficiency, the Spanish learners were able to identify unacceptable sentences with higher accuracy. The hypothesis of L1 transfer of a parameter value was confirmed by this experimental study.

In summary, applying the scientific method is a central feature of Gen-SLA from its outset. GenSLA is a cognitive science because it describes the cognitive psychological processes that happen in a learner's mind while she acquires language and when she uses it. GenSLA is a window through which one fascinating aspect of the human mind can be viewed.

1.5 Exercises

Exercise 1.1. How can we explain these facts about human language, using the set of assumptions we developed in this chapter?

- Commonality of basic grammatical structures.
- A child born to Korean-speaking parents is adopted into a French family and learns French as her native language.
- Any normally developing child acquires one (or more) language(s) without too many errors and without explicit teaching.

- The sentences in any language are innumerable, but the grammar of every language can be described by a finite number of rules.
- Language offers a means to study the nature of the mind that produces it.

Exercise 1.2. Watch the following video from the BBC website: http://www.bbc.co.uk/news/uk-17107435. The video is about 20-year-old Alex Rawlings who speaks 11 languages. He was an undergraduate student at Oxford University. Describe the conditions of acquisition of all his languages. Is there a limit to how many languages an individual can speak? Discuss what that limit would be, if you said that there is one.

Watch two more videos of polyglots available on YouTube, such as this one http://www.youtube.com/watch?v=eFpzeGoP-Kg. Then think of your own linguistic experiences in learning languages. Do you find anything in common among the people describing their linguistic experiences?

Exercise 1.3. Fill in the following table, after class discussion.

L1 property	L2 property	What behavior would L1 transfer predict?
Null subjects	No null subjects	
SVO	SOV	
Past tense marking with a morpheme such as -ed	No dedicated past tense morpheme	
No definite and indefinite articles	Definite and indefinite articles	
The preposition comes at the end of the prepositional phrase	The preposition comes at the beginning of the prepositional phrase	
The adjective precedes the noun it modifies	The adjective follows the noun it modifies	

Exercise 1.4. "Semantics." Read the following question Kitt asked on Ask.com:

Tonight a friend and I were joking about how much of a hamburger he ate. He said it was 1/4. But I said it looked more like 1/5. Then he said, "Well, that's just semantics." Now, I thought that semantics was the study of meaning behind the words, like different connotations and how meanings change overtime... Example: 100 years ago, "gay" meant happy. Now it describes a person's sexual orientation. But he thinks that semantics is when people mean the same thing, just describe it differently. What is semantics, really? And what is my friend talking about?

> Describe Kitt's informal definition of semantics? Is it correct?
>
> Describe Kitt's friend's definition of semantics.
>
> How do you use "semantics" in everyday speech? Are you familiar with the two meanings mentioned above?

Read the following comment on Kitt's posting:

A & B are talking and A says "Why did you steal my jacket?" B replies "I didn't steal it, I just borrowed it without asking." A says, "That is just arguing semantics. You *stole* it!" This is a more proper use of the term "semantics" because it describes the connotation of the words (not the math). Your friend is correct that people could describe the same thing differently, but they often misuse words (and sometimes on purpose). When they get called on the error, they say it is a semantic argument.

> Do you agree with the comment? Is the series of questions in this exercise "just a semantic argument"?

Exercise 1.5. In this TED talk, the linguist John McWhorter discusses the difference between speaking and writing as language modes, but also very different types of language use. He convincingly argues that texting is "fingered speech"; texting is a language in which we write like we speak. There are new linguistic signs developing in texting that do not exist in speech and in formal writing. Here is your question: If a person is fluent in speaking, writing and texting, are they bilingual? Or trilingual? Watch the video, and discuss: http://www.ted.com/talks/john_mcwhorter_txtng_is_killing_language_jk.html

2

Language variation

In this chapter, we continue to discuss the language architecture and, more specifically, parameters throughout the history of the generative enterprise. This time around, we will take a chronological approach and describe how the concept of a parameter has changed over the years and what the current idea of a parameter is. We will keep in mind how these ideas influenced the research questions of L2 acquisition studies performed since the 80s and what we can expect for the future. We will constantly keep an eye on how this type of theoretical knowledge can improve classroom teaching efficiency. But first, we will look at a few examples of language differences.

2.1 How do languages differ?

Before we go into a discussion of how differences among languages have been captured, analyzed, and conceptualized, it is important to get a good idea of how it is that languages vary. The most obvious difference, of course, is in their lexicons: different languages have different words for the same entity. Take for example the English word *table,* the Bulgarian word *masa,* the Russian word *stol*, and the Vietnamese word *bảng,* all standing for a piece of furniture with a flat top and one or more legs, providing a level surface on which objects may be placed. All the words in a second language have to be learned, usually painstakingly and one by one, but there are shortcuts and regularities to that process as well, as we shall see in Chapter 9 on acquisition of the lexicon. Languages also differ in what sounds they employ and how they combine them, the so-called phonotactic constraints. For example, a sequence of the sounds /t/ + /l/ is unpronounceable in English at the beginning of a word, but perfectly fine in Bulgarian, as in the word *tləst* 'fat.'

Abstracting away from the lexicon and the phonetics/phonology, however, syntactic variation is not random, and that is clearly brought home by extensive work on linguistic typology, stemming from Greenberg's (1963) pioneering work on language universals. Describing the possible order possibilities between the main constituents of the sentence: S(ubject)–O(bject)–V(erb), for example, linguists have established that not all of the six possible orders appear with the same frequency among languages of the world. If you want to discover such regularities on your own, please refer to the *World Atlas of Language Structures*.[1] (However, be forewarned that this is an extremely addictive website.) There you can find a map of the world with the possible word orders marked clearly. Out of 1377 languages described, 565 utilize SOV (41%), 488—SVO (35.4%), and 95—VSO, while 189 languages display no dominant order.

What these numbers suggest, first of all, is that the order of the major sentence constituents cannot be described in absolute universal terms. Rather, we are dealing with universal statistical tendencies: SOV and SVO are the most frequent word orders, etc. Furthermore, and much more interesting from an acquisition point of view, there are certain other regularities that go together with the dominant word order. But before we look at these regularities, we need to brush up on the notions of "head" and "complement" of a phrase. The head is the most important word in the phrase, from a structural as well as meaning perspective. The head determines the category of the whole phrase. The complement represents additional information that completes the meaning. The noun (underlined) is the head of the noun phrase (e.g., *the leg of the table*); the verb is the head of the verb phrase (*see the leg of the table*), etc. Languages that place heads either at the end or at the beginning of the phrase are called *harmonic*. For example, if a language has O before V, it is likely that the language will also

---

[1] WALS, http://wals.info/cf. Haspelmath et al. (2005).

have postpositions (*the market to*); if a language has V then O, it is highly likely that it will have prepositions (*to the market*).[2] In fact, 94.5% of languages surveyed in the WALS are harmonic with respect to the order of V, O, and adpositions (Baker 2008). Other word order regularities that go together with the order of V and O are given below (Biberauer 2008):

(1)   If V–O, then Auxiliary–V, Prepositions, Noun–Adjective, Noun–Genitive, Noun–Relative Clause.
       If O–V, then V–Auxiliary, Postpositions, Adjective–Noun, Genitive–Noun, Relative Clause–Noun.

Now let us take a concrete example from Japanese and English, from Baker (2003). Notice that linguistic examples are given on three lines, the first line providing an approximate transliteration of the Japanese sounds, but already divided into grammatical and lexical morphemes. The second line gives English equivalents of these morphemes, called *glosses*, retaining their order in Japanese. The third line gives an idiomatic translation of the sentence meaning in English. For our linguistic analysis purposes now, pay attention to the second line first.

(2)   Taro is thinking that Hiro showed pictures of himself to Hanako.

(3)   Taroo-ga   [Hiro-ga   Hanako-ni zibun-no   syasin-o   miseta]
       Taro   Hiro   Hanako-to self-of   picture   showed
       to   omotte iru.
       that   thinking is
       'Taro is thinking that Hiro showed pictures of himself to Hanako.'

At first glance, it may seem that the two sentences in (2) and (3) are very different. In fact, if you read out the second line of (3), it sounds like gibberish. However, if you look closely, you can see that the typological generalizations given in (1) above are exemplified clearly in these two examples. English is V–O while Japanese is O–V. The auxiliary *is* precedes the verb *thinking* in English, while the auxiliary *iru* 'is' follows the verb *omotte* 'thinking' in Japanese. The English preposition goes in front of the noun phrase (NP) to make a prepositional phrase (PP) *of himself*, while in Japanese the postposition *–no* 'of' follows the NP (*himself of*).

---

[2] Prepositions and postpositions have a common label: they are called "adpositions."

Before going forward, find two other differences between English and Japanese that can be attributed to their word order difference. Hint: there is no relative clause in this example, but there is a subordinate clause that functions as an object.

More generally speaking, English seems to put new words (the heads) in the beginning of already constructed phrases (acting as complements), whereas Japanese seems to add new words at the end of phrases. If we have a look at Baker's simplified phrase structure trees of parts of these two sentences, we will see why. Note how the two phrase structures look like mirror images of each other. Secondly, if you compare line for line, you will see the opposite order of the constituents: Verb and Object NP, Preposition/ Postposition and NP, etc. One way to express this generalization is to say that English phrases are predominantly *head-initial* (the head comes before the complement), while Japanese phrases are predominantly *head-final*. This is known as the Head Directionality Parameter (Greenberg 1963, Stowell 1981, Dryer 1992).

(4)   English phrases (partial tree)   Japanese phrases (partial tree)

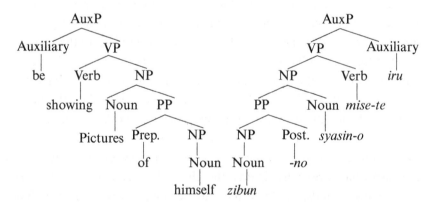

Next, to illustrate another level of language variation, we shall take a second paradigmatic distinction from Baker (2003), based on his work on the Mohawk language. Mohawk is a polysynthetic language, which means that "its sentences seem simple and fluid, but word structures are complex and rigidly structured" (Mithun and Chafe 1979, Baker 1996). Let us compare the two Mohawk sentences below with their English translations, the third line in the examples (5) and (6).

(5)   Rukwe'   wa-sh-ako-hsir-u   ne owira'a
      man   past-he-her-blanket-gave   the baby
      'The man gave the baby a blanket.'

(6)   Rukwe'   wa-h-uwa-hsir-u   ne owira'a
      man   past-him-she-blanket-gave   the baby
      'The baby gave the man a blanket.'

Let us start from the translations this time. Clearly, the meanings of the two sentences are exactly the opposite in terms of who is performing the action of giving and who is the recipient. Next, focus on the second line of the examples and notice that the word *rukwe'* 'man' is before the verb in both examples, but in one sentence he is the doer of the action while in the other he is the recipient. This fact illustrates the free word order in Mohawk, and it is very different from English, isn't it? In English, *John kissed Mary* and *Mary kissed John* do not denote the same event. Unlike English, the words in a Mohawk sentence can be put in any order without affecting the basic meaning. Now, look at the rich information encoded on the verb, in the form of tense and agreement morphemes. In (5), there is a morpheme showing that the event is past, then another morpheme pointing to the subject (3rd person, singular, masculine), and another indicating that the direct object is 3rd person, singular, feminine. Right before the verb, you see that the whole object *hsir* 'blanket' is "incorporated" into the verb. If you now compare the second and the third morphemes on the verb in (6), they indicate that this time the recipient is masculine while the giver is feminine, hence the different meaning. Mohawk speakers can also drop the nouns in these sentences altogether, if they are already mentioned in the discourse or known to the interlocutors. The event of giving in both languages has three participants: the giver, the recipient, and the object that changes hands, all three have to be obligatorily expressed. Baker proposes that the parametric difference between English and Mohawk can be formulated like this:

(7)   Mohawk: Express every major participant in an event inside the verb that names the event.

      English: Don't express the participants in an event inside the verb that names the event.

Apart from this major difference, visible in every sentence, note that there are similarities between the two languages, too. The obligatory nature of the three event participants is one similarity; the constraint that only the direct object, but no other participant, can be incorporated into the verb is another similarity. Although English doesn't have noun incorporation, it has verbal compounds such as *gift-giving,* while *baby-giving* (even if attested) can only have the meaning that the baby is the object that changes hands, but cannot be the recipient or the giver.

Teaching relevance

These are just two examples of how human languages differ parametrically, or in a predetermined way. We are interested in differences between languages, because they are what second language learners have to acquire. Furthermore, we would like to be able to describe those differences in a systematic way that makes acquisition easy. For example, if an English native speaker is acquiring Japanese, she does not need to acquire all the typological generalizations one by one. Having acquired one of them, for example O precedes V, she will be able to hypothesize that Japanese is a head-final language and has postpositions, etc. If an English native speaker is acquiring Mohawk, she will expect that in every sentence, the event participants have to be marked on the verb. Such generalizations help language acquisition immensely.[3] There is empirical support for such generalizations in the work of Megan Smith and Bill VanPatten (2014).[4]

2.2 Principles and Parameters in history

In this section, we will take a chronological survey of the concept of parameters. In doing so, we are aiming to elucidate how the concept of parameter developed, and why it matters for SLA. During the 1960s and

---

[3] This generalization was tested at the outset of GenSLA research in the 1980s, in the seminal work of Suzanne Flynn (Flynn 1987a,b, Flynn and Espinal 1985).

[4] The researchers tested native English speakers, who had never studied Japanese before. At first, participants were exposed to some head-final Japanese phrases, and then tested them on congruous phrases that they had not seen in the training part of the study. After minimal exposure, the participants demonstrated awareness of the head-final nature of Japanese, as measured by longer reading times on ungrammatical sentences as compared to the grammatical sentences.

70s, the attention of generative linguists focused on the basic regularities of language structure and on how to capture the infinite surface realizations of the underlying finite structure. Attention was paid to fine-grained descriptions of individual languages in rewrite rules[5] (as well as transformations), as exemplified in (8), where the order of the constituents is important:

(8)   NP → Det N (as in *the dog*);   VP → V NP (as in *eat a melon*), etc.

These rewrite rules are to some extent notational variants of tree structures, where the arrow stands for the binary branching. They both symbolize a VP that immediately contains a V and an NP. The order of V and NP captures the fact that the verb precedes its object (as in English).

(9)   VP → V NP   =   VP
                                        ⟋ ⟍
                                       V   NP

Note the similarity with the English tree and the difference with the Japanese tree above in (4). To the extent that the grammar of individual languages was fully accounted for by such rules, it was said that the grammar was *descriptively adequate*.

Over time, descriptive rules proliferated, which was in conflict with another stated goal of the generative framework, that of *explanatory adequacy*. The latter attempted to elucidate how a child was able to acquire language, in such a short time and relatively error-free, on the basis of finite (and maybe limited) comprehensible input. The abundance of descriptive rules describing language specific constructions was difficult to square with the easy, effortless way children learn language. In short, the system of rules became too rich to explain language acquisition.

This inherent conflict between descriptive and explanatory adequacy brought about the Principles and Parameters approach (P&P) in the beginning of the 80s. Explanatory adequacy came to be of higher priority and more highly valued than descriptive adequacy.

---

[5] Rewrite rules are called that because what is on the left of the arrow gets rewritten on the right-hand side of the arrow.

Since solving the clash between descriptive and explanatory adequacy (satisfying both) was a major goal of the Principles and Parameters approach, linguists developed an elaborate but elegant technical apparatus to this end. The points of invariance and points of variation were unified by proposing parameterized (flexible) principles. The transition from rules to principles was complete.

From the perspective of SLA, there is nothing wrong with specific language rules, and that is how language instruction has traditionally proceeded. However, explanatorily adequate parameters offer a shortcut of added efficiency to the instruction and acquisition process. Furthermore, this emphasis on explanatory adequacy revealed linguistic properties that were part of the knowledge of language, but were not within educators' purview until that time. The language gates had opened.

We shall exemplify a parameterized principle with Subjacency, one of the earliest proposals that was also taken up and studied extensively by second language scholars. Chomsky (1973) proposed that the leftward movement of a *wh*-constituent (such as *what*, *where*, or *which student*), starting from its underlying position close to its related verb and moving to the initial position of the sentence, is constrained by the following metric. Such a constituent could move only in small steps that do not cross over more than one "bounding node." Bounding nodes in the initial proposal were the categories S (standing for sentence) and NP. Let us look at a declarative sentence first, such as the one in (10), where the object *the present* and the location *under the bed* are close to the verb *put*. Sentence (11) questions the location; the question word *where* has moved to the top of the embedded clause. Sentence (11a) can be analyzed as a result of the two steps illustrated in (11b) and (11c). First the location phrase is substituted with the question word *where,* and then it moves to the beginning of the embedded clause leaving a trace, or a copy of itself, marked with angled brackets. The lower copy is silent, but it is there. In this jump, the *wh*-phrase moves over one bounding node, the S, which makes the jump a legitimate one.[6]

(10)   Bill put the present under the bed.

---

[6] The NP *the present* was considered to be a sister node to the location phrase *where* on the tree, so it is not counted as being "jumped over."

(11) a. Jane knew where Bill put the present.

                       where

    b. Jane knew _____ Bill put the present ~~under the bed~~.

    c. Jane knew where [s Bill put the present<where>].
                 #

In example (12), we want to execute the same substitution and movement of the object; however, the question word *what* is forced to take a much longer jump to the front of the sentence, crossing over two S bounding nodes (marked with a number sign). This long jump renders the whole sentence unacceptable. Structures from which a constituent cannot be moved out is called an "island," evocative of no escape because the escape hatch has been closed off.

(12) a. *What did Jane know where Bill put?

                       what

    b. *   did Jane know where Bill put ~~the present~~ <where>

    c. * What did [s Jane know where [s Bill put<what> <where>]]?
              #   #

(13) a. What did Jane know Bill put under the bed?

    b. What did [s Jane know <what> [s Bill put <what> under the bed]]?
             #   #

    That this is the correct analysis is confirmed only after we examine (13), an acceptable sentence. The difference between sentences (12a) and (13a) is that the former has moved the location *wh*-phrase *where* to the beginning of the embedded clause.[7] Its presence there would block the object *wh*-word

---

[7] This position was identified as the Specifier of the Complemetizer (Spec,CP) position, or S-prime, in the terminology of the day.

what from stopping over in that same position on its way to the top of the sentence. If *what* could stop over in the position of *where*, it would, but it cannot since that position is already taken (the node is filled). Remember that this position is considered the escape hatch from the island. The sentence in (12) is unacceptable because the question word *what* is forced to make an illegitimately long jump to the top of the main clause; the sentence in (13) is acceptable because *what* is allowed to stop over half-way, leave a copy of itself, and continue on its way to the top of the sentence, thereby making two smaller jumps. Note that now we have two lower copies of *what*, neither of which are pronounced. But if the top copy of *what* in the escape hatch did not exist, we would not be able to explain the difference in acceptability between (12a) and (13a).

> Do an informal linguistic experiment by writing out sentences (10), (11), (12), and (13) on a piece of paper, and poll three (or more) of your friends about the acceptability of the sentences. To start with, ask whether they are acceptable or unacceptable. Then offer your "experimental participants" a scale of accept-ability, say 1 to 5 or 1 to 7, where 1 is unacceptable and 7 is perfect. Long sentences with *wh*-movement like these ones are never judged perfectly accept-able, because they are difficult to process. That is why I predict that example (10) will obtain higher ratings. See whether you will be able to confirm the lower acceptability of (12) in comparison with (11) and (13).

The reader has to appreciate the breathtaking elegance and attractive-ness of this analysis. This was precisely the type of data that the generative program was called upon to reveal and explain. It uncovered linguistic knowledge that speakers did not even suspect that they had. This data set and others like it embodied the inherent complexity and surface unpre-dictability of the linguistic input children were exposed to. Very often, analogy between possible linguistic changes in sentences is misleading (think of the paradigm in (11), (12), (13) above, among many other examples). At the same time, such data sets become part of children's grammatical knowledge easily. The argument from the Poverty of the Stimulus goes like this:

1. English native speakers generally agree that (11) and (13) are accept-able sentences, so the rules of generating these sentences are part of their grammar.

2. However, nobody teaches English children that sentences such as (12) are unacceptable. Nobody *can* teach English children that, because it is not part of speakers' explicit language knowledge.
3. Since children know the difference between (11) and (13) on the one hand, and (12) on the other, they derive this knowledge from the innate Language Acquisition Device, or Universal Grammar.

Let me unpack step 3 of the argument a little. It is conceivable that children hear sentences such as (11) and (13), but not (12), since the latter is ungrammatical and no one around them will pronounce it. Could it be that children capitalize on never having heard a sentence like (12) and generalize from the lack of evidence ("I have never heard this sentence") to evidence of lack ("this sentence is unacceptable in my language")? But there are many sentences that children have never heard, yet they produce them. The generalization going from lack of evidence to evidence of lack is fallacious. It must be the case, then, that children know more than they are exposed to. They know that some structures are illicit in their language. The explanation of this fact must lie in Universal Grammar, which has supplied children with this linguistic information.

The history of describing language variation continues. Subjacency was treated as a principle of UG, in the sense that no language allowed movement of a *wh*-phrase to cross over more than one bounding node. However, uncovering language variation, Rizzi (1982) proposed that Italian has different bounding nodes than English. In the clause structure, the S node is dominated by S-prime (S', or what we currently know as complementizer phrase, or CP). Rizzi proposed that not S but S' was a bounding node in Italian. This subtle difference allowed sentences of the type of (12) to be acceptable in Italian. It was also discovered that Russian was even more restrictive than English and Italian (Freidin and Quicoli 1989), and so S and S' were proposed to be bounding nodes. Languages that did not move their *wh*-phrases to the beginning of the clause, such as Mandarin Chinese, were considered not to exhibit Subjacency at all. Thus phrase structure and movement were both subject to the inviolable principle, Subjacency, but the precise manner in which this principle manifested itself in different languages was flexible, and constrained by parametric variation.

Not all principles were flexible and parameterized. For example, the Extended Projection Principle, which stipulated that every clause should have a subject, and the Theta Criterion, which postulated that each thematic role of a verb should be assigned to one and only one argument, were inviolable and universal. Subjacency, too, was initially thought to be an invariant principle (cf. Chomsky, 1973), but Rizzi's (1982) work revealed this assumption to be incorrect. Thus the Principles and Parameters framework was very much a research program, where accepted analyses were likely to change a few years later, with the discovery of exciting new data from fresh languages. As in normal scientific practice, this was considered a strength, not a weakness of the framework.

A second, and very important characteristic of the P&P style parameters was the notion of parameter clusters. The gist of this idea was Chomsky's famous metaphor, attributed to James Higginbotham, of parameters as light switches with two values: On and Off. Placing the switch in one position leads to a cascade-like effect with various other constructions becoming available in the grammar of a speaker. This was known as the *clustering effect*. The notion was conceptually attractive because the constructions in the cluster were superficially unrelated. If it was possible to show that they all depended on an underlying value of a single parameter, this would constitute a cogent argument for the existence of UG indeed. Based on historical evidence, Lightfoot (1993) proposed the condition that the parametric *trigger,* the cue for the setting of the whole parameter, had to be salient and easy to acquire, such as a piece of inflectional morphology.

We will exemplify this idea of a parameter cluster with the Null Subject Parameter already introduced in Chapter 1. It is a classic parameter, which held a lot of promise at the time. In languages such as Spanish and Italian, it is possible not to pronounce the subject of a clause when the information of who the doer of the action is comes from the agreement morphology on the verb, as shown in (14a). This is not so in English, French, and German, see the English translations of the examples below to compare.

(14)   a. Habl-a   español   (Spanish)
          speak-3SG   Spanish
          'She/he speaks Spanish.'

       b. Piov-e   (Italian)
          rain-3SG
          'It is raining.'

       c. Verrà   Gianni
          will-come-3SG   Gianni
          'Gianni will come. / *Will come Gianni.'

d. Chi   cred-i   che <chi>   verrà?
who   believe-2SG   that <who>   will come
'Who do you think that will come?'   (ungrammatical in English)

The proposed cluster of constructions included null expletives (dummy subjects) as in (14b), postverbal subjects as in (14c), a sequence of the complementizer *that* and a trace of the moved subject, known as the "*that*-trace effect" as in (14d), and rich subject–verb agreement (Rizzi 1982). The salient cue that is observable from the linguistic input is the unrealized pronominal subject. The constructions in the cluster appear to be superficially unrelated and of varying difficulty. However, all of them hinge on the availability of a null pronominal subject, let's call it *pro* (pronounced "small pro" or "little pro"). Recall the universal principle that every sentence must have a subject. This requirement is still satisfied in the sentences in (14), but by *pro*. This null subject appeared in "weather sentences" (14b) as the equivalent of overt *it* in English (*It rains.*) *Pro* allows the notional subject *Gianni* in (14c) to remain lower in the structure, creating this postverbal subject effect. Finally *pro* also helps the *that*-trace violation to be avoided, as in (14d), by allowing *wh*-subjects to be extracted from a lower position, while *pro* itself once again satisfies the subject requirement. The "rich" subject–verb agreement in Spanish and Italian supplies *pro* with the person and number features it intrinsically lacks.

The details of some of these analyses have changed over time; however, the basic point still remains: the constructions exemplified in (14) cluster in null-subject languages, while their exact opposites are acceptable in non-null-subject languages. The parameter's two values hinge on the existence or unavailability of *pro:* it is the basis of the underlying analyses of the whole cluster. The rich deductive structure of this parameter was the poster child in the quest for explanatory adequacy. Null pronominal subjects are relatively easy to notice in the primary linguistic data; and although *that*-trace constructions are rare and not so salient, they would come into the grammar for free (when all the other necessary linguistic properties are learned).

A significantly bigger challenge is acquiring the fact that *that*-trace sentences are NOT part of the grammar of non-null-subject languages such as English. The child is not going to hear the unacceptable sentence in (15) and others like it. However, the easy analogy between sentences such as (16) and (17) below suggests that (15) should be fine. No parent teaches children that extraction of a subject after an overt complementizer *that* is unacceptable, because this knowledge is not part of the explicit language knowledge speakers of English possess.

(15)   *Who do you think that will come?
(16)   Who do you think will come?
(17)   I know that he will come.

Knowledge of the unavailability of (15) is another case of the Poverty of the Stimulus. In this instance, knowledge will be supplied by the acquisition that *pro* is not part of the English grammar. Noticing overt pronominal subjects and especially dummy subjects *it* and *there* would lead the child to acquire the whole cluster. Keeping all of this in mind, one could predict that a child that had already acquired the Null Subject Parameter would gain knowledge of the whole cluster.

As Baker (2008: 352) noted, history has not been kind to the Null Subject Parameter as originally stated by Rizzi (1982). The parameter leads to various expectations: that null-subject languages will be morphologically rich, that morphologically poor languages will not be null-subject languages, that the properties exemplified in (14) will always cluster together, and so on. It was soon discovered that these predictions were not all borne out. For example, Icelandic and Russian are rich in verbal agreement morphology, but are not null-subject languages. One attempted remedy was to argue that the setting of some other parameter interfered with the Null Subject Parameter. Icelandic was a case in point, where the setting of the verb-second parameter was proposed to mask the effects of null subjects, but that explanation cannot be extended to Russian. Another research direction was to quantify exactly how rich "rich agreement morphology" has to be in order to license null subjects. Both attempts were ultimately unsuccessful. However, both were nice tries, and scientists can only be faulted for not trying to explain existing states of knowledge, not for their explanations eventually failing.

More recently, Snyder (2001) has proposed another parametric cluster that has better withstood the test of time and extended scrutiny. The Compounding Parameter unifies (at least) the following constructions in a parametric cluster: productive noun–noun compounds as in (18), the verb–particle construction (19), the double object construction (20), resultative predicates (21), and *make*-causatives (22). The property underlying all these constructions has to do with the availability of complex predicate constructions, commonly involving productive root-plus-root compounding:

(18) *spider box* (meaning: a box where spiders are kept, a box with a
      spider drawn on its lid, etc.), *soda lady* (meaning: a lady who sips
      soda, a lady who sells soda, a lady who is going to a soda conven-
      tion, etc.)
(19) Mary ate the sandwich up.
(20) Mary gave John a rose garden.
(21) John wiped the table clean.
(22) Mary made John leave.

From its very conception, this parameter unified child language acquisition data and typological observations. Snyder observed a one-way implication in the data from a sizable number of languages: If a language permits
the verb-particle construction, then it also allows free creation of novel
compounds like *spider box* or *soda lady*. The implication is unidirectional,
however: There do exist languages that allow this type of compounding,
yet lack the verb-particle construction. Snyder therefore proposed that
the grammatical pre-requisite for the English type of compounding
(i.e., the positive setting of the compounding parameter) is one of several
prerequisites for the verb–particle construction. A clear acquisition prediction can be made: Any given child acquiring English will either acquire
compounding first, or acquire compounding and the verb–particle construction at the same time. In no case will a child acquire the verb–particle
construction significantly earlier than compounding. This prediction received
strong support from the longitudinal production data of twelve children
(Snyder 1995, 2001).

2.3 The Minimalist Program

As illustrated in the previous section with some representative examples, a
number of prominent parameters from the 1970s and the 80s met with the
harsh reality of additional linguistic data. This situation led some
researchers to reject the usefulness of the parametric endeavor as a whole
and to question whether variation is really constrained (see, e.g., Newmeyer
2005). In this section, we will examine how the concept of parameters has
changed, partly under the pressure of new data, partly because of a new
phase in the Principles and Parameters enterprise, namely, the Minimalist
Program.

The Minimalist Program, and especially its conceptualization after 2000, radically changed the approach to descriptive and explanatory adequacy, aiming to go "beyond explanatory adequacy," which is the title of a programmatic paper by Chomsky (2004). The starting point of the Minimalist model is that the language faculty has to do its job in the most efficient manner possible, given the language architecture we discussed in Chapter 1. This approach in effect postulates that we have to start with the null hypothesis that language is "perfect" or "optimally designed," at least until we get incontrovertible evidence to the contrary. Chomsky's rationale was that research within the Principles and Parameters program had explained enough about the language faculty by the early 1990s, so that a new programmatic goal was possible that would drive scientific inquiry forward and answer novel research questions, such as, how did language evolve.

Even within the P&P analyses, economy of derivation, or the need for derivations to be maximally simple, had been used as a metric to evaluate them. The new Minimalist goal goes further: the number of purely language internal entities the theory postulates should be minimal. The simplified architecture comprises just the Lexicon, the Computational System (also known as the narrow syntax) and two interface components, PF and LF (see Chapter 1). The linguistic information flows from the narrow syntax to the two interfaces. Chomsky considers the operations at the interfaces to be of "virtual conceptual necessity," because there is no getting away from the fact that language is a linearized sequence of symbols (words making up sentences and discourse) coupled with their interpretation. Thus PF and LF are conceptually necessary because they interface with the Articulatory-Perceptual system (the sound or signs) and with the Conceptual-Intentional system (the meaning).

Now, the requirement that language is as perfect as possible leads to the (strong) assumption that the computational system is the same for all languages, that is, it is universal. For example, it cannot be the case that the recursive operation Merge,[8] the principal structure-building operation of the syntax, takes two syntactic objects in Language A and three syntactic objects in Language B. Merge always involves two objects (or nodes). Hence, parametric differences can no longer be captured by postulating

---

[8] "Recursive" means that the operation happens again and again, as many times as needed.

that the syntax of two languages differs. Syntactic operations are universal. Note that this leaves us with only three places of possible variation: the lexicon and the two interfaces. We shall look at these possibilities in turn. Linguists' efforts are currently concentrated on reconceptualizing, or reformulating, the "old" parameters in the new Minimalist spirit, using the simplified language architecture.

The proposal that all parameters are in the lexicon because they are associated with the grammatical features of functional morphology is not new: it was made by Borer (1984) and adopted by Chomsky later on. This idea has been labeled the Borer–Chomsky Conjecture (Baker 2008: 253). It is currently a core assumption in Minimalist theorizing and one of the most influential proposals in the ongoing debate on where language variation is located. All parameters of variation are attributable to differences in the features of particular lexical items, the heads of functional categories, which reside in the lexicon. It is not difficult to see the conceptual appeal of this proposal. If lexical items constitute the sole locus of parametric variation, then learning the vocabulary of a first or second language constitutes learning the parametric profile of that language. In the next section, we will encounter the Bottleneck Hypothesis, a concrete proposal to this effect for L2 acquisition. We will also elucidate what we mean when we say "functional features."

Reconsideration of all the parameters proposed during the 30 years of generative theory development is far from complete, and some parameters are better candidates for reformulation than others. For example, the Null Subject Parameter, in effect, specifies two lexical requirements: the subject–verb agreement morphology in a null-subject language has to be sufficiently rich, and a particular type of pronoun, null little *pro*, must exist in the lexicon. The requirements of the compounding parameter can also be formulated as properties of lexical heads. Let me point out just one advantage of this idea. If variation is relegated to the lexicon, then variety is restricted to easily observable properties of utterances, hence easily learned.

We will next look at proposals that language variation can be captured at the PF and LF interfaces. In order to understand how this might work, we need to look more closely at features and where in the language architecture they are manifested.[9] Features are properties of morphemes and words.

---

[9] The following discussion is based on Gallego (2011).

They can be of three types: *phonological features* such as [± sonorant], [± voice], building up the sound side of the linguistic signal; *semantic features* such as [± specific], [± definite], [± countable] for nouns and nominal phrases, [± stative] [± telic] for verbs and verbal phrases, etc.; and *formal morphosyntactic features* such as [Case: {Nom, Acc, Gen...}], [Person: {1, 2, 3}], [Number: {Sg, Pl}].[10]

But which features are involved in variation? An assumption shared by Chomsky and Jackendoff, for example, is that semantic features are not a source of variation, because all languages have to be able to express the same meanings. Formal features are also present in all languages, but variation is restricted to their actual manifestation. Hence, variation is down to the phonological features of the grammatical morphology, or to make this more precise, to the morpho phonological *expressions* of the syntactic and semantic features. Let me just reiterate this because it is very important: features and their expressions are different things. According to one approach, Halle and Marantz' (1993) Distributed Morphology, the latter are added to the linguistic message after the narrow syntax has produced a detailed phrase structure tree with all formal syntactic features on it evaluated, checked, and some of them deleted (more on this mechanism later on in the book) and the message has bifurcated into PF and LF interfaces.

One suggestion for capturing variation at PF goes as follows. At the end of the syntactic computation, the product is a syntactic (phrase structure) tree. Let us imagine that one item in this tree has moved from one position to another. We already described such movement when talking about Subjacency. The moved item is a copy of the initial item. In effect, after movement, we have two identical copies in two positions of the tree. One way this movement can be captured in the lexicon is to postulate that the attracting head has a feature that initiates the movement. An alternative way could be to think in terms of PF-features that determine which copy of a chain is ultimately pronounced. Some languages would choose to pronounce the top copy while others would choose to pronounce the bottom copy (Bobaljik 2002). In still other cases, which copy is pronounced may depend on the phonological makeup of the surrounding words (Bošković 2001). That would constitute variation at the PF interface. I am repeating

---

[10] See the following website and Adger and Svenonius (2011) for more advanced discussion: http://www.features.surrey.ac.uk/index.html.

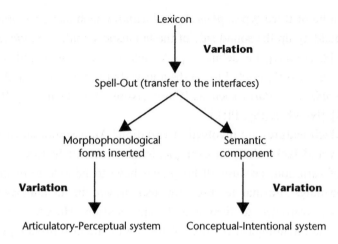

Lexicon

Variation

Spell-Out (transfer to the interfaces)

Morphophonological   Semantic
forms inserted   component

Variation   **Variation**

Articulatory-Perceptual system   Conceptual-Intentional system

Figure 2.1   Minimalist Language Architecture

here the language architecture from Chapter 1, so that the reader can visualize our discussion better (Figure 2.1).

Other researchers have proposed that variation is possible at the LF interface, as well. For example, Ramchand and Svenonius (2008) argue for the possibility that the conceptual systems are universal, but that the mapping between syntax and the C-I systems is non-trivial. More specifically, they propose that certain components of meaning, such as Tense and Aspect, are universally required to be represented in the syntax, while certain other meanings, such as definiteness and specificity, may be supplied by the context. The former constitute the backbone of the sentence. The functional category Aspect is necessary to link the verb with its arguments (e.g., *eat* and *a sandwich*) and give the shape of the event encoded in the verb phrase (ongoing, complete, etc.). The functional category Tense makes sure that the event (e.g., *eat a sandwich*) is linked to a time of utterance (*Mary ate a sandwich* = past, *Mary will eat a sandwich* = future). The entire sequence of functional categories must always be present (at the syntax–semantics interface) to ensure that the C-I system contains the basic skeleton of the sentence meaning.

On the other hand, definiteness is a meaning that is expressed by a dedicated morpheme in some languages (English *the, a*) but is not overtly expressed in some other languages (Mandarin Chinese, Russian, Hindi). How do speakers of these languages understand that a certain noun phrase is to be interpreted as definite? That meaning can be supplied by the context, or by other lexical means such as demonstratives. Other meanings that languages sometimes leave for the context to fill in are specificity, evidentiality,[11] and number. The interface, then, maps the information presented to it by the syntax and the information coming from the context. The actual variation is again captured in lexical items, but is also restricted by the requirements of the conceptual system.

Since different languages may employ different lexical items with different features to encode the same meaning, a crucial trait of this view of the grammar is underspecification, both in lexical and morpholexical (functional) morphemes. To take an example from Ramchand and Svenonius (2008), compared to the explicit dual marking in Northern Sámi personal pronouns *mii* 'I and others' and *moai* 'I and one other', English *we* is underspecified and can be disambiguated (but only if necessary) by adding lexical items (*I and others* versus *I and one other person*). Most of the time the context provides the missing information.

Finally, we will look at another proposal for the locus of variation, which is compatible with the conjecture that all variation is in the lexicon. The gist of this idea was proposed by Giorgi and Pianesi (1996), and it is currently assumed by many researchers. This type of variation applies to the way lexical items themselves are assembled. Universal Grammar provides a common store of atomic elements of meaning (such as semantic and grammatical features); languages select and assemble these features into lexical items (LIs). Now, one language may choose to assemble one array of these features into one LI, while another language may assemble a slightly different array into what superficially looks like an equivalent lexical item. A lexical item is nothing but a bundle of features, including phonological, grammatical, and semantic features. This process is illustrated in Figure 2.2, from Gallego (2011: 548).

Let us now recap the main ideas of this section. We discussed the Minimalist view of language variation, according to which most of the differences between languages of the world are encoded in the lexicon. This view is by no means accepted by all generative linguists, see Baker (2008) for one dissenting view. However, this conjecture is at the core of Minimalist theorizing. We also explored three proposals that are not incompatible

---

[11] Evidentiality encodes whether the speaker witnessed the event she is reporting, or it is hearsay.

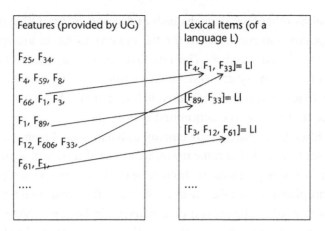

Figure 2.2   Assembling lexical items from features, following Gallego (2011)

with the Borer–Chomsky Conjecture. One proposal was that variation lies at the PF interface, while another proposal was that variation may also lie at the LF interface. Finally, we discussed how the lexicon itself may be a source of variation, through the assembly of different features (phonological, semantic, and grammatical) into actual lexical items of a language.

Why would we care about linguistic proposals on where the differences between languages are located? Particularly if linguists have not made up their own mind just yet? In any cognitive science, current knowledge is in a state of flux. However, we cannot stop research in SLA while waiting for linguists to resolve all their disputes.

> Some of the proposals for the locus of linguistic variation make diverging predictions about language acquisition. Think about what these diverging predictions might be.

2.4   What is the learning task for bilinguals?

In order to ponder what the learning task is in L2 acquisition, an important preliminary question that we need to answer refers to the L2 initial state. What do L2 learners bring to the process of L2 acquisition? There is almost universal consensus[12] that learners do not embark on the task with a clean slate, attempting to activate UG principles and set parameter values solely based on the L2 linguistic experience. They already have a grammar in their head, their native grammar. Following work described in White (1989), Schwartz and Sprouse (1994, 1996) argue that the whole of one's native grammar acts as the initial state of L2 acquisition. This position, known as "L1 transfer," entails that principles are available from UG or from the L1, and one cannot realistically tease these two sources apart. In addition, parameter values are initially transferred from the native language. If the L1 and the L2 have similar parameter values, no adjustment needs to occur; if the L1 and L2 parameter values differ, resetting of parameter values should be accomplished, if the L2 interlanguage grammar is to become targetlike.

While views on parameters in linguistic theory are frequently described,[13] there have been few attempts (but Lardiere, 2009 is a prominent one, to be discussed at length later on) to analyze what those views on parameters would mean for acquiring a second language after the initial L1 transfer. The way language variation is conceptualized virtually determines what a learner must "do" in order to acquire target language parametric values. The view of L1 transfer described above, enunciated most clearly by Schwartz and Sprouse, is firmly based on the Principles and Parameters framework. As the reader has appreciated in this chapter, generative positions on what parameters are and how they can be acquired have changed radically at least three times over the last 50 or 60 years. However, in the wider second language acquisition community some myths about generative parameters still persist, for example, the myth of parameters as on-and-off switches, and the associated idea of clustering. One of my major goals in this textbook is to show that the "new parameters" have already led to important new lines of research in generative SLA research, and that they hold much promise for the future.

In this section, we will preview some concrete applications of Minimalist parameters that follow logically from what we have discussed in this chapter. In keeping with the Scientific Method, L2 researchers insist on approaching the process of L2 development from the point of view of

[12] However, see Epstein, Flynn, and Martohardjono (1996) for a dissenting view.
[13] For excellent recent reviews see Biberauer (2008) and Gallego (2011). Holmberg (2010) presents a spirited and convincing defense of parameters.

learning tasks. These tasks spell out what properties have to be acquired in order for the learner to create in her mind the linguistic representations of the target L2 property. One such proposal is the Bottleneck Hypothesis (Slabakova 2008). The gist of this hypothesis is as follows. If language variation is (predominantly) captured in the lexicon, and more specifically in the functional lexicon, then it makes sense to think of language acquisition as acquiring the functional lexicon of the target language. As we mentioned above, this task would subsume learning the whole parametric profile of the new language. That would make it the most important task in language learning. Consequently, this is where learners and teachers have to concentrate their efforts.

The Bottleneck Hypothesis is also interested in what is difficult and what is easy to acquire in a second language. The motivation is again practical: more difficult areas of the grammar should get more instructional effort and attention, as compared to parts of the grammar that need not be taught because they will come to the learner for free. The predictions are based on current views of the language architecture and on the Minimalist proposals on what is to be acquired. Consequently, the hypothesis argues that there is ample evidence for successful acquisition of phrasal semantics and some universal pragmatics, because these properties are universal. It also predicts that (narrow) syntactic computations will not present insurmountable difficulty to learners, because they can transfer these syntactic mechanisms from their native language. On the other hand, acquiring the functional morphology of a second language, together with the related syntactic and semantic effects, should prove to be more difficult.

What would present the gravest difficulty for L2 learners? One of the hardest tasks would be to acquire a mismatch in the exponents of features.[14] This would be the situation when features are scattered across different lexical items. Recall the Spanish–English mismatch where the habitual action meaning is reflected by the simple past tense in English but in the imperfect tense in Spanish. We will see more examples in the exercises of this chapter and later in the book. L2 acquisition is also predicted to be especially difficult when the target parameter values are not fixed in overt functional morphology but signaled by various (lexical, word order) means or left to the discourse to supply. This is so because a specific

---

[14] As proposed by Lardiere (2009a,b), Ramchand and Svenonius (2008), and Slabakova (2009).

grammatical meaning (say, tense) is not predictably and uniformly signaled by one and the same morpheme every time it needs to be encoded. The learner has to attend to various cues and signals in the surrounding situation and the discourse in order to deduce the meaning. In sum, linguistic-theoretical proposals for parametric differences among languages are still our best tool in investigating second language grammars.

In this chapter, we focused on language variation, discussing several proposals on where the differences between languages may lie. Old-style P&P parameters were visualized as on-and-off switches, bringing clusters of unrelated constructions into the grammar. Minimalist parameters are closely tied to the acquisition of formal features. Mismatches and variation on feature expressions present hazards for successful acquisition.

2.5 Exercises

Exercise 2.1. Kayne (2005: 9) points to the following differences among English, Italian, and French.

a. We don't know **where** to go.
b. We don't know **whether** to leave.
c. *We don't know **if** to leave.

d. *Jean ne   sait   pas **si** part-ir   (French)
    Jean   NEG   know-3SG   not   if   leave-INF

e. Gianni non   sa   **se** part-ire   (Italian)
    Gianni NEG   know-3SG   if   leave-INF

Let us look at the English paradigm first, sentences (a), (b), and (c). The main clause subject (*we*) is the understood subject of the embedded clause. In other words, the people who don't know, and the people who need to go somewhere/leave, are "*we*." These are called control constructions. *Whether* is acceptable as the complementizer of the embedded clause, but *if* is not. (*If* has other requirements for its surroundings, which you may discover by creating your own examples.) Italian allows its equivalent of *if* to appear in structure (e), while French doesn't, as in (d). Discuss whether this is a parametric difference. Can it be described in terms of a binary choice? Is it possible to capture this difference in the functional lexicon of these languages? Is this difference pervasive in the grammar? Would you change your answer on taking the following additional data into account?

f. Jean veut   l'-achet-er   (French)
    Jean want-3SG   CLITIC-buy-INF
    'Jean wants to buy it.'

g. Gianni vuole   compr-ar-**lo**   (Italian)
    Gianni want-3SG   buy-INF-CLITIC
    'Gianni wants to buy it.'

Describe the different orders between object clitic (bold in the examples above) and infinitive in French and Italian. Do you see any connection with the sentences in (d) and (e)? Would English be relevant in the discussion of this difference?

Exercise 2.2. One of the cornerstones of the Principles and Parameters approach was the X-bar schema, which has retained its importance for the theory. It maintains that every phrase in language has the following components: a head of the phrase, a complement, and a specifier. They are in a hierarchical structure as shown below:

(i)

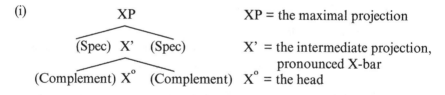

XP = the maximal projection

X' = the intermediate projection, pronounced X-bar

X° = the head

What you have in (i) is the general schema for all languages, but within each language, only one specifier and one complement are permitted. The intermediate levels can be repeated, but each phrase has only one head and only one maximal projection. Keeping the general schema in mind, draw the four logically possible phrase structures. The first one has been provided:

(ii)

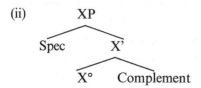

Next, recall the typological generalizations we made in Chapter 1, repeated here for ease of reference. These pervasive regularities in harmonic languages have been described as the Head Directionality Parameter.

(iii)   If V–O, then Auxiliary–V, Prepositions, Noun–Adjective, Noun–Genitive, Noun–Relative Clause.
        If O–V, then V–Auxiliary, Postpositions, Adjective–Noun, Genitive–Noun, Relative Clause–Noun
(iv)   The head of the phrase precedes/follows its complement.

For the time being, ignore the position of the Specifier (assuming it is always on the left) and focus on the relative positions of the head and its complement. Provide the structures of the following English phrases, where the heads are underlined. The first one is provided.

VP: _eat_ an apple; NP: _bone_ of contention; AP: _proud_ of his daughter; PP: _at_ the market

(v)

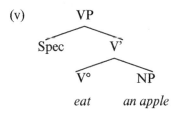

Are English phrases head-initial or head-final? Are all the complements NPs? Does English seem to be entirely harmonic, when you look at the orders in (i)?

Now, what are the predictions that you would make for the equivalent Japanese categories, VP, NP, AP, and PP? Draw their phrase structures.

The X-bar schema is another example of a principle that is also flexible. Describe how the Head Directionality Parameter provides the flexibility of the X-bar schema.

Exercise 2.3. This exercise is related to the one above, so do them in order. We have just seen above that the lexical categories (Noun, Verb, Adjective, Preposition) have the structure reflected in (ii). How about the functional heads Determiner, Tense, Aspect, and Complementizer, which project their own functional categories? Do you think they have the same structure? Would it be an acquisitional advantage if they did? Can you think of the structure of TP in English? What can it have as its complement? Think of examples such as:

a) John might go to Edinburgh.
b) John might have been to Edinburgh.
c) John is going to Edinburgh.

Exercise 2.4. Write down concrete predictions for the acquisition of the Null Subject Parameter in English by Italian or Spanish native speakers. What is the English value of this parameter?

Write down concrete predictions for the acquisition of the Compounding Parameter by English-native learners of Spanish. Spanish displays the opposite value of English. What would you expect the learners to know?

Exercise 2.5. The White (1985) study of the Null Subject Parameter (also known as the Pro-Drop Parameter) is a classic study in the generative SLA research framework. We mentioned it in Chapter 1. Find it on your library website and download it onto your hard drive. Here is the exact reference.

White, L. 1985. The Pro-Drop Parameter in adult second language acquisition. *Language Learning* Vol. 35, No. 1, pp. 47–62.

Answer the following questions:

1. Which three properties related to the NSP did the study investigate?
2. Why did the researcher include two experimental groups, French-speakers learning English and Spanish-speakers learning English?
3. What kind of test was used? Why were some filler sentences included that were unrelated to the NSP? Were all of the fillers acceptable? Why not?
4. How can you summarize the results? Was the level of proficiency a factor in accepting ungrammatical null subject sentences in English? How about in accepting post-verbal subjects?
5. Were the three NSP constructions acquired as a cluster, according to the findings of this study? Which construction presented the most difficulty?
6. One of the constructions in the purported cluster, the *that*-trace effect, is more complex than the others. The researcher is aware of that discrepancy in complexity. What prediction of the NSP does she

decide to look at in order to avoid this discrepancy (p. 57 of the article).

7. The unacceptability of missing pronominal subjects and of postverbal subjects seem to be of equal complexity, at least as compared to the *that*-trace effect, which is more complex than them. Did the loss of these two properties in the L2 English go hand in hand?

8. What is the author's interpretation of the results? Do you agree with it? Why, or why not?

3

The psychological reality
of language in use

In the previous chapter, we looked at how languages differ among themselves, and how these parametric differences were described throughout the course of generative linguistics. The new, minimalist view of parameters works together with the specific language architecture and the view of multiple spell-out at phases smaller than a sentence. We considered the possibility that language variation resides in the lexicon, through the grammatical features reflected in various lexical items and in various combinations, but also at the interface with sound (PF) and with meaning (LF). In this chapter, the language architecture and the grammar continue to be very important; however, we consider their relationship with the processing system. We will be interested in the psychological reality of language during the encoding and decoding of the linguistic message. In current generative theory, linguistic structure, acquisition, and use are intrinsically associated (Truscott and Sharwood Smith 2004).

3.1 What happens when we hear a sentence?

What happens when we hear a sentence? We listen out for the sounds and, as they come in, we store them in short-term memory until we have enough to make a word. Then the word is passed on to the mental lexicon, the word storage space where its meaning, morphology, and syntax are activated, and the sounds making up the next word start coming through. Again, the results of lexical processing are retained in short-term memory. We start combining the words into a syntactic structure as soon as we can, and we continue this process (called *parsing*) until all the words have been accommodated in the structure. We clear up any uncertainties about who did what to whom using knowledge of the world and discourse context, and we finally reach the full sentence meaning. Is language comprehension really that simple? Not at all, but we will start this section with a breakdown of the processes in order to understand what is involved in decoding a linguistic signal. The short answer: Quite a lot. We will briefly discuss phonological, lexical, morphological, and syntactic processing in this chapter in order to delineate the main ingredients of linguistic processing.

3.2 Phonological perception and lexical recognition

Speech, not writing, is the primary medium of language. Many languages do not have writing systems, many others only developed such systems in the last century or two. Reading is a relatively new capacity from an evolutionary standpoint. Children are quite good at their native language before they learn how to read, and arguably, writing does not aid their language acquisition.[1] Having established that spoken and heard language is the primary modality for language acquisition as well as for most communication, we start our discussion of processing from the acoustic signal. We should distinguish between phonological perception and word recognition, the process that happens when a proficient native speaker hears a word

---

[1] Later on in life, after they learn to read and write, children definitely expand vocabulary through those means as well. They are also exposed to structures that are more typical in written language (such as the passive) but that they also learn to incorporate in speech.

that is part of a sentence. We will leave the issue of how children break into the acoustic signal of their native language for Chapter 4.

Adult speakers of English have been estimated to know between 50,000 and 100,000 words. They are stored in something that linguists call the *mental lexicon*, an organized system of all those words that we know. When we hear the acoustic signal of a word, we start a search of our mental lexicon. This process does not resemble the search for a word in a dictionary. The frequency of individual words and even word parts (morphemes) is crucial for our vocabulary knowledge. That is because vocabulary knowledge depends on experience. You are quite confident that you know common words such as *coffee* and *problem* while you might not be so certain about words like *commensurate* and *berm*. It is possible that you know you have heard a word, but you are unable to give a definition or paraphrase its meaning.

But what happens when we hear a word that is part of a sentence? Well, that depends on whether we speak the language of that sentence or not. Imagine that you are played a sentence in a language such as Kikuyu. You will not know where one word stops and the next begins. What we do in a language we speak is *segment* the speech into words. Hearing speech is not at all like seeing the words written on the page, because they are already segmented in the written text. As an exercise, take a look at the waveform of a sentence given in Figure 3.1.

Try to figure out where the word boundaries are. In a normal speech situation, it is not the case that we hear silent spaces between words and, as a reflection of that, we do not see gaps in the waveform at the end of words.

   Onecouldthusthinkofthespeechsignalasatextwithoutspaces.

Another pervasive process in speech is *coarticulation*. The individual sounds change some of their qualities to blend together, to become more like the surrounding sounds, and that is true across word boundaries. Let us take an example of coarticulation with the pronunciation of the word *happy* whose phonetic representation is /hæpi/. Before you say anything, you will have moved your tongue into position for /æ/. Then, while you are saying /h/, it will sound a bit like /æ/. While you are saying /æ/, you will also be closing your lips for /p/. While your lips are together for /p/, you will be moving your tongue from where you had it for /æ/ to where you need it for /i/. Finally, while you are saying /i/, you will be opening your lips after /p/. The whole word will usually be uttered in less than half a second. To take another

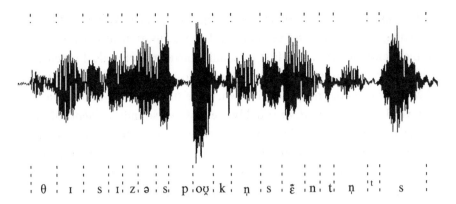

 θ ɪ s ɪ z ə s p ɔʊ k ŋ s ɛ̃ n t ŋ t s

Figure 3.1 Spectrogram of the sentence *This is a spoken sentence*

example, in French, a word-final voiceless consonant will often become voiced if followed by a voiced segment. So the word *avec* 'with' on its own is pronounced /avek/, but when it is followed by a word beginning with a voiced consonant such as /v/ in *vous* 'you' /vu/, we usually hear /aveg/. So the phrase *avec vous* 'with you' is often pronounced /aveg vu/. In short, speech is a continuous, connected stream of sounds, and sounds have a strong effect on other sounds that are adjacent or close to them.

In order to understand speech, the listener has to break down the continuous speech signal into a discrete sequence of words. Even before the listener gets to the lexical information, there are pre-lexical characteristics of the speech stream that help to achieve segmentation. Chief among pre-lexical cues is the rhythm of speech, the repetition of sequences of stressed and unstressed syllables that give the speech signal its specific rhythmic sound, not unlike music. In tone languages such as Mandarin and Thai, tone would be another pre-lexical cue for segmentation.

However, speech rhythm can only take the listener so far in the breaking of the stream of sounds. Adult listeners get crucial help in this process from their native vocabulary. The speech segmentation process goes hand in hand with retrieving word forms stored in our mental lexicon. Indeed, models of spoken word recognition have tried to explain how we find matches between sequences of sounds in the speech signal and word forms in the lexicon (e.g., Marslen-Wilson and Welsh 1978, McClelland and Elman 1986, Norris 1994). In these models, parts of the speech signal are matched with words that we have stored in our mental lexicon, until every part of the speech signal corresponds to a meaningful word.

The simplest version of lexical recognition starts with mapping the incoming signal onto the phonological representation of existing words in the mental lexicon. The first psycholinguistic model to deal specifically with the recognition of speech is the Cohort model of Marslen-Wilson (1987). This model proposes that when the first 150–200 milliseconds of the word is encountered, or roughly the first two sounds, a *cohort* of other words matching the word up to that moment is activated. For example, if encountering the beginning of the word *February*, /fɛ/, all words beginning with /fɛ/ are activated such as *fence* and *phenomenon*. Note that spelling doesn't matter. When the subsequent sound comes in as /b/, words that do not begin with /fɛb/ drop out of the cohort. This process is repeated until (optimally) the cohort is reduced to one member. *February*, for instance, can be recognized by the third segment, because no other English word begins with /fɛb/. This moment is known as the uniqueness point. The recognition point in this model can come well before the actual end of the word. As more input is heard, some words in the cohort become incompatible with the input sound and are filtered out. This would be phonetic-based filtering. But filtering can also be contextual: words that are incompatible with the syntactic or semantic context are also filtered out.

This latter claim suggests that not only the phonological representation is activated at the very beginning. Marslen-Wilson (1987) demonstrated this with an experimental task called (cross-modal) priming. When experiment participants are asked to recognize a *target* word written on a screen as a word or a non-word, the task involves lexical decision. However, when another word is seen for a fraction of a second before the target word, this other word is known as a *prime* and it influences the speed of recognition of the target word. If the prime is heard and the target is written, priming is called cross-modal because it spans two modalities. Marslen-Wilson found that semantic similarity between prime–target pairs such as *confess* and *sin* leads to faster recognition times of the target, as compared to a non-related prime such as *tennis* and *sin*. The researcher wanted to find out whether cohort meanings would be activated before the uniqueness point. He primed both *sin* and *wedding* with the word fragment *confe*, which could be the beginning of *confess* as well as *confetti*. He found facilitation effects in both cases, which suggests that when we hear a word, we do not only activate the meaning of that word, but also, very briefly, the meanings of its competitors in the cohort. More recently, Gaskell and Marslen-Wilson (2002) argued that the meaning activation is limited to just one or two meanings compatible with the speech input.

In the Cohort model, words are either a part of the word-initial cohort of activation, or they are not. However, other models of speech recognition, such as the TRACE model (McClelland and Elman 1986), introduced a refinement of the process. If a number of words are compatible with the initial portion of the word, but some are better candidates than others due to consistency with the input, then those better candidates will be more highly activated than the weaker candidates. Thus activation levels are on a continuous scale.

Mental lexicon researchers now agree on at least three aspects of spoken word recognition. First, there is consensus on the fact that multiple word candidates are activated in parallel as a word is being heard, constituting the word-initial cohort. Secondly, activation of word candidates varies with the degree of matching between the speech signal and stored lexical representations. Finally, all activated candidate words compete for recognition (Weber and Scharenborg 2012). Researchers also agree that word knowledge is the foundation on which knowledge of language rests.

Teaching relevance

Why is this important for teachers of language to know? It is important to appreciate how complicated the process of word recognition is in adult native speakers of a language, because one can then appreciate how much more complicated the process of word recognition is in bilinguals. Bilinguals have potentially double (although rarely so) the number of vocabulary items in their mental lexicon, some from their native and some from their second language. Imagine the mental lexicon of multilinguals. As a result of larger mental lexicons, the word recognition process in multilinguals takes longer. It makes sense that the following structure-building processes are going to be slower, too, compared to monolinguals. Note, however, that slower mental lexicon access does not really mean imperfect, or faulty, access.

3.3 Morphology

In the previous section, we discussed how words are picked out from the speech stream and accessed in the mental lexicon. In this section, we will look at another aspect of this same process: whether whole words or morphemes are being accessed, and what the factors affecting this process may be. It is often taken for granted that we access the words of the incoming sentence, but actually there is compelling evidence that this is not always the case. Before we can explain why, we have to go over some terms and the related concepts.

As you know, words can be divided into *morphemes,* the smallest meaningful units of language, and these units follow certain (morphological) rules when they combine to make up words. For our purposes here, it is essential to distinguish functional morphemes from lexical morphemes (see also Exercise 2.3 in the previous chapter). In the word *book-s, book* is a lexical morpheme (it can also be a word on its own, so it is a *free* morpheme) while *-s* marks the plural. The latter cannot exist on its own so it is classified as a *bound* morpheme. Morphemes that add grammatical meaning (plural, tense, agreement, etc.) to the lexical items are called *inflectional.* Note that they cannot change the word category (N, V, etc.) of the word they attach to. If *book* is a noun, then its plural is still a noun, as in *He reads* **book-s** *all the time.* If *books* is a verb as in *She* **book-s** *her flights well in advance*, then the *-s* marks that the present tense verb agrees with a 3rd person subject (not plural). What is known as *functional* morphology includes inflectional bound morphemes as well as free functional words such as *the, a, of, and*, etc., that is, all morphemes with some grammatical function. All functional morphemes are non-category changing.

Derivational morphemes, on the other hand, expand the lexical meaning of the original lexical morpheme or word, and can change the word category. In the word *boy-ish-ness,* the adjectival suffix *-ish* attaches to the noun *boy*, while the nominal suffix *-ness* attaches to the new word *boyish.* The structure of the word is as shown in (1). In English, the category of the whole word is the same as the category of the rightmost morpheme, in this case, *-ness.* There are no exceptions to this rule of word formation.

(1)   [[[boy $_N$] + -ish $_A$] + -ness $_N$]

Before you go on, think (on your own or with classmates) about the morphological structure of the following words: *desirability, ungentlemanliness, cooperatively,* and *examinations.*

Do these linguistic descriptions hold any relevance to how the mental lexicon is organized? A full-listing approach would have it that all complex words are stored whole so that the polymorphemic word *disenchantment* is accessed as a whole unit, the same way as the monomorphemic word *cat*. (How many morphemes in *disenchantment,* by the way?) Almost no one believes this is the case, however. The opposite proposal would be the affix-stripping, or a fully decompositional approach (Taft and Forster 1975), according to which all polymorphemic words are composed as they are being accessed, within the mental lexicon. As usual, the truth lies in between these two extreme proposals. It turns out that the most important factor affecting decomposition in the lexicon is a word's frequency: the more frequent a word, the higher the chance that it will be stored and accessed as a whole unit.

Decomposability is another factor, though. We will illustrate this with one of the longest and most important debates in contemporary cognitive science: the Great Past Tense Debate. As is well known, English has regular past tense forms such as *walk-ed* but also irregular ones such as *ate*. The latter is morpho phonologically opaque, meaning that it is not clear where the verb form stops and the past tense morpheme begins. In fact, it is quite clear that most irregular past tense forms are *not* decomposable into a lexical and an inflectional morpheme, although the two meanings are present in the form: *ate* = *eat* + |past|. These features of English past tense inflection allow researchers to contrast the whole-word and the decompositional approaches to lexical representation in a direct way. The debate has been waging since the mid-1980s and is also known as the Words and Rules Debate. Its significance is enhanced by the fact that it has become a proxy for comparing and contrasting two fundamentally opposed approaches to linguistic knowledge. The fundamental choice is whether rule-like behavior should be explained in terms of symbolic computation describable with a rule such as *verb + -ed = past tense verb* (Pinker 1999, Pinker and Ullman 2002), or in terms of connectionist learning systems, containing neither rules nor symbols but only levels of activation based on previous experience (McClelland and Rumelhart 1986, McClelland and Patterson 2002).

It is important to mention that it is not irregular verb forms that are under debate: both sides of the debate agree that irregulars are acquired and processed by a connectionist (usage-based) learning mechanism. The disagreement comes in the treatment of regular verbs. The connectionist approach holds that both regular and irregular verb forms are controlled by a single, integrated mechanism of word learning and access. This mechanism depends on phonological and semantic constraints operating together. The approach rejects the analysis that stem and inflectional morphemes are separable, and argues instead that inflected forms are learned and represented as whole forms. The more a verbal form (whether regular or irregular) is encountered and used, the stronger its associations within the neural network.[2]

On the other side of the debate, psycholinguists such as Pinker, Ullman, Marcus, Clahsen and colleagues argued vigorously in several papers over the years (e.g. Pinker and Prince 1988, Pinker 1999, Pinker and Ullman 2002), that regular past tense verb forms are decomposable, and that every time they are accessed, a symbolic rule operates in the lexicon to combine them into the needed form. In the mid 1990s, the nature of the evidence that the two sides were bringing to bear on the debate changed from studying behavioral observations and measures to looking at the underlying neural systems supporting the two types of forms. Marslen-Wilson (2007) reviews evidence from several studies investigating the behavior of people with brain lesions. These studies, according to him, point to the conclusion that decomposition processes are obligatory in the brain. They map the semantic and the phonological information of the verbal forms to brain regions that are separable although related. The on-line interpretation process integrates the use of these different brain regions. This conclusion can be extended (with caution) to all types of inflectional morphology in the mental lexicon.

3.4 The syntactic parser

Morphemes and words are just the ingredients of sentences and discourse. In order to understand linguistic processing, we now look at the processing of syntax. Syntactic processing is executed by the *syntactic parser*. Parsing involves the rapid and automatic assignment of grammatical structure to a sentence encountered in speech (Pritchett 1992: 1). Without assigning structure to the incoming signal, comprehenders cannot understand who does what in sentences such as *John kissed Mary*. Interpretation depends, among other things, on *thematic roles* such as Agent and Patient (also known as

---

[2] If you want to learn more about connectionist neural networks and how they work, refer to this source: http://plato.stanford.edu/entries/connectionism/.

Theme). When we hear a verb, its objects, and its subject, we attribute such thematic roles (a.k.a. theta roles) to the noun phrases surrounding the verb, depending on its meaning. For example, John is the Agent of the Mary-kissing event, and Mary is the Patient (the event was initiated by John and may have been without her active participation). Other such theta roles are Experiencer (*John dislikes his new boss*), Recipient (*John gave Mary a check*), Goal (Mary walked *to the farmers' market*), and others. We normally interpret theta roles without much confusion, because they constitute lexical information encoded in the verb.

Now look at the two structures in (2a) and (2b) representing *John kissed Mary*. The labels of nodes we will use in this chapter conform better to psycholinguistic practice, and are somewhat simplified. S stands for Sentence, NP for noun phrase, and VP for verb phrase.

(2) a.

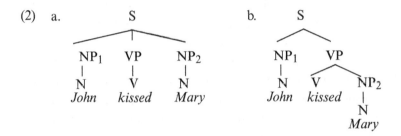

Note that the structure in (2a) presents the two NPs as equal partners, or sister nodes, to the VP. That structure predicts that the subject and object would behave in a similar fashion in various sentences. On the other hand, the structure in (2b) entails that the verb and the object come together, or merge first, and then as a second step, they merge with the subject. The relationship between the verb and the object is somehow closer than the relationship between the verb and the subject. This central syntactic fact is supported by a range of well-studied subject–object asymmetries, and we will glance at just two of them.

Marantz (1984) observed that while English has many idioms and specialized meanings for verbs in which the internal argument, the object, is the fixed part of the idiom and the external argument, the subject, is free, the reverse situation is considerably rarer. To put it in other words, the role played by the subject argument often depends on the filler of the object position, but not vice versa. Take Kratzer's (1996: 114) examples:

(3)   a. kill a cockroach
      b. kill a conversation
      c. kill an evening watching TV
      d. kill a bottle (i.e., empty it)
      e. kill an audience (i.e., wow them).

The killer of a bottle is a drinker, while the killer of an audience is a performer. As the examples above illustrate, the meaning of the verb within the verb phrase changes dramatically depending on the object, while this rarely happens when we vary the subjects. This fact supports structure (2b) as the correct analysis.

Secondly, we can have a reflexive pronoun in object position but not in subject position, and this is true universally for all languages. The reflexive *himself* is not self-sufficient in meaning: it takes its reference from its antecedent, in this case the NP_1 *John*. The antecedent has to *c-command* the reflexive, otherwise the sentence would sound awful as in (4b). C-command is a basic relationship between nodes in a tree structure. A node, say NP_1 c-commands another node NP_2 if NP_1 does not dominate NP_2, NP_2 does not dominate NP_1, and the first branching node dominating NP_1 also dominates NP_2. See for yourself how these relations play out above in trees (2a) and (2b). C-command has not only syntactic consequences, but interpretive ones, too.

(4)   a. John likes himself.
      b. *Himself likes John.

If our structure of a simple sentence were as in (2a) with NP_1 and NP_2 being on an equal footing, we would not be able to explain these facts, and especially the closer connection between the verb and its object. Remember, structure predicts syntactic behavior and interpretation. This is a potent fact.

When we have an ambiguous sentence, a sentence with two interpretations, unless the ambiguity is lexical,[3] it is usually diagrammed as two distinct phrase structure trees. Take for example the sentence in (5).

---

[3] An example of a lexical ambiguity are the two meanings of the word *port*: "haven" and "wine." These two meanings are equally possible in the sentence *They passed the port at midnight.* What are the two meanings: paraphrase them. Of course, in normal communication, the context usually disambiguates.

(5)   Mary ate the cake in the dining room.
- Interpretation 1: Mary consumed the cake that was in the dining room (but she may have left untouched the cake that was in the kitchen).
- Interpretation 2: Mary engaged in a cake-eating event in the dining room. It was in the dining room where that event happened.

(6)   Structure for Interpretation 1. (A triangle represents more detailed structure inside the node, but it is not shown because it is not relevant for the particular point we want to make.)

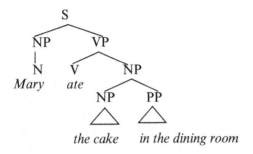

(7)   Structure for Interpretation 2

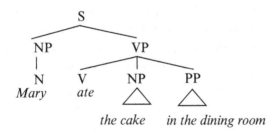

    In (6), the PP *in the dining room* modifies only the NP *the cake,* pointing to where that sample of baked goods is to be found. In (7), however, the same PP modifies the verb and the NP object together, signaling that the eating event happened in the dining room. See how structure determines interpretation?
    The representations in (6) and (7) are linguistic representations. But are they used by the parser? Psycholinguists argue about the relationship between real-time computation (parsing) and the underlying grammar (or grammatical representations). While the issue has not been solved

definitively and to everyone's satisfaction, the gamut of views ranges from a minimal relationship, or even a complete separation, to a functional dependency. Thus, one view is that the grammar just describes grammatical and ungrammatical sentences (through its rules and constraints) but is not directly implicated in real-time language processes (Sag and Wasow 2011). On the other hand, another view (Pritchett 1988, 1992, Phillips 2013) is that there is no need for the grammar and the parser to be separate, that they are aligned and the grammar can be implemented in on-line comprehension and production, with the addition of other psychological mechanisms. Juffs and Rodriguez (2015: 15) provide a useful analogy for the relationship of the grammar and the parser as the internal combustion engine at rest versus running. Do you see a parallel with Mark Baker's bread versus bread recipe metaphor?

[T]he grammar is the engine at rest, not driving the vehicle, but with the potential to do so. Parsing is the engine in motion, subject to stresses and possible breakdowns allowable by the system, and driving production or comprehension in real time. Just as an engine's function can be affected by fuel, availability of oxygen, oil level and road conditions, the operation of the grammar during processing may be affected by the quality of input, memory limitations, and interference from outside influences not related to the architecture of the grammar itself.

Current evidence favors the view that human grammatical abilities are best understood as a single structure-building system that assembles syntactic structures in a roughly left-to-right order and that the internal grammar is a key component of the parsing and production mechanisms. We shall now look at some concrete proposals. Consider again the ambiguous string of words in (5) and its two interpretations in (6) and (7). The sequence of words can be structured, or organized, in more than one way, consistent with the grammar rules of the language. Are ambiguous sentences harder to understand, compared to unambiguous sentences of similar word and structure complexity? If the answer is yes, then this fact would support the hypothesis that structure is indeed quickly built in parsing sentences. It could also be used to argue for an actual separation between the parser and the grammar, with the grammar proposing structures and the parser taking these structures for a test drive to choose the better option.

The short answer is that ambiguity does lead to longer reading times, and lower comprehension accuracy, although the preceding context can substantially modify these effects. In order to understand how listeners and readers attribute structure to sentences, linguists study the parsing of *temporarily ambiguous* sentences (also known as *garden path* sentences) such as (8).

(8)   The tomcat curled up on the cushion seemed friendly.

Temporarily ambiguous sentences contain a sequence of words that can be plausibly arranged in one structure, but half-way through the computation, the incoming words suggest that the first analysis was wrong and has to be changed. The comprehender ultimately arrives at just one global sentence interpretation, but was "led down the garden path" for a short time during the parsing. Imagine that you are reading on a screen the words or phrases of sentence (8), appearing one after the other, in the exact spot where they would be if the whole sentence were put up on the screen. This is known as the self-paced moving window presentation paradigm, because readers have to press a button every time they are ready for the next word to appear on the screen. It is assumed that the time between the appearance of a word and the button press for advancement is a function of how easy or difficult it is to accommodate the last word within the structure already built in the mind by that moment. Reaction times are calculated for each word or phrase slot.

(9)   Self-paced moving window presentation
    a. The tomcat _____ _____ _____ _____.
    b. _____ curled up _____ _____ _____.
    c. _____ _____ on the cushion _____ _____.
    d. _____ _____ _____ seemed _____.
    e. _____ _____ _____ _____ friendly.

Imagine that the sentence starts with step a), then step b). By the end of step c) *on the cushion*, the parser would be ready to fold up with the structure since this is a plausible sentence: *The tomcat curled up on the cushion,* with a subject NP, an intransitive verb and a location prepositional phrase (PP) analysis. When the next verb appears in step d), however, it becomes immediately clear that *seemed* is the main verb of the sentence and the grammatical function of *curled up* has to be reconsidered. The parser has to perform the additional step of reanalysis of the preceding structure into a reduced relative clause: *The tomcat (that was) curled up on the cushion,* where the words in parentheses are optionally omitted. That additional step takes longer to accommodate. In general, the longer it takes people to understand part of a sentence, the greater the processing load it imposes. When the final segment *friendly* appears, it just confirms the second analysis.

Before going further, try to analyze the following sentence (from Frazier and Rayner 1982) in such an incremental way:

(10)   While Susan was dressing the baby played on the floor.

What would be the first analysis, which segment would set off the reanalysis, and what would be the second analysis? Think about the properties of the verb *dress*. What property of this verb makes the temporal ambiguity possible?

The view that the language processor operates incrementally has enjoyed a lot of experimental support: it rapidly constructs a syntactic analysis for a sentence fragment, starting from left to right, merging syntactic constituents to establish a sentence node and then to expand it to the right. The processor also assigns each constituent a semantic interpretation, and relates this interpretation to world knowledge. In the next section, we will go over the classic models and debates of syntactic processing.

3.5 Models of syntactic processing

There is considerable controversy about when language users employ different sources of information during sentence processing. There is a major divide in the psycholinguistic literature depending on the following fundamental question: whether hearers/readers immediately use all relevant sources of information, or whether some sources of information are delayed relative to others? Based on the answers to these questions, sentence-processing theories can be divided into *interactive* accounts, in which all relevant information can be used immediately, and *modular* accounts, in which some information can be used immediately but some information cannot, and parsing has a somewhat cyclical nature.

We shall start by exemplifying the latter, among which the Garden Path model (e.g., Frazier 1987, Rayner et al. 1983) is the classic and most influential account. What does it mean that readers or listeners slow down their processing at step d) in example (9) above? It means that they have been making decisions about how to organize words into phrases and clauses before they have received sufficient information to be certain about the decisions they are making. In the moving window presentation, readers see that there are two more segments coming up, but that doesn't stop them from positing an analysis of a complete clause with the words that have appeared until that moment. Readers as well as listeners follow the *immediacy principle*: build as much structure as you can, as soon as possible (Just and Carpenter 1980). In the case of sentence (9), by the time they have heard step c) they build structure as in (11):

(11)

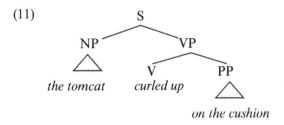

Only after they encounter the verb *seemed* do they go back and reconsider that analysis to come up with the correct one in (12).

(12)

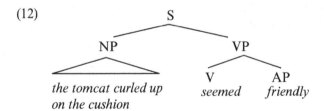

The idea that listeners and readers build and maximize structure immediately, even if it is the wrong structure, then get stranded along the garden path, after which they go back and reconsider their initial analysis at considerable processing cost, is at the foundation of Lyn Frazier's Garden Path model (Frazier 1979, 1987, Frazier and Rayner 1982). It is considered *a two-stage processing model* because she proposes that syntactic processing goes through an initial stage, at which the incoming words are analyzed to see what category they belong to: A, N, V, P, etc. No other information is available at that first stage, the parser only cares about categorical information and phrase structure rules. At the second stage of sentence interpretation, meaning is computed by applying semantic rules to the syntactic structure already built. That is why semantic information, frequency, and information from the context can only be taken into consideration at this second stage of processing. If we consider the debate mentioned in the beginning of this section, namely, at what stage of sentence processing people use different sources of information, the Garden Path model will be classified as a modular account. Modular models assume that the mind consists of modules that perform very specialized processes, and these processes are informationally encapsulated (closed off) in the sense that they use only information represented within that particular module (Fodor 1983).

The classic version of the model proposes two parsing heuristics, *late closure* and *minimal attachment,* that can be seen as embodying a drive for processing efficiency. Late closure postulates: Do not build more structure than strictly necessary, if possible continue to work on the structure that you are currently building.

> Going back to our examples, try to figure out how late closure explains the wrong initial analysis of sentence (9) as in (11).

Minimal attachment urges the parser to create structure with as few nodes as possible. In later work, these heuristics were augmented with the *main assertion preference,* which proposes that if the parser has any choice, it builds a structure where the new elements are related to the main assertion of the clause. In other words, they are arguments, not adjuncts.

Recent parsing findings suggest that the parser applies the heuristics in a flexible way. What heuristics are going to be applied in the sentence analysis will depend on the properties of the sentence, and most importantly, on the selectional requirements of the verb. As Traxler (2012: 151) points out, one of the main advantages of the Garden Path model is that it makes concrete predictions on where readers and listeners will experience processing difficulty. That means that the model is falsifiable, which is a fundamental requirement of all scientific proposals (think of the scientific method discussion in Chapter 1).

Alternative models of sentence parsing are *constraint-based,* or *interactive* parsing models (e.g., MacDonald, Pearlmutter, and Seidenberg 1994, Spivey-Knowlton and Sedivy 1995, Trueswell, Tanenhaus, and Garnsey 1994). Rather than building one structure at a time, constraint-based parsers are capable of pursuing multiple analyses of a clause at the same time. This is because the models adopt a parallel distributed processing architecture, similar to the TRACE model we discussed of lexical processing (see Section 3.2). This type of parser represents phrases and clauses not as grammatical structures as in (11) and (12) above, but as patterns of activation spreading over interconnected processing units. The units make up a neural network resembling the functioning of networks of neurons in the brain. While partial information can lead to partial activation of multiple mental representations, experience, frequency of association, and context decide which of the partially activated structures is the most likely analysis.

To come back to the example in (9), the constraints allow the parser to start building several structural hypotheses, using information from the lexical items, as well as syntactic and semantic knowledge, all at the same time. Because of this simultaneous employment of all possible resources, constraint-based models are known also as *one-stage models.* Of the multiple analyses being entertained, the more plausible ones are awarded with more activation while the less plausible ones lose out until they fade out completely. The activation levels presumably change with every incoming word. When two analyses remain highly plausible, hence activated, it takes a long time (relatively speaking) before the correct analysis wins the competition and the incorrect (but initially highly activated) analysis is inhibited. Thus competition results in processing difficulty and delay. Note that we cannot speak of reanalysis with this type of model, since both analyses are activated from the onset of the ambiguity. An attractive feature of the interactive processor allows it to immediately draw upon all possible sources of information during sentence processing, including semantics, discourse context, and information about the frequency of syntactic structures.

Most constraint-based models are also *lexicalist* in the sense that they assume that syntactic information is associated with words. As mentioned above, it is generally well established that verbs contain information about the arguments that they select. In addition, all verbal lexical entries are assumed to encode the frequency with which they occur in particular argument frames. For example, the verb *see* appears 9 times out of 10 with a direct object argument (e.g., *John saw Mary*). In 1 out of 10 cases, the verb is used intransitively (e.g., *I see*). This type of information is used during syntactic ambiguity resolution. Hence, many constraint-based models assume that there is a tight correspondence between sentence comprehension and production preferences: Structures that are produced frequently should be easier to process than structures that are infrequent. In a nutshell, these models highlight the role of experience and not so much linguistic creativity.

Next, let us delve deeper into the issue of whether and when semantic information is taken into account to constrain syntactic analysis, in a sense, to guide sentence processing. The following discussion is an illustration of how linguistic models make predictions about behavior, and how existing accounts are amended in order to accommodate new data. Semantic information can provide strongly constraining information over syntactic and lexical analyses in the cases of ambiguity.

(13)   They passed the port at midnight.

In the ambiguous sentence in (13), if the previous discourse context is about a party with various drinks being served, then the 'fortified wine' meaning of *port* will be much more activated than the 'haven' meaning. In cases of temporary syntactic ambiguity such as reduced relative clauses, the constraint-based models predict that semantic information such as animacy has an immediate effect on processing and even allows the comprehender to anticipate upcoming syntactic structure. The Garden Path model, on the other hand, would not predict such immediate effect, since according to this model the parser ignores semantic information as it is making its initial syntactic decisions. A number of studies have examined the effect of animacy and selection frequency in sentences such as the ones in (14), again involving a reduced relative clause:

(14)   a. The defendant examined by the lawyer turned out to be unreliable.
       b. The evidence examined by the lawyer turned out to be unreliable.

Sentences such as in (14a) are predicted to be hard by the Garden Path model because the first two words *the defendant examined* are likely to be immediately merged in an SVO structure "the defendant examined somebody" and not as the more complex reduced relative structure "the defendant who was examined." Furthermore, the model does not predict significant differences between sentences (14a) and (14b), as they have similar syntactic structure. The constraint-based model, on the other hand, predicts that the animacy of the subject in (14a) will create problems for comprehenders, because people and other animate things are more likely to initiate actions, move around and generally be movers and shakers, that is, thematic Agents. Therefore, a construal such as "the defendant examined somebody" is highly activated. The reduced relative construal, "the defendant who was examined," is also activated. When the parser reaches *by the lawyer*, the Agent assumption has to be abandoned. The defendant is not the initiator of the examining in this sentence, but its recipient, hence Patient or Theme; the second construal wins over the first one. However, the case in (14b) is much simpler: *evidence* is an inanimate object and thus not a likely Agent. On encountering a sentence such as (14b), a comprehender should not activate an Agent-plus-active-verb analysis very highly.

Thus, we have two contradicting predictions for these two sentences by the two leading parsing models. The experimental evidence comes down on the side of the fast contribution of the semantics. In experiments comparing the parsing of sentences such as (14a) and (14b), Clifton et al. (2003) and Trueswell et al. (1994) found that sentences with an initial animate noun do indeed impose more processing difficulties than sentences with an inanimate noun. Such findings, then, represent a problem for the Garden Path model.

In later work, Frazier and Clifton (1996) refined the Garden Path model to include the idea that the parser may sometimes build parallel structure simultaneously and that context may sometimes influence the parse very fast. One case in which this happens is in a sentence such as (14b), where the inanimate noun helps the parser reject that wrong structure very quickly, so that it can start building the correct structure almost immediately. Recently, alternative models have appeared that refine our understanding of the parser to include attractive features of both Garden Path and constraint-based models.[4]

An altogether different approach to native language processing is seen in the model proposed by Edward Gibson. Gibson's (1998, 2000) Dependency Locality Theory focuses not so much on sentence ambiguity but on structural complexity. At the bottom of the theory is the well-established finding

---

[4] E.g., the unrestricted race model, Van Gompel, Pickering, and Traxler (2000), Van Gompel, Pickering, Pearson, and Liversedge (2005).

that object relative clauses are more difficult to process in English than subject relative clauses, see examples in (15a,b).

(15) a. The reporter [who ____ attacked the senator] admitted the error.
                                                              (Subject Relative)
      b. The reporter [who the senator attacked ____] admitted the error.
                                                              (Object Relative)

Square brackets mark the relative clauses, while the underline marks the original position of the *wh*-word. In (15a) the reporter is the one who attacked someone, while in (15b) he was attacked. Since there is no ambiguity at any time, the robust finding of differential processing difficulty is hard to explain with parallel activation levels or structure reanalysis. Gibson proposes that these two types of relative clauses are processed differently because they vary in processing complexity. Two factors contribute to processing complexity: storage cost and integration cost. In other words, it is costly to store words in memory while processing, and it is cheap to integrate them as soon as possible. The former cost is incurred when a syntactic dependency between two words is *predicted* by the parser, and that dependency crosses over intervening referents. For example, in (15b) the relative pronoun *who* is thematically related to the verb *attacked,* but there is another intervening argument between them: *the senator*. Note that this is not the case in (15a), at least on the surface. If such a dependency has to be maintained in short-term memory during processing, the one in (15a) is shorter and less costly. On the other hand, integration costs arise when a syntactic dependency is *established*. On this count, too, the dependency in (15b) is costlier, since *the senator* intervenes between *who* and *attacked.* Gibson's model has been very influential in accounting for native language processing.

3.6 Working memory

Gibson's Dependency Locality Theory discussed in the previous section has given you a taste of how important working memory is for sentence processing. "Working memory" refers to the temporal storage and manipulation of linguistic elements in the course of language processing, and is thus different from our long-term memory. As illustrated above, it involves both

storage and processing of information. Working memory has been operationalized by psycholinguists and cognitive scientists as two different
constructs: phonological short-term memory (Baddeley 1999), and reading
span memory (Daneman and Carpenter 1980). The phonological short-
term memory is tested by asking research participants to memorize
unrelated digits, real words, or nonce (made-up) words. In a reading
span test, participants read aloud sentences and are required to remember the last word of each sentence, up to a set of six sentences. Thus, this
working memory test claims to check both processing (the reading of
sentences) as well as storage capacity (the memorization of words). Some
indication that the two types of tests may access different memory
systems is suggested by the fact that traditional span measures (using
digits, words) do not decline with age and do not correlate with sentence
comprehension impairment, whereas reading span does decline with age
and correlates with sentence comprehension scores (Carpenter, Miyake,
and Just 1994: 1078). While no consensus has been reached on whether
the two memory tests access different memory capacities, most psycholinguistic research on native language processing uses the reading span
measures, since this research often involves reading (Juffs and Rodríguez
2015: 45–46).

Much recent debate has centered around the question of whether the
working memory resources employed during syntactic processing are different from the working memory resources used for other, more conscious
verbal tasks. Just and Carpenter (1992) proposed the *shared resources
hypothesis*, according to which all linguistic tasks draw on the same limited
resource of working memory resources. The consequence is that when
working memory is taxed or its capacity is exceeded, a slow-down in
processing or excessive errors in judgments should result. A further consequence is that individual differences in working memory capacity among
readers and listeners should lead to measurably different behavior.

In contrast, Caplan and Waters (1999) proposed the *dedicated resources
hypothesis*: some working memory resources are dedicated to obligatory and
automatic linguistic processes (such as parsing) while different resources are
used for more strategic and controlled linguistic processes such as keeping
words in memory. Thus, if this account is correct, one would not expect to
find a correlation between accuracy on a processing task and a reading span
measure. Experimental results to date are mixed, but on balance, there is
more support for the dedicated resources account. We shall look at the results

of just one recent study, Sprouse, Wagers and Phillips (2012), on the connection of working memory and processing of islands.

Recall from Chapter 2 that "islands" are such linguistic structures from which a constituent word cannot be moved, or extracted. In examples (16a,b),[5] the extraction of the *wh*-word from the object position of the lowest clause is acceptable. The underlying position of the moved element (or the gap, in psycholinguistic parlance) is marked by an underscore. Examples in (17) illustrate, however, that not all extractions are acceptable, so that there are various constraints on this movement. In other words, those embedded clauses in (17) are islands. For example, extraction is not allowed from subjects, from adjuncts, from complex NPs, and when the lower clause is topped off with the word *whether*.[6]

In order to understand these structures, try to amend the sentences in (17) to get acceptable structures. What did you change?

(16)   a. What does Susan think that John bought ____?
       b. What does Sarah believe that Susan thinks that John bought ____?

(17)   a. *whether* island
          *What do you wonder [whether John bought ____]?
       b. Complex NP island
          *What did you make [the claim that John bought ____]?
       c. Subject island
          *What do you think [the speech about ____] interrupted the TV show?
       d. Adjunct island
          *What do you worry [if John buys ____]?

It has recently been proposed (Kluender 2004, Hofmeister and Sag 2010) that there are no grammatical constraints on extraction, but instead long-distance dependencies are too complex to process, and their unacceptability is due to the breakdown of the parser while reading or hearing them. Such

---

[5] The examples are from Sprouse et al. (2012: 82).

[6] The embedded clause can be topped off with any other *wh*-word moved there within the clause, as illustrated in Chapter 2, example (12), *What did Jane wonder where Bill put?* The more general name for this type of island is a *wh*-island.

an idea entails that one will find a correlation between working memory capacity measures and accuracy on islands such as (17a,b,c,d). Sprouse et al. (2012) tested over three hundred native speakers of English on the four island-effect types exemplified in (17), using two different acceptability rating tasks and two different measures of working-memory capacity. The researchers found no evidence of a relationship between working-memory capacity and island effects. Their findings suggest that island effects are more likely to be due to grammatical constraints than to limited processing resources.

3.7 The psychological reality of language and the grammar

Over the last several decades, there has been an enormous increase in interest in the psychology and neural substrates of language processing. Accordingly, there has been a proliferation of studies using new experimental techniques such as functional magnetic resonance imaging (fMRI), event-related brain potentials (ERPs), and eye tracking. They have revealed a great deal about how and when different types of information are integrated during real-time comprehension by native speakers of a language. We will discuss these new techniques when we focus on L2 processing in Chapter 12. However, this is probably a good place to explain why language teachers and language learners should know about processing language.

As I mentioned earlier in this chapter, the debate on the relationship between the parser and the grammar is not yet completely resolved. However, thinking about the psychological reality of language use (what psycholinguists engage in) has already influenced evolving linguistic theory (what theoretical linguists do). To take some examples, the language architecture proposed by Jackendoff (2002) takes language use into account.[7] Multiple spell-out, the idea that sentences are chopped into smaller chunks called phases and these chunks are sent to the two interfaces for interpretation right away, also reflects the computational needs of the processing system. Phases appear to offer computational advantages, enforcing locality of syntactic movement, thus reducing the information that must be held in "active memory" (Chomsky 2001, 2008). Finally, considerations of

---

[7] As a result, it is taken as a basis for a number of SLA proposals, such as the Bottleneck Hypothesis and MOGUL (Sharwood Smith and Truscott 2014).

processing limitations and excessive loads are now very frequent in explaining why child or adult language learners are taxed and challenged by certain constructions and certain properties. We shall see such analyses later in this textbook. The point that I want to emphasize here is that grammar and acquisition are difficult to discuss for a long time these days without mentioning processing. Theoretical proposals about grammar and especially about language acquisition have to be psychologically real. If this textbook had been written ten or fifteen years ago, it would not have had two whole chapters on psycholinguistics. That is why language-teaching practitioners should keep abreast of developments in this fast-growing field.

Linguistic theory is essential in these developments. The new approaches and the new techniques are most effective in elucidating human language processing when they are based on well-understood linguistic distinctions such as the distinction between lexical and functional morphemes, between nouns and verbs, between main and embedded clauses, etc. Although there are still significant disconnects between linguistic theory and the neurobiology of language (Poeppel and Embick 2005), there are also promising areas of investigation where the neurosciences intersect with linguistic research more closely than before (Poeppel, Emmorey, Hickok, and Pylkkänen 2012). Although much of the integration between linguistics and neuroscience lies in the future, there is no turning the clock back.

3.8 Exercises

Exercise 3.1. Read the following sentences and discuss whether each one offers a lexical or a structural ambiguity. Some of the examples have more than two meanings, and some may combine lexical and structural ambiguity.

(1) He gave her cat food.
(2) I saw her duck.
(3) They are hunting dogs.
(4) Wrap poison bottles in sandpaper and fasten with scotch tape or a rubber band. If there are children in the house, lock them in a small metal box. (*Philadelphia Record*)
(5) LOST Antique cameo ring, depicting Adam and Eve in Market Square Saturday night. (*Ad in Essex paper*)
(6) He strips the bark and leaves.

(7) "You know, somebody actually complimented me on my driving today. They left a little note on the windscreen; it said, 'Parking Fine.' So that was nice." (Tim Vine)

(8) "*Outside* of a dog, a book is a man's best friend; inside it's too hard to read." (Groucho Marx)

(9) The Rabbi married my sister.

(10) She is looking for a match.

(11) The fisherman went to the bank.

(12) I know women more beautiful than Julia Roberts.

Exercise 3.2. Crash blossoms.[8] The following are headlines from newspapers, which follow somewhat different conventions from normal sentences: they can be missing articles and other functional words for the sake of brevity. However, that allows for an unusually large amount of ambiguity. Discuss the following structurally ambiguous headlines, and more specifically, how lexical polysemy allows the ambiguity.

(1) Kids Make Nutritious Snacks

(2) Miners Refuse to Work After Death

(3) Teacher Strikes Idle Kids

(4) Red Tape Holds Up New Bridge

(5) Local High School Dropouts Cut in Half

(6) Stolen Painting Found by Tree

(7) Include Your Children When Baking Cookies

(8) Doctor Testifies in Horse Suit

(9) American Ships Head to Libya

(10) Enraged Cow Injures Farmer with Ax

(11) Gadhafi Forces Barrel Into Main Rebel Base

(12) Sting Proves Bing Copied Search Results

(13) Squad Helps Dog Bite Victim

---

[8] "Last August [2009], ... in the Testy Copy Editors online discussion forum, ... Mike O'Connell, an American editor based in Sapporo, Japan, spotted the headline 'Violinist Linked to JAL Crash Blossoms' and wondered, 'What's a crash blossom?' (The article, from the newspaper *Japan Today*, described the successful musical career of Diana Yukawa, whose father died in a 1985 Japan Airlines plane crash.) Another participant in the forum, Dan Bloom, suggested that 'crash blossoms' could be used as a label for such infelicitous headlines that encourage alternate readings, and news of the neologism quickly spread." (Ben Zimmer, "Crash Blossoms," *The New York Times Magazine*, Jan. 31, 2010.)

(14) Judge to Rule on Nude Beach
(15) Police Discover Crack in Australia.
(16) Satellite Tracks Cows From Outer Space

Exercise 3.3. Consider these garden path sentences.

  (1) Fat people eat accumulates.
  (2) The cotton clothing is usually made of grows in Mississippi.
  (3) Until the police arrest the drug dealers control the street.
  (4) The man who hunts ducks out on weekends.
  (5) When Fred eats food gets thrown.
  (6) Mary gave the child the dog bit a bandage.
  (7) The girl told the story cried.
  (8) I convinced her children are noisy.
  (9) Helen is expecting tomorrow to be a bad day.
 (10) The horse raced past the barn fell.
 (11) I know the words to that song about the queen don't rhyme.
 (12) She told me a little white lie will come back to haunt me.
 (13) The dog that I had really loved bones.
 (14) The man who whistles tunes pianos.
 (15) The old man the boat.
 (16) The tycoon sold the offshore oil tracts for a lot of money wanted to
       kill J.R.
 (17) The raft floated down the river sank.
 (18) We painted the wall with cracks.

Work on adding the disambiguating words in brackets, so that the sentences
are no longer garden paths. The first example is done for you.

(The) fat (that) people eat accumulates.   (So true!)

Some of the sentences in exercises 1–3 are borrowed from the following
websites:

  http://www.byrdseed.com/ambiguous-sentences/
  http://www.fun-with-words.com/ambiguous_garden_path.html
  http://allthingslinguistic.com/post/36385656700/my-favourite-garden-
     path-sentences

There are numerous blogs and websites devoted to fun with ambiguities and garden paths out there.

Exercise 3.4. C-command is a fundamental relationship between nodes on a syntactic tree, but it is also essential in language processing. Practice c-command. Look at the following tree and state the relationship between the nodes, answering the questions exhaustively. Refer to the definition of c-command above.

(i)

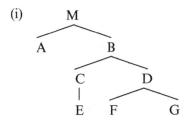

What does M c-command?
What does A c-command?
What does C c-command?
What does E c-command?
Does D c-command A?
Does B c-command A?
Does E c-command C?
Does E c-command D, F, and G?
Does F c-command G?
Does G c-command F?

Exercise 3.5. To illustrate how psycholinguists make predictions about various models, let's look at some predictions following the classic Garden Path model. Consider the sentences in (i) and (ii):

(i)   The burglar blew up the safe with the rusty lock.
(ii) The burglar blew up the safe with the dynamite.

The sentence in (i) should be ambiguous. Look at the structures (6) and (7) in the chapter and say whether they can accommodate the ambiguity. Count the nodes of the structure it takes to represent the intended meaning.

Paraphrase each one, giving an explicit version of the meaning. Which structure, (6) or (7), is simpler, i.e. has fewer nodes? Which meaning would the minimal attachment principle predict that readers would assume? Will the parser then send an error message, and why?

Would sentence (ii) be easier to parse, and why?

It makes sense to assume that speakers would use a sentence like (i) with the meaning as in (6) only if there are two safes in the available context, and we have to distinguish one from the other, right? In this sense, if a test sentence such as (i) is introduced by context as below, that might help to disambiguate it (Altmann and Steedman, 1988):

A burglar broke into a bank carrying some dynamite. He planned to blow open a safe. Once inside, he saw that there was a safe with a new lock and a safe with an old lock.

In Altmann and Steedman's Experiment 1, sentences such as (i) were read **more quickly** preceded by such context. What does this suggest for the Garden Path model? Why? Does this finding support constraint-based models?

Answer: The parser does not automatically take the simpler analysis as in (7), the so-called VP-attachment analysis, if the context favors an NP-attachment analysis as in (6), even though the latter has more nodes. Hence, the minimal attachment does not obtain, because the context militates against it.

Exercise 3.6. It would go against constraint-based parsing models if the parser sometimes favors less likely structures over more likely ones. Consider the sentence in (i):

(i)   The athlete realized her shoes somehow got left on the bus.

The athlete realized her shoes is not a plausible sentence, right? That's because the verb *realize* is most often followed by a complete clause, such as *She realized that she was hungry.* We can assume that this verb's preference to be followed by a clause would influence the parser right away and readers would not slow down at the noun *the shoes.* How would that follow from constraint-based models? In the eye-tracking experiment reported in Pickering, Traxler, and Crocker (2000), readers did slow down on *the shoes.* What does this finding suggest? How does it support the principle of minimal attachment?

PART II

Language Acquisition

In this part of the book, I situate SLA in the big picture of language acquisition. I shall demonstrate how comparisons between the different language acquisition contexts and conditions are relevant to understanding SLA. All acquisition conditions will be treated from the perspective of two seminal issues, which are the main focus of this book: the Critical Period Hypothesis and the importance of linguistic input for language acquisition. The position I will argue for throughout this part of the book is that sustained high-quality comprehensible linguistic input emerges as the indispensable condition for successful language acquisition, overriding potential critical periods (at least in some modules of the grammar).

PART II

Language Acquisition

4

The Critical Period Hypothesis

4.1 The view from biology

If language development is like other neurological development processes, it
is likely to have a critical period early in life, after which no amount of
experience can bring the development to normal ranges. Hubel and Wiesel
(1970) demonstrated such a critical period in the ocular development of
kittens. By depriving them from using one of their eyes, they showed that the
kittens did not develop areas of the brain receiving input from both eyes,
something that is needed for binocular vision. The forced ocular dominance
in the early months of life turned out to be irreversible.

   With respect to language, the Critical Period Hypothesis was first discussed
by Montreal neurologist Wilder Penfield (e.g., Penfield and Roberts 1959).
Later, Eric Lenneberg's (1967) seminal work popularized the idea and

especially its implications for language as a biological phenomenon. In essence, Lenneberg argued that there are maturational constraints on first language acquisition due to brain lateralization, which he assumed started at 2 and finished at puberty.[1] If language is not acquired by puberty, some aspects of language such as the lexicon can be learned, but nativelike mastery of grammatical structure cannot be achieved. Some empirical support for this observation comes from the cases of Genie[2] and other children deprived of language input while growing up.

During most of the 20th century, the consensus among neuroscientists was that brain structure is relatively immutable after a critical period during early childhood. This belief has now been challenged by findings revealing that many aspects of the brain remain plastic even into adulthood. Many researchers nowadays argue that language development may have a sensitive period, after which some impairment normally occurs, but problems can be compensated for and reversed (e.g., Hensch 2004). New knowledge about the development and functioning of the brain highlights its plasticity instead. Decades of research have now shown that, in response to experience, substantial changes can occur in the neocortical processing areas[3] that can profoundly alter the pattern of neuron activation. Neuroplasticity is exhibited on a variety of levels, ranging from cellular changes caused by learning, to larger-scale changes, and up to cortical remapping in response to injury.

Of course, a lot of research remains to be done, but neurocognitive studies already indicate that experience can actually change both the brain's physical structure (its anatomy) and functional organization. To cite just one of

[1] This is no longer believed to be the case. Brain lateralization is thought to be complete by early infancy and maybe even at birth (Hahn 1987).

[2] Genie was 13 years old when discovered. She had been kept strapped to a potty chair and was wearing diapers. Her father had judged her retarded at birth and had chosen to isolate her, and so she had remained until her discovery. She appeared to be entirely without language. Although this case of domestic abuse was a tragic event, it afforded scientists a glimpse at "a forbidden experiment:" what happens if a child experiences total lack of language until the age of 12. Although Genie was exposed to ample language input and taught language after that age, she was unable to acquire English completely (Curtis 1977). The degree of her neurological damage (due to the abuse) and the degree to which she acquired language are disputed.

[3] The neocortex is the roof of the cerebral cortex that forms the part of the mammalian brain that has evolved most recently. It makes higher brain functions possible, such as learning.

many examples, a study by Polk and Farah (1998) found that Canadian postal workers were more adept at manipulating the letter and number representational systems, relative to American postal workers. The explanation was that Canadian postal codes include both numbers and letters while US postal codes include numbers only. Neuroscientists are currently engaged in a reconciliation of critical period studies demonstrating the immutability of the brain after development, with the more recent research showing how the brain can, and does, change.

4.2 The two positions in second language acquisition

It is of paramount importance to keep in mind that Lenneberg's formulation of the critical period for language is not a valid description of the second language acquisition process (Lenneberg 1967: 176). L2 speakers already have a native language that was properly engaged at birth, so the brain lateralization argument does not apply to them. While no researcher is disputing the significance of linguistic input for the normal development of child language acquisition, there is still much dispute in this respect within the field of L2 acquisition.

The two positions have recently solidified without getting much closer to each other. On the one hand, Long (2005), DeKeyser and Larson-Hall (2005), and Hyltenstam and Abrahamsson (2003) argue that it is impossible for adult near-native speakers to attain nativelike grammars, when all facets of the grammar such as pronunciation, perception, syntactic representation, and processing are investigated. In these researchers' opinions, the incidence of nativelike performance among early-onset bilinguals is also less common than it was previously assumed.

On the other hand, Birdsong (2005), Donaldson (2011), Flege (2009), Montrul (2009), Muñoz and Singleton (2011), Rothman (2008), Singleton (2005), and Slabakova (2006, 2008) argue that a much more nuanced approach to nativelike attainment is warranted, where quality and quantity of linguistic input as well as language proficiency play bigger roles than previously assumed, and where sensitive periods for some but not for other modules of the grammar, and even for specific grammatical properties, can be uncovered. The critical period is not absolute.

However far apart the two positions may appear to be, they are not irreconcilable. For example, critical period proponents have recently started calling it a sensitive period (see the new edited volume Granena and Long 2013). It is possible to piece together a composite picture of ultimate attainment in a second language. We will attempt to see what such a picture might look like, after we discuss some more variables involved in the process of second language acquisition. But first, let's turn to some of the evidence for and against a critical period for language.

4.3 Global nativelikeness versus different sensitive periods for the separate parts of the grammar

Three large-scale studies addressing the Critical Period Hypothesis (CPH) will be presented first, those of Johnson and Newport (1989), Abrahamsson and Hyltenstam (2009), and Abrahamsson (2012). These studies offer considerable improvements over previous work addressing the CPH in terms of number of subjects, variety of tests, and statistical treatment of the data. They offer substantial support for the view that complete, in all respects nativelike linguistic performance is impossible for adult L2 learners to achieve.

The classic study in this respect is Johnson and Newport (1989). In this study, the participant's intuitive knowledge of English grammar was measured through a grammaticality judgment task involving listening to and evaluating sentences. Scores on this task obtained from 46 Korean and Chinese long-term residents in the United States were correlated with the participants' age of arrival (AoA) in the country. There was a strong negative correlation between AoA and grammatical knowledge among the early starters (AoA 3–15; $r = -.87$, $p < .01$), and little individual variation was observed. Very early starters (AoA 3–7) invariably performed like native control participants. However, after the AoA of 15, the significant negative correlation with the grammaticality judgment scores disappeared ($r = -.16$, $p > .05$) and was instead replaced by great individual variation. After that age, individual characteristics rather than age determined the grammatical scores. Despite criticism and some indisputable methodological problems, Johnson and Newport's study remains a very influential milestone in this field of research.

Abrahamsson and Hyltenstam (2009) reports on a large-scale, labor-intensive study of the competence of L2 speakers of Swedish, perceived to be near-native by native speakers. The researchers started out with 195 native speakers of Spanish who were very advanced learners of Swedish and were living in Sweden. A panel of ten native judges evaluated the nativelikeness of those participants' speech samples, interspersed with some native speaker speech samples. The findings demonstrated that only a small minority (5%) of those bilinguals who had started their L2 acquisition after age 12 were perceived as native speakers. However, a majority (62%) of those with an age of acquisition below 12 were deemed to be nativelike by at least nine of the ten judges. A second experiment involved 41 participants that were considered nativelike by a majority (>6) of the native judges; these were divided into a group of child learners and a group of adolescent to adult learners. The experiment comprised ten tests covering a range of phenomena from phonetic perception and production, to grammar and inferencing, to formulaic language. An important advantage of this experimental design was that it established native-speaker ranges for all tests, which allowed the researchers to then check how many of the L2 speakers fell within those ranges. Only three of the child learners and none of the adolescent or adult learners performed as native speakers on the whole array of ten linguistic tests. The authors concluded that complete nativelike acquisition after puberty is impossible.

The findings of Abrahamsson's (2012) study are largely in line with the Johnson and Newport (1989) study. Again, a large number of participants distributed in roughly equal numbers across AoA points ranging from 1 to 30 were tested on a grammaticality judgment task and on a Voice Onset Time (VOT) discrimination task. The latter task measures whether a perceiver distinguishes between a voiceless stop (*p, t, k*) and a voiced stop (*b, d, g*) in Swedish. VOT is the length of time that passes between the release of a stop consonant and the onset of voicing, with the languages involved, Swedish and Spanish, differing in this respect. Abrahamsson found a robust negative correlation between earlier acquirers (AoA < 15) and scores on the two tasks, but a lot of variation among later acquirers.

In sum, these and other studies show that, although sounding nativelike in everyday conversation, when their phonological, perceptual, grammatical, and lexical abilities are examined in detail, people who have acquired their L2 after puberty (12–15) perform significantly below the native-speaker range, and their global L2 performance is distinct from that of native speakers. Researchers who document such performance very often link it to the distinction of implicit versus explicit linguistic knowledge. This link goes back to Lenneberg (1967: 176), who stressed that what disappears around puberty is the ability to attain "automatic acquisition from mere exposure," the way children learn their native language. After puberty, language acquisition typically involves "a conscious and labored effort." The implication is that, successful or not, language acquisition achieved through explicit learning is irrelevant to the Critical Period Hypothesis. Keep this distinction in mind as we will revisit it below.

On the other side of the debate, many researchers have argued on theoretical grounds, and continue to demonstrate, that nativelike attainment is possible for some learners with respect to some modules of the grammar, as attested by nativelike judgments or performance on individual properties within these modules. There are many studies documenting such successful acquisition in various parts of the grammar, so I have to be fairly selective here. One study representative of this line of research is Donaldson (2011). The researcher used comprehension tasks that examine intuitions and preferences, but he also recorded the production of ten near-native speakers in natural conversation with native speakers. The author was interested in tracking how the near-native learners used *Left Dislocation*, a syntactic construction that marks Topic, as in (1).

(1)   Marie$_i$, elle$_i$ vient cet après-midi.
       Marie, she is coming this afternoon
       'Mary is coming this afternoon.'

In order to use this construction with nativelike frequency and accuracy, L2 speakers of French have to coordinate syntactic knowledge with monitoring who is already mentioned in the discourse. It is precisely this coordination of two types of information (grammar and discourse) that has been argued to present extraordinary difficulty to learners (Sorace, 1993, 2011, Sorace and Filiaci 2006).

Analyzing the near-native speakers' production of left dislocations—the syntactic accuracy of the dislocated subjects and objects, the obligatory resumptive pronoun[4] in the main clause, and how speakers used the construction to promote different types of discourse referents to topic status— Donaldson contends that the near-native participants' mastery of this aspect of discourse organization converges on that of native speakers. Donaldson's near-native speakers demonstrated nativelike performance on a property

---

[4] A resumptive pronoun is a pronoun that refers to the moved argument, in this case the subject in example (1).

that could not have been transferred from the native language and is rarely explicitly taught in language classrooms.

An earlier study, Montrul and Slabakova (2003) set out to test whether very advanced learners of Spanish with English as their native language had nativelike intuitions on the meaning of the aspectual tenses (Preterit and Imperfect past tenses). These interpretations are deemed to be particularly difficult for learners of Spanish. The test instruments targeted both semantic knowledge that is taught in language classrooms (e.g., the Preterit denotes a complete event in the past; the Imperfect conveys a habitual sequence of events in the past) as well as semantic entailments that are not taught in language classrooms and are difficult, even impossible, to deduce from positive input alone (see Exercise 4.4 for some actual test items).

To take a concrete example, one such subtle meaning distinction is the interpretation of the impersonal subject *se* in the context of Imperfect and Preterit aspectual tenses. In sentences with Imperfect verbs as in (2) *se* refers generically to everyone and is equivalent to the impersonal pronoun 'one.' In sentences with Preterit main verbs as in (3) *se* refers to a specific group of people already mentioned and is equivalent to 'we.'

(2)   Se comía-IMPF bien en ese restaurante
      'One ate well in this restaurant.'

(3)   Se comió-PRET bien en ese restaurante
      'We ate well in this restaurant.'

As the reader can ascertain for herself or himself, instruction of such meaning subtleties is quite unlikely to be offered in many language classrooms. In general, such semantic differences are not often discussed explicitly among speakers of a language (unless they happen to be linguists). Therefore the authors argued that this particular semantic contrast represents a Poverty of the Stimulus learning situation.

It was established that 15 out of 17 near-native participants, 5 out of 23 superior participants, and even 2 out of 24 advanced speakers (so 22 out of a total pool of 64 participants) performed within the range of native speakers on a truth value judgment task probing these interpretations. These findings, as well as Donaldson's findings mentioned earlier, address the implicit versus explicit learning issue introduced above. If we assume that L2 learners who attempt L2 acquisition after puberty are only capable of labored, conscious acquisition that depends on rote learning of rules, Montrul and Slabakova's (2003) and Donaldson's (2011) results remain unexplained. No speaker can reach such advanced state of knowledge through learning explicit rules. Slabakova (2006) and Rothman (2008) make the same argument and give many additional examples of successful acquisition of properties exhibiting poverty of the stimulus. They argue that such results are in direct contradiction to a strict critical period claim.

In summary, this section presented some evidence for the two positions on the critical period for language. Of course, we cannot do justice here to the literature that has been growing over the last 40 years and comprises over a hundred published studies. But I hope to have demonstrated that the issue is no longer "Is there or isn't there a critical or a sensitive period for language acquisition?" The answer is more complicated. One conclusion that we can all agree on is that if age of acquisition is after puberty, there are very few individuals in a group, and frequently none, who display a complete mastery of the second language, including phonetics and phonology. However, looking at specific properties of morphosyntax and meaning acquisition, research frequently uncovers successful adult learners. The last 30 years have revealed considerable complexity in the overall picture of L2 acquisition, and it appears that other factors are at least as important, if not more important, than age of acquisition. We will review more studies in the next sections, where we discuss other factors that can and do affect nativelike acquisition.

4.4 The first and the second language as communicating vessels

The notion of first and second language interference, or interaction, has gathered some credibility in the discussion of critical or sensitive periods. In a nutshell, the idea is that the more the native language grammar is established (entrenched) in the learner's mind/brain, the more difficult comparable acquisition of a second language becomes. A useful visualization of this idea is to imagine the first and the second languages of the bilinguals influencing and interacting with each other as liquid in communicating vessels (Bylund, Hyltenstam, and Abrahamsson 2013).[5] In his Speech Learning

---

[5] See animation at http://en.wikipedia.org/wiki/File:ANIMvasicomunicanti.gif.

model (Flege 1995), James Flege conceptualizes the native language as one factor that can interfere with nativelike mastery in the second language. The model assumes that the sounds of the L1 and L2 are related to one another and exist in a common "L1±L2" phonological space. Being in contact, the sound systems of the L1 and L2 may mutually influence each other. The key word here is "mutually."

A large-scale study, Yeni-Komshian, Flege, and Liu (2000), assessed the global pronunciation of 240 L1 Korean–L2 English bilinguals divided in ten groups according to age of arrival in the US or Canada: AoA 1–3, AoA 4–5, AoA 6–7, etc. They were recorded as adults, reading and repeating sentences in Korean and English. Ten monolingual judges evaluated the accentedness of the bilinguals' speech in both languages, Korean and English, on a scale of 1 (very strong accent) to 9 (no accent). The bilinguals who had emigrated at a very young age (AoA 1–5 years) had relatively high pronunciation ratings in English, but as a group they were still distinguishable from monolingual speakers. In this respect, the Critical Period Hypothesis was supported in the area of pronunciation. However, another important finding was the significant negative correlation $(r = -.47)$[6] between L1 and L2 pronunciation for bilinguals who had started acquiring English before the age of 12, but not for the those participants who arrived at higher ages. Interestingly, one group, who arrived when they were 10 or 11 years old, had roughly equal ratings in English and in Korean. The authors interpreted their findings as partially supporting the interference hypothesis: the more strongly the native language is represented in the brain, the more strongly it will interfere with the second language. The communicating vessels metaphor works for this and other studies with similar findings: you just have to imagine the communicating vessels tilted to one side, then the other.

However attractive this explanation may seem, another recent study which sets out to test precisely the communicating vessel view of ultimate attainment, Bylund, Abrahamsson, and Hyltenstam (2012), comes to the opposite conclusion. The researchers examined the L1 and L2 knowledge of L1 Spanish–L2 Swedish bilinguals, whose AoA ranged between 1 and 11, but their mean length of residence (LoR) was 23 years. This study focused on grammatical competence and semantic intuitions, which they tested

---

[6] A negative correlation is a relationship between two variables such that as the value of one variable increases, the other decreases.

through an aural grammaticality judgment task and a cloze test.[7] When compared at the group level, the bilinguals did not perform as well as the native speakers. However, when individual results were scrutinized, it turned out that around half of individual learners performed within the native speaker range. Importantly for us in this section, however, those who did well on Spanish, their L1, also did well on Swedish, their L2. The higher scores were correlated with higher language aptitude (as measured by a standard aptitude test). Thus the negative correlation, or interference, between the first and the second language uncovered by Yeni-Komshian et al. (2000) was not detected in this study. However, this discrepancy can very well be due to the fact that the former study tested pronunciation, while the latter tested grammatical and semantic knowledge.

In sum, research shows that the entrenchment of the first language hampers the establishment of the second language, but it is also possible that this could be the case only in the area of pronunciation. In the other areas of the grammar, however, the native language does not block the achievement of nativelike L2 proficiency.

4.5 Effects of bilingualism: Is the bilingual two monolinguals in one mind?

Put very simply, *bilingualism* is the ability to use two languages. But, as François Grosjean (1989) famously quipped, the bilingual is not two monolinguals in one mind. It has been suggested (Ortega 2009) that, in all fairness, bilinguals should not be compared to monolinguals, and that bilingualism itself makes this comparison flawed/erroneous. This is a line of argumentation certainly worth considering. However, defining bilingualism has turned out to be problematic in more than one respect. Let's unpack this issue a little.

---

[7] A cloze test is a test of global language proficiency, involving lexical, grammatical, and pragmatic knowledge. Some words are omitted from a complete story and the speaker is invited to fill in the gaps. In some versions of the cloze, every sixth or seventh word is deleted, so the gaps can be grammatical morphemes but also full lexical items. The exact word scoring method is appropriate for such a cloze test, and even native speakers do not score close to 100% on such a test.

Who is a bilingual? Definitions of bilingualism start from minimal proficiency in two languages and range over to nativelike command of two languages. An example of the former would be a British English native speaker with high-school French conversing with a local taxi-driver on a visit to Paris. An operational definition of this minimal level of bilingualism is being able to produce comprehensible and grammatical sentences in the second language. An example of the latter would be a person who grew up bilingual in French and English in Montreal, Canada or a speaker of Spanish as a heritage language who grew up in California. In yet another definition of bilingualism (Grosjean 2001), a person is considered bilingual if she or he uses two or more languages in everyday life; this type of definition capitalizes on frequency and functionality of use.

When we consider the effects of bilingualism on nativelike attainment, we should probably adopt a middle-of-the-road but flexible definition: one that is beyond the incipient view but stops long before full command of two languages. In this sense, a bilingual and an L2 learner are the same, for the purposes of this textbook. The reason for assuming such a practical definition is the robust evidence showing that the two languages of a bilingual are constantly activated, even in situations when only one language is needed to carry out a task. It seems it is virtually impossible to switch off the language not in use. Parallel activation of a bilingual's two languages can be observed in reading, listening, and in planning speech. This parallel activation happens not only at initial stages of acquisition but in advanced proficiency stages as well. As Bialystok puts it, "[T]his situation creates a problem of attentional control that is unique to bilinguals—the need to correctly select a form that meets all the linguistic criteria for form and meaning but is also part of the target language and not the competing system" (2009: 3–4).

Let us review some hard evidence that this parallel activation is happening. Within the mental lexicon, accessing a word in one language leads to the activation of related words in the other language, both in comprehension (Spivey and Marian 1999, Van Heuven, Dijkstra, and Grainger 1998) and in production (Colomé 2001, Costa, Miozzo, and Caramazza 1999). Within syntax, grammatical information from the irrelevant language is constantly available in bilingual individuals processing language. For example, Hartsuiker, Pickering, and Veltkamp (2004) found that Spanish–English bilinguals, describing cards to each other in a dialogue game, used the passive construction in English significantly more often after they had heard it in Spanish than after an intransitive or active sentence. The authors argued that their findings support a view of syntactic representation being integrated between the two languages of the bilingual.

Secondly, recent brain studies have shown that the neural systems engaged by the bilingual's two languages are largely the same. Since there is a high level of interaction between the two language systems, it has been shown that, unsurprisingly, the native language influences the second language, but more surprisingly, the second language also influences the native language in various ways. A demonstration of this influence is offered by a study on English–Welsh bilinguals, Thierry and Sanoudaki (2012), which showed that even when reading in English, early bilinguals were mentally open to the Welsh order of Noun–Adjective, even though it is ungrammatical in English. In short, a bilingual's two languages may come to function somewhat differently than either language in a monolingual native speaker (Kroll, Bogulski, and McClain 2012).

If a bilingual's mind functions differently from a monolingual's mind, then a comparison between the two is not only unfair but uninformative with respect to nativelike ultimate attainment. By this logic, bilinguals will never be able to achieve monolingual levels, since their mental lexicons and grammatical systems will be influenced by their second (or multiple other) language(s). Their competence will not be deficient with respect to the monolingual gold standard; it will just be different. Comparing monolinguals and bilinguals, then, will be like comparing apples and oranges. Many researchers have indeed adopted the position that age effects on nativelikeness should only be tested among early and late bilinguals, and that the monolingual native speaker's performance should not be used as a yardstick against which the bilingual performance is evaluated (Birdsong 2009, Muñoz, and Singleton 2011).[8]

A related question that deserves our attention is whether bilingualism (the effects of two languages in one mind) completely rules out nativelikeness, irrespective of age of acquisition. The short answer is no, and the evidence in this respect is quite strong. We shall cite some examples concerning the performance of simultaneous bilinguals and of adult bilinguals, both tested on meanings of functional morphology. One caveat to keep in mind, though, is that research to date rarely reports whether the control groups

---

[8] However, it is a worthy scientific goal to understand the mind of bilinguals and the minds of monolinguals. It is just not fair to use monolingual standards in judging bilinguals.

of native speakers are indeed really monolingual or whether they might also be bilingual in another language (not tested). Thus we are not in a position yet to evaluate bilingual achievements in a two-way comparison: with a monolingual control group and with a bilingual control group.

Kupisch (2012) examined knowledge of specific (e.g., *The cats are on the mat*) and generic nominals (e.g., *Cats are beautiful animals*) in simultaneous bilinguals of German and Italian, individuals who grew up speaking both languages from birth (see next chapter). Some of her participants were dominant in Italian, while some were dominant in German, and there was a positive correlation between dominance and length of stay in one of the countries. Those who grew up in Italy were Italian-dominant, whereas the opposite held for German. The Italian-dominant bilinguals scored at ceiling with accuracy of 97 to 100% at judging the acceptability of bare, definite, and indefinite nominals in Italian. German-dominant bilinguals faced considerable problems in contexts in which Italian differs from German. Such results show that bilingualism on its own does not automatically lead to deviant grammars and that language dominance, obviously conflated with length of exposure and language use, has a crucial effect. This study did not employ a control group but just showed that the dominant bilinguals performed at ceiling in the dominant language.

Studies addressing the same issue, the effect of bilingualism, but looking at adult-onset bilingualism are the Montrul and Slabakova (2003) and the Donaldson (2012) studies discussed in Section 4.3. Since these studies showed that groups of learners as well as individual learners can be demonstrated to perform within the ranges of native speakers, we have to conclude that bilingualism on its own does not preclude nativelikeness in a second language. It is also quite clear that neither age of acquisition nor the effect of bilingualism prevents nativelike performance among nonnative speakers, in some areas of the grammar. We turn to other factors likely to influence bilingual performance in the next section.

4.6 The importance of the input

We already pointed out the importance of this factor when discussing the Kupisch (2012) study above: simultaneous bilinguals with two languages learned at birth, who had not maintained a relatively good balance between their two languages, were not as proficient in their weaker language as they were in their dominant language. This and many other studies point to the conclusion that age of acquisition is not an all-important or completely decisive factor for ultimate attainment. Maintaining full and diverse linguistic input in the L2 through constant contact and varied usage of that language can be an equally important factor.

As we saw above, researchers who argue for the Critical Period Hypothesis, or at least age effects in second language acquisition, show that the earlier an L2 learner is exposed to the second language, the more likely she is to achieve nativelike competence. Summarizing over the present research, for example, Long (2013: 5) maintains that with respect to pronunciation, nativelike performance is most likely (although not guaranteed) for those with an AoA between 0 and 6, still possible but less likely with an AoA between 6 and 12, and impossible after that. Nativelike morphology and syntax are most likely if the L2 was acquired between the ages of 0 and 6, but highly unlikely after the mid teens. These are strong pronouncements indeed. The flaw of this argument is that it only focuses on one, however important factor, while ignoring other important factors. For instance, as Flege (2009) argues, Long's claims imply that late learners receive input equal in quality and quantity with early learners, but they do not use it in similar ways so as to reach a nativelike grammar. However, there is a dangerous confound in such an interpretation, since in most cases early learners have enjoyed decades of native input while late learners have received significantly less exposure. Furthermore, the differences in the input available to learners can be of different length, but also of different quality. We shall look at both quality and quantity of input below.

Even among simultaneous bilinguals acquiring two languages from birth, quantity of input can influence language development. Elin Thordardottir (2015) reports on vocabulary acquisition in French–English bilingual children in Montreal using the one parent–one language system. Those children who had equal amounts of exposure to the two languages, as measured by parental reports, exhibited monolingual-like receptive vocabulary skills. Those children who did not receive equal exposure to French or English had stronger vocabularies in the language to which they had more exposure. These findings suggest that reduced quantity of communicative interaction with the language provider (the parent) impacts even simultaneous bilinguals.

In order to illustrate the significance of the input, we move from child bilingualism to foreign language learning. The relative effects of input exposure and starting age on foreign language acquisition[9] were investigated by Muñoz (2014). The author analyzed the oral performance of 160 learners of English in Spain and related it to various input measures: number of years of instruction, number of hours of curricular and extra-curricular lessons, number of hours spent abroad in an English-speaking setting, and current contact with the target language. She measured oral performance through lexical diversity, speech rate, syntactic complexity, and overall accuracy on a film retell task. Muñoz shows that input has a stronger association with measures of oral performance than age of acquisition. She argues that cumulative exposure and especially contact with high quality input are better predictors of oral performance in the foreign language than AoA.

The clinching point in this debate is offered by the case of heritage speakers (Montrul 2008), who should be more successful than adult learners since they are child learners and actually are native speakers of the heritage language. When a heritage speaker starts school (or preschool), the majority language exposure and use typically increases considerably, as measured by hours in a typical day, but also in communicative importance, while the home language typically recedes in all these respects. Remember the tilted communicating vessels metaphor? It is certainly true for the hours in a day when a bilingual speaker comprehends and produces her heritage language or the majority (second) language: the more L2, the less L1. Thus the native language, although chronologically first and hence native, gets strong competition from the communicative input of the majority language. What happens as a result? To cite just one example, Montrul (2009) reported overall findings from a large-scale study comparing 70 post-puberty L2 learners and 67 adult heritage speakers in different areas of Spanish morphology and syntax. She demonstrated both comparable error patterns for the two groups and advantages for the early bilinguals in some areas, arguing that an early start may not be crucial in language acquisition, while the input quantity and language use may be just as important. In other words, age of acquisition cannot be the most important factor for nativelike linguistic performance, since heritage language learners have spoken that language from birth, but are not comparable to those native speakers who

---

[9] Foreign language acquisition refers to learning a language in a country where that language is not the national language, such as English in Spain.

have maintained constant usage (receptive and productive) of that language. In some respects, heritage speakers' knowledge is comparable to the knowledge of adult L2 learners. We will expand on this issue in Chapter 6.

How about quality of the linguistic input? Imagine the situation when a Russian-speaking child is growing up in the USA, in the family of two Russian native speaking parents and even some grandparents. While the child is being raised at home, it is possible to maintain the input quality (and quantity) roughly comparable to those of a monolingual child being raised in Russia. But when the same child starts school, the English spoken there often becomes the dominant language. In addition to the change in hours of language practice, the bilingual child's two languages can become differentiated according to topics or areas of life normally discussed in one or the other language. It is often the case among heritage bilinguals that they can talk freely and fluently about every day, home-related topics in their heritage language but they are more comfortable discussing political events or professional topics in their second language. This functional differentiation affects the mental lexicon as well as the syntactic complexity in the two languages. For instance, it is well known that the English passive construction (*The truck was hit by the car*) is not frequent in everyday communication, while it is more frequent in written language and more elevated registers.[10] Hence, we can expect higher accuracy with the passive in speakers of English as a second but dominant language, who use it for academic and professional purposes.

What kind of linguistic input is most useful for successful acquisition? In other words, what is high quality input? It has to be diverse, wide-ranging and rich in registers (home language, school language, professional language, etc.). It also has to be socially and communicatively important for the individual. Even if we disregard the different length of exposure, which we should not, there is some evidence that the quality of the linguistic input to which younger and older L2 learners are exposed may be different. Jia

---

[10] A register is a variety of language used for a particular purpose or in a particular social setting. In formal versus informal settings, speakers unconsciously change their way of speaking according to the situation. An example of a formal setting would be talking to a policeman or appearing in court; an example of an informal setting would be talking to one's friends at a party or in the pub.

and Aronson (2003) is a longitudinal study monitoring Mandarin-speaking children and teenagers acquiring English in a naturalistic environment. The study uncovered that the youngest children (ages 5–9) had much richer communicative interaction with native peers while the teenagers (aged 12–16) had less rich social interactions and linguistic environment. The authors attribute the quick change of language dominance, from Mandarin to English, among the younger children to their rich linguistic input.

Finally, a requirement of the linguistic input that is often overlooked is comprehensibility in a communicative situation. It is highly unlikely that one will learn a language by listening to the radio, even if one is exposed to it eight hours a day. Why is that? There are numerous cases in language acquisition when a perfectly acceptable sentence is inappropriate in the context of the previous conversation. A simple illustration would be using a pronoun such as *he* (e.g., *He is coming*) when no referent for that pronoun has been mentioned in the preceding discourse. In that case, the interlocutor is justified in asking, "*Who is coming?*" The utterance *He is coming* is grammatically complete, but contextually inappropriate. Knowing a language includes being able to produce grammatical sentences, but also knowing in what context they are appropriate and relevant. Thus, it is imperative to heed O'Grady, Lee, and Kwak's (2009: 72) warning that "[i]n considering the role of input frequency in language acquisition (first or second), it is vital to bear in mind a key point: what counts is not how many times learners hear a particular form—it is how many times they encounter mappings between a form and its meaning." In sum, language input is useful only when the communicative discourse situation can be mapped onto the linguistic sign and the fit between the two can be evaluated in social interaction.

4.7 An indirect way of appreciating the importance of input

In the previous section, we surveyed some evidence for the claim that the quantity and quality of the linguistic input is a crucial factor in achieving nativelike proficiency in a second language. In this section, we will consider another type of evidence for the importance of input: the effect of linguistic input on monolingual first language acquisition. I will be using two terms widely applied to linguistic performance: variability and optionality. Variability in language acquisition refers to the inconsistent application of the target language rules, or the deviation from such rules.[11] Optionality refers to the simultaneous use of more than one form with the same meaning, e.g., *I no like chess* and *I don't like chess* at the same stage of development. The two terms are often used interchangeably.

The effect of variable input on child grammar development is demonstrated in a fascinating recent study by Miller and Schmitt (2010). The authors take advantage of existing dialectal differences in Spanish to test a situation that they could not have created experimentally. Chilean Spanish and Mexican Spanish differ in phonetic realization of plural morphology. In Mexican Spanish, plural is overtly realized as [s] on nouns, adjectives, and determiners, while in Chilean Spanish (subject to sociolinguistic variation) this piece of inflectional morphology undergoes a regular process of lenition (weakening) to aspiration or to nothing. In this way, plural morphology is not completely absent in Chilean Spanish, but it is rendered unreliable as linguistic evidence, being pronounced about 50% of the time. Miller and Schmitt (2010) report on the production of adults as well as children (mean age of 5;2–5;3) from different socio-economic groups: middle class and working class, tested by three different tasks. Both younger and older Mexican (working class) children were significantly more accurate on comprehension of plural than their Chilean counterparts. The authors argue that the more variability/ambiguity in the input there is, the longer it will take the learner to converge on the adult grammar.

While Miller and Schmitt (2010) studies the effects of variability in the input on child grammars, Meisel, Elsig, and Bonnesen (2011) addresses the effects of quantity and quality of the input on adult native grammars. French has a variety of interrogative constructions, some used more often in colloquial speech and others used in more formal varieties. For example, subject–verb inversion as in example (4) is almost non-existent in the input to children before they go to school and are exposed to standard French there.

(4)   Quand arrive le train?
      when arrives the train
      'When does the train arrive?'

---

[11] Variability can also refer to the different rates of acquisition and different outcomes of the process, e.g., not all L2 learners attain the same proficiency after a set amount of exposure, say, two years of high school Japanese or ten years in the L2-speaking country.

The researchers wanted to investigate what happens if children are not exposed to an interrogative construction before they go to school. They reasoned that this construction will then be learned as a second language construction and will be inherently unstable in their grammar. Meisel et al. (2011) employed a grammaticality judgment task and tested adult French native speakers. All of their participants performed consistently on the standard interrogative constructions that are supported by evidence in colloquial French (subject–clitic inversion, complex inversion). In contrast, the question types as in (4) that are only present in standard French exhibit a lot more cross-individual variety as well as more inconsistency within the performance of the same individuals. The authors interpret this behavior of native speakers as essentially indistinguishable from that of second language speakers. Characterizing their native participants' grammar, the authors say: "They do, of course, acquire knowledge about these constructions, but as is evidenced by the broad range of variability in their ratings, it is afflicted by persistent optionality as is typically encountered in L2 acquisition" (Meisel et al. 2011: 380).

This conclusion brings us back to the very interesting question of what constitutes native and nonnative knowledge of language. Obviously, if limited exposure to particular constructions results in optionality in native grammars, then nonnative grammars, also characterized by variability and optionality, are highly nativelike indeed, at least as far as these constructions are concerned. This type of reasoning is supported by another recent body of work, that of Dąbrowska and colleagues (see the epistemological issue of the journal *Linguistic Approaches to Bilingualism* 2:3 for a review and commentaries). One study, Street and Dąbrowska (2010), argues that simple sentences employing the quantifier *every* (e.g., *Every cat is on a mat*) and the reversible passive voice (e.g., *The soldier was hit by the sailor*) present a comprehension challenge to native speakers of English with a low level of education. This is because they do not encounter such sentences often enough to learn them. However, after a brief explanation and practice of the constructions with the adult native speakers, comprehension improved dramatically and for the long term.

A training study, Wells, Christiansen, Race, Acheson, and MacDonald (2009), systematically manipulated participants' exposure to relative clause constructions (e.g., *The senator [that the reporter attacked _____] admitted his error*) over the course of three sessions spanning nearly a month. Two groups of undergraduate students were matched for verbal working memory: their measures on a reading span test were at the low end. Over three training sessions, the experimental group was exposed to equal amounts of subject and object relatives. The control group received an equivalent amount of complex sentences, but without the inclusion of relative clauses (i.e., they read complex sentential complements and conjoined sentences). After training, the two groups' reading times on relative clauses diverged such that the speed of processing of the experimental group resembled the pattern for high-reading-span individuals, whereas the control group showed the kind of reaction time profile associated with low-reading-span individuals. These findings suggest that the attested differences in processing relative clauses were due to the amount of experience with this structure and not to differences in working memory. Let me reiterate the main argument of this section: variable linguistic performance is attested in monolingual native speakers, too, and it is clearly related to lack of exposure to a certain construction or to input that itself exhibits optionality.

4.8 Conclusions

We set out in this chapter to examine the issue of whether there is a critical period for second language acquisition, after which bilingual individuals cannot achieve nativelike performance. There are several parts of this question that are up for debate. First of all, researchers these days talk of sensitive periods, or age effects in language acquisition. Sensitive periods most likely differ for the different areas of the grammar, with mastering the sounds and intonation of the L2 to nativelike levels being considerably more difficult than mastering the sentence structure or the interpretation of sentences and discourse. It is fairly well established that if L2 acquisition comes after adolescence, complete and global nativelikeness is difficult, by some accounts impossible to achieve. Such nativelikeness will not only make an L2 speaker difficult to distinguish from native speakers, but she will have to perform in the range of native speakers on a variety of challenging and rigorous tests spanning phonology, syntax, and semantics. Linguistic theory offers principled answers to the questions of why some areas of the grammar are more attainable to nativelike levels than others.

We also considered the effects of bilingualism on nativelike attainment, pointing out that the brain of a bilingual and that of a monolingual speaker, if not morphologically different, are perhaps functionally different as they process language in distinctive ways. Age effects and the effects of bilingualism on nativelike language use can augment each other. Perhaps the most significant challenge to strict critical period claims come from instances of language acquisition where quantity and quality of linguistic input trump age of acquisition, as is the case with heritage speakers. Even among monolingual native speakers, the effects of exposure to a particular grammatical morpheme (the plural) or grammatical construction (passive, relative clause) can lead to variable production and comprehension. If we assume that L2 speakers have fewer opportunities to interact with meaningful language in communicatively significant situations, then their nonnative performance may be due to the input factor. Age of acquisition is certainly of great importance, but the linguistic input may override its importance in the achievement and maintenance of nativelike linguistic competence.

Finally, as in every complex learning process, it is very likely that a variety of factors influence successful acquisition of a second language, including factors such as language aptitude and the learner engagement with the language, also known as motivation. I focused on the importance of bilingualism, exposure and input in this chapter, because these are the factors most closely related to the learner's internal linguistic system, which is at the center of this textbook. For an appreciation of the other factors and their contribution, see the special issue of the journal *Language Acquisition* (2014, issue 4) edited by Carmen Muñoz.

Teaching relevance: Away with the pessimistic message

Why would we worry at all about the Critical Period Hypothesis when we teach a foreign or a second language? How about for psychological reasons? People want to know whether what they do is futile or whether it can make a difference. Of course pronunciation is not taught in most language classrooms with the aim of learners eventually sounding like native speakers, but rather with the aim of comprehensibility. However, teachers should know that their efforts in the classroom are not futile, and that their students can, eventually, become nativelike in many other respects of language competence. We should approach language acquisition with the message of what is possible to acquire, which areas of the grammar students can make real progress in, and where they should concentrate their efforts: the acquisition of morphology, syntax, semantics, and pragmatics.

4.9 Exercises

Exercise 4.1. The following Q and A exchange was found on Yahoo. Read it carefully and discuss. How would YOU answer the question? Make a list of skills or capacities that would help an individual to be classified as a near-native speaker. At all times, consider what the range of native speakers might be.

Question: I am a native speaker of English and I have been describing myself as a "near-native" speaker of Greek ever since I discovered the term. I would just like to check that my definition conforms to the popular consensus:

I started learning my second language (Greek) when I was 8 and this process was continued up until I was 22 (I'm nearly 24 now). I spoke it all the time with my grandmother and have her accent and, like her (who was Cypriot), I am always mistaken for an Athenian because my accent is rather posh for a Cypriot - but still, it's a native Greek one. Following the years of study, practice, immersion (both in and out of Greece and Cyprus) and lessons I can confidently say I'm fluent. The thing is, like anyone, I still make mistakes in phrasing which give me away as an Englishman and not a Greek.

My understanding of a "near-native" speaker is someone who has no trouble understanding anything that is said to him or that he reads and no nuance or play on words is missed and speaks well enough that native speakers feel confident that they can talk at native speed and speak as freely as they want, not restricting themselves to facilitate the understanding of the "foreigner". Also, he can speak so well to a point that until there's a slip up in word-choice or phrasing, the listener believes they are speaking to a fellow-countryman.

I feel I fit into that above category and will be including it on my CV. However, that description might be wrong and I have been mis-using the term to describe myself for ages. Please, tell me your opinions and share your own definitions if mine is incorrect.

Thank you.

One answer: A near-native speaker understands almost 100% of a novel or a paper, listens to a native speaker and understands almost everything, can write with "dignity", recognizes the different "languages" (formal, informal, semi-formal etc.), usually uses good syntax, understands 99% of humor in the foreign language, can follow a phone conversation with a native speaker, is fluent when he speaks etc. From my own experience the most difficult thing to get is a PERFECT PRONUNCIATION. There is usually a "little something" almost "invisible" there that shows you are a foreigner.

I've heard many foreigners in my country who speak very well but whose accent has "something" if they immigrated after when they are 12 years old or the like. The vocabulary level depends a lot on how many books you have read, if you have studied Geography, Biology, Physics, Chemistry, etc. in your near-native language. I think that according to what you say, you could be called a near-native.

Exercise 4.2. Figure 4.1 is from Abrahamsson (2012) (his Figure 2). The study tested 200 participants, Spanish-native L2 speakers of Swedish (LoR in Sweden > 15 years), on an auditory grammaticality judgment task (GJT) and on perception of voice onset time (VOT) with the pair of words *par* and *bar*. Recall that VOT is the length of time that passes between the release of a stop consonant and the onset of voicing, and is heard as how much voicing you put on your consonants.[12] Recall also that Spanish and Swedish, the L1 and L2 of the learners, differ in VOT values. The individual results are plotted below. Each little quadrangle corresponds to the average performance score of an individual, while the line represents central tendency. *R* is the measure of the correlation between the two plotted variables: age of onset of acquisition and performance score. The higher its value, the stronger the correlation.

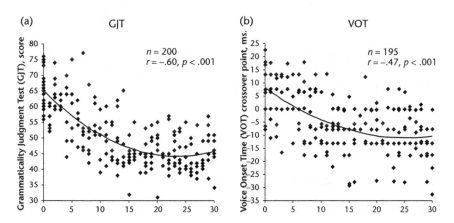

Figure 4.1   Grammaticality Judgment Task scores and VOT crossover points plotted against Age of Onset of acquisition, from N. Abrahamsson (2012)
Reproduced with permission

[12] For additional explanation of VOT with spectrograms, see the following video: https://www.youtube.com/watch?v=b9NuwOLiyss. For a layman's explanation of VOT, check out this one: https://www.youtube.com/watch?v=NKQBWnXMpns.

Looking at Figure 4.1, answer the following questions:

Question 1: What is the range of scores of the native speaker controls on the two tasks?

Question 2: Are there individual learners who score higher than the natives? On which task?

Question 3: Are there individuals who score within the native speaker range at all ages of onset of acquisition?

Question 4: Do you see a critical age in the graphs, after which no individual learner is within native speaker range?

Question 5: Do you think these findings support or refute a strict version of the Critical Period Hypothesis?

Exercise 4.3. Part 1. Abrahamsson (2012) posed another research question: to establish whether the GJT scores and the VOT scores would correlate for early learners, but not for late learners and native speakers. The author explains the theoretical motivation of this hypothesis as follows:

Behind the prediction lies the assumption that grammatical and phonetic intuitions should develop more or less simultaneously and to a similar degree if the language has been acquired automatically, incidentally, and implicitly as an interdependent or interconnected whole, but not if it was learned consciously, intentionally, and explicitly as independent, separate parts of a whole. This, in turn, would potentially suggest that early and late L2 learners use fundamentally different systems: Although children automatically acquire the morphosyntactic and phonetic–phonological system "from mere exposure" (Lenneberg, 1967, p. 176) through innate, domain-specific mechanisms [. . .] and by using mostly procedural memory resources [. . .], adults have lost most of these abilities and instead must learn the L2 consciously, through formal instruction, and via their domain-general cognitive system, using mostly declarative memory resources. The consequence is that early learners develop implicit linguistic competence (or intuition) very similar to that of native speakers, whereas adults typically end up with mostly explicit (some of which can be equated with metalinguistic) knowledge, which cannot be used as efficiently for spontaneous and effortless language production and perception. (Abrahamsson 2012: 209–10)

Question 1: Do you agree with this reasoning in general? Why or why not? In particular:

a. Why should GJT and VOT scores correlate in early learners but not in natives?

b. Consider the distinction between *implicit, unconscious acquisition,* where different parts of the linguistics system are acquired simultaneously and systematically versus *explicit, intentional learning* where conscious effort and attention is involved. This distinction is made by Paradis (2004, 2009) and other scholars. They relate implicit acquisition with procedural memory and explicit acquisition with declarative memory, arguing that the latter is predominantly used in SLA after puberty. Does it follow from the implicit–explicit distinction that L2 learners would either learn the phonetics or the syntax of the second language, depending on what they decide to pay attention to?

c. To cite Abrahamsson again:

> ...the adult learner treats the different levels and sublevels of the L2 as independent puzzles, some of which the learner can choose to focus on in depth, and some of which can—consciously or unconsciously—be disregarded as either uninteresting, unnecessary, or unlearnable, if not left entirely unnoticed." (Abrahamsson 2012: 194).

Do you agree with his logic? Why or why not?

Part 2. Consider the results of the correlations plotted in Abrahamsson's Figure 3, which are reproduced in Figure 4.2.

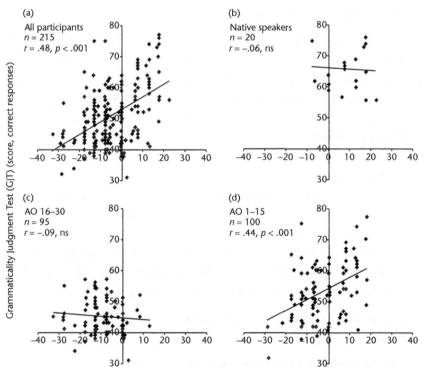

Figure 4.2 Scatterplots with Pearson's correlations between Grammaticality Judgment Task scores and VOT measurements in (a) all participants including the native speakers, (b) just the native speakers, (c) just the late learners, (d) just the early learners, from N. Abrahamsson (2012)

Reproduced with permission

Question 2: Describe what you see in each quadrant. Look at some individual results in quadrants (c) and (d). Point to learners who are good at phonetics and not so good at grammar. Do you see learners who are good at grammar but not nativelike at phonetics? Circle such individual results.

Question 3: Which group shows a significant correlation between the two types of scores (that is, between grammatical and phonetic intuitions)?

Question 4: What does this mean? Are these results in support of Abrahamsson's prediction?

Part 3. Niclas Abrahamsson, the author of this study, writes that the results supporting the prediction of early versus late acquirers using different mechanisms of acquisition is only partially supported by the data, therefore "the empirical results as well as their theoretical interpretation are of a more suggestive and tentative nature."

Question 5: Do you agree with him? Why, or why not?

Question 6: Can you think of a better way to test whether late learners acquire implicit linguistic knowledge?

Exercise 4.4. In the Montrul and Slabakova (2003) study, learners were asked to evaluate the truthfulness of the test sentences in the context of the preceding story. Each story was followed by only one test sentence; the same story with the second test sentence appeared elsewhere in the experiment. Read the stories and test sentences that appear below and answer the following questions:

(i) Generic event story:
     Según el periódico, el restaurante de la calle Jefferson era muy bueno y el servicio era excelente. Lamentablemente el restaurante cerró el verano pasado y nunca tuvimos la oportunidad de ir.
     'According to the newspaper, the restaurant on Jefferson Street was very good and customers were always happy with the service. Unfortunately, the restaurant closed last summer and we never got to go.'

     a. Se comía-IMPF bien en ese restaurante.   True
        'One ate well at that restaurant.'

     b. Se comió-PRET bien en ese restaurante.   False
        'We ate well at that restaurant.'

(ii) Specific event story:
      Según la mayoría de la gente, el restaurante de la calle Jefferson era muy bueno y el servicio era excelente. Fuimos allí a celebrar el

cumpleaños de Carlos y a todos nos gustó mucho. ¡Qué lástima que lo cerraron!

'According to most people's opinion, the restaurant on Jefferson Street was very good and the service was excellent. We went there to celebrate Carlos's birthday and we all liked it a lot. It's a pity that it closed!'

a. Se comía-IMPF bien en ese restaurante.   True
   'One ate well at that restaurant.'

b. Se comió-PRET bien en ese restaurante.   True
   'We ate well at that restaurant.'

Question 1: What is the only difference between the two sentences under each story?

Question 2: What is the tense in the English translations? Is this a syntax–semantics mismatch, in the sense that two Spanish aspectual tenses are translated with the same tense in English?

Question 3: Is knowledge of this syntax–semantics property likely to be implicit or explicit?

Question 4: Recall that we mentioned that meaning can only be learned if the linguistic signal is mapped to an extralinguistic situation exemplifying that meaning. Discuss possible acquisition situations in which this distinction in meanings could have been acquired from observation of extralinguistic situations (such as in these stories) paired with sentences such as these.

Question 5: What kind of feedback should a learner have received, so that she could have learned the mapping of story (i) and that test sentence (b) is not possible? Is it likely that learners hear such corrections from their interlocutors or teachers?

Question 6: Create another quadruple of two stories, one describing a habitual, generic event and the other a similar complete one-time event. Add two test sentences which differ only in the aspectual tense. If you speak Spanish, create the stories and test sentences in Spanish. Other Romance languages such as French and Italian also have similar tenses: check if they work just like Spanish. If you do not speak a Romance language, create the stories in English.

5

First language acquisition, two first languages

In this chapter, we will discuss how children acquire their native language, paying attention to both the stages in this process as well as the various components of language: sounds, words, and syntax. Why are we interested in knowing the milestones of this process? If we want to argue that the L2A process is a natural acquisition process guided by the innate Language Acquisition Device, it is imperative to compare the two processes at various milestones. We are pretty sure these days that the two processes (monolingual L1A, adult L2A) do not unfold in exactly the same way, but we would still like to know which aspects of the processes may be similar and which may be different. Furthermore, simultaneous acquisition of two languages, or 2L1, is even more pertinent to compare with adult L2A because both conditions make the individual a bilingual.

5.1 Acquisition of the sounds of one's native language

Children need to acquire (a) the sounds of their native language, what linguists call the segmental inventory of that language, (b) the phonological

processes (or rules) that involve these sounds, (c) the restrictions on phonotactics (which sounds may combine in their language and which may not),
the word prosodic structure, and larger prosodic units that define the adult
grammar.[1] Most importantly, children have to build a lexicon in which
phonological representations of words are stored. Two acquisition issues
discussed in the literature are the phoneme categorization problem and the
segmentation problem.

How do babies know which of the sounds functioning in the languages
of the world distinguish words in their own language? After all, there are
around 600 consonants and 200 vowels in all human languages (Ladefoged
2001). Each individual language uses a unique set of about 40 distinct
elements, or *phonemes*, which distinguish between words. Phonemes actually comprise a number of similar but non-identical sounds, called *phones* or
phonetic units, which are functionally equivalent in the language. For
example, [l] and [r] belong to different phonemes in English (e.g., *lake* and
rake), since they differentiate words, but [l] and [r] happen to belong to a
single phonemic category in Japanese, the phoneme /r/.[2] A baby's task is to
figure out the composition of the 40-odd phonemic categories of her language. Japanese-learning infants have to group the phonetic units [r] and [l]
into a single phonemic category whereas English-learning infants must
uphold the distinction in order to separate *rake* from *lake*.

Babies solve this problem by starting big and eliminating options. It turns
out that infants are capable of distinguishing all the sounds of the world's
languages. Very young infants discriminate not only native, but also nonnative phonetic differences (Eimas, Siqueland, Jusczyk, and Vigorito 1971,
Streeter 1976), differences that the adult speakers of their native language
are not aware of. For example, the [d] sounds in the context of "this doll"
versus "our doll" are acoustically different, although they belong to the
same phoneme /d/ in English. However, the dental and retroflex variants of
[d] belong to different phonemes in Hindi, as they distinguish between the
Hindi words for *lentils* and *branch*. Werker and Tees (1984) demonstrated
that both English and Hindi-learning infants discriminate this contrast at
6–8 months of age, but only the Hindi-learning infants continue to do so at

---

[1] Prosody (also known as suprasegmental phonology) includes those aspects of speech
that go beyond phonemes and deal with the auditory qualities of sound, e.g., pauses,
pitch or intonation, stress or emphasis, volume, and others.
   [2] We generally enclose phonemes in slanted lines and sounds in square brackets.

age 10–12 months. In a series of experiments, Janet Werker and her colleagues showed young babies' sensitivity to various non native sounds and contrasts. Speech perception scientists interpret these findings as indicating that infants are born with special sensitivity to all linguistically important sounds.

But how do scientists know what babies are sensitive to? After all, the infants in these experiments cannot speak, so they cannot tell us about their perceptions. Scientists take advantage of a behavior at which infants are singularly good: sucking. Babies depend on sucking for their sustenance, but they also engage in sucking behavior between feeding, as becomes obvious when you give them a pacifier. During the initial, or habituation, period of an experiment, a machine measures how fast and how often the baby sucks when no stimulus is presented. This establishes a baseline sucking rate and amplitude (how hard she sucks). When a new stimulus is presented aurally, the baby starts sucking with more force and more frequently. When the same stimulus is repeated for some time, however, the baby's sucking gets down to habituation levels, as if signaling that she is "bored" with the old stimulus. If a new stimulus, for example, a new sound, is played at that moment, and the baby notices the change, she is said to dis-habituate, that is, she starts sucking harder again. The whole experimental paradigm is known as the high-amplitude sucking paradigm, or HAS. This paradigm is very widely used in speech perception research. That's how we know that new born babies and infants distinguish various sounds.

In fact, the native phoneme categorization problem is even more complex than I suggested above. When a female speaker pronounces *lake*, the acoustic features of the signal are different from when a male speaker pronounces the same word. Using detailed acoustic analysis, research has established that the phonetic characteristics of any speech sound diverge in the way different speakers pronounce it, and even in the way the same speaker pronounces it at different times. Obviously, some acoustic differences lead infants to phoneme differentiation, while others don't. While infants are sensitive to non native phonemic contrasts, they are not sensitive to acoustic variation that does not lead to phoneme differentiation. Infants may be able to detect a multitude of phonetic contrasts, but by their first year of life they have largely sorted out which contrasts do matter in their language and which don't. In doing this, they have mapped the different variants of a native phoneme onto the same category, while maintaining the differences between phonemes.

> Think about whether the phoneme categorization problem applies for L2 speakers as well.

Another all-important acquisition task babies face is the so-called speech segmentation problem: where does one word finish and the other start? Recall the spectrogram of *This is a spoken sentence* in Chapter 3, which had no gaps between words. You may have experienced this problem if you tried to listen to an unfamiliar language on the radio. The problem is particularly acute if that language has different prosodic characteristics, for example, if a Spanish speaker listens to a tone language such as Mandarin Chinese, Vietnamese, or Thai. In fact, this problem persists in native speakers for words that they don't know. For example, a high school teacher, A. Greene, published a collection of word analysis errors that her students made, one of which is the following (cited in O'Grady 2005: 18):

(1)   In 1957, Eugene O'Neill won a Pullet Surprise.

If you read this sentence aloud, you would immediately understand that the student was trying to write: *Eugene O'Neill won a Pulitzer Prize.* Not knowing the words, the student came up with a reanalysis of the word boundary.

Teaching relevance: segmentation

Segmentation is an especially difficult problem for L2 learners, too. Think of any examples you have heard from your students, or produced yourself, when you could not distinguish the actual word boundaries. What could a teacher do in order to make segmentation easier for her students?

Is it possible that children learn some words when spoken in isolation, such as *Daddy*? Yes, although this is not going to take babies all the way to solving the segmentation problem. Many of the child's first 50 words are those that the child has heard in isolation. But extensive observation of caretaker speech suggests that only 6 to 60 words produced by a caretaker within an hour are produced in isolation. Think of how that knowledge continues to give in the segmentation enterprise. If you have already isolated *Daddy* as a word, then it follows that the rest of the sequence in the utterance *Daddy knows* should also contain a whole word or words.

What are some other cues that the baby has access to? I already mentioned prosody, and that is indeed a cue that grows in importance after the baby is born. The prosodic bootstrapping hypothesis[3] proposes that children pay attention to prosodic characteristics of the speech signal because they can identity word boundaries (although not perfectly). Word stress is a crucial prosodic characteristic. For example, about 90% of disyllabic (two syllable) words in English employ the *trochaic* stress pattern, meaning that the first syllable is stressed, or pronounced louder, while the second is relatively less so. In order to appreciate the pattern, pronounce the words *baby, sponsor, money* twice: first in the regular way, then make the second syllable louder (and slightly longer). The second way is very unnatural for those words, right? The fact that trochaic words are a great majority in the English language is a significant cue to segmentation: if babies assume that each stressed syllable is the beginning of a new word, they will be right about 90% of the time. Of course, this claim is oversimplifying the matter, but the point is that we have identified two segmentation cues already: words pronounced in isolation, and prosody (stress), which obviously complement each other.

A third cue likely used by older babies to supplement the other cues and cut into the speech signal is *phonotactics*. Phonotactic information is unique to each language, and it comprises the possible combinations of sounds in that language for each syllable position (*onset*, *nucleus*, and *coda*, or the beginning, middle, and end of each syllable). For example, in English a combination of the consonants [t] and [l] cannot start a syllable, so the sequence *fatlump* has to be divided into *fat lump* and never *fa tlump*. However, in Bulgarian this combination of sounds is allowed in the beginning of words, hence of syllables, (e.g., [tləst] 'fat'), so a Bulgarian-learning baby cannot safely decide that the syllable or word boundary is between [t] and [l]. Another example would be the segmentation of the phrase *thisplace*: it can only be segmented into *thisp lace* or *this place* but not into *thispl ace*. Think of other words that finish in *–isp* and *–is* in English: you will never be able to come up with a word that finishes in *–ispl* because this coda does not obey English phonotactic contraints.

[3] The name of this hypothesis (and others, as we shall see later) come from the expression "to pull yourself up by your bootstraps," meaning, to help yourself. A famous literary character, Baron Münchausen, attempted to do just that, when trying to go to the moon.

Production of native sounds and words is another matter altogether. It is well known that children's first words approximate but do not match adult productions. Research into child production has argued that children gradually build up a system of phonological contrasts, phonotactics, and prosodic structure, describing typical processes like segment deletion, substitution, consonant harmony, and metathesis (reordering the sounds in a word). Exhibiting substitution, Daniel, an English-speaking child, produced [gak] for *clock, sock, rock, quack*, and he used metathesis (switched sounds around) when he said [deks] instead of *desk*. An intriguing research question is whether children's phonological system of representations differs from that of adults. The fact that they recognize words that they cannot pronounce suggests that there is continuity between child and adult representational systems. Since adult L2 speakers do not have production problems that are commensurate with babies', however, we shall leave this issue aside.

To recapitulate, babies acquire segmental inventories and knowledge about phonotactic and prosodic structure largely in the absence of a lexicon. In fact, that knowledge *has* to be acquired before lexical learning starts, since it guides word learning. It is likely that children use all the cues available to them (prosody, phonotactics, distributional cues, etc.) in conjunction, so that the various cues can reinforce each other.

5.2 Learning word meanings

Children produce their first word around the first year of their life, give or take a couple of months. It takes them about six to eight months to get to 50 words, that is, at first, word learning is quite slow. However, after that age, something called "the great vocabulary spurt" takes place: a time when children learn one or two new words a day (McMurray 2007). At later ages, children learn even faster: about ten words a day at ages 2 to 6 years. The average six-year-old has 14 000 words in her mental lexicon, while the average high school graduate knows about 60 000 words (Bloom 2000). Compare this amazing rate of learning to word learning in L2 acquisition, which is typically much slower. Not only the rate of acquisition is amazing: children can deduce the meaning of a word from hearing it used a couple of times; older children can learn a word from one occurrence in speech. We call that *fast mapping*.

This is an astonishing feat of deduction on another account, too: the child has to overcome a significant Poverty of the Stimulus. The same Poverty of the Stimulus is to some extent present for L2 learners in communicative classrooms, and especially true for naturalistic ones. This problem of acquisition is discussed wittily and convincingly by the philosopher Quine who dubbed it the Gavagai Problem (Quine 1960). Imagine that a child is in the company of an adult caregiver, and they see a bunny rabbit running away in the distance. The adult says "Gavagai." What is the child to assume as the meaning of the word *gavagai*? It can mean "rabbit", but it can also mean "running", or "running away from us" or "furry animal" or "two ears" or "let's eat him." The information on the object to be named, provided by the extralinguistic situation does not allow the learner, whether child or adult, to identify one and only one possible meaning.[4] Children employ several cognitive strategies to resolve this word-learning problem. As in the speech segmentation problem, children entertain hypotheses, but not all logically possible hypotheses.

The first strategy that can help children with the Gavagai Problem is the so-called *whole object assumption*. It proposes that children who are exposed to an object and a name will assume that the name stands for the whole object and not for parts of it. That means that they will not assume *gavagai* names the bunny's tail or legs, but the whole bunny. In general, infants as well as adults have a natural predisposition to treat novel words as labeling the whole object (Markman and Hutchison 1984). Of course, this assumption has to be overruled when the words for body parts, such as *leg* and *fur*, need to be learned.

Next, there is *the type assumption* (Clark 1993). In order to exclude individual names such as Flopsy or Jack, children should assume that the word labels a whole type of similar animals, not one individual rabbit. Finally, another well-studied assumption is the *basic level assumption* (Hall and Waxman 1993). It postulates that labels of objects will be assumed to refer to basic-level terms (e.g., PERSON) not a context-restricted kind (e.g., PASSENGER). A new count noun applied to an unfamiliar solid object should refer to a basic-level kind of object and not to a kind that distinguishes its members based on the stage or situation they are in.

---

[4] Recall that this learning situation is called "poverty of the stimulus." We discussed it in Chapter 2.

Another learning assumption that saves a lot of effort when it comes to labels of objects is the *mutual exclusivity assumption* (Clark 2003, Markman and Wachtel 1988). Proposed by Ellen Markman, it postulates that no two words in a language should have exactly the same meaning. O'Grady (2005) rightly calls this an organizational assumption. In one experiment, children were shown a familiar object, e.g., a spoon and an unfamiliar object, e.g., a whisk. Then a researcher called the unknown object *a fendle* (a made-up word obeying English phonotactic rules) and asked the children to bring the fendle over to them. The children brought the unknown object to the researcher. They reasoned that they knew what a spoon was, there were two objects around, and they had to get the fendle. If one of the objects was a spoon, then the fendle had to be the other object, since a spoon could not be called a *spoon* and *fendle* at the same time.

The mutual exclusivity assumption works well for children with small vocabularies. It helps children to override the whole object assumption. In one possible scenario, if a child already knows the word *dog*, and the adult who is sharing a book with the child points to a picture of a fluffy dog, saying "fluffy", by mutual exclusivity, the child should assume that the new word is not naming the object again, but is referring to a property of the dog. That would be the correct assumption.

Acquiring the meanings of verbs present an even bigger challenge than nouns. First of all, consider that verbs are cognitively much more complex than nouns, especially the first nouns in the child vocabulary, which mostly describe objects. Knowledge of verbs crucially includes knowing the number of participants in the verb event. For instance, knowing the verb *eat* includes the thematic roles of the two participants in an eating event: one of the participants (the Agent) has to be a sentient being (a person, a rabbit) and the other participant (the Theme) has to be edible. *Charlie ate his shoe* is not ungrammatical but pragmatically odd because shoes are not normally edible items. However, recall the film The Gold Rush (1925), in which Charlie Chaplin plays a tramp who eats his own shoe.

Linguists debate whether knowing the meaning of the verb gives rise to correct sentence syntax or whether knowledge of the syntactic frames in which a verb appears "bootstraps" children into acquiring verbal meanings. In other words, this is a debate on whether lexical semantics comes first and syntax follows, or the other way around. These two opposing views are called "semantic bootstrapping" and "syntactic bootstrapping," respectively. To understand syntactic bootstrapping, we need to know what is meant by syntactic frames. If you hear a novel verb in a sentence where you know the rest of the words, chances are you will be able to guess at its meaning. Take the sentence in (2):

(2)   Mary *clessed* the toy car to her baby brother.

The made-up verb *cless* has three arguments in this sentence: Mary, the toy car, her baby brother. A plausible assumption will be that the sentence denotes a (past) verbal action akin to acting upon (such as showing or passing) the inanimate object (the car) to bring it to the attention or possession of the animate participant (the brother). That is how the verbal frame Noun−Verb−Noun−*to* Noun might bootstrap acquisition of *cless*, if it were a real verb. In a sense, the speaker translates the syntactic frame into the semantic frame Agent−Verb−Theme−Recipient. Undoubtedly, transitive frames ("Mary *clessed* the toy car") present more difficulty, hence lead to more variable hypotheses about verbal meaning.

The syntactic frame Noun−Verb−Noun happens to be mapped onto Agent−Verb−Theme (where the Theme is the affected participant in the verbal action) around 75% of the time in English child-directed speech (Kline and Demuth 2013). No wonder young children sometimes overextend this causative meaning to intransitive verbs as in (3) (Bowerman 1974):

(3)   a. Don't giggle me.   (a child at age 3;0)
      b. I'm singing him.   (another child at 3;1)

It has been established that frequencies of occurrence of each syntactic frame have an effect on comprehension and production of novel verbs in sentences. As we mentioned above, the most frequent frame is the transitive one as in (4). Next comes the Agent−Intransitive Verb frame as in (5) with 16% frequency, followed by the Theme−Intransitive Verb frame as in (6) with 9%.

(4)   Joey is closing the door.
(5)   Joey is walking.
(6)   The door is closing.

Accuracy with verb meanings follows these frequency distributions (Kline and Demuth 2013). At age 3, children show remarkable command of the syntactic frames by producing intransitive sentences that respect the event restrictions (who is doing what) and animacy cues (the affected participant (the Theme) is likely to be inanimate). They demonstrate comprehension of verb frames even at the age of 2. What is debated at present is whether children achieve that accuracy learning verb-by-verb (the gradual development view) or rapidly, generalizing across syntactic frames (the early generalization view). In sum, word learning is at the heart of language acquisition, and many of the psychological processes involved in monolingual acquisition are relevant for second language acquisition as well.

5.3 Acquisition of functional morphology and syntax

Examining verb learning brings us to the next area of grammar building, that of morphosyntactic development. When we combine words in some order, that order is crucial for understanding the sentence, at least in English and other languages. But the word order is not the whole story in attributing the sentence a representation that leads to correct comprehension. Speakers also need to pay attention to the endings of words *(-ing, -ed)* or the little words (auxiliaries, definite articles, prepositions, etc.) that signal the grammatical meaning (see Chapter 3). Language researchers pool these grammatical morphemes under the label *functional morphology*. To use whole sentences in communication, children have to learn to decode what the order of the words entails for the meaning of the whole sentence (in comprehension); they have to learn to line up their words in the appropriate order (in production), as well as decode/signal grammatical meaning.

At this point, it is worth emphasizing the difference between lexical and grammatical meaning. In this chapter, children's early knowledge of nouns and verbs was assumed to suggest they know the *lexical meaning* of the items, that is the idiosyncratic denotation of each lexical item such as "chair" denotes a PIECE OF FURNITURE USED FOR SITTING), "push" denotes an ACTION OF MOVING AN OBJECT ALONG A SURFACE, etc. Children do learn lexical meanings one by one but may also generalize meanings to whole classes of words. *Grammatical meanings* are of another order altogether. They reflect cognitive universal concepts (time, space) that are also linguistically relevant in the sense that languages of the world tend to mark them in their structure. Examples of such concepts include [plural noun], marked by the *-s* affix and [past state or event] signaled by *-ed* in English. It is also important to distinguish between grammatical meanings and their *linguistic expressions*. For example, the plural meaning is expressed by reduplication in Indonesian and Malay, or left unexpressed morphologically in Acehnese. The past meaning is not signaled by dedicated inflectional morphology in Mandarin Chinese, Vietnamese, and Thai. The World Atlas of Language Structures http://wals. info/ is a precious online resource compiling linguistic research on grammatical meanings that you can explore at your leisure. See the map for past tense distribution here http://wals.info/feature/66A#2/25.5/148.4.

Children are very good at acquiring regular morphological inflections, such as the plural *-s*. This is demonstrated in a classic experiment performed by Jean Berko Gleason in 1958. Young children were shown a drawing of a made-up creature, described by the pseudoword (or nonce word) "wug," in this way. In this case, the creature looked somewhat like a bird and was blue. Then another creature of the same shape appeared, and children had to produce the correct word ending. You can see a historical footage from this test in this YouTube video https://www.youtube.com/watch?v= MgB2iMuEZAA.[5] Preschoolers at the age of 4 and 5 accurately produced the suffix 75% of the time.[6] This high accuracy on some, though not all, novel tokens represents children's ability to formulate a grammatical rule: when there is more than one noun, add an *-s*. The Wug test is probably the most famous experiment in language acquisition research.

Rule-learning is implicated in acquiring another inflectional suffix, past tense morphology in English. (Gleason tested it in the Wug test, along with the plural and other affixes.) Recall the Great Past Tense Debate we discussed in Chapter 3. Even though the majority of verbs create a past tense form by adding the regular *-ed*, there are irregular verbs whose past tense forms are marked in other ways: *eat–ate, sing–sang, go–went*, etc. Children's behavior with these forms is indicative of how learning of functional morphology involves both token learning and generalized rule learning. It can be modeled by an idealized U-shaped learning curve. At first, the child produces a few tokens of the correct irregular form of frequent verbs,

---

[5] You can see the whole experiment at the following blog: http://www.onbeing.org/ blog/sunday-morning-exercise-take-wug-test/2510

[6] They were less accurate when the pseudowords ended in a sibilant sound such as *kash* and the correct ending needed a vowel in front of the -s: *kashes,* pronounced [ka∫ɪz]. See Berko Gleason (1958).

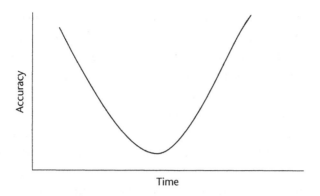

Figure 5.1 Idealized illustration of U-shaped development

say *went, had, took, gave*. Then she learns a lot of regular verbs (*looked, dropped*), figures out the rule and behaves as if she has unlearned the correct irregular form by over-applying the new rule. At this stage she produces *goed* and *went* interchangeably. Finally, she relearns the correct irregular forms and keeps them separate from the regular forms. Plotting the accuracy on verb past tense forms against the number of verbs learned, we get the following idealized shape of the letter U (Figure 5.1).

However, this U-shaped behavior is not uniform, in the sense that it does not affect all the irregular verbs at the same time (Marcus et al. 1992). That is, there are phases of over-regularization for different verbs at different times. Frequent verbs are over-regularized much less often than infrequent ones. There are indications that the past tense is not the only overgeneralized affix in English. Children also over generalize the plural suffix as in **mans, *tooths* and the comparative and superlative affixes of comparatives: **gooder, *powerfullest,* among others. They can certainly find regularity where it doesn't exist, as in the following exchange. Explain which affix is overgeneralized where.

(7)   a. Parent: No booze in the house!
          Child: What's a "boo"?

      b. [After being told it was going to snow.]
          Child: "It did! It snew!"

As we already mentioned in Chapter 3, linguists and psychologists have been debating how best to explain this sort of behavior. One account proposes a dual lexical access mechanism, where regular and irregular verbs are retrieved in different ways (Marcus et al. 1992, Pinker and Prince 1988). On the one hand, children memorize past marking on separate lexical items; on the other hand, they learn a rule of regular past tense inflection. Another account argues for a single lexical access mechanism and contends that U-shaped development is due to changes in vocabulary size (Plunkett and Marchman 1991, 1993). The mental representation of verbs is a set of connections in a network instead of rules, and learning involves forming associations between sound sequences and meanings. Eventually the correct form wins out by establishing the strongest connection. It is during this period of competition that overregularization occurs because the connections for the irregular verbs are still not strong enough to always overtake the regular morpheme. Whatever explanation turns out to be correct, the process of (unconscious) over generalization of inflectional morphology is a fact of learning language, and we will see it exemplified in SLA learning as well.

It is worth making a conscious detour from functional morphology at this time. When we pondered the distinction above between grammatical meaning and its expressions, we mentioned the need to keep in mind that grammatical meanings are universal, while their expressions are language specific. If you access the WALS map of tense, you will see that roughly half of the languages studied do not mark tense, the morphological expression of time (the white circles). The fact that Mandarin Chinese, for example, uses no past tense morphology does not mean that Chinese speakers do not express temporality, i.e., cannot situate an event or state on the time line. They signal temporality with other, non-morphological linguistic means, such as context, time adverbials, and aspectual morphemes (Smith and Erbaugh 2005). So when we discuss the acquisition of functional morphology, we have to acknowledge that very often we are examining the acquisition of grammatical meanings and their various expressions in a specific language, which might not always be functional morphemes.

Let's take the following learning situation as an example. Children acquiring Chinese have a different problem compared to children acquiring English. Acquiring grammatical meanings in the absence of dedicated morphology may be even harder than acquiring tense markers, because children are forced to identify other markers of temporality, which come from various areas of the grammar: adverbials in the lexicon, grammatical morphemes reflecting other grammatical meanings, and pragmatic principles. To master the temporal system, Mandarin-speaking children need to learn not only how to use formal temporal devices (the aspectual particles, for example) but also how to convey implicit references to past or future events. In her pioneering research on this issue, Erbaugh (1992) suggests that learning "less" is actually more difficult. There are indications that learning to signal temporality is not yet accomplished by Mandarin-learning children at the age of 3;2 (Huang 2003). Children's abilities to use discourse-pragmatic resources may still be rather limited at that age. That is why they rely on situational context (the here and now) and not so much on discourse context (previously mentioned temporal adverbials) in their marking of temporality. End of detour.

The idea that, in learning morphosyntax, children are building a mental grammatical system came to the forefront of language acquisition studies in the 70s. The towering figure of this line of research is the psychologist Roger Brown, with his description of longitudinal data from the linguistic behavior of three children (who he called Adam, Eve, and Sarah). The children's speech was followed over a period of 15 to 21 months, starting at roughly 2 years of age. Brown (1973) observed that the children acquired 14 grammatical morphemes, which he called functors, in roughly the same chronological order.[7] DeVilliers and DeVilliers (1973) confirmed the findings with cross-sectional data. The seminal idea was that all children acquire their first language in a fixed, universal order, regardless of the specific grammatical structure of the language they learn.[8] The progressive -ing morpheme was acquired first, then came prepositions in and on, followed by regular plural -s, and so on. Brown argued that this order reflected the cumulative grammatical complexity of the morphemes, measured in the number of features and sometimes, depending on the grammatical theory, in the number of rules they employ. See Table 3 in the exercises of this

[7] Brown (1973) defines functors as "forms that do not, in any simple way, make reference. They mark grammatical structures and carry subtle modulatory meanings. The word classes or parts of speech involved (inflections, auxiliary verbs, articles, prepositions, and conjunctions) all have few members and do not readily admit new members" (p. 75). Is he defining what we discussed as morphemes with grammatical meaning?

[8] In his APA address, Brown summed up his view of language development in a sentence: "All of this, of course, gives a very 'biological' impression, almost as if semantic cells of a finite set of types were dividing and combining and then redividing and recombining in ways common to the species." (Cited from Roger Brown's obituary by Steven Pinker.)

chapter for the full list of functor morphemes. In later years, researchers explored other factors to explain this order of acquisition, for example, the frequency of these morphemes in child-directed speech as well as the phonetic salience of the morphemes (how easily they are perceived in the speech signal). Although there is no consensus on the issue, it is clear that the acquisition order may be due to a variety of factors.

To add a typological perspective to the acquisition of inflectional morphology, we should briefly consider the instructive research of Wolfgang Dressler's research group (Laaha and Gillis 2007). The researchers compared the rate of acquisition of verbal and nominal inflectional paradigms in nine languages that they categorized as weakly inflecting, strongly inflecting, and agglutinating (three languages in each category). Agglutinating languages such as Turkish, Finnish, and Yucatec generally express one meaning per inflectional morpheme. In "strongly inflectional" languages such as Russian, Greek, and Croatian, in contrast, one morpheme can carry several grammatical meanings. "Weakly inflectional" languages (French, German, Dutch) mark fewer meanings with inflectional morphology. The researchers computed the mean paradigm size of these groups of languages and correlated this size to child acquisition data of the same morphology. The overall conclusion was that the richer noun or verb morphology in the input, the more rapidly the child developed that morphology. It is as if the child is rising up to whatever challenge the morphosyntax of her language throws at her.

Children's syntax grows rapidly in their third year of life. As demonstrated already in Brown's and much later work, the vast majority of the sequences of words they produce obey the word order of the language they are learning. Researchers of child language usually distinguish a *one-word stage*, a *two-word stage*, and a *multiple-word stage* in children's syntactic development. Children's early utterances represent snippets from longer potential sentences expressing a more complicated proposition. For example, most two-word sequences contain a verb and one argument, but that argument can have various thematic roles, e.g., *Mommy fix* (Agent–Verb), *give doggie* (Verb–Recipient), and *put light* (Verb–Location). The complex proposition that children are able to express later is probably limited at the two-word stage by a processing bottleneck.

One widely used measure of children's syntactic development is mean length of utterance (MLU). It is a way to monitor syntactic growth over time. This is accomplished by counting the number of morphemes (both

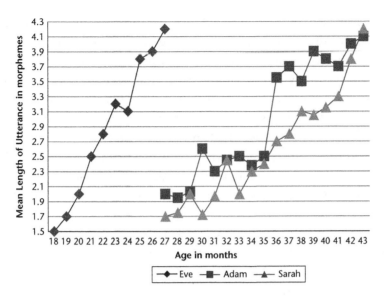

Figure 5.2 Mean length of utterance and chronological age for the three children from the Brown corpus, following Brown (1973)

lexical and grammatical morphemes) in a set of 100 sentences, and then dividing by 100. You will have the opportunity to try this for yourselves at the end of this chapter. Figure 5.2 following Brown (1973) illustrates the MLU development in Eve, Adam, and Sarah.

As you can ascertain visually, Eve's syntactic development is quite rapid, and she reaches MLU of over four in the course of eight months, while the other children's syntactic spurt starts a bit later and lasts a little longer.

Since we cannot do justice to the vast topic of syntactic development here, I shall exemplify more complex structures in child language with *wh*-question formation. The first patterns that appear in child production, (e.g., *What's this? What's that? What this? Who that?*) suggest that children use these word sequences as unanalyzed chunks, as sequences that do not have internal structure. However, it is also notable that English children produce spontaneous *wh*-initial strings (e.g., *where go? what hit?*) that they cannot be repeating. (Think about why not?) While *wh*-words appear sentence-initially in child English, they appear sentence-internally in child Indonesian, a language where *wh*-words appear *in situ* (Cole et al. 2001). This distinction suggests that the *wh*-movement parameter, which regulates whether *wh*-words move to the beginning of the sentence or not, is set rather early.

Stromswold (1995) examined the spontaneous speech of 12 English-learning children from the CHILDES database, in order to establish whether subject or object questions appeared first. The results seem to be mixed (O'Grady 1997), without clear preference for one pattern over and above what can be explained by frequency in parental speech. However, in forced-production experimental tasks, clear preference for subject questions emerged: children made fewer errors in subject questions (Wilhelm and Hanna 1992, Yoshinaga 1996). This has also been found for languages such as French, Italian, and Hebrew. Why is this important? Because it sheds light on the child's process of building a mental grammar.

In trying to explain children's superior accuracy on subject questions over object questions, O'Grady (1997: 135) notes that subject questions do not, at least on the surface, exhibit movement of the auxiliary over the subject (subject–auxiliary inversion):

(8)   Who is helping Mary?
      subject–aux–verb–object

(9)   Who is Mary helping?
      object–aux–subject–verb

(10)

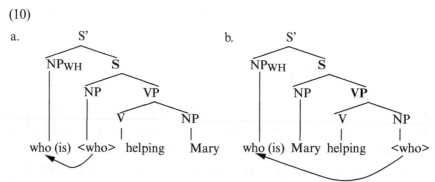

This subject–object asymmetry cannot be due solely to frequency in parental speech, as ascertained by Stromswold (1995). A structural reason suggested by O'Grady (1997: 136) is the added complexity of the object questions. He formulates it as follows:

(11)   "A structure's complexity increases with the number of XP categories (S, VP, etc.) between a gap and the element with which it is associated."

Recall that we mentioned structural complexity while discussing Gibson's Dependency Locality Theory in Chapter 3. This is essentially the same explanation. Let us look at the approximate structures in (10a) and (10b), corresponding to sentences in (8) and (9). S stands for Sentence and the node above S is S′ (S-bar), a higher functional category where *wh*-phrases land. Angled brackets < > mark the original position of the *wh*-word, subject or object of *helping*. The position from which movement originates is also known as "the gap." In moving to S′, the subject *who* crosses only one category, S. To land in the same position known as "the filler," the object *who* has to cross at least two categories, VP and S. This larger number of crossed nodes makes the object questions structurally more complex, hence more difficult for children.

If this structural complexity explanation is on the right track, it makes predictions about child language: the longer the structural distance between filler and gap, the more difficulty children will experience. Hildebrand (1987) used an imitation task to check this prediction. In this task, children are invited to repeat a sentence verbatim. It is considered that they can correctly repeat a sentence only if it is allowed by their grammar and can be correctly parsed. Some of Hildebrand's test sentences appear below; Table 5.1 shows the percentage of correctly repeated sentences in the task. Keep in mind that the words in the angled brackets are not pronounced; these are the original positions of the moved *wh*-words, or the gap. Square brackets stand for nodes that have to be crossed in *wh*-movement to the filler; those are additionally marked underneath with a number sign (#).

(12)   What did   [s the little girl   [vp hit <what> with the block today?]]
               #   #

(13)   What did [s the little boy [vp play [pp with <what> behind his mother?]]]
                    #   #   #

(14)
What did [s the boy [vp read [np a story [pp about <what> this morning?]]]]
             #   #   #   #

Table 5.1 Percentage of correctly repeated sentences in Imitation Task, Hildebrand (1984). Presented following O'Grady 1997: 137

Example sentence	4-year-olds	6-year-olds	8-year-olds	10-year-olds
(12)	83	94	97	100
(13)	46	80	86	97
(14)	31	78	89	89

Conspicuously, the majority of the errors involved children reducing the structural complexity of the sentence they had to repeat: e.g., *What did he play with?* was repeated as *What did he play?* These results have been corroborated with other experimental techniques in comprehension as well as production.

Let us ponder the issue of competence versus performance in this case. If you need to, review these concepts introduced in Chapter 1 and the structural complexity discussion in Chapter 3. After the initial stage of repeating unanalyzed strings, children may acquire the way English creates *wh*-questions (the *wh*-word moves to sentence initial position, there is subject-auxiliary inversion[9]) in stages. It makes sense to assume that children acquire a general rule of grammatical feature-based operations, and not separate rules for each kind of question (subject, object, object of a preposition, adjunct). If this is the right explanation, the structural complexity proposal by O'Grady and Gibson can manifest itself mainly in processing: children have underlying knowledge of both types of questions but object questions are more difficult to process, leading to more errors. Surveying a large body of data, Roeper and de Villiers (2011: 239) come to the similar conclusion that length of derivation is "both guiding and constraining acquisition." In other words, children know the rules for how to create questions, they just make more errors in performance with the more complex sentences.

Teaching relevance: structural complexity

Do you think that structural complexity will affect adult second language acquisition? Why or why not? Is it possible to ameliorate structural complexity so as to aid learners at initial stages in acquisition? These questions can all be answered in the affirmative. If teachers know what is structurally complex (from personal experience and from linguistic theory), then they can break down the acquisition process into manageable steps by reducing complexity.

---

[9] Although we have not discussed subject–auxiliary inversion in this chapter, the name illustrates the process: the subject and the finite auxiliary switch places in question formation. This type of inversion is illustrated with the statement *We **should** buy apples* and the corresponding question *What **should** we buy?*

Finally, let us consider a frequently made claim: normally developing children acquire (the morphosyntax of) their native language by the time they are four years of age, thereby entitling them to be called "linguistic geniuses" who have "cracked the language code" (Pinker 1994). This is a curiously widespread myth, but a myth nonetheless. To demonstrate that, I shall continue with examples from *wh*-acquisition. A recent experimental study on specifically language-impaired children, Van der Lely, Jones and Marshall (2011), included three groups of typically developing children at the ages of 6, 7, and 8. They were tested with three standardized tests to ensure they fell into the normal range of grammatical and verbal abilities. All the children were given sufficient context and were asked to judge the grammaticality of simple *wh*-questions such as *Who kicked Cookie Monster?* and *Who did Cookie Monster kick?* The ungrammatical test sentences included a no-tense error (*Who kiss Miss Piggy?*), doubly marked tense (*Who did kicked Cookie Monster?*) and no *do*-support (*Who Tinky Winky tickled?*). All the groups were highly accurate in accepting the grammatical sentences and semantic control sentences. The accuracy of the children in rejecting the ungrammatical sentences appears in Table 5.2.

Can you comment on the performance of the 6-year-old participants? Does performance reach ceiling in the older participants? Van der Lely et al. observe that only four (36%) of the youngest children performed statistically differently from chance in rejecting these errors, while even among the oldest participants, 2 out of 12 children failed to reject the badly formed sentences. These are hardly isolated results; they surface in study after study. The conclusion is that successful acquisition of syntax is hardly accomplished at 4, and may continue until 7 or 8, depending on different properties.

Table 5.2 Percentage of correctly rejected sentences in Grammaticality Judgment Task, selected from van der Lely et al. (2011)

Type of error	6-year-olds	7-year-olds	8-year-olds
No tense	63.6	76.7	78.5
Double tense	55	85	87.7
No *do*-support	50	73.4	81.5

5.4 Acquisition of semantics and pragmatics

If there are complex structures that take more time to master, are there some grammatical meanings that are more difficult than others? Research has uncovered an interesting disconnect between children's fairly quick and accurate acquisition of some functional morphology and their knowledge of the actual meaning of that same morphology. For example, in several experiments checking the interpretation attributed to the Imperfect tense in Italian, the imperfective aspect in Polish and the Imperfect and Progressive tenses in Dutch, Angeliek van Hout established that children have interpretations curiously diverging from the adult interpretations, even though they produce these morphemes fairly early. These are all expressions of the grammatical category of viewpoint aspect, where speakers can choose to present the verbal action as ongoing at some past moment and incomplete (unfinished), but not as completed. Children in the age range of 3 to 5 allowed (correctly) imperfective forms to refer to incomplete or ongoing events but also to completed events. Adults did not allow the latter interpretation. Van Hout (2005) argues that what is missing in the child grammar at this stage of development is how to anchor the described events in the time sequence of the larger discourse. Kazanina and Phillips (2007) demonstrated the same comprehension problems with Russian children's performance (aged 3–6) on interpreting imperfective morphology. The study also shows that the children's performance improves dramatically when they are given an explicit temporal clause with respect to which to interpret the incomplete, or ongoing event (e.g., *While the boy was watering flowers, the girl was cleaning the table.*) It seems that assuming this temporal perspective without verbal support is not impossible, but just very hard for the developing mind.

The findings on the acquisition of another type of meaning are relevant here, the so-called scalar implicatures. Sentences with scalar implicatures refer to meanings that are not overtly expressed but just implied. Let's illustrate this with an experimental situation. In a study of Greek-speaking children, Papafragou and Musolino (2003), the experimenters acted out with toys the following situation in front of their subjects. A number of horses played in a meadow, then one by one they jumped over a white fence. At the end, all the horses were on the other side of the fence, having jumped over it. The reasonable expectation is to describe the situation with a sentence like (15):

(15)   All the horses jumped over the fence.

However, the researchers had a puppet describe the situation with (16):

(16)   Some of the horses jumped over the fence.

Note that the utterance in (16) is logically true: if all the horses jumped over the fence, then some of them jumped over the fence, too. However, the utterance in (16) is not maximally informative. The quantifiers <*some, all*> constitute an implication scale, where the use of the weaker member, *some*, implies the negation of the stronger member, *not all*.[10] In other words, the description in (16) is logically true but pragmatically infelicitous. Greek adults rejected this infelicitous description with 92.5% accuracy. However, Greek 5-year-olds rejected it only 12.5% of the time, a significant adult–child discrepancy. It is as if children do not "take into account" the other, more felicitous description of the same event in (15), which helps adults reject (16) as infelicitous, or not informative enough.

These two hurdles in the child language acquisition of meaning, the interpretation of imperfective grammatical morphology and scalar implicatures, suggest that not all meanings are created equal, even if they belong to a universal inventory of grammatical meanings that all languages have to express in one way or another. Some researchers have argued that cognitive maturity is a factor in developing these and other interpretations: children up to puberty are just not mature enough to take a perspective different from their own in the here-and-now. They have difficulty seeing the world through the eyes of another speaker. Other researchers (e.g., Guasti et al. 2005, Reinhart 2006) point to successful acquisition when the different perspective is made explicit, and argue that in fact processing considerations come into play. Comparing the child's own perspective with some other person's perspective is cognitively more demanding, since one has to keep both in working memory for the extent of the comparison. This type of

[10] Sentences like (16) are said to be violating Grice's (1968) Maxim of Quantity: the speaker should strive to be as informative as is required. The hearer assumes that the speaker has been maximally informative, and if the speaker has not produced the stronger scalar term, then the weaker scalar term is invoked. Note the involvement of two perspectives in this meaning computation: the speaker's and the hearer's.

computation uses up a lot of processing resources. When children's processing power proves unequal to the task, children often resort to guessing.

Analogous to structural complexity, Reinhart (2006) formulates this issue
as one of *computational complexity,* and I will return to this issue in later
chapters. Note that computational complexity does not completely overlap
with derivational complexity demonstrated in the case of forming *wh*-ques-
tions. Scalar implicatures appear in very simple sentences. In semantics and
pragmatics, computational complexity refers to comparing two possible
construals and choosing the appropriate or relevant one among them. It is
still processing complexity in the sense that the language processor and
working memory resources are involved, but of a slightly different type.

Concluding the sections on child language, let us recount the challenges in
language development we have mentioned. Children have to break into the
speech signal, and they do this making use of various cues. Children learn
words at an amazing rate and utilize various strategies to help organize the
items in their mental lexicon into word classes (verbs, nouns, etc.) as well as
into similar types within each class (transitive verbs, causal verbs, etc.).
Acquisition of functional morphology is fast and relatively error-free. The
bigger the inflectional paradigm in a language, the faster it is acquired.
Children are not only fast but also efficient in extrapolating grammatical
rules from comprehensible speech. Complex structures (long *wh*-questions,
relative clauses) are not produced or comprehended accurately until later
ages (5–8 years), probably because they are difficult to process. They also
may not be evidenced in the comprehensible input as often as earlier
acquired structures. Since the acquisition of meaning depends on observation of the extralinguistic situation in which a sentence is appropriate,
some subtle meanings, not evidenced frequently, also take many years to
develop. Akin to structural complexity in syntax, we invoked the concept
of computational complexity in the acquisition of semantic and pragmatic
interpretations.

5.5 Bilingual first language acquisition

Children who grow up acquiring two languages from birth are known as
simultaneous bilinguals. I mentioned quite a few studies involving simultaneous bilinguals in Chapter 4, Section 4.5. In this section, I will review the
central issues that have been discussed in the literature on this topic:

Namely, does the child grow up with two differentiated linguistic systems, and if so, do these two systems influence each other later in life? The main point I will try to make, following the bulk of the literature on cross-linguistic influence in bilinguals, is that if language A influences language B, this happens in highly constrained and linguistically motivated ways.

But let me start with the basic question: Is it possible to acquire two languages simultaneously? The research in the last 30 years suggests that the answer is yes. Starting with the seminal work of Genesee (1989), Meisel (1989), and De Houwer (1990), the evidence on morphosyntactic acquisition demonstrates that bilingual children acquire them as largely independent systems. Three main arguments are presented in support of this view: (i) bilingual babies separate their languages from early on, (ii) bilingual children pass through the same developmental stages as monolingual children (sometimes more slowly or more quickly), and (iii) bilingual children commit the same types of error as monolingual children. In addition, as Hoff et al. (2012) demonstrates, in children exposed to two languages, the rate of development of each language will vary as a function of the children's relative amount of exposure.

Is it possible to acquire two languages to monolingual standards, if you start from birth or soon after? That is a different story altogether, and I already touched upon this topic in Chapter 4, arguing that the monolingual yardstick is probably not the best one with which to measure bilingual development. This is because it is hard to imagine that the two languages of a simultaneous bilingual do not interact and influence each other. For this to be true, bilingual children should have had two brains, not two languages in one brain. A major impetus to this line of investigation has been the work of Müller and Hulk (2001). These researchers proposed that cross-linguistic influence occurs in areas of the grammar that are difficult for monolingual children, as well, such as the interface between the syntax and discourse.[11] They also suggested that interference may occur where the two languages overlap on the surface. If a structure in language A can be analyzed in two different ways, that is, if it is structurally ambiguous, and language B has evidence for one of the two possible analyses, that analysis would be reinforced in language A. For example, if a child is acquiring a null-subject language (say Greek or Italian) and a non-null-subject language (Dutch,

---

[11] There is quite a lot of evidence suggesting that cross-linguistic influence occurs in other domains, too.

English), this hypothesis would predict oversuppliance of overt subjects in the null-subject language.

Can you discuss the different logical steps of this prediction?

More recent research on the effects of having two grammars has brought other explanatory factors to the limelight: choosing the most economical way to derive a complex structure. Strik and Pérez-Leroux (2011) makes use of this notion of economy to explain why children learning Dutch and French leave their Dutch *wh*-words in their argument position (*in situ*, as linguists say), an option not allowed by that language. French–Dutch bilingual children sometimes produce sentences like (17) instead of the target one with the *wh*-word *what* moved to the front of the sentence and with the subject and verb inverted.

(17) Jij   doe   wat   giraffe?
      you   do.2SG   what   giraffe
      'What are you doing giraffe?'

Even when they do move the *wh*-word to the beginning of the sentence, they sometimes fail to invert the subject and the verb. We already saw that constructions can be compared based on how many categories a *wh*-word crosses over in its movement. A similar notion is that constructions can be compared based on how many Merge operations are involved in the computation (Jacubowicz 2005). The less complex construction, involving fewer terms, will be favored. In this particular study, French has more types of interrogative constructions, including one with the *wh*-word *in situ*, and the derivationally simpler construction is transferred to Dutch, although it is not grammatical in that language.

Further evidence for cross-linguistic influence over time is provided by a large study of bilingual children, aged between 6 and 10 (Sorace, Serratrice, Filiaci, and Baldo 2009). Bilingual children were tested on whether they knew which antecedents null and overt pronouns refer to in null-subject languages. When null pronouns appear in the subject position of embedded clause (see the empty set symbol Ø in (18)), they typically refer to the main clause subject, and we say it is an already mentioned Topic. When overt pronouns appear in the same position, they indicate that the Topic has shifted, i.e., the previously mentioned (main clause) subject is no longer the pronoun referent. Note that the English translation of (18) is ambiguous while the Italian sentence has only one interpretation per pronoun. The null pronoun refers to the mother, while the overt pronoun can only mean that the daughter (or someone else), but not the mother, is putting on a coat.

(18)

La mamma dà un bacio alla figlia   mentre **lei/ø** si mette il capotto
the mother gives a kiss to the daughter,   while she   REFL puts on the coat
'The mother kisses her daughter, while she is putting on her coat.'

When they had to choose pronoun referents in a forced-choice task, the bilingual children made significantly more errors as compared to monolingual children. The fact that this was true for English–Italian as well as Italian–Spanish bilinguals[12] suggests that the two grammars in the mind of the bilingual affect how well the bilinguals can perform these subtle mappings between syntactic form to discourse function.

To be sure, other factors also influence which grammar of a bilingual affects the other. For example, language dominance (better knowledge of one language over the other) can cause transfer, as can the relative frequency of a structure in the two languages. Research on bilingual children is challenging because internal and external factors are difficult to control with actual children out there in the world. However, when these factors are controlled for and grammar interdependence is still attested, there is a strong indication that the linguistic factors of processing economy and processing complexity that we discussed are also at play.

In this section, I related the research consensus that even if children are acquiring two languages from birth, they are building two different grammatical systems that they are able to differentiate. Furthermore, we surveyed some studies pointing to the conclusion the two mental grammars interact in complex but linguistically predictable ways. These factors will remain important in the grammar-building process of adult learners, too.

---

[12] Recall that both Italian and Spanish are null-subject languages, hence have the same null and overt pronoun referents.

5.6 Exercises

Exercise 5.1. We concluded in the section on bilingual first language acquisition that building two grammars at the same time is possible and is frequently accomplished by bilingual children. However, even in simultaneous bilingual acquisition, the two grammars interact and influence each other. Discuss what this conclusion implies for the Critical Period Hypothesis and the frequent comparison of adult L2 learners with monolingual native speakers. (Hint: should we compare adult L2 learners with monolinguals. Why or why not?)

Exercise 5.2. Please see Table 5.3 below based on Brown (1973). The morphemes are arranged in a developmental sequence: if a child knows the morphemes at the bottom of the table, she certainly knows the ones at the top. A child producing the regular third person morpheme -s should already be accurate with regular plural. Check whether this is true in Alison's and Kathryn's speech samples below the table.

Table 5.3 Developmental sequence of morpheme acquisition, following Brown (1973)

Morpheme	Example	Age of Mastery[*] (in Months)
Present Progressive	-ing: Mommy driving	19–28
In	Ball in cup	27–30
On	Doggie on sofa	27–33
Regular plural	-s: Kitties eat my ice cream. Forms: /s/, /z/ and /iz/ cats, dogs, classes, wishes	27–33
Irregular past	came, fell, broke, sat, went	25–46
Possessive	's: Mommy's balloon broke Forms: /s/, /s/ and /iz/ as in regular plural	26–40
Uncontractible copula (Verb to be as main verb)	He is. (Response to "Who is sick?")	28–46
Articles	I see a kitty.	28–46
Regular past	-ed: Mommy pulled the wagon Forms: /d/, /t/, /id/ pulled, walked, glided	26–48
Regular third person	-s: Kathy hits Forms: /s/, /z/, and /iz/	28–50
Irregular third person	Does, has	28–50

Uncontractible auxiliary	*He is.* (Response to "Who is wearing your hat?")	29–48
Contractible copula	*Man's big* *Man is big*	29–49
Contractible auxiliary	*Daddy's eating* *Daddy is eating*	30–50

* Used correctly 90% of the time in obligatory contexts. Adapted from Bellugi and Brown (1964); R. Brown (1973); and J. Miller (1981).

ALISON

Age 1;4

Child: (picks up toy) cow. cow. cow.

Child: (tries to stand it on chair) chair. chair.

Mother: (child gives cow to mother for help) what, darling?

Child: Mama.

Age 1;4

Child: (offers biscuit to mother) Mommy

Mother: Oh, thank you.

Child: (looks at cup) juice.

Mother: Shall we have some juice?

Child: (looks in cup) cup. (picks out two cups and holds one cup out to mother) Mommy. juice.

Mother: Mommy juice.

Child: No. (puts down one cup) Baby!

Mother: Baby.

Child: (picks up another cup) Mommy. Juice.

Age 1;9

Child: (wearing a jacket and pointing to her neck) up. up.

Mother: What?

Child: Neck. up.

Mother: Neck? what do you want? what?

Child: Neck.

Mother: What's on your neck?

Child: (points to zipper and lifts her chin up) zip. zip. zip.

Age 2;4

Child: (Mother is wearing a microphone) I want to try that – that necklace.

Mother: You want to try this necklace? Okay. you know what this is called?

Child: Something.

Mother: See, it's a microphone. there. (puts the microphone on Alison)

Child: I don't want it.
Mother: You don't want it?
Child: No. you want it on. you have it on.

Age 2;4
Child: (climbing on chair) I'm gonna sit on her. may I? I wanna sit on here.
Child: (later) oh, I don't want drink it out cup. I want drink it out can.
Mother: Oh, what did I say about that? what did I say about drinking it out of the can?
Child: Mommy, I want it.
Mother: You want it?
Child: I want drink it out can.

Age 2;10
Mother: (a baby boy is in the room) oh, maybe he'd like to see the truck?
Child: He – he may want to play with the truck.
Mother: Okay.
Child: Maybe he'll play with the truck. he can play with the truck. I think he'll play with the truck.
Mother: Yes, I think he likes the truck.

KATHRYN
Age 1;9
Child: (picks up red bean bag shaped like a frog) Santa Claus.
Mother: Santa Claus? that's a frog, honey, that's not Santa Claus. that's a frog. red frog.
Child: Frog. (puts frog on car) sits.
Mother: Yes, he is sitting down. that's right.

Age 2;9
Child: (looking under her skirt) I just have see
A: (language researcher has come to visit. The child hasn't seen her for six weeks) hi.
Child: Hi.
A: Hi, Kathryn. I haven't seen you in such long time.
Child: You came. you come a lot of days.
A: I do come a lot.
Child: You come lots of weeks. again and again and again.
A: I didn't come last week.
Child: So you came this week.

Age 2;11

Child: (playing 'airplane trip' with the language researcher) mow, why
    don't we shut the doors?

A: Hmmm?

Child: Why don't you shut your – shut your door? shut so no air can come
    in.

A: I did.

Child: Let's get. ssh! ssh! and some nurses bring some – some food.

A: Who?

Child: The – the – the – the – lady who lives in the airplane.

A: Who is the lady who lives in the airplane? what did you call her?

Child: A lady

A: Did you call her a nurse or a stewardess?

Child: A stewardess.

Data from Bloom, L. and Lahey, M. (1978). *Language Development and
Language Disorders.* New York: Wiley.

Exercise 5.3. Using Anne's production data from the CHILDES database,
provide an MLU calculation in morphemes for two of the files from the
beginning and the end of data collection. In the first file, Anne is 1 year 10
months old (1;10) and in the second file she is 2;9. You can retrieve the files
from the CHILDES database using the link below. Anne's data is part of
the Manchester corpus. To get to the original files you have to open this
link, then download the folder called Manchester.zip and unzip it. All
Anne's files are there: open the files called "anne01a.cha" and "anne34a.
cha" using a word processing application such as Microsoft Word.

http://childes.psy.cmu.edu/data/Eng-UK-MOR/http://childes.psy.cmu.edu/
data/Eng-UK-MOR/

This is how to calculate MLU:

Exclude from your count: imitations, elliptical answers, unintelligible utterances, false starts and reformulations within utterances, noises, discourse
markers, identical utterances.

Count as one morpheme: uninflected lexical morphemes, contractions,
inseparable linguistic units, irregular past tense, plurals which do not
occur in singular form.

Example: *The boy's father slowly filled the glass with juice.*

The	boy	's	father	slow	-ly	fill	-ed	the	glass	with	juice
1	2	3	4	5	6	7	8	9	10	11	12

This is one sentence containing 9 words and 12 morphemes. You can find some of the conventions of the transcripts here: http://childes.psy.cmu.edu/manuals/CHAT.pdf.

Exercise 5.4. Here are some more examples of errors children make in complex constructions.

> A. Children close to five years of age were not at all capable of correctly repeating relative clause constructions with genitives such as the one below (Frizelle and Fletcher, 2013).
> There is the girl **whose toy** Anne broke in the garden.
> B. At 4;1, a child produced erroneous sentences such as these (Guasti, Thornton, and Wexler 1995).
> a. What did he didn't wanna bring to school?
> b. What did the spaceman didn't like?
> C. English-speaking kids aged 4;1–5;4 produce the following in an elicitation task (Thornton 1990):
> a. What do you think which animal says "woof woof"?
> b. What do you think which Smurf really has roller skates?
> c. What do you think what Cookie Monster eats?
> d. How do you think how Superman fixed the car?
> D. 12 English-speaking kids aged 4;5–6 produced the following question where the adult target wh-word is whose (Gavruseva and Thornton 2001).
> a. Who do you think's flower fell off?
> b. Who do you think's sunglasses Pocahontas tried on?
> c. Who do you think's Spiderman saved cat?

The construction in C is called medial wh and is an attested option in languages such as German. The construction in D may also be analyzed along the same lines. Think about the elements of the sentence that the children repeat. In which syntactic positions do you find them? What do these further examples mean in light of our discussion of structural and derivational complexity as factors in acquisition? In each case, explain exactly where the complexity lies, and what the children are doing to ameliorate it.

6

Child second language, multilingual and heritage language acquisition, language attrition

Starting in the previous chapter and in this one, we are thinking about individuals with two or more languages in their brain. There is one issue that unites all bilinguals and multilinguals, no matter when the other languages were learned: their minds/brains are not identical in their functionality to those of monolinguals, precisely because the former operate with two and more languages. This fact is of paramount importance when discussing multilingual linguistic behavior. It may confer a broader cognitive benefit, but in day-to-day language use, it may also make lexical access harder and processing more taxing.

In this chapter, I will look at various language acquisition and change conditions. I will briefly introduce the process of adult L2 acquisition, which is the focus of this book. Next, I compare child and adult L2, to see if these are qualitatively different processes. I will then present L3 or Ln language, or multilingual, acquisition. Heritage language speakers are bilingual speakers who are using their native language while speaking another, dominant language. Language attrition, the loss of the native language, may arise under the conditions of bilingualism even if speakers are late bilinguals. All of these conditions of incrementally adding or losing a language will help us think about the important factors affecting these changes. This chapter paints a multifactorial picture of language acquisition. At the end of this chapter, you will be able to appreciate some of the important factors and variables that researchers take into account in order to investigate the process. But first, let me introduce adult native speakers.

6.1 Adult L2 acquisition

Who can be considered an adult L2 acquirer? The current cutoff point for considering someone an adult L2 learner is 7 or 8 years of age, based on Johnson and Newport's classical (1989, 1991) studies. However, there has been some variation in this respect in the literature. For example, Lenneberg proposed 6 years of age to be the end of the Critical Period for language acquisition. Another commonly used cutoff point is puberty (between 11 and 14 years of age nowadays). As the rest of this textbook deals with the way adults acquire a second language, we will not spend too much time in this section describing acquisition routes. However, remember that the conditions of acquisition (in the country where the language is spoken or not), type of exposure (naturalistic or classroom), and length of language exposure and use may matter at least as much as age for the convergence of the speakers on a nativelike mental grammar.

6.2 Child L2 acquisition

When the *initial* exposure to the nonnative language is approximately between the ages of 4 and 7, we define it as child L2 (cL2) acquisition (Schwartz 2004, Meisel 2011). The reasoning for the lower limit is that 4 is considered the age when the bulk of the native grammar is roughly in place.[1] The age of 7 or 8 has been argued to be the critical age after which acquisition may not proceed as in child L1. Although opinions in the literature vary, there is some experimental support for these cut off ages. For example, the classic studies by Johnson and Newport (1989, 1991) identified children who started to acquire the L2 before this age as most likely to fall in native ranges of competence.

My approach here will follow Bonnie Schwartz's groundbreaking work on this topic (Schwartz 1992, 2004, 2009, see also Lakshmanan 1995). She calls the child–adult L2 comparison "the perfect natural experiment" (Schwartz 2004: 17). Why would that be? What is the rationale for considering L2 children such an important population, with respect to the UG issue? Recall from Chapter 4 that, according to the Critical Period Hypothesis, second language acquisition cannot proceed as child language acquisition, if the learner is already an adult (aL2). This logic can be extended as follows: if the learner is not an adult, that is, between the ages of 4 and 7 or 8, L2 acquisition should proceed differently. For example, in Johnson and Newport's (1989) study, the child acquirers were generally more successful than those who started as adults, and a negative age-to-nativeness correlation was observed. Thus, if research uncovers evidence that the developmental *paths* of L2 children and adults look the same, in the sense that they make similar errors and exhibit the same developmental stages, this would constitute evidence that they are both going the UG-sanctioned route. If, on the other hand, the developmental course of the adult L2 learner diverges from that of the child L2 learner, this would be evidence that adult L2 acquisition is not UG-constrained and may be due to rote learning, various problem-solving strategies, and superficial noticing of linguistic rules. The L1–cL2–aL2 comparison, then, can address a seminal research question, namely, the question that we have been pondering in this textbook from the very beginning.

What are some similarities and differences between the three populations we are considering here? Although the latter may be more mature, L1 and cL2 learners are children, that is, they fall within the window of opportunity of the Critical Period for language. On the other hand, cL2 and aL2 learners are similar in that they have a previously acquired language, their native language. In contemplating whether the same underlying processes are

---

[1] Although we saw in the previous chapter that a lot of complex constructions are not acquired by children until much later than the age of 4.

involved in L1, cL2, and aL2, Schwartz (2009: 66) makes the important distinction between linguistic development and ultimate attainment in child and adult L2ers. She argues that looking only at the end states of child and adult L2 acquisition is not sufficient because they may have reached the same end state via different routes. Instead, it is important to look at language development over time. Schwartz (2009) proposes the Domain by Age model that we shall discuss in some detail below.

To illustrate common developmental stages between cL2 and aL2, we shall take an example from Unsworth's (2005) work (as cited in Schwartz 2009). The Dutch language allows an operation called "scrambling," or movement of the definite object over negation, as (1) and (2) illustrate.

(1)   Base word order in Dutch, SOV
       Nijntje gaat **niet de bloem** plukken.
       Miffy goes not the flower pick

(2)   Scrambling of definite DO: DO Neg V
       Nijntje gaat **de bloem niet** plukken.
       Miffy goes the flower not pick

(3)   cL2 and aL2 order: (S Aux) Neg V O
       *(Nijntje gaat) niet plukken de bloem.
       Miffy goes not pick the flower
       'Miffy is not going to pick the flower.'

When learning the possibility of the object scrambling over negation as in (2), both child and adult L2 learners go through a stage that is not attested in child L1 development. Under the influence of English, they produce sentences as in (3), in which the object appears after the verb and negation. Later on, they go through a stage when they produce both the attested and the unattested order, before they converge on the target word order as in (2). Children acquiring Dutch as a native language do not make such errors because they are not influenced by a previously learned language.

Unsworth (2008b) compares the scrambling behavior of low-proficiency, intermediate-proficiency, and high-proficiency children and adults L2 acquirers. The behavior that emerges is as follows: while the low proficiency children and adults fail to scramble where they should, intermediate and high-proficiency children and adults scramble more or less consistently.

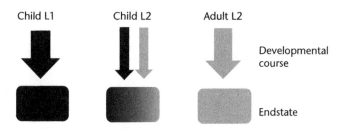

Figure 6.1   Illustration of the Domain by Age model by Schwartz (2009)

Thus, in this experiment, participants pattern together on the basis of proficiency, not on the basis of age. The L2 children and adults were observed to pass through the same developmental sequence, and hence their behavior was consistent with the claim that UG is involved in adult L2 acquisition.

Capitalizing on such findings, Schwartz proposes the Domain by Age model (Figure 6.1), essentially proposing that child L2 acquisition proceeds like adult L2 acquisition in the domain of syntax (dark grey (black) arrows), but it is like L1 acquisition in the domain of inflectional morphology (light grey arrows). The rationale for the second part of this claim came from work by Weerman (2002), which documents overgeneralization errors with Dutch adjectival morphology.[2] These overgeneralization errors go away by age 6 for Dutch L1 children, but they persist for child L2 learners.

However, more recently Schwartz (2009) brings forward unpublished data from Tran (2005), to update this latter part of the Domain by Age model. Tran investigated whether a well-supported fact in child German is also manifested in cL2 German. German children move the verb in second position in the sentence only when it is finite, that is, it is correctly marked with person, number, and tense inflectional morphology. When the verb is in its infinitival form, it takes sentence-final position in child speech. The data in (4) and (5) illustrating this contrast comes from Poeppel and Wexler's work on the production of Andreas, a monolingual German acquirer at age 2;1.

(4)   V2 (OVS) (Poeppel and Wexler 1993: 14, (13b))
      Ein Fase hab ich
      a vase have I

---

[2] L1 and L2 children produce a schwa in contexts where there should be no schwa.

(5) V-final (SOV) (Poeppel and Wexler 1993: 11, (11))
     Thorsten Caesar haben.
     Thorsten C. (=doll) to.have

Tran tested native English children learning German in Honolulu. While the high-proficiency learners had already acquired the above contingency, the mid and low-proficiency children had not. They placed 57% of non-finite forms in the verb-second position in marked contrast to Andreas. Schwartz suggests that these data support the observation that cL2 learners may get to the desired targetlike state of knowledge, but they take different routes from L1 children.

Additional data in this respect come from Herschehnsohn, Stevenson, and Waltmunson (2005), who tested 6-year-old cL2 learners of Spanish in an immersion context, a year and a half after immersion started in kindergarten. The researchers looked at one inflectional morpheme—the marking of number in 3rd person subject agreement—and tested it by eliciting answers to questions. The children were only 38% accurate on the first testing occasion and 56% accurate on the second testing occasion, two months later. At the same time, it is well documented that child L1 learners of Spanish make very few commission or substitution errors[3] with this inflectional morpheme. This study, again, supports the conclusion that cL2 development is not like cL1 development, even in the area of inflectional morphology. Another recent study on cL2, Li (2012), will be discussed in Exercise 6.4. While more data and further confirmation with fresh language pairs is always needed, the overall picture at this moment in time remains as in Figure 6.2 (see e.g., Blom 2008, Sopata 2010).

In summary, there is accumulating evidence that cL2s are like aL2 learners both in the area of syntax as well as in the area of inflectional morphology. They go through similar developmental stages and experience difficulties with inflectional morphology marking. A fundamental reason for this situation may be the presence of an already learned language in the mind/brain of the learners, that is, bilingualism itself. We shall discuss common characteristics of cL2, aL2, and heritage speakers in the last section of this chapter.

---

[3] A commission error is when a speaker produces a morpheme where it is not needed, e.g., *You works.* An omission error is when a speaker does not produce a morpheme where it is needed, e.g., *He work.* A substitution error is producing one morpheme instead of another, e.g., *He working.*

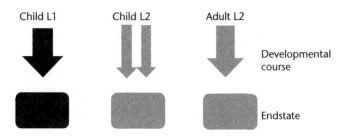

Figure 6.2   Illustration of the Domain by Age model, second version

6.3 L3/Ln acquisition

Although the focus of this text is on adult second language acquisition, a relatively new and vigorously developing area of investigation is third (L3) language acquisition, defined as the sequential acquisition of another language beyond a second language. In this section, when I write L3, I will actually include additional language (Ln) acquisition as well. How is L3 acquisition relevant to L2 acquisition? Studying multilinguals can actually help us to understand a lot about the linguistic representation of the second language in the mind. The essential issue, and one that is hotly debated among generative L3 acquisition researchers, is whether it is the grammar of the first or the second (or any subsequent) language that can influence the L3/Ln. The answer to this question is still related to the Critical Period Hypothesis, although in a slightly roundabout way. Here is the rationale. If the first language and the second language are equally capable or influencing the acquisition of subsequent languages, then they must have equal cognitive and epistemic status in the mind of the learner. If the learner is using her *entire* linguistic repertoire of grammatical features, constructions, functional morphemes, etc., then the linguistic knowledge of the second language must be represented in the mind in a way that makes subsequent transfer possible. If, on the other hand, the native and the second languages are learned in a qualitatively different way and result in qualitatively different representations, we cannot expect the L2 to have but a superficial influence on the L3/Ln.

Researchers in this field ask whether and when "transfer" takes places in the L3 interlanguage development. Transfer is defined as linguistic knowledge that can be traced back to prior linguistic experience (see definition in Chapter 2). To take an example given in Rothman (2015), consider the case of English native speakers who also speak Spanish as an L2 and are learning Portuguese as an L3. English marks gender only on pronouns (*he, she, it*), while in Spanish and Portuguese every single noun is specified as feminine or masculine. In addition, adjectives agree with nouns for gender and number. We call the latter "grammatical" gender. A learner of L3 Portuguese with L2 Spanish will already be sensitive to grammatical gender being marked on all nouns and to adjective–noun agreement, exhibiting "early knowledge of morphological and syntactic reflexes for grammatical gender features" (Rothman 2015: 182).

In L3 acquisition, researchers consider the potential sources of transfer from any of the previously known languages, both in the initial state and in subsequent development. The specific interplay between the L1, the L2, and the L3 parameter values is being investigated. Does transfer in L3 acquisition come exclusively from the L1 as in L2 acquisition, as Leung (2006) has proposed? Does it come exclusively from the L2 (Bardel and Falk 2007) because it was the grammar most recently learned? Can it come from both languages, as Flynn, Foley, and Vinnitskaya (2004) have argued, or from no prior experience (Håkansson et al. 2002)? All of these possible sources of transfer have been evaluated, and found support from (some) experimental data. Linguists have also discussed whether transfer can be only facilitative (beneficial), or it can also be harmful, so that the L3 property is not really acquired, or is acquired with great difficulty. In this respect, the Cumulative Enhancement model (Flynn et al. 2004), as the name itself suggests, argues that transfer from the L1 or the L2 can be only facilitative, while Slabakova and García Mayo (2015) show that transfer of a very frequent and salient property can stand in the way of complete L3 acquisition. Needless to say, language proficiency in the second language will always be an important factor for transfer: after all, a learner cannot transfer what she has not really acquired.

Another variable that appears to play a role in L3 acquisition is what is usually referred to as the typological proximity of the languages. Let's take for example Spanish and Portuguese, which are closely related languages belonging to the Romance language family; they can be considered typologically closer to each other than to English, a Germanic language. The idea of the Typological Primacy model (Rothman 2011, 2015), based on Kellerman (1983), is that the learner will transfer properties from the grammar, be it L1 or L2, which she perceives to be typologically closer to the L3. This typological relation may only be perceived, not real.

Finally, another issue debated in generative L3 acquisition research is whether transfer happens "wholesale" at the initial state, or whether it happens property by property and even feature by feature, from the initial state and into the development process. The Typological Primacy model (Rothman 2015) argues for the former view, while the Scalpel model (Slabakova 2015), defends the latter view. At present, there is no clear evidence that can answer this question definitively. Future research aiming to tease these positions apart should involve a longitudinal study of a third language, studied in adulthood *ab initio*, where the L2 and the L3, or the L1 and the L3, are typologically similar.

With so many variables to control, research on L3 acquisition involves complicated research designs. I shall look at three studies to give the reader a taste of the variety of language combinations studied. Flynn et al. (2004) is a pioneering study, one of the first to demonstrate empirically that the L1 is not the only source for L3 transfer at the level of formal syntactic features and functional categories. The authors examined the production of restrictive relative clauses in L1 Kazakh/L2 Russian/L3 English speakers. Relative clauses, as we have seen in Chapter 2, can have their head on the right or on the left of the clause. Head directionality in Kazakh is the same as in Japanese, while Russian and English work in similar ways. The researchers surmised that, if transfer is always from the native language, L3 acquisition of English by L1 speakers of Kazakh should resemble L2 acquisition of English by L1 speakers of Japanese (there is ample literature on this acquisition for comparison). However, the L1 Kazakh learners had an easier time acquiring the head directionality of the English relative clauses. Flynn et al. proposed that the L2 Russian had a facilitative effect on the acquisition of this particular L3 construction. More generally speaking, Cumulative Enhancement argues that experience in any previously acquired language can be taken advantage of in the acquisition of any subsequent language.

Rothman and Cabrelli Amaro (2010) investigated two L3s, French and Italian, where English was always the L1 and successfully acquired Spanish was always the L2. They examined properties related to the Null Subject Parameter. French is like English in this respect, while Spanish and Italian work similarly, that is, they are null-subject languages. For easier reference, the configuration is given in (6), where the italicized languages work the same way and the non-italicized languages work the other way.

(6)

$$L1\ English\ -L2\ Spanish \begin{cases} \nearrow & \textit{L3 French} \\ \searrow & \textbf{L3 Italian} \end{cases}$$

In addition, two groups of learners of French and Italian as second languages were tested. For this part of the experiment, five groups of participants judged the grammaticality (acceptability) of ten sentences in four conditions: null and overt expletive subjects (*It rains*) and null and overt pronominal subjects (*He snores*). The authors demonstrated that both groups of L3 learners transferred from Spanish, which is actually the wrong choice for L3 French. Even though English, the native language of the learners, could have helped in the acquisition of French, the learners were influenced by the typologically related Romance language. This finding is especially clear when we compare the learners of French as an L2 and as an L3, in Figure 6.3. These experimental results showed that transfer can be harmful, including when the transfer is from the language perceived to be typologically closer to the L3. In other words, they found support for the Typological Primacy model.

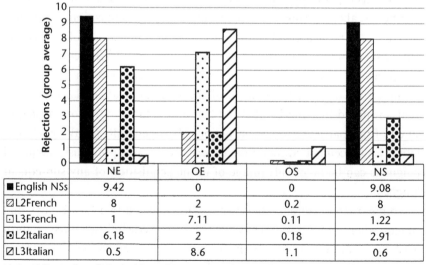

	NE	OE	OS	NS
■ English NSs	9.42	0	0	9.08
☑ L2French	8	2	0.2	8
☐ L3French	1	7.11	0.11	1.22
◙ L2Italian	6.18	2	0.18	2.91
☑ L3Italian	0.5	8.6	1.1	0.6

Notes: NE = null expletive subject; OE = overt expletive subject; OS = overtpronominal subject; NS = null pronominal subject

Figure 6.3 Group average rejection of null and overt subjects in a grammaticality judgment task, from Rothman and Cabrelli Amaro (2010)

> Before going forward, let us spend some time understanding the figure. What is plotted, here, acceptance or rejection? What is the highest score each group of participants could have achieved? Each column stands for a score of one participant group in one condition; conditions are grouped together. Look at the first column in each group. Do the English native speakers behave predictably? Now look at the next two columns in each group. These are average scores of learners of French. Are their grammaticality judgments of null and overt pronominal and expletive subjects different? What can you say about the learners of Italian? The crucial groups of columns to notice are the first and the last ones, where the L3 French learners do not reject null expletive and pronominal subjects as they should, under the influence of their L2 Spanish.

Finally, another recent study demonstrated non-facilitative transfer, too, but from a first as well as a second language. Slabakova and Garcia Mayo (2015) investigated knowledge of English topicalization as in (7), a construction which moves the object to the front of the sentence when it is known, or already mentioned.

(7) A: Did Janice like the wine?
     B. Oh, **the wine** she didn't drink (***it**). She stuck to lemon ices.

(8) El libro   lo   compr-amos   ayer.
     the book   ACC.CL.3M.SG   buy-PAST.1.PL   yesterday
     'The book, we bought yesterday.'

The languages under investigation were Basque and Spanish as L1 or L2, English was the third language, as (9) illustrates. Again, the presence/absence of italicization indicates similar constructions. As in Rothman and Cabrelli Amaro, there was a group of native Spanish speakers learning English.

(9) **L1 Basque** – *L2 Spanish* – **L3 English**
     L1 Spanish – **L2 Basque** – **L3 English**

While English and Basque work similarly with respect to topicalization, the Spanish construction[4] in (8) requires a clitic pronoun *lo* to double the moved

---

[4] Known as "clitic left dislocation."

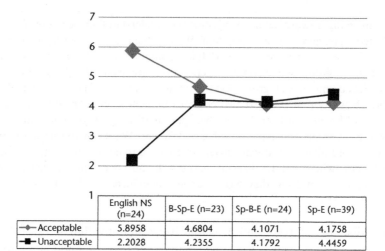

	English NS (n=24)	B-Sp-E (n=23)	Sp-B-E (n=24)	Sp-E (n=39)
◆ Acceptable	5.8958	4.6804	4.1071	4.1758
■ Unacceptable	2.2028	4.2355	4.1792	4.4459

Figure 6.4 Mean ratings of topicalization by four groups of participants, from Slabakova and García Mayo (2015)

object. Therefore, the unacceptable test sentences in English had a pronoun in the object position, as in (7). The experimental design involved listening to recorded conversations and evaluating the acceptability of test sentences with and without resumptive pronouns, on a scale of 1 to 7. Figure 6.4 plots the mean ratings of all the participant groups.

Look at Figure 6.4 and explain what you see. Do the native speakers exemplify a contrast between acceptable and unacceptable topicalization? What do mean ratings of around 4 signify in the learner groups' performance?

Slabakova and García Mayo argued that non-facilitative transfer from Spanish is exhibited in their results, no matter whether Spanish was the first or the second language of the trilinguals. The bilingual results also buttress this conclusion.

Teaching relevance: "Concealed" L3 learners

It is very interesting that after researchers started paying attention to L3/Ln acquisition, it turned out to be the case that many classroom learners are in fact not L2 but L3 learners. For example, it is most often the case in the US college system that students come to Portuguese or French or Italian classes with some or a lot of Spanish L2. It is useful for teachers of such students to be aware of how the Spanish grammar can facilitate these other Romance languages as L3s.

In summary, the vigorously developing research in L3/Ln acquisition focuses on the issue of the source of cross-linguistic influence. Transfer can come from the first or the second language of the learners, and it can be facilitative or harmful. As in generative linguistic research in general, transfer is understood not as a superficial phenomenon of influence, but on a deeper level of grammatical competence and development. Generative language acquisition researchers do not perceive L3/Ln acquisition as a simple extension of L2 acquisition, because of the complex sources of transfer available to multilinguals.

6.4 Heritage language learners

We brought forward the importance of heritage language speakers for the Critical Period debate in Chapter 4. In this section, we will expand on the characteristics of this important population's language knowledge.

The term *heritage speaker* was first introduced in the mid-1970s (Cummins 2005) but has been gaining ground in the acquisition literature since the 1990s. Broadly defined, heritage speakers are child and adult members of a linguistic minority who grew up exposed to both their home language and the majority language. For some researchers, this definition also includes indigenous languages, not just immigrant languages (Fishman 2006). Spanish, South Asian, Russian, East Asian, and Arabic speakers in the US who are the so-called second generation immigrants are representative examples. While the parents are either monolingual or dominant in their native language, the children grow up in homes where both the majority language and the native language are spoken. Very commonly, the heritage language is the individual's native, or consecutively first language, learned in a naturalistic setting in a family environment. The heritage language could also be one of two simultaneously acquired L1s. However, the dominant language of those individuals is the majority language of the country and the community, exerting educational and social pressures over the weaker, heritage language. Once the majority language is introduced, the heritage language becomes restricted to family-centered uses and situations. Figure 6.5 and 6.6 from Montrul (2012) illustrate the typical development of heritage and L2 languages, where the length of the columns is meant to represent proficiency with respect to adult norms.

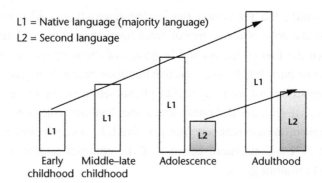

Figure 6.5 Typical development of a first (L1) and second (L2) language (after puberty) in a majority language context, after Montrul (2012)

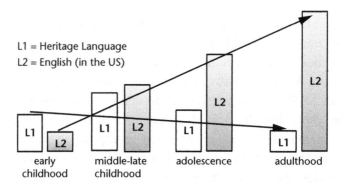

Figure 6.6 Typical development of a heritage language (L1) in a majority language context, after Montrul (2012)

Who exactly falls into this rather heterogeneous group of heritage speakers? According to Montrul (2011b), this group may include:

(a) simultaneous bilinguals, those exposed to the heritage and the majority language before the age of 3–4; (b) sequential bilinguals or child L2 learners, those exposed to the heritage language at home until age 4–5 and to the majority language once they start preschool; and (c) late child L2 learners, children monolingual in the heritage language, who received some elementary schooling in their home country and immigrated around ages 7–8. (Montrul (2011b: 157)).

This is a good place to reinforce an important distinction in bilinguals and multilinguals. One should be careful not to confuse *language dominance* with *language chronology* or *nativeness*. Heritage speakers have acquired their heritage language chronologically first and from birth. It is their mother tongue. However, they later become dominant in another language, spoken by the wider community around them. Very often they sound nativelike in that second language. Countries with consistent streams of immigration through the years, such as Canada, the UK, and the US are full of such people, the so-called second-generation immigrants (Silva-Corvalán 1994). Teachers of foreign languages in such countries encounter many individuals fitting this profile in their classrooms. When tested in their weaker, non-dominant language, these speakers may be more or less proficient. Indeed, according to some sources, about 30% of undergraduate students in American colleges and universities may be heritage speakers of an immigrant language; in California, this percentage may be even higher, at around 40% (Carreira and Kagan 2011).

> **Teaching relevance: Dominance versus chronology**
>
> Identifying specific areas of linguistic knowledge in which the heritage language speakers and L2 learners may or may not differ informs materials development, classroom-based instructional intervention, or language program direction. The educational needs of these two populations are just not the same. It is important for teachers to be aware of just how different heritage speakers are from adult L2 learners.

Which aspects of language suffer when the consecutively first language gets used less and less over the years, until it becomes a weaker language of a bilingual? Recent research into the competence of these speakers has uncovered significant gaps in their linguistic competence, making them very different from age-matched monolingual speakers.[5] In general, adult heritage speakers are better at aural comprehension than oral production. This is not surprising if we keep in mind that they continue to overhear the heritage language in their family circles although they may not speak it on a regular basis. Furthermore, their written language skills are worse, compared to adult L2 learners, because they typically do not have the benefit of schooling in the heritage language.

---

[5] See Benmamoun, Montrul and Polinsky (2013a,b) for a recent overview and linguistic treatment.

An important early series of studies, Au et al. (2002) and Knightly et al. (2003), compared beginning L2 learners of Spanish to Spanish native speakers with only a receptive knowledge of the language. They labelled the latter speakers "overhearers." The researchers found that the heritage speakers were significantly more nativelike on the phonetics/phonology and pronunciation measures, while their performance on morphosyntactic measures, around 60% accurate, was similar to the L2 performance. Advantages of heritage speakers on phonetic discrimination and pronunciation have been confirmed for various heritage languages: Saadah (2011) for Arabic, Lukyanchenko and Gor (2011) for Russian, Chang et al. (2008) for Mandarin Chinese.

Although heritage speakers enjoy some advantages in phonetics/phonology, their linguistic systems share many similarities with adult L2 speakers. Many of the problem areas typical of L2 learners, such as inflectional morphology, complex syntax, syntax–semantics mismatches, and discourse-related meanings seem to be problematic for heritage speakers as well. We will illustrate the parallels between heritage and adult L2 learner grammars with some concrete studies below.

One representative study of heritage speaker case morphology, Song, O'Grady, Cho, and Lee (1997), investigated the ability of monolingual Korean and heritage Korean children to use case marking for distinguishing the doer of the action in a transitive situation. In Korean, the order of the object and the subject can be reversed without any additional changes, because the arguments are marked with Nominative and Accusative case. Participants heard a scrambled Korean sentence as in (10) (similar to the scrambling in Dutch we saw earlier). They had to choose one of two transitive construals (who is hugging who), as illustrated in Figure 6.7.

(10) oli-lul   thokki-ka   anacwue   OSV
     duck-ACC   rabbit-NOM   hug
     'It is the duck that the rabbit is hugging.'

Whereas the monolingual children responded above chance (50%) by age 4, even the 8-year-old heritage children did not reach chance level on these structures. Since Korean case marking depends on four interrelated factors—grammatical function, focus, animacy, and definiteness—the researchers concluded that the input the heritage speakers received was

Figure 6.7   Sample picture used to test the attentiveness to case in the interpretation of sentence (10) by Korean monolingual and heritage children, from O'Grady et al. (2011) Reproduced with permission

not sufficient for them to establish a difficult form-to-meaning mapping of this sort.

In another recent study, Albirini, Benmamoun, and Saadah (2011) investigated the narrative production of Arabic-speaking heritage speakers of the Egyptian and Palestinian dialects. They attested quite a high level of proficiency among these speakers. Still, some significant gaps in their knowledge became visible, in comparison to monolinguals. They had problems with agreement and tense morphology. For example, where inflected verbal forms were expected in the narratives, these speakers frequently substituted a simpler participial form. The researchers contend that the heritage speakers use this participial form as default, when access to the verbal paradigm fails them. Transfer from English word order was also attested.

To exemplify how heritage speakers deal with complex syntax, we shall mention the findings of Polinsky (2011) on comprehension of relative clauses in heritage Russian. Polinsky tested prepubescent heritage speakers, age-matched monolingual Russian children, and adult Russian speakers. The child heritage speakers performed on a par with the monolingual children. Meanwhile, the adult heritage speakers had significant problems with relative clauses. A very interesting feature of their linguistic competence was uncovered: they performed at chance on object relative clauses (*The dog that the girl saw ____*) but were close to the other experimental groups in their comprehension of subject relatives (*The girl who _____ saw the dog*). Polinsky argued that the nativelike grammatical knowledge of relative clauses that the child heritage speakers showed had been reanalyzed by the adult heritage speakers into a new system allowing only subjects, but not objects to be heads of relative clauses.

The study of heritage speakers' competence, just as the study of cL2A, has been developing very vigorously in the last ten years. Three major explanations have been proposed for the linguistic development of heritage speakers. Of course, all such explanations have to refer to differences between heritage speakers and monolinguals, as well as to the similarities between heritage speakers and adult L2 learners. One line of explanation proposed by Montrul argues that heritage speakers exhibit signs of *incomplete development* (Montrul 2008). The reduced situational, family-based usage can cause "arrested development" in the heritage language or lead to incomplete acquisition of some constructions. Another explanation, proposed by Polinsky maintains that heritage languages have in fact been acquired completely, but have subsequently reduced by *language attrition* (loss of native language, see the following section) (Polinsky 2011, among others). A third explanation, argued for by Sorace and Rothman separately, directly relates heritage language competence to reduced input, not only quantitatively but qualitatively. Heritage speakers receive input primarily from speakers—first-generation immigrants and other second-generation speakers—who are themselves living in a language contact situation and hence may be consistently providing them with *linguistically changed input*. Thus, individual attrition may be reinforced through intergenerational attrition (Sorace 2004, 2012, Rothman 2007, Pascual y Cabo and Rothman 2012). Of course, it is likely that all of these factors work in consort to some extent. The common thread running through these three explanations is that the linguistic input, variable both in quantity and in quality, and the reduced language use, are the chief reasons why heritage grammars are different from monolingual grammars. This is true even though heritage language speakers are native speakers.

6.5 Language attrition

The term *language attrition* refers to native language regression or loss. The speakers of such a reduced language are dubbed *attrited speakers*. Attrition research examines the potential erosion of native language competence after long exposure to another language. Although they are related, heritage language competence and language attrition have to be clearly delineated. In the case of attrition, a given property of language has been fully acquired by a speaker who has typically reached a stable native grammar state, but is subsequently lost due to reduced exposure to the native language. Attrition is much easier to demonstrate in adults than in children: the latter may or may not have acquired the linguistic property completely in the first place. Recall from the previous section that Polinsky (2011) argued for attrition being the cause of heritage speaker differences by comparing heritage children who exhibited knowledge of object relatives with heritage adults, who didn't. Only this type of research design can rule out incomplete acquisition and support attrition as the sole cause of the grammatical deviation from native norms.

In cases of native language attrition, exposure to an L2 is often sustained and intense and may be accompanied by a sharp decrease in exposure to the L1. The typical attrited speaker is the first-generation immigrant, who may be the parent of heritage speakers. The definition of attrited speakers, similarly to heritage language, encompasses attriters with a wide variety of linguistic situations and profiles (Schmid 2011). Under a broad definition, attrition can be studied in balanced simultaneous bilingual or childhood L2 learners, adults, as well as heritage speaker bilinguals. A narrower definition focuses on loss of (some parts of) the language faculty after the putative critical period.

Language attrition is typically minimal if attriters lost contact with their native language in adulthood. For example, Schmid (2002) found that, after more than 30 years of living in the US, German Jews exhibited some transfer from English but made very few morphosyntactic errors that could be attributed to L1 attrition. No adult speaker, who comes into contact with a second language and starts living in a new environment, is likely to forget the verb conjugations, the native sound contrasts, and how to ask questions in their native language (Keijzer 2007). But less dramatic, although still measurable, changes in native grammars may be documented when potential attriters are compared to recent arrivals or native speakers in the country of origin (Gürel and Yılmaz 2013, Sorace 2005).

However, not all cases of attrition are relatively mild and superficial. Iverson (2012) discusses a case study of extreme attrition of native Spanish in contact with Brazilian Portuguese. The bilingual speaker, called Pablo (not his real name), was tested in his fifties. He was born in Chile, where he went to school until age 13, then worked in Chile and in other Spanish-speaking countries until he moved to Brazil in his early twenties. At the time of the testing, Pablo had spent 30 years in Brazil with minimal contact with Spanish. He never visited Chile nor did he speak to family members there on a regular basis. He is a street artist, married to a Brazilian Portuguese-speaking woman and is the father of a Brazilian Portuguese-speaking daughter. He rarely encounters other Spanish speakers.

Iverson obtained spontaneous speech samples which demonstrate that Pablo intersperses many Brazilian words in his Spanish narrative, not only nouns, but verbs as well. Sometimes he produces words that are neither Spanish nor Brazilian Portuguese but amalgamations of both, such as *enton* 'then' from the Brazilian *então* and the Spanish *entonces*. His speech, which he considers Chilean Spanish, is not recognized as such by native speakers. Iverson further tested Pablo, as well as two control groups of monolingual Brazilian Portuguese and Chilean Spanish speakers of the same socio-economic status as Pablo, and speaking the same dialects. A range of tasks probed judgments of verb–subject word order, overt pronoun use in discourse-neutral contexts, null objects in complex syntactic contexts and/or with definite antecedents, interpretation of embedded overt subject pronouns in ambiguous contexts, and relative clause attachment in ambiguous contexts. Although Spanish and Brazilian Portuguese are closely related Romance languages, the tested areas represent contrasts between those grammatical systems. The findings were extremely robust: Pablo's performance diverged dramatically from the Spanish control group on the whole range of the tested constructions. He consistently performed qualitatively (and often quantitatively) like the Brazilian Portuguese control group. Iverson's conclusion is that the whole of Pablo's native Spanish grammar may have restructured under the influence of the second language grammar in the circumstances of extreme cessation of native input and usage.

In summary, we speak of language attrition to describe changes in the native grammar when immigrants stop using their native language and carry out most of their communication in the second language, the language of their new linguistic community. There could be personal and societal pressures for such disuse. Research to date has shown that the changes to the native grammar, in most cases, remain superficial and are manifested in loss of processing accuracy and speed, as well as labored access to lexical items and complex constructions. However, extreme cases such as Pablo's are also attested. Future research should address the factors making possible and accelerating such restructuring of a native grammar through disuse.

6.6 Commonalities and differences between the four acquisition contexts

In Chapters 5 and 6, we have been describing various types of bilingual situations, as well as the effects of the first language on the second and the effects of the second language on the first. In Chapter 5 we discussed bilinguals who have two first languages (2L1), or simultaneous bilinguals. In Chapter 6 we discussed child second language (cL2) and adult second language (aL2) learners, multilinguals, heritage native speakers, and attrited native speakers. Now is a good time to take stock and identify which are the central and decisive factors affecting all of these language development processes. We shall consider Age and Input as crucial impacts, admittedly simplifying matters and summarizing a lot of studies for the sake of gaining some overarching insight into bilingual language use and maintenance.

6.6.1 Is age the crucial factor in bilingual acquisition?

The short answer is no. Evidence supporting this negative answer comes from three relatively well-established facts. One fact is that even if a child starts acquiring two languages from birth, one of them is likely to be the weaker language as a function of relative hours of exposure and hours of use. There are many indications that the mere fact of becoming a (proficient) bilingual has ramifications for both linguistic systems. For example, Flege (1987) demonstrated that bilinguals pronounce some phonemes with some intermediate value in both their languages, a value that is not attested in either language. Dussias (2004) found a similar bidirectional interference effect with respect to grammatical processing strategies. Such findings suggest that the monolingual norm may be something that bilinguals can never fully attain, not necessarily because they have reached the limit of their acquisitional potential but simply by virtue of being bilingual.

A second fact militating for a negative answer to Age as the crucial factor is that child and adult native speakers follow the same developmental paths and make similar developmental errors. As Schwartz and others have argued, if Age were the crucial factor, we would expect to see children and adults diverge in the stages of acquisition they exhibit and the type and rough percentages of errors they make, but they don't.

A third factor is possible ultimate attainment in some areas of the grammar, even if one starts in adulthood. Although it is true that not all bilinguals become near-native speakers, it is possible for many to become such speakers in the areas of syntax, semantics, or pragmatics. The level of proficiency attained is usually a better predictor of truly nativelike behavior than age of acquisition (Wartenburger et al. 2003). Although age and proficiency may be very difficult to disentangle, and they are seldom controlled for, there are studies which point to the possibility for highly proficient L2 speakers who started learning the language across a range of ages to apply the same processing mechanisms as natives (Herschensohn 2007). To give just one example among many, Montrul and Slabakova (2003) investigated knowledge of aspectual semantics in very advanced-proficiency bilinguals and identified around 30% of them who performed within native speaker norms. If age is not crucial for the successful acquisition of such properties, then the critical period claim is too strong indeed.

6.6.2 The Critical Period Hypothesis and the importance of the input

If age is not the absolutely crucial factor, then what is? Some of the points discussed in the previous sections indicate that actually input is the crucial factor. To elaborate, simultaneous bilinguals are exposed to two languages from birth, but the effects of bilingualism are mitigated by the amount of time they spend using the weaker and the more dominant language. Heritage speakers are also exposed to the family language from birth, but the disuse of that language in later years in favor of the majority societal language leads to dramatic reduction of fluency and accuracy, and in many cases even to restructuring of the native grammar. Finally, attrited speakers who left their native country in adulthood, and thus interrupted their native language flow of communication, also lose some fluency and experience lexical and constructional access difficulties. In extreme cases, they may undergo changes in underlying mental representations, not just processing preferences. The common thread between these three different populations: simultaneous bilinguals, heritage speakers, attriters, is the loss of usage and reduced availability of native language input. When input is lost or diminished, there are consequences for the nativeness of the grammar.

6.6.3 What kind of input?

Is any input going to be sufficient for language maintenance? The short answer is that, for a language acquired to completeness to be maintained, the input has to be copious, sustained, and continuous. Communication (give and take) in that language is essential. Communication has to be on diverse topics, allowing the language users to comprehend and produce a variety of constructions of different complexity. Reading in the language, not just oral communication, is also considered beneficial for language maintenance, because there are different constructions and aspects of language exemplified in oral and written varieties. For example, it is a well-known fact (and easily checked) that heritage speakers tend to be good at aspects of language that are reinforced in family communication, such as household, food, and vocabulary related to everyday life. They have been exposed to the lower frequency, academic-oriented vocabulary, and the complex structures of the more formal registers in their second language in school settings, and they may not have learned that more specialized vocabulary or registers in their native language.

6.6.4 Which areas of the grammar suffer with reduced input?

The answer to this question comes from looking at the performance of bilingual speakers in reduced input conditions on a variety of linguistic properties. Benmamoun, Montrul, and Polinsky (2013a,b) cite morphology, complex syntax, semantics, and discourse pragmatics as areas of the grammar where heritage speakers display non nativelike characteristics. For example, Montrul and Ionin (2010) identified non targetlike interpretations of the definite article and the bare noun in generic contexts. Heritage speakers accepted sentences such as *Leones son peligrosos*, 'Lions are dangerous,' which is good in English but unacceptable in Spanish. Heritage speakers have been shown to omit case marking or misuse it (Montrul, Bhatt, and Bhatia 2012, O'Grady et al. 2011). Polinsky (2006) showed that Russian heritage speakers who cannot write in Russian had reanalyzed the gender system to contain two genders instead of the monolingual Russian three. Kim, Montrul, and Yoon (2009) studied the interpretation of three local and long-distance reflexives by Korean heritage speakers. They found that while the monolinguals had a three-way anaphor system, the Korean heritage speakers had a simplified system with only two pronouns.

In sum, studies have uncovered morphological instability, high variability, and nonnative knowledge of definiteness marking, gender agreement, case marking, lexical aspect, grammatical aspect, mood, and inflected infinitives. As this already sizable body of data indicates, native speakers in circumstances of reduced input demonstrate nonconvergence, simplification, and/or reanalysis of various areas of their native grammar. Frequently, these have been shown to be the effect of the dominant second language. It appears that all areas of the grammar can be affected by reduced input, with the possible exception of phonetics/phonology. However, it is still an unanswered question why some properties within an area of the grammar are affected while others are not. For example, Håkansson (1995) found that Swedish heritage speakers did not have problems with the Verb Second rule, a complex grammatical rule. Furthermore, while Russian heritage speakers have severe problems with gender and case, Spanish heritage speakers typically have fewer problems with these grammatical morphemes. Theoretical answers to these questions should include an array of experience factors affecting linguistic knowledge, as well as principled proposals based on linguistic theory.

6.6.5 Are first and second language acquisition qualitatively different?

The short answer is no, first and second language acquisition are not qualitatively different. If the Language Acquisition Device were permanently altered after the acquisition of the native language in such a way that subsequent languages were acquired in a qualitatively different way, then the acquisition of the dominant language of heritage speakers cannot be explained adequately (see Figures 6.3 and 6.4). Furthermore, if we find, as we do, that even adult L2 learners attain similar proficiency to monolinguals in some areas of the grammar, then the same language acquisition mechanisms must be at work. It is as simple as that: if language acquisition processes (L1A, L2A, L3/LnA, heritage L1A, heritage L2A) start at different ages but lead to comparable attainment levels, the mechanisms cannot be qualitatively different.

This interpretation of the L1–L2A fundamental difference remains controversial. Proponents of a strong version of the Critical Period Hypothesis argue that it is a special cognitive-based and measurable aptitude that makes some but not all individuals better language learners, leading to performances quantitatively comparable to monolinguals (Long, DeKeyser, Meisel). According to this line of reasoning, even if they are better language learners, these successful individuals do not learn language in the way L1 children do, because they rely on general cognitive skills, as well as metalinguistic patterns of observation and explicit explanation. This type of argument is only countered by demonstrating that successful L2 learners have mastered properties that are not taught in language classrooms and that are not easy to acquire based on observation of natural language input. Such research findings exist, and we will see them discussed at length in Chapter 10. Suffice it to mention just one study here, Slabakova (2003), which shows that successful interpretation of taught and untaught semantic contrasts is demonstrated by Bulgarian learners of English even at intermediate levels of proficiency.

At the same time, if we maintain that L1 and L2 acquisition are fundamentally similar processes, we must explain the wide discrepancy in attainment levels for the two types of acquisition. While a typically developing first language is always acquired to completeness, a typically developing second language is not *guaranteed* 100% success. Could the solution lie in the fact that acquiring a second language creates a bilingual individual? Bilinguals experience complex demands on their language faculty because they must constantly negotiate two competing systems at the same time, both in production and comprehension. Even if they are able to establish fully targetlike underlying knowledge of the L2 grammar, they may fail to apply it deterministically due to the competing linguistic systems and the heightened demand on processing resources. In order to use her weaker language, a bilingual has to expend a great deal of effort at inhibiting the deeply entrenched routines used by her dominant and stronger language. This inhibition can sometimes fail, allowing the output from underlyingly intact rules to show influence from the dominant language.

It stands to reason that all types of bilinguals (consecutive, sequential, and adult) should show evidence of such "bilingualism effects." In other words, we should find more widely variable outcomes with all types of acquisition leading to bilingualism but no such variation with monolingual acquisition (barring impairments and traumas, of course). Interestingly, such evidence comes from the area of simultaneous bilingualism. "Raising children to speak a single language has a 100% success rate except in some cases of impairment. Raising children to speak two languages only has a

75% success rate." (De Houwer, 2007: 421). Why would that be the case, even with consistent exposure to two languages from birth? We can also construe the heritage language findings discussed in this chapter in this light: while competence in one language goes up, competence in the other language might go down, see Figure 6.6.[6]

A clinching argument comes from a recent study by Hopp and Schmid (2013). The idea was to compare the performance of late L2 learners against that of other, similarly fluent and proficient bilinguals, who share the effects of cross-linguistic influence but who have acquired the same language from birth. The two researchers compared data that they had collected separately[7] on some comparable measures. Hopp's body of data was from near-native speakers of German with English and Dutch as their native languages; Schmid's was from German attriters in Dutch and English environments. Since the two populations took a C-test[8] measuring proficiency, their global proficiency could be compared directly. The ranges of the attriters on the C-test were much larger, but the means were comparable, and lower than the monolingual control group.

An investigation of perceived foreign accent among these groups of speakers revealed that a minority of the L2ers (37.5%) and a majority of the L1 attriters (72.5%) were perceived to be within the monolingual range. However, 80% of all L2ers fell into the range delimited by the attriters. Schmid (2013) further compares the rate of morphosyntactic errors per minute, taken from a spoken speech sample. Although the topics and the duration of the samples were not exactly the same, Schmid collated errors in four categories: lexical errors, word order (syntax) errors, and two morphological errors (case and gender) (see Figure 6.8).

Let's examine the interesting contrasts between attriters and near-natives on the data in Figure 6.8. The near-native L2 speakers of German are less accurate on the lexicon (which Schmid suggests could be due to the specific

---

[6] The reader should not extend these arguments to suggest that there is only room for one language in the brain and if you add another, the first will inevitably get worse. This is not the case. All I am suggesting here is that languages suffer from loss of input.

[7] Hopp (2007) and Schmid (2007).

[8] A C-test is a type of language test in which learners read a brief paragraph in the target language. The first two sentences are left intact. Thereafter, every other word is left intact but for each alternate word, only the first half of the word is written out while the second half is represented by a blank space for each missing letter. This is what it looks like: every oth_ _ word i_ left int _ _ _.

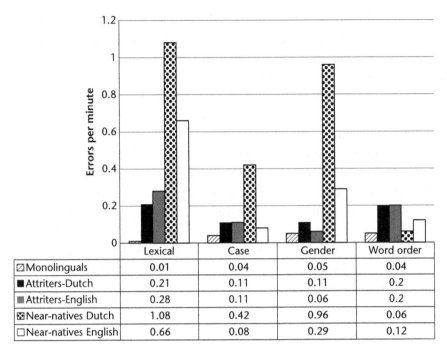

	Lexical	Case	Gender	Word order
▨ Monolinguals	0.01	0.04	0.05	0.04
■ Attriters-Dutch	0.21	0.11	0.11	0.2
▤ Attriters-English	0.28	0.11	0.06	0.2
⊠ Near-natives Dutch	1.08	0.42	0.96	0.06
☐ Near-natives English	0.66	0.08	0.29	0.12

Figure 6.8 Errors per minute in the production of four experimental groups, from Schmid (2013)

speech topic), but they are extremely accurate on word order, even more so than the attriters. With respect to case marking, the English native speakers are again out performing the German attriters. Gender-marking, on the other hand, which is relatively unproblematic for the attriters, seems to be hard for the near-natives. This is particularly prominent for the Dutch-native learners of German, although Dutch has a system of gender-marking that is quite similar to German. We shall look at the acquisition of grammatical gender later (in Chapter 7), suffice it to say here that it is considered one of the hardest functional categories to acquire due to the high level of lexical learning involved. The overall results of this interesting and rare comparison suggest that it is *possible* for L2 learners to become as successful as bilingual natives on many linguistic measures, while monolinguals outperform both, at least at the group level. As the research design keeps constant the effect of managing two linguistic systems online, both the similarities and the differences between the two populations must be due to the underlying competence or the performance of the two groups.

In sum, the position emphasized in this chapter is that continued diverse and comprehensible linguistic input and rich communicative use emerge as the indispensable conditions for successful language acquisition, overriding potential critical periods (at least in some modules of the grammar). At the same time, Universal Grammar principles and parameters constrain learners' hypotheses and can facilitate subsequent language acquisition. Bilingualism or multilingualism effects, such as the necessity to manage two or more competing grammar systems in production and comprehension, may go a long way towards explaining the higher variability in additional language attainment (no matter whether that is from birth, in childhood, or in adulthood). It could be the case that the language aptitude some researchers correlate with attainment is directly related to the ability to navigate two competing grammatical systems, although this remains an empirical question. I have argued that the null hypothesis of L2 acquisition is that it is fundamentally similar to L1 acquisition,[9] because both are processes of *human language acquisition*.

6.7 Exercises

Exercise 6.1. Montrul et al. (2008) revisited the question originally posed by Au et al. (2002): whether early exposure to the language confers an advantage in linguistic ability to heritage speakers (n = 42) over L2 learners (n = 44). This study investigated syntactic knowledge of gender agreement in three tasks: a comprehension task, a written morphology recognition task, and an oral production task. While the native speakers performed at ceiling on all tasks (with almost 100% accuracy), the two experimental groups were significantly less accurate. Yet, the results also revealed interesting *task effects*. Within the L2 group, speakers were significantly more accurate on the two written tasks (M = 89.5 and M = 88.5) than they were on the oral production task (M = 72.1). The heritage speakers, by contrast, were more accurate on the oral task (M = 89.7) than on the two written tasks (M = 84.6 and M = 83.3). Oral versus written accuracies are significantly different within groups. Furthermore, comparing between groups, L2 learners were more accurate than heritage speakers on the two written tasks,

---

[9] See also Hopp (2007).

while the heritage speakers were more accurate on the oral task than the L2 learners.

Discuss whether these task effects change substantially, or change at all, the interpretation that we have espoused in this chapter: that heritage speakers' competence is comparable to L2 competence, due to their reduced language input and language use.

Exercise 6.2. Find the study from Exercise 6.1 in your local library or online, read it and discuss whether the interpretation of the authors coincides with the interpretation stated above. Discuss whether written or oral tasks better capture implicit linguistic competence. What do the overall results tell us about the linguistic competence of these two groups on the property under investigation?

Exercise 6.3. Still on the same study, consider the Figures 6.2, 6.4, and 6.7. In which group is there more variability? How is that captured in the graphs? Now look at Table 10. How were the individual results calculated? Discuss whether the individual results support the group findings and your comments on variability within groups.

Exercise 6.4. A recent longitudinal study of the initial state in child L2 acquisition, Li (2012) studies six 7- to 9-year-old Chinese-speaking children learning English in an immersion context in the US. The children had resided in the US between four and five months at the beginning of the study. The school instruction and environment was in English only. The children's spontaneous productions were recorded once a month, for eight months in interactions with the researcher. There was not much development in the children's data over that time. The findings of the study are summarized in Table 6.1. Note that commission errors (producing a wrong morpheme) on tense and agreement are around 13%.

Lardiere (1998) describes the production of the adult L2 learner Patty. Find the article, print it out, and read it. Answer the following questions:

Table 6.1 Percentage of correct usage in the spontaneous production of six English-learning children

Correct use of verb inflections				Syntactic properties	
3PSG -s	Regular -ed	Irregular past	Copula be	Overt Subjects	Nominative Subjects
16%	13%	38%	93%	~100%	~100%

Question 1: Compare the personal characteristics of Patty and the children in Li's study. Then compare the rates of correct suppliance for Patty and the children on the properties listed in Table 6.1. Make a combined table. Do you see a similar pattern?

Question 2: How does Lardiere explain the discrepancy between the accuracy reflected in the first three columns in Table 6.1, and in the last two columns? Do you think that Lardiere's explanation of Patty's performance can extend to the children's performance?

Question 3: Lardiere describes Patty as a fossilized learner. Why? Do you think that the children in Li's study are fossilized learners, and why?

Exercise 6.5. In Section 6.3, we discussed various models attempting to describe the L3/Ln acquisition process. Looking at the experimental designs described in this section, provide experimental configurations of languages and properties to test the following hypotheses:

Hypothesis A: Transfer can come only from the L1;
Hypothesis B: Transfer can come only from the L2.

What findings would support hypothesis A? What findings would support hypothesis B?

PART III

Second Language Acquisition

At the outset of the second part of the book, devoted to second language acquisition, it is profitable to discuss the whole process in general outline. The concept of "interlanguage" is central to the wider field of SLA and the generative L2A enterprise in particular. Due to Larry Selinker's seminal publication in 1972, this term describes the linguistic system we can see in learner language when the learner attempts to convey meaning in the target language (Selinker 1972). The term "interlanguage" embodies the idea that learner language is not a hodgepodge collection of random errors, but that there is a *system* to the errors. The interlanguage rule system may be different from the target rule system used by its native speakers, and it may be different from the rule system of the learner native language. However, that system is indicative of an internal grammar and describable on its own terms.

Before interlanguage, the prevalent theory of SLA was contrastive analysis. This approach assumed that errors were caused by the differences between the first and the second language of the learner. Thus, it was sufficient to compare the two, in order to predict what errors a specific learner would make. There is still a large dose of truth in that contention; however, it is far from sufficient in explaining all learner errors. For example, contrastive analysis can tell us that a native Russian speaker learning English will make errors with articles (most likely drop articles), because Russian does not mark definiteness with specific morphemes while English does. An interlanguage approach, as represented in Tania Ionin's work, for example, will hypothesize that learners are making these errors because they are not sure whether *the* in English marks definite noun phrases (familiar to the speaker and the hearer) or specific noun phrases (known to the hearer and somehow noteworthy). This hypothesis immediately predicts that learners would overuse *the* in specific indefinite contexts, which is actually supported by experimental data. Thus, the concept of the learner grammar being systematic allows the researcher to make predictions and *explain*, not just describe, behavior.

The concept of interlanguage also implied that if linguistic development is systematic, one can describe developmental sequences for some more complicated constructions that the learner needs to acquire. Such developmental sequences were described for negation, question formation, and relative clauses (Lightbown and Spada 2006), where researchers showed that learners from different linguistic backgrounds go through the same progressive sequences in discrete stages. The language acquisition process was firmly established as having an initial state, various interlanguage stages at which deterministic changes are discernible, and a final state, which Selinker termed "fossilized state," and at which developments are no longer evident.

Within the generative L2A framework (White 1989, 2003), the concept of interlanguage was fully embraced and given new content. It was still viewed as the learners' transitional linguistic system that can be viewed in terms of evolving developmental stages; however, these stages were proposed to be described as parametric changes. Learners have free access to linguistic principles, the information that is common to all languages, and they have to reset their parameter values from the L1 setting to the L2 setting. This process of parameter resetting manifests itself in developmental sequences (White 2003). It is likely that a developmental stage very close to the initial state will have a few basic parametric values reset, especially ones that are supported with a lot of evidence in the input. At later developmental stages, one can expect to see more parametric values reset. A complete convergence, according to some theories to be discussed later in the book, is possible; however, it is contingent on a lot of input-dependent factors (Schwartz and Sprouse 1996). Crucially, at every stage of development including the initial state, the interlanguage grammar represents parametric values that may not be targetlike, but are still UG-sanctioned and thus possible in other languages. In other words, an interlanguage grammar is a system of UG-provided principles and parameter settings; it is a fluid system changing with the evidence coming from the target language input. The reader should keep this general perspective on SLA throughout our discussion of the development within the separate language modules.

In this part of the book, we reap the benefits of having established the big picture of what language is, and what language acquisition is, in order to delve deeper into the second language acquisition process. This is the core part of the textbook, where I concentrate on adult SLA. I shall examine the acquisition of functional morphology, syntax, the mental lexicon, the syntax–semantics interface, discourse–pragmatics interface, and L2 processing.

The exposition and the exercises of the previous chapters have hopefully prepared the attentive reader to tackle the survey of findings that is to come. One overarching idea that same person, the attentive reader, should keep in mind while scrutinizing the material in this chapter and the next is the following: What is relatively easy to acquire, and what is relatively harder to acquire, for adults in a second language? The answer to this research question is not always straightforward, and some gross overgeneralization is inevitable, but it is always extremely pertinent to the applied concerns of developing theory. Very simply put, the idea is that if language teachers and even learners themselves know what areas of the grammar are likely to trigger the most difficulty, or likely to remain problematic even after many years of acquisition, teachers and learners will pay more attention to these areas and expend more efforts for practicing those areas. If, on the other hand, some features and even whole areas of the grammar are easier to acquire, then again, knowledge of which these properties are is likely to increase language teaching efficiency. This is the underlying idea of the Bottleneck Hypothesis, to be discussed in more detail in Chapter 13. In this chapter, we embark on a comprehensive survey of inflectional morphology acquisition because this part of the grammar is at the core of the linguistic system.

7

Acquisition of (functional) morphology

Functional morphology is considered to be the locus of language variation.[1]
It hosts the features that regulate how a specific language grammar functions.
Functional morphology has three essential aspects: a) it has morphophonological form (it is pronounced and is frequently attached to another word as a
prefix, suffix, or infix); b) it carries grammatical meaning (e.g., tense, aspect,
gender, case); and c) it has syntactic consequences by regulating which
phrases move around in the sentence and which stay where they merged.
After learning the vocabulary items of the second language, the functional
morphology is the single most important form–function mapping that learners have to master. Without the inflectional affixes and the function words,
the message of a sentence may be comprehensible in communication, but the
sentence is not well formed and no native speaker would produce it that way.

---

[1] See Chapters 1 and 2 for the language architecture and how that affects acquisition.

Since functional morphology is visible, some of it even salient, and highly frequent, it can be tested in naturalistic or elicited production. The most common method of evaluating knowledge of morphology has been to use a sample of transcribed learner speech in order to count the environments in which a native speaker of the language would use a particular piece of morphology. These are known as obligatory contexts. For example, a plural context is a noun phrase of this sort: *two book___*. A speaker of English would produce *two book-s*, while a learner of English might drop the *-s*. An obligatory context for the progressive *-ing* suffix would be *I am go___ to the market*. The researcher counts how many times the individual learner produced the appropriate morphology in the obligatory context. The result should be reported both as a raw count and a percentage.

> Why might it be important to report accuracy in obligatory contexts both in raw count and as a percentage?

However, one should never disregard meaning. The features that regulate meanings are called "interpretable features," and we will see them exemplified in this chapter. Meaning is not visible on the surface, and we can't directly record meaning. Of necessity, we need to create experimental situations to extract speakers' interpretations. One clue as to what meaning learners attribute to a morpheme may be appropriate usage in production, but this clue can also be misleading. Extensive research has indicated that children and other learners might not attribute an adultlike interpretation to function words and morphemes, even if they produce them correctly. For example, it is well known that while English-speaking children produce correct object pronouns as in *Mama Bear is touching her*, half of the time they actually interpret such a sentence to mean *Mama Bear is touching herself* (Chien and Wexler 1990), which is not at all the same meaning, is it? Therefore, caution should be used in assuming that if a morpheme is used correctly, it is actually fully acquired.

7.1 Morpheme studies

The acquisition of functional morphology has been of great interest to L2 researchers since the 70s. This interest was sparked by Roger Brown's seminal work on child language acquisition (Brown 1973), which we reviewed in Chapter 5. In this work, Brown tracks the grammatical developments in three children's speech by counting the correct usage of what he called "functor" morphemes, or grammatical morphemes. He established that Adam, Eve, and Sarah acquired these morphemes in the same order, though not at the same age. Until that time, work on native language transfer in SLA had taken a behaviorist perspective[2] and engaged in contrastive error analysis. Inspired by Brown's work from a more psychological, generative perspective, a series of studies in the early 1970s tested the idea that child L2 acquisition follows the same milestones and the same route as child L1 acquisition. Dulay and Burt (1973, 1974) proposed the Creative Construction Hypothesis, according to which children acquiring a second language were guided by the innate principles of grammar, causing them to formulate "certain types of hypotheses about the language system being acquired, until the mismatch between what they are exposed to and what they produce is resolved" (1974: 37). This hypothesis rings true even today.

The data supporting this hypothesis came from a standardized test of English (later extended to Spanish), known as the Bilingual Syntax Measure, whose purpose was to elicit functional morphology and evaluate the accuracy of its use in required contexts. The method used seven cartoonlike pictures and 33 questions. For example, the experimenter pointed to two houses in one of the pictures and asked "What are these?" The expected answer would include a plural morpheme as in *house-s*. In one experimental study, Dulay and Burt (1973) compared BSM scores from 5 to 8-year-old Spanish-native children acquiring English under different circumstances and amounts of exposure.[3]

---

[2] The Behaviorist (behavioral) approach asserts that languages are learned in the same way as any other behavior. Language acquisition is habit formation, so existing habits could be reinforced through imitation, conditioning, stimulus, and response (Skinner 1957). As discussed above, contrastive error analysis was a method of explaining why some features of a second language were more difficult than others to acquire. This method was prevalent in the 1960s and early 1970s, couched in the behaviorist view of language acquisition popular at the time. Difficulty depended on the distance between the learners' native language and the language they were trying to learn.

[3] The children in the Sacramento group had the most exposure to English, as they were born in the US. The San Ysidro group of children were exposed to English only in school, as they went back to their homes in Tijuana every day after school. The Puerto Rican children in East Harlem were recent immigrants and had not been in the US for more than a year. They were exposed to a dual immersion program in school, where subject matter was taught both in Spanish and in English.

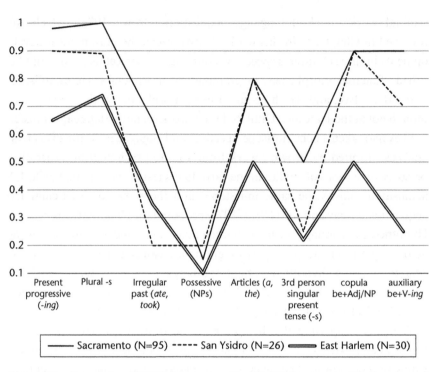

Figure 7.1 Comparison of BSM scores on English L2 functors by three groups of Spanish-speaking children, from Dulay and Burt (1973)

In Figure 7.1, the functor morphemes are plotted on the X axis (not all of Brown's functors were tested), while the mean functor ratios are plotted on the Y axis. The latter were calculated as follows: for each functor, the denominator was the total number of obligatory occasions for that functor for all children across a group, and the nominator was the sum of the scores obtained for each obligatory occasion. What is immediately visible is that although the composite ratios differ among the groups, they vary largely in consort. Look, for instance, at the low ratios on the possessive morpheme.

Even more astonishing, and with a slightly higher number of functors, are the findings of Dulay and Burt (1974). Figure 7.2 illustrates the same congruence of accuracy on the functors for two groups of children from very different linguistic backgrounds: Chinese and Spanish, acquiring English. In this study, Dulay and Burt used two methods of calculating the BSM (group score and group means), only one of which is plotted here.

Bailey, Madden, and Krashen (1974) investigated whether a similar order of acquisition would emerge in adult L2 learners. The learners they tested on

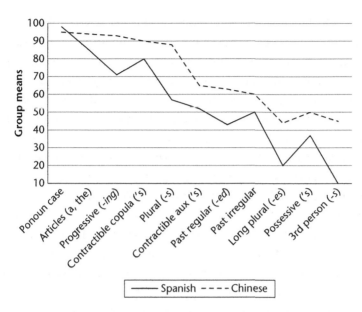

Figure 7.2 Comparison of group means on English L2 functor acquisition by Spanish-speaking and Chinese-speaking children, from Dulay and Burt (1974)

the BSM were divided into Spanish-native and non-Spanish-native, the latter group comprising a variety of typologically different native languages. Such a design was rightly criticized for making it impossible to test the effect of the native language. Bailey et al. discovered that the progressive -*ing*, the contractible copula (*I'm late*), and plural -*s* emerged as the early-acquired morphemes, while possessive '*s* and 3rd person singular subject -*s* were produced with much less accuracy. The order of functor acquisition so established, with slight variation between child L1, child L2, and adult L2 learners, indicated that there could be a certain fixed order to the acquisition of the various functional morphemes (free morphemes and inflectional affixes). The researchers suggested that the fixed order reveals the "creative construction" of a common L2 grammar.

These studies were very influential, although various facets of their methodology were widely criticized. For example, many researchers felt that the morpheme order studies underrepresented the influence of the native language. Luk and Shirai (2009), for instance, uncovered that the order of English morphemes was different for native speakers of Spanish, on the one hand, and for speakers of Japanese, Chinese, and Korean, on the other. The original studies also sparked a lot of replications and new research trying to elucidate why the order of acquisition is as it is (see Exercise 7.1 for various explanations of the order proposed in the vast literature on the issue).

The most substantive criticism of the early morpheme studies concerns the interpretation of the findings. Do accuracy orders really reflect developmental sequences? Some doubt on this strong claim is cast by the realization that if a learner accurately supplies a specific morpheme in all the required contexts, but also overuses the same morpheme in contexts where native speakers would not use it, this learner would score 100% on the BSM, while her successful acquisition of the morpheme would be suspect. One such case was uncovered by Wagner-Gough and Hatch (1975). Five-year-old Homer, an Iranian child learning English, used the -*ing* progressive morpheme early and pervasively, as other children do. However, further inspection of Homer's production shows that he did not contrast this tense–aspect morpheme with other tense–aspect marking forms. He also overused the -*ing* to signal immediate intention, distant future, past events, and imperatives. For the latter functional meaning, see the example below (Wagner-Gough and Hatch 1975: 303).

(1)   Imperative meaning:
      Okay, sit down over here! *Sitting* down like that!
      (= Sit down over here. Sit down like that!)

It is not difficult to improve the BSM scoring method by taking into account extensions of meaning leading to overuse of some morpheme. One such improvement was offered by Stauble (1984). In investigating the verbal morpheme accuracy of six Spanish and six Japanese learners of English in a quasi-longitudinal study, Stauble (1984: 329) used a different method for calculating targetlike usage. First, she counted the accurate suppliance of a morpheme in obligatory context. Say, a learner provided the -*ing* morpheme in five of the ten obligatory contexts, for an accuracy score of $5/10 = 50\%$. However, the learner also overused the -*ing* on three further occasions, such as in (1) above. Stauble would add 3 to the denominator of the previous calculation, $5/(10+3) = 5/13 = 38\%$, a more realistic numeric equivalent of the learners' performance on this morpheme.

The discussion of calculating a certain percentage that is purported to reflect a learner's accuracy, that is, targetlike performance on a certain functional morpheme opens a much more significant and fundamental issue. It is related to the question we pondered above: Do accuracy orders really reflect developmental sequences? One might paraphrase it like this:

When can we assume that a certain morpheme has been acquired? Of course, the answer to this question depends on one's assumptions of what "to be acquired" means, for a specific morpheme. Let us continue with the example of *be* + *-ing*, the English progressive tense. Leaving aside modal meanings and vastly oversimplifying, its semantics reflects an ongoing event in the past, present, or future. The function of this aspectual tense requires that it be used when the intended meaning is of a process with its completion left open (*Mary was eating a sandwich when I came in*). With respect to form, both a finite, correctly inflected instance of *be* and an *-ing* participle are required. Correct form–meaning mapping would suggest that the learner *contrasts* this aspectual tense with, for example, the past simple tense (*Mary ate a sandwich*). For such a contrast to be demonstrated, the same learner must use both simple and progressive tenses and must know the meaning difference between them. Only then could one argue that the functional category of Aspect has been activated in the learner's grammar. This formulation is just shorthand for "the learner has acquired the progressive form–meaning mapping, that is, what grammatical form is paired with the ongoing event meaning."

But what percentage of targetlike usage in naturalistic or elicited production should we take to be indicative of successful acquisition of such a grammatical contrast? Views on this issue vary. Brown (1973) used the 90% correct usage in his study of Adam, Eve, and Sarah's linguistic production. He assumed that the child had acquired a linguistic contrast when she or he produced the functor morpheme in 90% of the cases where an adult English speaker would produce it. Another cutoff point for assuming successful acquisition of functional morphology is 60%,[4] presumably because it is significantly different from chance. Finally, another cutoff point proposal comes from the child language literature, one as low as first productive use in children, followed soon after by regular use (Stromswold 1996, Snyder 2007). The logic of the latter is that if a child produces a certain construction freely and without imitation, and uses it with a variety of lexical items, then this construction has entered the child's grammar. Snyder (2007) gives an example from the acquisition of the verb–particle construction (*She drank the coke up*) by Sarah. At first, two isolated uses of the construction are found in the transcripts but they are not followed by regular use, hence they are not deemed to be indicative of a new construction in the grammar. Soon after

---

[4] This cutoff was used by Vainikka and Young-Scholten (1994). Note, however, that it is far below adult native speaker norms.

that, a veritable "geyser" of examples of verb plus particle is attested in the transcripts. The age of 2;06,20 (two years, six months, and 20 days) is established as the first of repeated uses (or first clear use, followed soon after by repeated use), and that is considered to be the age when Sarah acquired the verb–particle construction.

While the first of repeated uses seems justified for child language acquisition, the case for using this criterion to gauge successful acquisition in the second language is far from clear-cut. One important difference is that children very rarely make errors with functional morphology: the large majority of their errors are simply omissions. While omissions are also attested in L2 acquisition, there are also the so-called errors of commission, such as using one form of a functor where another one is required. Furthermore, in order to establish whether a functional category has been acquired, we have to take into account not only production of the correct form but also comprehension of the correct meaning. In the next sections, I consider several theoretical proposals on the form–meaning mapping, with respect to functional morphology, in adult L2 acquisition.

7.2 Syntax-before-morphology, White (2003)

In her textbook on generative second language acquisition, Lydia White (2003) frames this debate in an even more interesting light. In addressing the issue of when we can consider that a functional category has been acquired, she argues that another type of information is also crucial to consider: not only surface morphology and grammatical meaning, but also syntactic information related to that category. To take an example from the functional category of Tense Phrase (TP), consider the following example:

(2)   He often take -s the bus.

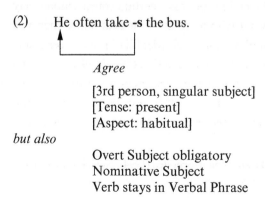

Agree

[3rd person, singular subject]
[Tense: present]
[Aspect: habitual]

but also

Overt Subject obligatory
Nominative Subject
Verb stays in Verbal Phrase

> Three reflexes of the Functional Category Tense Phrase (TP)
>
> Morphophonology: -s;
> Meaning: present, habitual event;
> Syntactic information: subject agreement, obligatory subject, nominative subject, verb in VP.

The subject pronoun carries the features [masculine], [3rd person], and [singular]. These features are interpretable, that is, they contribute to the meaning of the sentence. The features on the verb ensure agreement with the subject, and so they are not important for understanding the sentence meaning. We call them "uninterpretable".[5] The latter features are extremely important for triggering and establishing syntactic dependencies, (essentially, the case when the form of one category depends on another). According to this fundamental distinction, the presence of an uninterpretable feature in a derivation forces a search for a matching (interpretable) sister feature. When this match is achieved through the process of Agree, the uninterpretable feature is deleted from the derivation. However, it has already executed its function of creating a syntactic dependency, including movement of phrases. Thus, only interpretable features survive into the syntax–semantics interface. In oversimplified terms, interpretable features remain to be taken into account in the meaning calculation while uninterpretable features regulate core syntactic behavior.

However, that's not the only function of the agreement morphology. The morpheme -s has additional features: it also signals that the verb is in the present tense and denotes a habitual activity. In addition to agreement, tense, and aspect, a host of other obligatory facts are captured by the features of the tense morphology: the fact that in English the subject is obligatory, that it is in Nominative case, and that the verb stays in VP, as signaled by its being on the left of the VP-edge adverb *often*. All these properties are English-specific; tense inflections in other languages signal different values. For example, the subject in Russian can be Dative, the subject in Spanish and Mandarin can be null (unexpressed), and the main verb in French and Italian go on the other side of adverbs such as *often*. As

---

[5] Chomsky (1995: 277ff). For an accessible review of this topic, see Adger and Svenonius (2011). See also Adger (2003), Chapter 2, for more examples of features across languages.

the reader can easily establish, the little morpheme -*s* on the verb packs a lot of information which impacts on the form and meaning of the whole sentence. All of that *morphological, semantic, and syntactic* information has to be acquired, in order for the morpheme to be properly acquired. However, it is also conceivable that a learner does not acquire all of that information at the same time.

More generally speaking, the set of functional categories constitutes a submodule of the computational system, namely, the Functional Lexicon (and a very important submodule, at that). Each functional category is associated with a lexical item, or items, specified for the relevant formal features. (For example, TP is associated with -*ed*, -s, and various auxiliaries.) A language's parametric choices come from a blueprint made up of a finite set of features, feature values, and properties. One such property regulates whether a certain feature will induce phrasal movement or not, what we call "strength of features." Learning L2 functional categories comprises acquiring the properties of a set of functional lexicon entries. Part of this knowledge involves syntactic reflexes *superficially unrelated* to the morphophonology of these lexical entries, like displacement of a phrase away from its position of merging. It is precisely this syntactic information that White (2003) and Lardiere (1998a,b) argue is important as an indication that a functional category has been acquired. The logic goes like this: if all of these formal features, including the meaning, construct the functional category, then knowledge of at least one type of information (morphological, syntactic, or semantic) can attest to the successful acquisition of a category.

But which one comes first, knowledge of syntax or accurate suppliance of morphology in production, in the building of the second language grammar? One approach, dubbed "morphology-before-syntax" by White (2003: 182), proposes that acquisition of the actual morphophonological reflexes of the functional category drive acquisition of the syntax (Clahsen, Penke, and Parodi 1973/74, Radford 1990). Proponents of this approach for SLA include Vainikka and Young-Scholten (1996, 1994) and Hawkins (2001). The opposite claim, named "syntax-before-morphology," finds support from data like the following in Table 7.1 (see also Table 6.2 in Chapter 6, White 2003, p. 189).

Evidence for the separation of syntactic knowledge and morphological accuracy comes from child and adult production of L2 English (Lardiere 1998a,b; Li 2012). Lardiere's subject, Patty, is a Hokkien and Mandarin-bilingual adult learner of English (see more in Exercise 7.3). Li's participants

Table 7.1 L2 English suppliance of functional morphology in obligatory contexts (in %)

	3 sg. agreement	Past tense on lexical verbs	Suppletive forms of *be*	Overt subjects	Nom. case	V in VP
Lardiere (1998a,b)	4.5	34.5	90	98	100	100
Li (2012)	16	25.5	93	100	100	–

are six Mandarin-native children aged 7 to 9 acquiring English in a naturalistic environment in the US. Patty's performance is considered to be at end-state, in the sense that she will not develop it further. The children's performance is captured longitudinally for eight months, starting when they had been in the US for four months.

What is especially striking in the data presented in Table 7.1 is the clear dissociation between the incidence of verbal inflection (ranging between 34.5% and 4.5%) and the various syntactic phenomena related to it, like providing overt subjects, marking nominative case on the subject, and the verb staying in VP (above 98% accuracy). It seems that Patty and the children do not produce the overt morphemes *-s* and *-ed*, but they know what the morphemes stand for and what other syntactic processes they regulate in the sentence. Knowledge of all the properties reflected in Table 7.1 is purportedly knowledge related to the same underlying functional category of Tense Phrase and its features. In view of such data, it is hard to maintain that omission of functional morphology is indicative of lack of L2 morphosyntactic features.

Data from acquisition of grammatical meaning also supports the morphology-before-syntax view. In a little twist of the logic of the argument presented above, Slabakova (2003) investigated English L2 knowledge of various meanings associated with the functional categories Tense and Aspect. These meanings included the ongoing interpretation of the (present) progressive tense (*I am eating an apple*), the habitual interpretation of the simple tense (*I eat an apple every day*), and the temporary state meaning of the progressive tense with stative verbs (*I am being lazy today*). The native Bulgarian of the learners does not mark these meanings with verbal inflectional morphology. However, all these meanings are taught in language classrooms, at least in Bulgaria, from the first days of classroom exposure. It could have been the case that English L2 speakers were so accurate on these meanings because they had learned explicit rules about temporal and aspectual interpretation. That is why another, related, meaning was included and tested in the experimental study: the complete event interpretation of bare verbs as in *I saw Jane cross the street.* Jane must have crossed the street to the other sidewalk, for this sentence to be True. This meaning is not taught, but learners were as accurate on it as they were on the other, instructed, meanings. The researcher concluded that once the functional categories are activated, all the attendant meanings come into the grammar of the learners.

7.3 Representational Deficit Hypotheses

The opposite approach to the one described in the section above is to postulate that there is no meaningful separation between the morphological, syntactic, and semantic information making up knowledge of a functional category. The immediate and logical consequence is to assert that inferior or poor performance on functional morphology is indicative of incomplete or non-stable grammatical competence (Johnson, Shenkman, Newport, and Medin 1996). Have we seen this assertion made before? This type of logic is also in evidence in the morphology-before-syntax view and in the morpheme order studies, as discussed above. Recall that we asked the question whether targetlike performance on functional morphology is tantamount to, or at least indicative of, linguistic knowledge. The answer is a qualified yes on the representational deficit view and a qualified no, on the full functional representation view, exemplified by the Missing Surface Inflection view (see next section).

For theories adopting a representational deficit view, learners' problems with inflectional morphology are caused by missing or defective syntactic features that trigger morphological agreement. But what exactly does the representational deficit view hold? Several researchers over the years, notably Roger Hawkins and Ianthi Tsimpli, have argued that abstract morphosyntactic features, including those relevant for agreement and case marking, are only accessible to adult L2 learners if they are instantiated in their native language, but not otherwise (e.g., Hawkins and Casillas 2008, Tsimpli and Dimitrakopoulou 2007). In an effort to discuss morphology and syntax separately, as far as possible, I shall expand on this approach in the next chapter. In this chapter, the discussion is confined to this view's assumption that a strong link exists between inflectional morphology and syntax in L2 grammars. A common thread among representational deficit positions[6] is that morphosyntactic representations of adult L2 learners are somehow impaired and that errors with morphology are indicative of deeper problems with syntax. For example, early approaches to missing inflection in the verbal domain argued that absent or incorrect agreement morphology on verbs in the initial state of SLA reflected either missing functional projections such as Inflectional Phrase (IP, equivalent to TP in later analyses) and Complementizer Phrase (CP) (Vainikka and Young-Scholten 1996, 2013) or unvalued "inert" features in the IP projection (Eubank 1996).

One study that upholds this position with data from inflectional morphology is Hawkins and Liszka (2003). This is a study that compares the incidence of past tense morphology in oral production (a film retell task) by five German, five Japanese, and two Chinese speakers learning English. The Chinese learners produced significantly fewer -*ed* morphemes (63%) as compared to the Japanese and German speakers (92%). According to Hawkins and Liszka, this discrepancy is due to the Chinese learners' impaired representation of the Tense functional category. The reason for this impairment is that, according to some syntactic proposals, the Chinese language lacks TP. However, Hawkins and Liszka did not report on their Chinese learners' knowledge of the other syntactic properties (overt subject, Nominative subject, etc.) and how that knowledge compares with that of the German and Japanese learners'. At issue remains what compels the Chinese learners to produce the past tense morphology in the 63% that they do it correctly. The representational deficit response to such a question is that successful performance is due to superficial noticing of the morpheme and imitation of native speakers. In other words the Chinese learners are "faking" correct performance without a correct underlying representation.

Several further studies by Hawkins and Franceschina (Franceschina 2001, 2005, Hawkins and Franceschina 2004) on the L2 acquisition of gender in the Noun Phrase (NP) are also relevant to this issue. In order to understand the concrete claims of this research, we need to resort to the distinction between

---

[6] Over the years, the impairment view/approach/position has included the Valueless Features Hypothesis (Eubank 1993/4), the Local Impairment Hypothesis (Beck 1998), the Failed Functional Features Hypothesis (Hawkins and Chan 1997) and the Interpretability Hypothesis (Hawkins and Hattori 2006, Tsimpli, and Dimitrakopoulou 2006).

interpretable and uninterpretable features as defined above. In the area of gender marking, the inherent gender feature of nouns marked in the lexicon is considered to be interpretable. However, the same feature on adjectives agreeing with the noun in the so-called gender concord is uninterpretable. Note that both features are reflected in inflectional morphology. The following examples come from Harris (1991):

(3)   a. Mi sobrino/padre (*m*) es inteligente (*m*)/alto (*m*)
         'My nephew/father is intelligent/tall.'
      b. Mi sobrina/madre (*f*) es inteligente (*f*)/alta (*f*)
         'My niece/mother is intelligent/tall.'

The Interpretability Hypothesis (Hawkins and Hattori 2006, Tsimpli and Dimitrakopoulou 2006) makes use of this distinction to argue that interpretable features are acquirable, because they are vital for interpretation, while uninterpretable features are not acquirable, except when they come in the L2 grammar through the native grammar. In their work on nominal features, Hawkins and Franceschina show that even highly advanced L2ers whose L1s do not have grammatical gender experience difficulties acquiring gender concord in L2 Spanish. For example, Franceschina (2001, 2005) reports data from a case study on Martin, an English learner of L2 Spanish, who had supposedly reached a steady state grammar. Martin was nearly natively accurate with gender assignment on nouns (where these features are interpretable); however, he demonstrated considerable variability with gender assignment on determiners and adjectives, favoring the masculine gender as default. Franceschina also reports that Martin was accurate to a native level with number assignment across nouns, determiners, and adjectives. This dissociation of accuracy on number and gender is significant. Since English has grammatical number, but not grammatical gender, she interprets this difference in morphological performance as evidence of the fact that new uninterpretable L2 features cannot be acquired. Thus, both Hawkins and Franceschina argue that the mental representation of grammatical gender for L1 English adult learners of Spanish is necessarily different from native Spanish speakers.[7]

---

[7] However, see Sagarra and Herschensohn (2013) for findings of the opposite type, namely, intermediate learners of Spanish demonstrating sensitivity to gender concord, as attested by a processing task.

7.4 The Missing Surface Inflection Hypothesis

The opposing view of L2 speakers being impaired in their linguistic representations can be dubbed Full Functional Representation. There are several proposals within this position that we will examine in the next sections. The common thread between these hypotheses is that it is deemed possible for second language learners to acquire nativelike functional representations and thus achieve grammars that are not *qualitatively* different from those of native speakers, though they may be *quantitatively* different. For example, in Section 7.2, we were able to appreciate the fact that inconsistent, seemingly random suppliance of inflectional morphology might underrepresent actual knowledge of functional categories. I argued, following White and Lardiere, that knowledge of syntactic and semantic reflexes of a functional category also attests to knowledge of the category itself, because all three types of features (morphological, syntactic, and semantic) go together to construct the category. This is essentially a charitable view of second language knowledge: speakers actually know more than we give them credit for.

There is no doubt that *morphosyntactic variation* is the biggest challenge to the view that L2 acquisition is possible and attainable in adulthood. Individuals vary on the correct suppliance of (the morphophonology of) inflectional affixes, even if they are at the same level of proficiency. They vary in the accurate production of the morphology depending on the time of the day and whether they have had coffee that morning. Patty, Donna Lardiere's subject, is a highly functional English speaker and a professional with a successful career in a US company, but she produces the past tense ending only 35% of the time. In comparison, children rarely make mistakes with such affixes, and after they acquire a certain functional category, it seems that they know all there is to know about it. (Sometimes it just seems so, but that's another story.)

Pervasive and extensive variation is what all second language researchers have to explain, then. We should also keep in mind that variation is most visible in production, but that may not be the whole story. The Missing Surface Inflection Hypothesis (MSIH) (Haznedar and Schwartz 1997, Prevost and White 2000) provides one explanation of the relationship between suppliance of functional morphology and knowledge of the syntactic properties underlying this morphology, or associated with this morphology's feature bundle. This theory is, in a way, a direct extension of the syntax-before-morphology view discussed above. Under this view, there may be no representational deficits in learners whose language production of the morphology is not optimal. However, there may be a mapping problem between abstract features and surface morphological forms, such that incorrect production underrepresents underlying knowledge. In a nutshell, some rupture occurs between syntax and morphology such that the morphology is somehow missing, but only on the surface. Hence the name of this hypothesis.

Evidence for this view comes again from child and adult learners. Haznedar and Schwartz (1997) reported findings from the production of a four-year-old Turkish-speaking child, Erdem. Erdem's development in English was followed with regular recordings over 18 months. In child first language acquisition, producing finite verbal forms is related to the obligatory suppliance of overt subjects, in the sense that finite verbal forms and overt subjects have to come together in learner grammar. Erdem started producing subjects long before his use of verbal inflection in obligatory contexts rose to nativelike levels. This dissociation suggests that the relationship between the use of inflectional morphology and overt subjects is broken, at least for him. Haznedar (2001) presents robust evidence for his use of nominative pronoun subjects, suggesting that Erdem's case assignment works well. Haznedar and Schwartz argue that the uninflected forms produced by Erdem are in fact finite forms and they function as such, but that their overt inflections are missing.

Prévost and White (2000a,b) examine similar evidence from the production of children and adults acquiring French and German in naturalistic ways (two Moroccan-Arabic learners of French and two native speakers of Spanish and Portuguese learning German). Again, the distribution of finite and nonfinite verbal forms is under investigation, in its relation with overt subjects (clitics and strong pronouns), as well as negation. Very simply expressed, if learners have knowledge of finiteness, finite forms should not occur in nonfinite positions. The researchers found that their adult learners did not typically use finite forms in nonfinite positions. It is also true that the learners used infinitive verb forms in both nonfinite and finite positions, suggesting that infinitive verb forms are unspecified for finiteness. Thus, the argument is that adult L2 learners have an abstract representation for finiteness that is concealed by their "misuse" of French/German infinitive forms. These results converge with Haznedar and Schwartz's findings.

The question arises of what grammatical process allows this sort of separation between unimpaired syntactic knowledge and haphazard morphological realization. Note that in the case of English-acquiring Erdem, the nonfinite verb forms were just bare verbs, so inflection was truly missing. In the case of Prévost and White's German and French acquiring subjects, however, the nonfinite verbal forms do carry infinitival morphology. Prévost and White explain the separation, or dissociation, they uncover as a mapping problem between the lexical items of the inflectional affixes and the feature specifications of the syntactic nodes where the inflected forms are inserted.

In order to understand this claim, we need to take an excursion into a linguistic proposal called Distributed Morphology (Halle and Marantz 1993) and more specifically, its claim of late lexical insertion. According to this proposal, the syntactic tree for the sentence to be produced provides terminal nodes in which all morphosyntactic features have been checked and validated (different approaches to feature checking would have different validation mechanisms). For example, if the subject is *John*, the verbal form has to be specified for 3rd person singular features, among others (*John like-s sushi*). The next step in the derivation involves competition between fully specified lexical items for insertion into the syntactic nodes. An inflected (finite) form such as *like-s* is associated with grammatical features such as tense, person, and number (in some languages even gender) as part of its lexical specification. In lexical insertion, the features of a lexical item should be consistent with the features of the syntactic node where it is inserted, but the most highly specified item wins the competition for insertion. The requirement is that the features of the syntax node and the lexical item match, but the latter can also be a subset of the former. In the case of mapping breakdown, learners may not have easy access to the fully specified best candidate for lexical insertion, and they may instead access a less specified but more accessible item.

For Prévost and White (2000), L2 learners acquire the relevant grammatical features of the terminal node in the syntax via the native language, UG or the L2 input, but they might not have fully acquired the feature specifications of the associated items from the functional lexicon. Verbal paradigms are hard to learn, and in some languages more than others. Prévost and White propose that learners sometimes reach for "default forms" such as infinitives because they are easy to access in their mental lexicons, being basic and frequent. Under this analysis then, there is no syntactic deficit in interlanguage grammars but performance limitations, sometimes resulting from communication pressures, may lead to omission of inflection or use of default forms (2000a: 129). In other words, failure to produce consistent inflection is attributed to difficulties in accessing the relevant lexical items by which inflection is realized, particularly when speaking.

Note that an immediate prediction of this account is the following: omission and use of default forms should happen more in production than in comprehension, and more when the learner is tired, distracted, or under some communicative pressure. This is because variability in morphology is linked to lexical access, which is arguably more difficult in production. McCarthy (2008) set up an experimental study to check the former prediction. She tested English learners of Spanish on production and comprehension of Spanish object clitics, and looked at agreement in gender and number. McCarthy discovered that for her intermediate learners, morphological variability was attested in production but extended to comprehension as well. She argued that there may be representational problems with the inflectional morphology, as well as access problems, for these learners. Furthermore, she documented the use of default forms in production as well as comprehension. For instance, the masculine object clitic *lo* was more likely to be interpreted as referring to a feminine object. However, McCarthy did not uncover such variability in the comprehension of the feature number, and the use of the singular as default was only attested in production. Furthermore, the acquisition of the gender feature has proved very difficult for learners (Unsworth 2008a), probably because there is a lot of lexical learning involved in acquiring the gender specification of each noun one by one.

Support for McCarthy's findings comes from a recent processing study, Reichle, Tremblay, and Coughlin (2013). The researchers measured ERP responses of intermediate learners of French reading sentences in which subject–verb agreement was violated. In an interesting twist, the researchers employed two conditions: in one the agreement violation was local (the subject and verb were close together); in the other it was long distance (the subject and verb were separated by another nominal). They also tested the working memory span of the learners. The learners' responses revealed N400 effects when they encountered subject–verb agreement violations. This ERP effect is a well-known response to lexical and semantic violations, suggesting that the learners did not treat these as morphosyntactic violations (as they did in their native English). Furthermore, the size of the L2 learners' N400 effect decreased when the subject noun was not adjacent to the verb as compared to when it was. The latter type of sentence taxes working memory and increases its load. The authors found that:

L2 learners who excel at performing simultaneous linguistic operations such as reading sentences for meaning and holding sentence-final words in memory (i.e., reading-span task) also excel at holding subject nouns in memory when processing non-adjacent agreement dependencies (i.e., ERP task).

These findings indicate that, at intermediate proficiency levels at least, mental lexicon access may be involved in processing agreement morphology, modulated by learners' working memory capacity.

In summary, the MSIH capitalizes on the three types of linguistic knowledge that together comprise knowledge of a functional category: the morphophonological, syntactic, and semantic reflexes of that category. The hypothesis proposes that even if the syntactic side of a functional category has been acquired, the morphological forms may not be always supplied adequately in production, due to a mapping issue between the syntax and the functional mental lexicon. A substantial body of research from child and adult learners lends support to this separation of syntactic and morphological knowledge (e.g., Hyams 1994). McCarthy's (2008) research suggests that problems with the morphology may affect comprehension as well, but only among intermediate learners. Research that aims at directly supporting the MSIH should demonstrate higher variability for inflectional morphology in the same individuals, under different production and comprehension conditions.

Teaching relevance

It might be helpful for teachers to know that failure to produce correct inflectional endings is a work in progress. Such failure may not reflect underlying problems with grammatical information. Errors may be more pronounced in production than in comprehension. Since the problems are of a superficial nature and are related to lexical retrieval, ample practice of grammatical morphemes in language classrooms is warranted. Such practice will improve the automatic lexical access for function words and inflections.

7.5 The Prosodic Transfer Hypothesis

Still within the Full Functional Representation position, another proposal to at least partially explain morphosyntactic variation is Goad and White's Prosodic Transfer Hypothesis (PTH) (Goad, White, and Steele 2003, Goad and White 2004, 2006). It is compatible with the MSIH in the sense that it offers another reason why learners might not produce verb endings or other functional morphology. Just as the MSIH, the PTH suggests that L2 learners' syntactic representations are appropriate for the target language (that is, there is no representational deficit). However, L2 learners may delete functional material in production, since the prosodic structure of their L1 may differ from the L2, leaving no way of building the correct prosodic structure for the L2.

But let's look at prosodic structure and how it may be relevant for second language acquisition (Nespor and Vogel 1986, Selkirk 1984, 1996). It should come as no surprise to the reader of this book that phonological structure is proposed to be hierarchical, in the sense that units merge together to form bigger and qualitatively different units. Scholars of phonology have discovered that segments are organized into a syllable, syllables are organized into a foot, feet are organized into a prosodic word (PWd), and prosodic words are organized into a phonological phrase (PPh). Note the resemblance to syntactic structure trees.

(4)   Phonological Phrase (PPh)

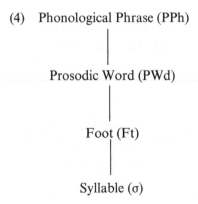

Prosodic Word (PWd)

Foot (Ft)

Syllable (σ)

Where a certain sound or a certain affix is attached within the prosodic word or the phonological phrase is important for language acquisition. For example, children pronounce coda consonants more often (instead of dropping them) in syllables of longer duration. Since grammatical affixes, especially in English, frequently consist of a single sound /s, z, t, d/, prosodic effects are attested on the acquisition of the functional morphology. A recent experiment (Sundara, Demuth, and Kuhl 2011) discovered that 2-year-olds noticed the difference between grammatical (e.g., *Now she cries*) and ungrammatical sentences missing the agreement marker *-s* (e.g., *Now she cry*). However, when the agreement marker was inside the sentence (*She cries now* vs. *She cry now*), the same children did not show sensitivity to the difference. Clearly, the position of the functional morphology determines its perception. In another example, 2;3-year-olds were shown to be more likely to produce the definite article when it followed a monosyllabic word (e.g., *Tommy kicks the rabbit*) than a disyllabic verb (*Tommy catches the rabbit*). The explanations of both findings have to do with the prosodic structure of the utterance and its effect on acquisition, perception, and production of grammatical morphology. Scholars of child language (e.g., Demuth 2001, 2014) argue that the variable emergence of early grammatical morphemes are *prosodically licensed,* as well as grammatically licensed.

It is hardly surprising, then, that such effects are being discovered in second language acquisition as well. This is exactly what Goad and White (2004, 2006, 2008) propose. Languages differ in the way they prosodify (attribute prosodic structure to) functional morphemes, and differences between the L1 and L2 may turn out to be significant for production of affixes. To date, these researchers have studied production and comprehension of functional morphology (past tense, agreement, articles) in Chinese-English and Turkish-English interlanguage. The main idea is as follows: learners may not produce inflectional morphology while they have fully engaged the functional category of that morphology and obey all the syntactic and interpretive consequences of that successful acquisition.

To take an example from past tense morphology, Goad and White (2006) start by showing that the prosodic structure of words ending in consonant clusters is different for regular and irregular past tense expression.

(5)   a. English regular past tense   b. English irregular past tense

In English, the regular *-ed* ending as in (5a) is realized as adjoined to the prosodic word, while the irregular ending, that looks similar, actually has a different structure, all organized within the prosodic word. In Mandarin, on the other hand, the only inflection is aspectual, and it is organized within the prosodic word, just as in English irregular past tense.

(6)   PWd

      mai3   lə5
      buy   PERF 'bought already'

Assuming that the prosodic structure required to pronounce English past tense endings and past participles is absent in Mandarin, Goad and White predicted that initial learners' production accuracy would be depressed. However, at later stages of development, learners will be able to minimally adapt their native prosodic structure to new configurations and will be able to pronounce the endings. Compare the predictions of the representational deficit account with respect to the production of past tense endings. If learners have impaired past tense representations, it will make no difference whether they are trying to pronounce regular or irregular verbs: they will be equally incorrect. Hawkins and Liszka (2003) acknowledge that this prediction is not supported by their data.

Goad and White (2006) administered an interpretation test and a production task on the same stimuli. First, participants had to choose the correct continuation (past or present) for a past adverbial lead in, as follows:

(7)   Last night after dinner,
      you showed me photos of your daughter.
      you show me photos of your daughter.

The ten learners, who were of intermediate proficiency, achieved 83% accuracy in choosing the correct continuation. After they had registered their choice, they were asked to read it out loud. Only correct choices were counted in the second task. Results show that learners were highly accurate on the production task as well, with accuracy percentages between 87 and 94 on the various types of stems. No significant differences emerged between regular and irregular past tense forms. Although the prediction of the PTH for a differential accuracy on regulars and irregulars was not supported by this group of subjects, it is entirely possible that learners at earlier levels of development could show such support. Importantly, these Mandarin learners of English demonstrated both high levels of suppliance of morphology as well as superior knowledge of interpretation, which are two clues for successful acquisition. Goad and White (2008) offered a detailed examination of the phonetics of learners' past tense and article production. They showed that many of the learners' outputs cannot be due to what the second language input offers them. In particular, learners produce tense and articles in ways that are not found in either the L1 or the L2 (fortis release on tense inflection and stress on articles). The researchers argue that transfer from native prosodic structures, which learners then try to adapt to the target prosodic structures, explains their findings best.

In sum, some (although not all) of the variation in functional morphology production may be due to the necessity to adapt native prosodic structures to target language prosodic structures. UG supplies the template of how to do this, but it is a learning process that takes time. Goad and White specifically argue that their hypothesis does not apply to perception; in other words, prosody does not act as a filter for comprehension.

7.6 The Feature Reassembly Hypothesis

Lardiere's Feature Reassembly Hypothesis (FRH) (Lardiere 2009a,b) is a theoretical proposal that builds on the observation that successful acquisition involves acquiring the set of formal features of the second language. As we remember, formal features include phonological, syntactic, and semantic features, bundled together on the lexical items of every language.[8] Languages differ in what features they encode in the various pieces of functional morphology. Where do all these features live? A mainstay of the Minimalist Program is the proposal that features come from a universal repository, made available to the child together with the computational procedures of how to combine these features on lexical items, check and delete uninterpretable features, etc.

Of course, acquiring a second language involves acquiring a second set of features, different from the native one. It is often the case, as Lardiere (2007,

---

[8] Borer (1984), Chomsky (1995): the so-called Borer–Chomsky Conjecture (Baker 2008).

2009a) notices, that "[a]ssembling the particular lexical items of a second language requires that the learner reconfigure features from the way these are represented in the first language into new formal configurations on possibly quite different types of lexical items in the L2." (Lardiere 2009a: 173). Thus, learning lexical items with bundles of features in possibly new configurations appears to be the most important learning task. I shall illustrate this with one extended example from the feature [±past] (Lardiere 2007, Slabakova 2008). This feature captures the temporal relationship between the event and the speech moment: past events happened before the speech moment; non-past events either hold at the moment of speech or in a future time interval. Languages can choose to represent or not represent this feature with an overt morpheme. The oft-cited languages that differ in this respect are Mandarin Chinese, without past tense marking, and English, with past tense marking. However, the mapping between meaning and form in English is considerably more varied than this simple, one-to-one mapping configuration may suggest. As Lardiere (2005) points out, it is a many-to-many mapping. First of all, the -ed morphology encodes perfective aspect in English (Smith 1997), as the example in (8) demonstrates.

(8)   We devoured the pizza on the terrace (and there is no more pizza left).

The pizza-devouring event in this sentence is not only in the past, it is also complete, so uttering the second clause in (8) as a continuation of the first is not a contradiction.[9] Secondly, the past morphology is used as a marker of uncertainty and hence politeness in requests:

(9)   I was wondering whether you would be free tomorrow.

In (9), both past tense forms *was –ing* and *would* stand for a present state ("I am wondering as I speak") and a future state ("are you going to be free tomorrow?").

Thirdly, past morphology can be used in sequence of tenses to refer to a non-past state or event, leading to ambiguity.

---

[9] To understand this, compare the sentence in (8) with its progressive alternative:

(8′) We were devouring the pizza on the terrace when he came.

In (8′), there is no guarantee that the pizza is all gone.

(10)   Jane said that Joyce was pregnant.

The utterance in (10) can mean either that Joyce was pregnant at the time when Jane and Joyce saw each other, but Joyce has given birth since; or it can mean that Joyce is still pregnant today, at present. In this utterance the past form is actually ambiguous between a present and a past temporal reference. Note that all these meanings of the past morphology are not equally frequent in the input, learners may not encounter some of the meanings every day, and as a consequence, might not learn all of the meanings at the same time.

Finally, historical present usages are very common in everyday speech and in fiction. The following excerpt is from Marc Nesbitt's short story "Gigantic."[10]

(11)   *"I rake dead bats from the hay floor of the bat cage and throw them in a black plastic bag. ... I pick up a sign that says, "Quiet! _____ sleeping!," slip in the "Bats" panel, and place it up front, where all the kids can see it. An hour till we open, I go see our one elephant, Clarice."*

Note that all the events described by the underlined verbs denote a sequence of closed events in the past and not ongoing, future, or incomplete events. This usage of the present simple (a.k.a. the historical present) is a pragmatic convention of English (Smith 1997).

Sticking to English past tense morphology and barely scratching the surface, I have demonstrated, following Lardiere (2005, 2007, 2008), that *-ed* in English can encode [+past] but also [–past], politeness, *irrealis* mood in conditionals, and perfective aspect in events, among other grammatical and pragmatic meanings. On the other hand, the simple present tense can also encode a sequence of complete events in the past. Thus, a mapping of many-to-many exists between English past tense meanings and forms.

A further comparison between English, Irish, and Somali points to another source of mismatch: the lexical categories on which a feature is expressed may differ across languages.[11] Irish expresses the tense distinction on its complementizers in agreement with the tense in the embedded

---

[10] Published in *The New Yorker* on July 9, 2001, p. 76.

[11] The examples are from McCloskey (1979) and Lecarme (2003, 2004), as cited in Lardiere (2005: 180).

clause as in (12) while in Somali [past] is encoded on nouns within the noun phrase, (13).

(12) Deir   sé   gurL   thuig   sé   an scéal   Irish
      says   he   that-Past understood   he   the story
      'He says that he understood the story.'

(13) a. árday-gii   hore   Somali
         student-Det.Masc.Past   before
         'the former student'

      b. (weligay)   dúhur-kii   baan   wax   cunaa
         (always)   noon-Det.Masc.Past   Fem.1S   thing   eat-Pres
         'I always eat at noon.'

      c. Inán-tii   hálkée   bay   joogta?
         girl-Det.   place-Det.   Fem.3S   stay-Fem.
         Fem.Past   Masc.Q   Pres
         'Where is the girl?'

The mismatches don't stop here. The expressions of the *-ed* past morpheme in English are phonologically determined: they surface as /-t/, /-d/ or /-ɪd/ depending on the preceding sound. Furthermore, if one considers the frequent irregular verbs with their (partly) phonologically determined classes of past tense marking, it becomes abundantly clear that the one form–one meaning mapping in the functional morphology of human languages is very rare indeed. Thus what are crucial to acquire are not only the meanings and the morphophonological forms of the affixes but also the conditioning environments in which they appear.[12]

Research applying the predictions of the FRH to the acquisition of second language properties is just beginning to pick up steam. However, this hypothesis has engaged the imagination of SLA scholars[13] and research is proceeding apace. In fact, this is one of the more promising future directions for SLA research, because it compels researchers to build a

[12] Lardiere (2009a) provides an extended comparison between Mandarin and English plural, and the reader is encouraged to tackle the original article at this point.

[13] See Dominguez, Arche, and Myles (2011), Gil and Marsden (2013), Cho and Slabakova (2014), Guijarro-Fuentes (2011, 2012), Shimanskaya and Slabakova (2014).

more complex picture of the acquisition process and to pay attention to meaning as well as syntactic expression, conditioning environments of the functional morphology, learning features of the same affix one by one, and so on. I shall take one example here from Shimanskaya (2015) (see Shimanskaya and Slabakova 2014), a study which looks at personal pronouns in English-French interlanguage.

English and French personal pronouns differ in many respects, the most visible one being that French has clitic pronouns that attach to the left of the verb (*Je l'aime* 'I love him'). Moreover, while English encodes gender only in the case of [+Human] referents (biological gender), French uniformly encodes grammatical gender in determiners, accusative clitics, and strong pronouns. A distinction not studied before involves another feature: while English pronouns *lexically encode* the [±Human] distinction (*him/her* versus *it*), in French the same accusative clitics (*le, la*) are used to refer to [+Human] and [−Human] antecedents. In the sentence *Je **la** vois* 'I see her/it' the feminine clitic *la* can refer to *la table* 'the table' and *la fille* 'the girl'. Note how in English we have to choose between *I saw her* and *I saw it*. Thus, the feature [±Human] is active in the English pronominal system but is not expressed in the French pronominal system. It was predicted that since the L1 lexically encodes the feature, anglophone L2 learners would initially attempt to establish a similar contrast in the L2, and they will transfer this feature from the L1. Three groups of French learners at different levels of proficiency took a forced-choice picture selection task (among others), in which they read context sentences as in (14), after which they had to choose which picture corresponded to the test sentence.

(14) Context: On Tuesday evening, Nicolas goes to the library to meet Anne and David.
Nicolas: Parfois, je **la** vois près de la fenêtre. (Sometimes I see **her** near the window)

(a) referent #1 (gender appropriate)	(b) referent #2 (gender inappropriate)	(c) both referents are possible	(d) gender-matched distractor
Anne	David	Anne and David Les deux sont possibles	la table
☑	☐	☐	☐

The test sentence contains the feminine clitic *la* and, thus, can only be interpreted as referring to *Anne* (or the distractor *the table*). A gender error in the example above would be choosing David.

Animate and inanimate referents were counterbalanced in the experimental design. Beginning and intermediate learners made significantly more gender errors with inanimate than with animate nouns. This pattern of behavior suggests that the learners experience relatively more difficulty in using grammatical gender to refer to inanimate nouns. The natural gender in their native English (*he*/*she*) helps them with the grammatical gender in French, but only within the set of humans at first. Biological gender takes precedence over grammatical gender when disambiguating pronominal reference in L2 learners whose L1 does not have grammatical gender. By advanced proficiency levels, the new feature of grammatical gender is added to the L2 grammar, and accuracy reaches 99%. The take-home message of these experimental results is that the reassembly process is not instantaneous, and that it is undoubtedly influenced by the native features.

In conclusion, we have seen in this chapter that learning the functional morphology in a second language is crucial because it is where languages differ. This acquisition is complicated because a functional meaning may be represented on one lexical category in the native language and on another lexical category in the second language, or not at all overtly represented (cf. Irish, English, and Somali expressions of Tense). It is also complicated because a functional meaning, say 'past,' can be expressed with dedicated morphology in one language, while in another language it is expressed only optionally or not expressed at all; it can also be expressed with forms lacking this morphology (the historical present). Finally, acquiring a functional form is difficult, even if it has constant meaning, because it may have varied expressions depending on different phonological and morphological environments. As the form–function mismatches discussed above attest, the learning task involves much more than a simple pairing between meanings and pieces of functional morphology.

I have argued that the current findings advocate for two (tentative) conclusions. First, even if the functional morphology is not produced with high accuracy, this is not a necessary indication of impaired underlying representations but can be due to lexical access difficulties (the MSIH) or prosodic constraints on pronunciation (the PTH). Secondly, it is possible that getting together the complete feature bundle of an L2 functional category is a nonlinear (hence fragmented) and extended process, affected by the native feature composition and the evidence for each feature in the input. Since acquisition of the functional morphology is most important for correct production and comprehension in the L2, it should get the lion's share of attention in language classrooms.

7.7 Exercises

Exercise 7.1. Here are some explanations of the morpheme order findings:

a) This is a natural acquisition order of acquiring English grammatical morphemes. Since it is guided by universal principles, it does not depend much on the native language (e.g., Krashen 1977).

b) It is a combination of five factors (perceptual salience, semantic complexity, morphophonological regularity, syntactic category, and frequency) that predicts about 71% of the variance observed in the studies included in Goldschneider and DeKeyser's (2001) meta-analysis.

c) The influence of the native grammar has been underestimated so far. It does exist (Luk and Shirai, 2009).

d) Learners are building a mental grammar of the L2 (in this case English), and the order reflects the hierarchical organization of the clause structure that is being acquired: CP-over-TP-over-VP (Hawkins 2001).

Discuss these explanations in turn, paying attention to whether they are mutually exclusive or not. Can you find a way to reconcile explanations c) and d)? Can you see the connection between explanations a) and d)?

Exercise 7.2. Debate the relative merits and shortcomings of the different cutoff points for accepting that a piece of functional morphology (a functor, in Brown's terminology) has been acquired. Recall that 90% and 60% of required contexts have been proposed, as well as evidence of first productive (non-chunk) use.

Exercise 7.3. In this exercise, we will scrutinize the production of Patty (not her real name), the fossilized learner whose linguistic production is

Table 7.2 Summary of Patty's English

Structure	Use	Grammatical property in Hokkien and Mandarin	Has she learned it?
Present tense -s (3sg subject)	4–5%	No overt tense morphology	
Past tense -ed	35%	No overt tense morphology	
Case marking	Nativelike	No case marking	
Overt subjects	100%	Null subjects allowed	
Definite determiner	84%	No articles	
Question formation	Nativelike	Wh-in-situ	
Passives	81%	Passives are marked differently	
Possessive pronouns	Near nativelike	With a particle	
Plural marking	84%	No overt morphology	

described in Lardiere (1998a,b; 2007). Patty's characteristics as an L2 learner are as follows (see Table 7.2[14]):

- Hokkien and Mandarin bilingual speaker (dominant in Hokkien), English is (at least) her fourth language.
- Resident in US since her early 20s.
- Company executive, master's degree.
- Married to a Vietnamese L1 speaker and later to an English L1 speaker.
- Recorded at age 32 (after ten years of residence in the US) and at age 40 (after 18 years of residence)

Some examples of Patty's English include:

1. I feel like I should buy the other one too.
2. Something that have to show the unbeliever that you are in spirit.
3. He have the inspiration to say what he want to say.
4. I don't know if everybody can speak in tongue.
5. But I know that I have doubt.
6. That's the gift of wisdom that we have to manifest.

---

[14] Thanks go to Laura Domínguez for allowing me to use the summary table she created.

7. Everyone who believe it can get it.

8. When you pray what you want you got what you want.

9. Yesterday they open until five.

10. He call me last night.

11. She give me a lot of help.

12. Why do you want me to go?

13. You don't know who you should associate with.

14. She was chosen from forty people.

15. We spoke English to her.

16. He make me uh spending money.

17. She keep asking me to get a concert . . . and asked him to go to this place.

18. And uh that's why M, at that time M want to go too, but her, her sister said no, that's why she never come.

19. They kick him.

Discuss Patty's production, using both the table and the examples. Find examples that would support each line of the table.

Look at the second column of the table. Can you assert that Patty's production is affected ONLY by her native languages?

Discuss what you would answer in the last column of the table, for each property. Reconsider your answer keeping in mind complete acquisition of functional categories (which includes morphological, semantic, and syntactic reflexes).

Exercise 7.4. Based on Montrul (2011). Montrul (2011) is a study comparing the morphological production of adult anglophone L2 learners and heritage speakers of Spanish residing in the US. I will provide some of the findings below, so that you can answer the following questions.

To test production and affix recognition in the grammatical area of tense and aspect, Montrul used an oral and a written task. The oral task involved pictures of Little Red Riding Hood and asked participants to retell the story in the past. The written task was a forced choice of preterit and imperfect morphology (so chance was 50%) in a story told in the past. Here is an example:

(i)   El jefe le **daba/dio** el dinero a la empleada para depositarlo en el banco. La empleada **trabajó/trabajaba** para la compañía pero no **estuvo/estaba** contenta con su trabajo y **quiso/quería** otro trabajo. La mujer **necesitó/ necesitaba** salir del pueblo.

Table 7.3 Percentage accuracy on tense–aspect and mood morphology in the written recognition and oral production tasks

Group	Tense–aspect		Mood	
	Preterit	**Imperfect**	**Indicative**	**Subjunctive**
L2 learners (*n* = 72)				
Written recognition	87.1	84.2	87.8	72.5
Oral production	94.3	88.0	86.2	42.6
Heritage speakers (*n* = 70)				
Written recognition	85.7	70.1	83.1	65.7
Oral production	98.2	95.0	93.3	69.6
Native speakers (*n* = 22)				
Written recognition	98.9	97.4	99.1	98.3
Oral production	100	100	100	100

'The boss **gave** the money to the employee to have it deposited in the bank. The employee **worked** for the company but **was** not happy with her job and **wanted** another job. The woman **needed** to leave the town.'

To test production and comprehension of indicative and subjunctive mood, the latter unattested in English as widely as in Spanish, she used broad questions designed to elicit opinions and advice (e.g., *What are your plans after graduation and what is your ideal job? What advice would you give to a friend of yours who is an alcoholic? What would you recommend he/she do?*) Some of the contexts required the use of subjunctive forms, while in others it was optional. The written task checking recognition of the mood distinction was in the same format as example (i) above. Table 7.3 presents accuracy percentages.

Questions for you.
Is the oral production of correct functional morphology across the three experimental groups comparable? Is the written recognition comparable? Which group is better at what? Why do you think this is the case?
Discuss the effects of the native language on the L2 learners. Discuss the effect of the dominant English language on the Spanish heritage speakers. Discuss the possible effect of classroom instruction on the results. Discuss the possible effects of linguistic experience on the differential accuracy.
Are these findings in support of representational deficit hypotheses? Are these findings in support of the Missing Surface Inflection Hypothesis? Are

these findings in support of any other hypothesis we have discussed in this chapter? Support your answers with concrete data.

Can we say that one of the experimental groups has superior morphological competence? Which task is better at capturing this competence?

Find the original study and compare your answers with Montrul's discussion of her results.

Exercise 7.5. Find H. Hopp (2013), Grammatical gender in adult L2 acquisition: Relations between lexical and syntactic variability. *Second Language Research* 29: 33–56, doi:10.1177/0267658312461803.

Download it to your hard drive. The author argues that his "findings support lexical and computational accounts of L2 inflectional variability and argue against models positing representational deficits in morphosyntax in late L2 acquisition and processing." Does he mean the MSIH or some similar account? Make a list of his findings that support this interpretation.

8

Acquisition of syntax

In this chapter, we turn to the acquisition of syntactic properties. Syntax is all about the organization of clauses and sentences: word order and movement of constituents. It was argued in Chapter 2 that syntax proper involves universal operations that fall from the feature specifications of the different languages. We are going to expand our ideas on how morphosyntactic parameters work, and how acquisition researchers have sought to explain their acquisition.

8.1 A historical excursion into the notion of parameter (through the ages)

The acquisition of syntax was the first area of the grammar to develop in generative L2A, and it is still the area most closely associated with generative linguistics. In this chapter, we will review the adult L2 acquisition of syntactic parameters, still keeping in mind the overarching question of this book: what is easy and what is hard to acquire. In order to understand the notion of parameter correctly, we need to start from the beginning and see how that notion has developed.

The original idea of language acquisition within generative linguistics (Chomsky 1981, 1986) was that, apart from universal properties called principles, language-specific properties could be described by parameters, understood as (a small number of) options provided by Universal Grammar for controlled variation, which, once set, would offer the basis for further parameter setting. A light switch that could be turned on and off was an apt metaphorical illustration of the idea.[1] Recall from Chapter 1 that one of the first parameters described in child language acquisition was the Null Subject Parameter (NSP) (Hyams 1986). Nina Hyams argued that English-speaking children start out with the null subject value of the parameter, only to reset it to the correct value later. The switch metaphor contributed to the perception of instantaneous, successful acquisition: switches are either on or off, with no in-between state.

Conceptually, it was attractive to think of parameters as changes that would bring a host of superficially unrelated constructions into the grammar, all of them dependent on a single parametric value. For the NSP, the proposed cluster of constructions included null subjects (1a), null expletives (1b), postverbal subjects (1c), *that*-trace effects (1d), and rich subject–verb agreement (Rizzi 1982). We already saw this cluster in Chapter 2, but I will repeat the examples for ease of reference. *That*-trace effects refer to the possibility of having a complementizer followed by the trace of the moved subject (signaled by *t*). Notice the ungrammaticality of that construction in the English translation of (1d). Once a learner—child or adult—acquired null subjects, the whole cluster of associated constructions would also become part of that individual's grammar. As the reader can ascertain, these constructions are not only superficially unrelated, but of different complexity as well.

(1) a. Ø Mangia come una bestia.
          eat-3SG like   a beast
          'He/she eats like a beast.'

     b. Ø Piove oggi
          rain-3SG today
          'It is raining today'

---

[1] Attributed by Chomsky to James Higginbotham.

c. Ha telefonato uno studente.
has telephoned a student
'A student called.'

d. Chi cred-i   che *t* verrà?
who think-2SG that t come-FUT
*'Who do you think that will come?'

Unfortunately, even the earliest L2 generative studies related to the Null Subject Parameter (White 1985, Hilles 1986, Phinney 1987, Liceras 1988, 1989) did not find support for the clustering of these properties in English interlanguage. White (1985) probed this parameter in the grammar of native Spanish and French speakers learning English. The prediction was that Spanish learners would have initial difficulty learning not to produce null subjects, while the French learners would not, as French is not a null-subject language, hence there is no parameter to reset. The Spanish learners accepted ungrammatical English sentences where the subject was missing more than the French learners in this study, and their improvement was gradual. It is notable that some French beginners also accepted null subjects in English. More importantly, the purportedly related constructions of the cluster did not come into the grammar simultaneously, thus calling into question the concept of the parameter as a switch. Research on other parametric clusters, e.g., the Verb Movement Parameter (White, 1990), led to mixed results, as we shall see below.

The Feature Reassembly Hypothesis (Lardiere 2009a,b), which we discussed in the previous chapter, dealt a fatal blow to the notions of instantaneous acquisition and parametric clustering. But those ideas had been undermined by research findings, such as the ones on the Null Subject Parameter, long before that. Lardiere placed the emphasis on the acquisition of formal features, in what bundles they appear on the functional morphology, what functional morphology acts as an exponent for (a bundle of) features, and what the conditioning environments are for the use of that morphology. By 2009, Lardiere had enunciated what many in the field had been discussing for some time.

However, it is premature and counterproductive to dismiss the notion of parameter altogether. Parameters still have their place in linguistic theory and in generative SLA. In commenting on the FRH, Montrul and Yoon (2009) argued that the notion of lexically encoded parameters, as widely accepted in the Minimalist Program (Borer 1984, Chomsky 1995) is still our best hope for describing principled and not haphazard parametric variation among languages of the world and making astute predictions about what is hard to acquire in a second language. The grammar of a language is defined by a selection of formal features from a universal inventory and bundling these features on the lexical items. These lexical items (some of them residing in the lexicon, some of them in a subset thereof, the Functional Lexicon) are accessed by the universal computational system, in order to construct syntactic expressions. It is in the syntax where features are active: they trigger various syntactic processes such as Agree and Move. Interpretable features remain in the derivation and pass on to the syntax–semantics interface where they are interpreted. Uninterpretable features trigger agreement and movement of syntactic objects. After they fulfill their function, they get checked and deleted. All of these computational syntactic processes are part of the innate language faculty and do not need to be learned through input.

While the emphasis on formal features and their assembly and reassembly on lexical items is welcome, there are still principled questions linguistic theory has to answer with respect to parameters. Montrul and Yoon phrase them like this:

- Just what sorts of formal features can be selected?
- What are the formal features that UG makes available to begin with?
- Since features are assembled into lexical items, what constraints, if any, exist on the assemblage?
- Is there a logical order in which features are acquired? That is, does the selection of a feature entail that of another?
- Are parameters independent? That is, does choosing a value for a parameter for one class of lexical items have consequences for other classes? (Montrul and Yoon 2009: 296)

The cluster of constructions associated with a certain parameter is no longer a premise of generative linguistic theory because it is difficult to express in lexical terms. The research questions enunciated above are just beginning to be addressed, and the answers are frequently sought in general principles of human cognition and processing. In particular, how come we express so many grammatical meanings while we have so few syntactic operations? Linguists are trying to address the tension between the austerity

of the computational system and the universally determined set of hierarch-
ically organized functional categories. To exemplify the current syntactic
thinking, I will summarize one recent proposal, Ramchand and Svenonius
(2014), but other accounts exist, too. Ramchand and Svenonius start from
the observation that the sentence structure in any language can be divided
into three main domains: the Verb domain, the Tense domain, and the
Complementizer domain. No language exhibits these domains in any
other order. Analogs of these domains exist in the structure of nominal
expressions as well. Why should that be the case? These domains constitute
a hierarchy that is not innate, and not given by the computational mechanism, but is rooted in human cognition.[2]

The V domain represents the conceptual primitive Event (e), containing
the verb and its arguments (the participants of the event). The T domain
contains the V domain and adds another function: it anchors the event or
state in time and makes it a Situation. Finally, the C domain contains the
T domain, adding a connection to the discourse and making the whole
sentence a Proposition with a truth value. To illustrate, think of the verbal
phrase *Mary eat a sandwich* which gives us the type of event the sentence is
about: an eating event with Agent and Theme arguments. That event has
participants but is not anchored in time. In order to anchor it, we need some
tense (and possibly aspect) inflection: *Mary will eat a sandwich* or *Mary ate a
sandwich*. Finally, we link the sentence to discourse by leaving it as a
statement or making it a question as in *Will / Did Mary eat a sandwich?*

According to Ramchand and Svenonius, events, situations, and propositions are cognitive primitives grounded in "extralinguistic cognition:
A cognitive proclivity to perceive experience in terms of events, situations
and propositions (with analogous ontologies for other extended projections)" (2014: 34).[3] While this is a deceptively simple picture, it is an
illustration of how linguists are beginning to address the question of where
the functional categories come from and why they are ordered in functional

---

[2] Note that for a hierarchy to be innate and to be rooted in human cognition amounts
to the same thing in practice: it is available to all language learners and does not need to
be relearned in SLA. However, this distinction is theoretically important. It is not clear
where innate properties come from (yes, UG, but what is UG?) while extralinguistic
cognition is truly universal in the appropriate sense.

[3] Wiltschko (2014) has an analogous proposal with four domains: discourse linking
(C), time anchoring (T), point of view (Asp), and classification (V). Earlier proposals of
similar spirit exist, too.

hierarchies. Clearly, much work remains to be done, but it is already clear that general cognition impacts the grammar.

In the next sections, we will review some views of the possibility of parameter resetting. When discussing the evidence, we will be pointing out the lexical base of what has to be learned, in each case.

8.2 Representational Deficit versus Full Functional Representation accounts

If we understand parameters as sketched above—limited to the formal features that are selected from a universal inventory, assembled on functional categories and accessible from the Functional Lexicon—we have to conceptualize parameter resetting as adding or subtracting features from the feature bundles of the L2 functional categories. Recall Figure 2.2 in Chapter 2 to visualize this process. If a formal feature does not exist in the L1 but is active in the L2, then the L2 grammar needs to add it. That would be the case of grammatical gender on English pronouns and French nouns and pronouns. If a feature is expressed in the L1 but not in the L2, then this feature needs to be preempted, or deleted from the grammar. This would be the case of the feature [±Human] in English pronouns (*him/her* versus *it*), absent from French (clitic) pronouns (*le/la*) (see the discussion in Section 7.6). Finally, if a feature exists in the L1 and L2 but has a different value, or is differently bundled, or is expressed on a different syntactic category, then parameter resetting would entail feature reassembly.

In the case when a feature has to be added, we are mostly looking at uninterpretable features regulating agreement or movement. This is because a slightly different learning situation is true of interpretable features, to be addressed below. There are two major positions on the possibility of acquiring a new uninterpretable feature in the L2 grammar. In a nutshell, the Representational Deficit view argues that the mental representations of L2 learners cannot *in principle* achieve native standards because uninterpretable features not coming from the native language cannot be successfully acquired. This view subsumes the Valueless Features Hypothesis (Eubank 1996), the Local Impairment Hypothesis (Beck 1998), the Failed Functional Feature Hypothesis (Hawkins and Chan 1997), the Interpretability Hypothesis (Hawkins and Hattori 2006, Tsimpli and Dimitrakopoulou 2007) and the Fundamental Difference Hypothesis (Bley-Vroman 1989, 1990, 2009).

The Interpretability Hypothesis, for example, posits the impossibility of attaining uninterpretable features unavailable from the native language, if a learner is post-critical-period. The recent version of the Fundamental Difference Hypothesis invokes domain-general problem-solving strategies as well as transfer from the native language as the only mechanisms of acquisition available to adult L2 learners. Researchers supporting this general position have to explain *successful* acquisition of properties that are predicted not to be acquirable.

Counter to the Representational Deficit view, the Full Functional Representation view (Schwartz and Sprouse 1994, 1996, Prévost and White 2000, and many others) contends that nativelike linguistic representations are possible *in principle*, although they may be very difficult to attain in practice. Researchers defending this position have to explain variation in L2 production and comprehension, and distance from native speaker norms, that is, *unsuccessful* acquisition. Some of the hypotheses explaining variation, such as the Missing Surface Inflection Hypothesis and the Prosodic Transfer Hypothesis were presented in the Chapter 7. Other explanations will be discussed below.

One interesting thing to note is that representational deficit views can only be investigated in learning situations where the L1 and L2 differ, that is, there is an uninterpretable feature to be added or preempted (e.g., the Null Subject Parameter in Spanish and English). If research looks at a learning situation where the parameter value is the same (e.g., the Null Subject Parameter in French and English), and if successful acquisition is attested, one cannot be certain whether this knowledge came through the L1 or Universal Grammar.[4] Obviously, in the case where no parameter resetting is involved but knowledge is not yet complete, as in the French learners of English null subject in White's (1985) study, we have to invoke other explanations than parameter resetting.

In the next sections, three properties of syntax will be used to exemplify the two views: word order, verb movement, and *wh*-movement. They all depend on uninterpretable features; at issue is whether those features can be successfully acquired.

---

[4] In the context of L2 acquisition, Hale (1996) argues that the distinction between knowledge derived from the L1 and knowledge drawn directly from UG becomes impossible to test empirically in studies of L2 acquisition because the fundamental properties of any L2 grammar are also manifested in the L1 grammar.

8.3 Word order

The positioning of the subject (S), verb (V), and object (O) in an informationally neutral clause (without topic and focus) is one of the major differences among languages (see Chapter 2). Permutations of the three clause ingredients can give six possible word orders. However, not all six are equally attested in the world languages. Typological generalizations show that in the vast majority of human languages, the basic word order is either SOV (about 45% in the World Atlas of Language Structures) or SVO (about 35.4%) while orders like VSO (9%) or OSV (0.5%) are much less frequent or extremely rare. It has been suggested that these strong tendencies can be explained cognitively in terms of the prototypical transitive action scenario, in which an animate agent acts forcefully on an inanimate patient to induce a change of state. The most cross-linguistically prevalent word order patterns reflect the most natural ways of linearizing and nesting the core conceptual components of actions.[5] This type of cognitively based explanation is akin to the tripartite functional structure of the sentence we discussed above, and illustrates the current efforts by linguists to embed some aspects of language in general cognition principles. If these explanations are on the right track, the significant corollary for L2 research is that switching between parameters that are cognitively supported should be easier than acquiring less cognitively supported, less frequent word orders.

To date, most L2 research has focused on acquisition of one or the other most prevalent word orders. How does a learner acquire basic SVO when their native language exhibits SOV, or vice versa? The theoretical conceptualization of this parameter has changed over the years. At the time when researchers were interested in OV/VO word order acquisition, the prevalent analysis was that the ordering of the verbal head and the object in the VP was a parameter provided by UG and fixed on the basis of ample linguistic experience.[6] The structures are illustrated in (2).

[5] See Kemmerer (2012). Note that the subject does not always carry the Agent thematic role, the object is not always the Theme, (e.g., *The key opened the door*), so assuming strict mapping is misleading.

[6] For example, Travis 1984.

(2)   a. Head-initial VP (English, Romance) b. Head-initial VP (Japanese, German)

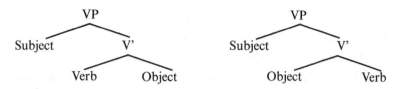

In the 1990s, an influential proposal by Kayne (1994) suggested that SVO was the universal underlying word order, and all other attested orders were a product of constituent movement. In the 2000s, the analysis shifted again to reflect a minimalist UG cleansed of all parameters. It is now widely accepted that the VP is built through the operation of Merge, satisfying the selection features on the verb (e.g., the verb *eat* is transitive and hence needs to merge with two arguments, an Agent and a Theme). Once the VP is built, the linearization of the string, that is, where each constituent is pronounced in the surface string, is calculated at the interface between syntax and the sensory-motor system, and depends on a diacritic on the verb. Essentially, the lexical information of the verb in English contains the information that the verb goes before the object, while the lexical information of the Japanese verb contains the opposite information, that the verb follows the object.

The acquisition of word order in the VP was a big part of the debate on the initial state of L2A in the mid 1990s. This debate was couched in terms of the relationship between two sources of L2 knowledge. One source is the native grammar, and how much of it constitutes the initial hypothesis for the L2 grammar. *Full transfer, partial transfer*, and *no transfer* were all proposed. The other possible source of knowledge, relevant for later stages of acquisition beyond the initial state, was access to UG, based on the L2 linguistic experience. Thus, *full access, partial access*, and *no access to UG* were discussed. Theoretical proposals varied in their claims on the two sources of L2 knowledge and how they combined. For example, Full Transfer Full Access (Schwartz and Sprouse 1994, 1996) declares its claims in the very name of the hypothesis. The Minimal Trees Hypothesis (Vainikka and Young Scholten 1994, 1996) proposed transfer of lexical categories but not of functional categories, so partial transfer. This hypothesis, however, still argued for full access to UG. The No Transfer Full Access option was also proposed (Epstein, Flynn, and Martohardjono 1996).[7] Note that all three positions

---

[7] Although the researchers didn't give this name to their hypothesis.

that diverge on transfer argue for full access, understood as follows: UG makes all parameter values and features available to the learner, as they are needed in accounting for the L2 input and building L2 functional categories. Successful acquisition is in principle possible, based on the L2 linguistic experience, although in certain areas of the grammar where input may be misleading, full convergence is not guaranteed (Schwartz and Sprouse 1996).

The position advocating partial access to UG was represented by the Failed Functional Features Hypothesis (Hawkins and Chan 1997). This hypothesis proposed that although lexical categories such as the VP and its headedness were learnable, functional features not available from the native language cannot be acquired. However, as Meisel (2011: 93) correctly points out, the lines between the partial UG access and the no UG access positions were blurred. If partial access is *only* through the native grammar, then there is no effective direct access to UG, for functional categories and features not instantiated in the native language.

Let us consider the experimental evidence now, with respect to the word order in VP property (OV vs. VO). A common assumption of The Full Transfer Full Access Hypothesis and the Minimal Trees Hypothesis is that learners initially transfer their native word order in the languages they are acquiring. For learners of German (SOV) whose native language is a Romance language (SVO), the expectation is that they will initially transfer SVO and will place the verb (both finite and non-finite forms) before the object. This assumption is supported by findings in Meisel, Clahsen, and Pienemann (1981), where verbs initially appeared in second position. Supporting findings also come from Vainikka and Young-Scholten's work: Korean and Turkish learners of German are observed to prefer verb-final constructions initially, while Italian and Spanish learners tend to use left-headed VPs. The fact that learners use their native VP word order appears to be empirically well established.

How about acquisition of word order more generally speaking? Beyond the order of constituents in the VP, surface word order is regulated by uninterpretable features. One of the most important of such features, known as the EPP[8] feature for historical reasons, controls whether subjects have to move to the TP projection, or whether another constituent or a null subject can check the feature. Also regulated by uninterpretable features is

---

[8] EPP stands for External Projection Principle, a feature which ensures that every clause must have a subject.

the movement of nominal and other constituents called "scrambling" (think: scrambled eggs). In the languages where scrambling is licit, such constituents can appear in positions different from where they were merged, sometimes optionally, sometimes to satisfy language-specific constraints. We shall look at examples of such feature acquisition next.

But first let us update the predictions. With the focus on features in L2 research, the "access to UG" source of knowledge has to be reformulated as follows: are uninterpretable features, externalized by the functional morphology and demonstrable through correct movement and agreement, acquirable in a second language if they differ in the native and target grammars? If research findings attest to successful acquisition of uninterpretable features so expressed, full access to UG approaches will be supported and representational deficit positions, e.g., the Interpretability Hypothesis, will be in question. If, on the other hand, it is demonstrated that learners cannot attain such knowledge even at advanced levels of proficiency, then full functional representation will be challenged.

I will summarize here the relevant findings of Papadopoulou et al. (2011), a large study investigating knowledge of word order and its interaction with case marking and specificity in the interlanguage of Greek native speakers, beginning and intermediate learners of Turkish. Greek exhibits SVO word order while Turkish is an SOV language so learners have to establish a new word order in their second language. The battery of tests in this study included a cloze test, an online grammaticality judgment task, and a picture selection task. Learners were significantly more accurate on verbal inflection (agreement) than on nominal inflection (case endings), as established in the cloze test. Accuracy percentages for the beginner group were 42% versus 21%, respectively. At the same time, learners got progressively better in supplying correct case endings, with increased proficiency (95% for verbal inflection, 49% for case in the most proficient group).

In the grammaticality judgment task, which utilized only simple transitive sentences, learners viewed each word centered on the screen for 2 seconds. A "?" at the end of the sentence prompted them to record whether they found the sentence acceptable. Response times were measured. The study findings attest to the target SOV word order of Turkish being acquired even by the lowest proficiency group. However, on non-canonical word orders, learners did not do so well. Look at the following examples.

(3) a. gazete-ler-i   çocuk   oku-du.   O$_{ACC}$ SV
         newspaper-PL-ACC   child   read-PAST
         'The newspapers were read by some child.'

     b. *gazete   çocuk   oku-du   *O$_{ABS}$S V
         newspaper   child   read-PAST
         'Newspapers were read by some child.'

In Turkish, specificity and case marking interact with word order. When the subject is generic (referring to some unspecified child, in this case) and the object is specific (known to the speaker), the object is marked for Accusative case and obligatorily appears in sentence-initial position. The acceptable (3a) and the unacceptable (3b) illustrate this. Note that this word order is different from the canonical SOV. It is probably very rare, and it is only allowed with Accusative case-marked objects. Papadopoulou et al. (2011) found that their beginning and intermediate learners had not acquired this word order, although they showed some sensitivity to it. Taken together, the results of this study suggest that the uninterpretable features responsible for the Turkish canonical SOV are acquirable, but intermediate proficiency learners have problems with non-canonical word orders, especially when there is an interaction with case, which is still shaky in their grammar. Thus, this study provides support for accounts such as the Bottleneck Hypothesis and the Feature Reassembly Hypothesis that place lexical learning of the functional lexicon at the heart of acquisition. Interaction between features (in this study, word order and case) obviously increases the complexity of the learning task, and acquisition just takes longer.

Papadopoulou et al.'s (2011) experimental participants were intermediate learners of Turkish. This leaves us with the unanswered question of whether non-canonical word order is acquirable in the longer term. To see one answer to this question, we turn to Hopp's (2005) study. Hopp tested English and Japanese native speakers who were advanced learners of German. He used a contextualized grammaticality judgment task to probe their knowledge of "remnant movement," a complex German construction which moves parts of the embedded clause to sentence-initial position. In order for the reader to appreciate the high complexity of this German word order, part of the tested paradigm appears in examples (4) and (5). The symbol *t* stands for the position where the moved phrase, in square brackets, started.

(4)   Remnant topicalization (across-scrambled phrase) across finite clause
      boundary, acceptable:

      [t₁ Zu reparieren]₂   glaube   ich [t′₂   hat Peter   [den Wagen]₁
      to repair   think   I   has Peter   the car
      schon t₂   versucht].
      already   tried
      'I think that Peter already tried to repair the car.'

(5)   Remnant scrambling across short-scrambled phrase, unacceptable:

      * Ich glaube, dass [t₁ zu reparieren]₂ Peter [den Wagen]₁ schon t₂
      I think   that   to repair   Peter the car   already
      versucht hat.
      tried   has
      'I think that Peter already tried to repair the car.'

Knowledge of the whole paradigm (allowed and disallowed scrambled sentences) depends on uninterpretable features beyond those responsible for topicalization.[9] In addition, Japanese learners would have an advantage over English native speakers in learning these constructions, since Japanese also allows scrambling. Thus the "scrambling" feature, whatever it is, would be available to them from their native language, while it would be new for the English natives. Hopp's results attest to ultimately successful acquisition, in that all English and Japanese learners robustly repeated the evaluations of the native German speakers. He also uncovered native language influence. Hopp made the case that knowledge of the allowed and disallowed sentences could not have come through classroom instruction or observation of the native input. Since complete knowledge of this paradigm involves rejection of unacceptable constructions that cannot come from astute observation of the input and pattern-noticing, Hopp argued that this is a Poverty of the Stimulus learning situation. The input simply does not contain unacceptable sentences of the sort of (5). The input does not contain unacceptable sentences, period. Furthermore, they look suspiciously similar to the acceptable sentences in (4), and both are pretty complex. Still, advanced learners distinguish between them reliably.

---

[9] Topicalization is a construction marking old discourse information structure, available in English, recall the discussion in Chapter 6.

In summary, let us discuss the relative merits of the two opposing positions, with respect to word order phenomena. Proponents of representational deficits can take heart from findings such as Papadopoulou et al.'s (2011), because they document lack of successful acquisition of non-canonical word orders. For full functional representation proponents, however, findings such as Hopp's (2005) provide a clinching argument: acquisition of uninterpretable features cannot be *impossible*, if at least one such documented case of successful acquisition exists. It is crucial that successful acquisition involves knowledge of ungrammaticality, which cannot be due to noticing patterns or imitation. However, pattern noticing and imitation are the only ways in which deficit accounts can explain learner success with uninterpretable feature acquisition.

8.4 Verb movement

After discussing headedness in the VP and movement of non-verbal constituents in the sentence structure, this section looks at another poster child of UG parameters: verb movement. This is a parameterized language distinction also triggered by uninterpretable features and featuring a cluster of constructions that has been extensively researched in L2 acquisition.

The Verb Movement Parameter studies (White 1990, 1991, and others) provoked a lot of heated discussion in the debate on new parameter value accessibility. At issue is a distinction like the following (Pollock 1989) illustrated in (6), (7), and (8), examples from White (1990):

(6) a. Jean embrasse   souvent   Marie.   French: S–V–Adv–O
         John kisses   often   Mary
     b. *John kisses often Mary.
     c. *Jean   souvent   embrasse Marie.
         John   often   kisses   Mary
     d. John often kisses Mary.   English: S–Adv–V–O

(7) a. Marie   n'aime   pas Jean.   French: S–V–Neg–O
         Mary   likes   not John
     b. *Mary likes not John.
     c. Mary does not like John.   English: S–Aux–Neg–V–O

(8) a. Aime-t-elle   Jean?   French: V-S-O?
         likes-she   John
     b. *Likes she John?
     c. Does she like John?   English: Aux-S-V-O?

As examples in (6) show, the French verb moves to the left of the adverb *souvent* 'often,' which is argued to mark the edge of the VP. In English, however, the verb stays in VP, as its position to the right of the adverb demonstrates. Examples from negative sentences in (7) illustrate the same fact: the French verb appears to the right of the stable (non-clitic) negation marker *pas,*[10] while in English the positions are reversed. Finally, (8) shows that it is possible (although not obligatory) for the French verb to invert with the subject to create interrogative clauses. This would be the equivalent of (8b), which is of course unattested. To mark a sentence as interrogative, English main verbs need *do*-support (although auxiliary verbs are different in this respect). These three properties make for a beautiful paradigm, don't they? Pollock's linguistic analysis explains all of these examples by postulating that the verb moves out of the VP and up to T and C in French, while it remains in VP, in English.

(9)

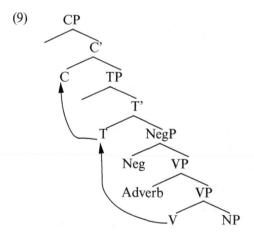

As demonstrated in the examples and the tree structure in (9), the Verb Movement Parameter associates three superficially unrelated constructions, united by a common analysis in linguistic theory. That is why this parameter was investigated as another showcase of grammar restructuring: parameters are responsible for clusters of superficially unrelated constructions becoming part of the grammar once the triggering feature of the parameter has been acquired. In this case, movement of the verb over adverbs and negation, as well as knowledge of V-to-T-to-C movement in question formation, were predicted to be correlated (although the putative trigger, rich verbal morphology, was not tested).

In an ambitious and carefully designed study, White and her colleagues (White 1990, 1991, White, Spada, Lightbown, and Ranta 1991) tested francophone adolescents (the average age was 11) on adverb placement before and after a teaching intervention. During a two-week-long period, one experimental group was exposed to instruction on adverb placement, while the second experimental group was taught question formation. A post-test and a delayed post-test on adverb placement were then administered. Parameter theory (at the time) predicted that instruction on one property in a cluster associated with lack of verb movement in English would generalize to the other property in the cluster.

The francophone adolescents' knowledge of adverb placement was probed with three different tasks: a grammaticality judgment task, a preference task where acceptable and unacceptable sentences were shown side by side, and a word order manipulation task where learners had to arrange words written on cards into acceptable combinations. Recall that the prediction would be that both the question group and the adverb group should improve on adverbs if question formation and adverb placement are both reflexes of the verb-raising parameter. The results were devastating for parameter theory. While accuracy on adverb placement increased dramatically in the adverb group, there was no change of behavior in the question group. Even the gains of the adverb group proved to be short-lived: as White (1991) reports, after exactly one year post-intervention, the children's accuracy on adverbs had reverted to the pre-test values. In addition, Trahey and White (1993) exposed another group of francophone adolescents to a flood of Subject–Adverb–Verb–Object naturalistic examples, without any focus on form. The results revealed that while the adolescents acquired the grammaticality of the English adverb placement, they did not preempt the French placement. In other words, they ended up with a grammar containing optional S-V-A-O and S-A-V-O. The researchers argued that a flood of positive input (without negative evidence) may not be sufficient to restructure the grammar, in some cases. Possible explanations of these results touched on the issue of quality and quantity of the (unambiguous) input available to learners, with respect to adverb placement, as well as the length of the teaching interventions. Whatever the explanation, such results would obviously support representational deficit accounts.

Related to verb movement is the so-called Verb-Second (V2) parameter. In German and other Germanic languages, an uninterpretable feature requires that the verb is always second in the clause. If another constituent other than the subject moves to clause-initial position as in example (10) below, the (auxiliary) verb has to follow it and so comes to be pronounced before the subject.

(10)   a. Er hat sie im Park   gefunden   (Meisel 2011: 32)
          he had her in the park found
          'He found her in the park.'

       b. Im park   hat er sie gefunden
          in the park had he her found
          'He found her in the park.'

The structure illustrating this movement will be along the lines of (11) (leaving numerous details aside), where the copies of the moved constituents are crossed out.

(11)

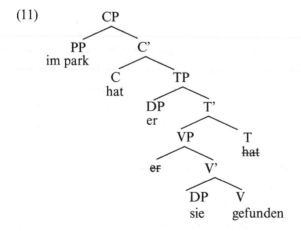

In languages with the "on" value of the V2 parameter (German), the verb moves to C, while in languages with the "off" value (English), the verb stays in T. I shall use this parameter to illustrate an influential recent account of child language acquisition that unifies parameter setting with general learning mechanisms based on frequency of relevant evidence in the input, Yang's Variational Learning Model (Yang 2002, 2004, 2010). The main idea is that a parameter supported with abundant and unambiguous evidence in the input will be learned earlier than a parameter for which the supporting evidence is scarce. More concretely, this learning model considers the frequency of unambiguous input (what Yang calls a parameter "signature") in proportion to all the input relevant to that parameter. An example of a parameter set very early is that of *wh*-movement in English (which we shall discuss in the next section). Supporting evidence for this parameter amounts to about 25% of all child-directed input.[11] On the other hand, Yang gives the V2 parameter in German as an example of a late acquired parameter. It is unambiguously evidenced only by sentences where the object or some other constituent is in the sentence-initial position and the verb precedes the subject. Taking into account all the child-directed relevant sentences, such evidence comes in only 1.2% of them, which results in a relatively late acquisition at the 36th–38th month (Clahsen 1986).

This account can be extended to second language acquisition. If Yang's metric is on the right track for the establishment of the V2 parameter value in the second language, we should find experimental evidence for late V2 acquisition in adult learners as well. Such evidence exists. Wahlstrom McKay (2001) tested oral production of beginning to intermediate instructed learners of German (3rd and 4th semester of German classes). She found that students violated V2 in 49.3% of obligatory contexts. However, Conradie (2006), Prévost (1999), and Tran (2005) present evidence for successful acquisition of the V2 rule. Conradie used a battery of tests to investigate knowledge of V2 in South African English-speaking learners of Afrikaans and argued that parameter resetting in their grammars is complete by the time of testing. Prévost (1999) tested Spanish-native intermediate learners of German on a variety of properties, including V2. His learners obtained 100% accuracy for verb placement on the production task. Prévost showed that these learners were also accurate in rejecting V3

---

[11] Stromswold (1995); see also Yang (2004: 455: Table 1).

structures (possible in Spanish), and they only rejected correct V2 utterances where an argument was fronted (topicalized) without sufficient context. Finally, Tran's (2005) study tested English-native children (aged 9–13) learning German in an instructional setting. Her experimental data consist of oral productions of fronted (topicalized) time adverbials and direct objects. Her results indicate that the high proficiency learners make very few errors with the V2 placement of the finite verb. The results of all four studies mentioned above point to initial difficulties and subsequent successful acquisition of the V2 rule.

Recently, the V2 parameter has been used as an illustration of another proposal on how language acquisition unfolds: the Multiple Grammars hypothesis by Amaral and Roeper (2014). The authors argue that it is *in principle* possible to maintain incompatible subgrammars in human language. This state of affairs can explain dialectal variation in adult grammars, diachronic language change, variation, and optionality in first and second language acquisition. For example, while German has a V2 rule active in the whole of the grammar, that is, a generalized V2 rule, English has a lexically limited V2 rule. Subject–auxiliary inversion is allowed after the negative polarity adverbs *never, rarely*, etc., for emphasis. Of course, the non-emphatic variant in (12b) is also an option.

(12)   a. Never/rarely have I seen such a beautiful garden!
       b. I have never/rarely seen such a beautiful garden!

Note how the V2 parameter is not deterministic any more, and is relegated to a V2 rule. Amaral and Roeper argue that the input from any language is usually ambiguous due to such lexically triggered exceptions. As a result, multiple grammatical rules coexist in the human mind. The incompatible rules are distinguished by diacritics, or little notes "attached" to the rule to specify environments in which they are manifested. To take another example, an adult English speaker knows that *it seems cold* and *seems cold* are both colloquially possible in English, although the latter is the signature of a null subject grammar while English is not a null-subject language. *Seems cold* is lexically restricted, then, to main clauses and to diary and colloquial registers. Rules are kept separate by the diacritic and accessed independently: the English speaker knows that inversion after any old adverb is not appropriate, see (13a):

(13) a. *Occasionally have I seen him smoke.
      b. Occasionally, I have seen him smoke.

While the linguistic aspect of this hypothesis is simple and satisfying, the psycholinguistic side is not sufficiently developed yet. That is, it is not very clear how the mind keeps the multiple grammatical rules separate in language use so that massive optionality and variation do not occur.

To recap this section, here we discussed a series of experiments on the Verb Movement Parameter in French–English interlanguage, whose general findings do not support parameter restructuring in a cluster-engaging fashion. On the other hand, we also mentioned several studies documenting successful acquisition of the V2 rule in German. Yang's Variational Learning Hypothesis is in a position to explain why V2 is a difficult rule to acquire, while the Multiple Grammars approach proposes that incompatible rules like generalized V2 (in German) and lexically restricted V2 (in English) can co-exist in the mind of a German–English bilingual.

8.5 *Wh*-movement

In this last section, we will use the acquisition of *wh*-movement constraints (a.k.a. island constraints) to discuss the issue of Poverty of the Stimulus in the second language. We already alluded to this issue in discussing German scrambling in Hopp's (2005) work. The argument in a nutshell is as follows. Acquiring the fact that some construction is ungrammatical (also known as preempting) constitutes a learnability problem because the relevant information is not available in the positive input that the language acquirer is exposed to. Superficial observation of grammatical *wh*-movement may lead to the wrong generalization that *wh*-movement is essentially free of constraints. Thus, demonstrating knowledge of unavailability of certain constructions by rejecting them in experimental conditions attests to innate linguistic knowledge that could not have come from the observation of the input or simple analogy.

But let us first look at what there is to acquire. The big initial divide is between languages that allow their question words to remain where they were merged, in argument positions, versus languages that move their question words to the beginning of the clause, to the CP projection. Chinese is what linguists call a *wh-in-situ* language:

(14) a. Hufei   mai-le   shenme   (Mandarin Chinese)
          Hufei   buy-PERF   what
          'What did Hufei buy?'
      b. John bought WHAT?   (echo-question)
      c. *John bought what?   (regular question seeking information)
      d. What did John buy?

Both Mandarin and English are SVO languages, but English cannot allow the question word for the object to remain after the verb. (14b) is acceptable as an echo question with emphasis on the question word. These questions are used when we have not heard properly. However, (14c) is ungrammatical as a regular question seeking information, while the correct way to ask for the object is (14d). The *wh*-movement parameter captures this linguistic distinction.

Now, as we have already seen in this textbook, the movement of the *wh*-word to the top of the sentence, in languages that require such movement, is constrained in a complicated way. The examples below are based on Belikova and White (2009), and they illustrate the cases when *wh*-movement in English is allowed and when it is prohibited. The ungrammatical constructions are called islands, as a metaphor for a spot from which one cannot escape (if we disregard boats and ships). The underline stands for the original position of the *wh*-phrase, also known as "the gap."

(15) a. This girl danced with Mark.
      b. Who did this girl dance with ____?

(16) a. You said that this girl danced with Mark.
      b. Who did you say that this girl danced with ____?

(17) a. You wondered whether this girl danced with Mark.
      b. *Who did you wonder whether this girl danced with ____?
                                                              (wh-island)

(18) a. You spread a rumor that this girl danced with Mark.
      b. *Who did you spread a rumor that this girl danced with ____?
                                                        (complex NP island)

(19) a. You met a girl that danced with Mark.
      b. *Who did you meet a girl that danced with ____?
                                                    Relative clause island

(20) a. You met this girl after she danced with Mark.
      b. *Who did you meet this girl after she danced with ____?
                                                        Adjunct island

Chomsky (1973) proposed that the disparate constraints illustrated in the examples above have the same underlying explanation, having to do with the necessity of the *wh*-phrase to take short steps on its way to the top of the sentence, but not longer jumps. This unifying principle was called the Subjacency condition: a constituent may not move over more than one "bounding node" at a time. The bounding nodes could differ across languages (Rizzi 1982) but in English NP and IP (what is now TP) were proposed to be bounding nodes. We introduced this constraint in Chapter 2.

In their classical work on the Critical Period Hypothesis, Johnson and Newport (1991) focused specifically on the acquisition of Subjacency. They tested Chinese native speakers who had arrived in the US between the ages of 18 and 38, on NP complements as in (18), relative clauses as in (19), and *wh*-islands (17). It is no wonder that the Chinese native speakers did not perform as well as the English native speakers on these complex sentences: they are understood much better if context is provided. However, the learners distinguished reliably between the acceptable and unacceptable sentences, demonstrating that their judgments are not indiscriminate (though they may not be completely nativelike). We shall come to this issue again.

A very important study for this particular topic (*wh*-movement) in SLA was Gita Martohardjono's (1993) PhD dissertation. Just as Johnson and Newport, she tested native speakers of Indonesian, Italian, and Chinese, all languages argued not to obey Subjacency in the same way that English does. Martohardjono tested rejection rates of ungrammatical constructions of two types: extractions of subjects and objects of relative clauses. By that time, the theory had identified that these two extractions differed in acceptability. Sentences such as (21a) still violated Subjacency, but did not lead to strong ungrammaticality: these were called weak violations. They should contrast in the reader's judgments with strongly unacceptable sentences as in (21b), which violate Subjacency and another linguistic principle, the Empty Category Principle. The latter were considered to be strong violations.

(21) a. ??Which car did John spread [NP the rumor [CP that the neighbor stole ____?]]

b. *Which neighbor did John spread [NP the rumor [CP that ____ stole a car?]]

Table 8.1 Rejection rates of strong and weak violations, in percent (based on Martohardjono 1993)

Native language	Strong violations	Weak violations
English	99	78
Indonesian	87	42
Chinese	76	38

The distinction between the acceptability of the two types of sentences as in (21a) and (21b) is clearly present in the judgments of the native English speakers, as can be seen in Table 8.1 by their 99% rejection rate for strong violations versus their considerably lower 78% rejection rate for weak violations. That is why the example in (21a) is marked with two question marks only, while (21b) is rated completely ungrammatical with an asterisk. This difference in acceptability constitutes a Poverty of the Stimulus situation for learners because neither type of sentence appears in the input. It is remarkable, then, that the same pattern of acceptability demonstrated by the native controls is exhibited by the learners as well. As the ratings of the learners on the strong violations are significantly above chance, Martohardjono argued that these learners have been successful in acquiring *wh*-movement. It is important to emphasize that the successful acquisition here differentiates between two relatively complex and unacceptable types of sentence, which the learners have never heard pronounced, which they cannot transfer from the native language, and they have not been taught to reject. Their behavior, then, is suggestive of access to universal grammatical principles and parameter values.

We should mention two more studies attesting successful acquisition of *wh*-movement, both looking at Chinese native speakers acquiring English. Li's (1998) study tested 180 adult learners and documented nativelike judgments. White and Juffs (1998) compared the performance of two groups of Chinese learners: one group that had never left China, and hence consisted of foreign language learners, and another group that was studying in Canada at the time, having been exposed to naturalistic English input. Not only were the learners' judgments highly accurate, but the two groups differing in type of exposure to English were also not statistically different.

> ### Teaching relevance
>
> When we are speaking of successful acquisition of *wh*-movement and other properties, we are mentioning mostly research results from groups of participants. Group results may hide individual differences, of course. While it is clearly the case that some participants in those studies have acquired the constraints on movement of *wh*-phrases in English, acquisition is not uniform, and not guaranteed. For some test participants, an L1-based analysis of some constructions will continue to predominate. For all learners, though, rich input in natural situations provides all they need in order to restructure their native grammar.

We just reviewed some studies arguing that acquisition of *wh*-movement by L2-ers can be successful. How would proponents of the Full Functional Representation position explain why learners are never as accurate as the native speakers on such constructions? They don't have to. What L2 acquisition studies are trying to show is that learners have established a contrast in their mental grammar between acceptable and unacceptable structures. That's what knowledge of language really means. Learners don't have to be statistically indistinguishable from native speakers in all respects. Bley-Vroman (1983) cautioned against comparing natives and learners directly. It would be a Comparative Fallacy to do so, he argued. It is a welcome result if learners perform as well as the natives in some study, but that need not be the case for successful acquisition to be established. The more complex the linguistic construction, the more variation in learner performance is to be expected, related to individual differences dependent on processing resources. We will talk a lot more about individual variation in processing in Chapter 12. Suffice it to say here that more variation is expected in L2 processing as compared to native language processing, because there are two languages at play in the mind.

On the other side of this debate, taking the opposite view, is the Representational Deficit position. Recall that this view postulates the impossibility of acquiring uninterpretable features and explains cases of successful acquisition as only seemingly successful, or superficial. We shall exemplify supporting evidence for this view from studies of resumptive pronouns. Hawkins and Chan (1997) tested the acquisition of restrictive relative clauses by Chinese and French speakers. French and English relative clauses have a similar analysis, while Chinese relative clauses arguably do not involve *wh*-movement and allow resumptive pronouns. Compare the sentences in (21).

(22)

a. The girl [$_{CP}$ who [$_{TP}$ I like _____] is here.]

b. *This is the boy [$_{CP}$ who [$_{TP}$ Mary described [$_{NP}$ the way [____that Bill attacked_____.]]]

The sentence in (22a) is acceptable because the *wh*-word *who* has made a small manageable jump to the beginning of the relative clause CP. The sentence in (22b) violates Subjacency because the second step involves jumping over two bounding nodes (NP and TP). Chinese relative clauses do not exhibit movement of the *wh*-phrase, and they allow a pronoun in the original gap, which would sound something like (23a) in English, if it were allowed:

(23) a. *This is the girl I gave a present to **her**.

  b. [$_{CP}$ [$_{TP}$ Wo song liwu gei **ta** $_{TP}$] de $_{CP}$] neige nühai
    I gave present to her "that" the girl
    'This is the girl I gave a present to.'

Ta in the Chinese relative clause in (23b) is the equivalent resumptive pronoun. Hawkins and Chan argued that Chinese learners of English would not acquire the correct way of forming relative clauses in English, which does not allow resumptive pronouns. We have to mention that the French learners of English behaved as expected on all the test sentences, although they reached native levels only at advanced proficiency. The Chinese learners, though, performed differently, see Table 8.2.

The arrows in this table point to the direction of accuracy improvement. While it seems that the Chinese learners are acquiring the ungrammaticality

Table 8.2 Accuracy rates by Chinese learners of English on restrictive relative clause violations, in percent (based on Hawkins and Chan 1997)

	Correct rejection of resumptive pronoun	Correct rejection of *wh* - island	Correct rejection of complex NP
Chinese elementary	38	63	71
Chinese intermediate	55	54	61
Chinese advanced	90	41	38
English natives	98	98	85

of resumptive pronouns, their correct rejections of Subjacency violations is slipping down, as the arrows show. Hawkins and Chan suggest that the elementary learners are rejecting the ungrammatical *wh*-islands and complex NPs at rates higher than the advanced learners because they do not see in them the resumptive pronouns they are looking for. The Chinese advanced learners, on the other hand, perform better on rejecting resumptive pronouns, which suggests that they are acquiring the surface form of English restrictive relative clauses. However, they perform much worse on detecting Subjacency violations, which points to an incorrect analysis of the structure without *wh*-movement. Hawkins and Chan's careful experimental study shows how important it is to keep in mind that if a learner group is accurate on an experimental task, this does not necessarily mean that the learners have the same analysis as the native speakers.

Continuing with the acquisition of resumptive pronouns, we will look at two further studies, one a partial replication of the other. Tsimpli and Dimitrakopoulou (2007) looked at Greek learners of English. Since Greek optionally allows resumptive clitics, the authors hypothesized that it would be impossible for Greek learners to preempt resumptive pronouns in their mental grammars for English. In addition, the authors hypothesized that various other interpretable features, such as animacy, may be able to aid the learners in learning superficial structure. Here are some examples from the acceptability judgment task:

(24) Grammatical and ungrammatical subject extraction, with and without complementizer *that*:
  a. *Who do you think that Ø met Katerina?
  b. *Who do you think that he met Katerina?
  c. Who do you think met Katerina?
  c. What do people think Ø makes American cinema popular?
  d. *What do people think it makes American cinema popular?

(25) Grammatical and ungrammatical object extraction, animate and inanimate *wh*-phrase:
  a. What did you say that Maria forgot Ø when she was leaving home?
  b. *What did you say that Maria forgot it when she was leaving home?
  c. Who do you think that Susan would marry Ø?
  d. *Who do you think that Susan would marry him?

Table 8.3 Percentage of correct rejection of ungrammatical sentences in T&D's experiment

	Subject ($-that$)	Subject ($+that$)	Object
Intermediate	63.9	59.6	59.5
Advanced	68.4	66.5	78.6
Native speakers	96.7	95.5	96.7

As the accuracy scores in Table 8.3 suggest, even advanced learners of English were far from accurate on rejecting sentences with resumptive pronouns, although they were slightly more accurate on object versus subject extractions. Tsimpli and Dimitrakopoulou concluded that "(un)interpretable formal features... cause learnability problems even at advanced stages of acquisition" (2007: 237).

Leal Méndez and Slabakova (2014) set out to replicate this study with Spanish native speakers. Why was a replication deemed necessary? Spanish, like Greek, makes resumptive clitics available in informal registers. The researchers divided their English learners into those who accepted resumptives in their native Spanish (the +R group), and those who did not (the –R group). The hypothesis was that the group that did not like resumptives in the L1 would have an easier time with resumptives in the L2. Leal Méndez and Slabakova used the same test sentences as Tsimpli and Dimitrakopoulou, but embedded in a context and pronounced in a natural way by a native speaker (Table 8.4; see also Exercise 8.1).

The –R advanced group is on average over 10% more accurate than the +R advanced group, suggesting that individual preferences against resumptives in their native Spanish do have an effect in the L2 English. That is, learners may be transferring an individual (processing) tolerance to resumptives from their native language.[12] Importantly, however, both +R and –R advanced learners have established a syntactic, grammatical contrast in

---

[12] There is a tension between processing and grammar in the usage of resumptive pronouns. While they are generally not grammatical in English, sometimes they alleviate Subjacency violations. Ross (1967) is the classical treatment. Example (i) is a spontaneously produced example while examples like (ii) were elicited experimentally by Ferreira and Swets (2005).

(i)   We are afraid of things that we don't know what **they** are.

(ii) This is the donkey that I don't know where **it** lives.

Table 8.4 Percentage of correct rejection of ungrammatical sentences in LM&S (in press)

	Subject (−*that*)	Subject (+*that*)	Object
−R Intermediate	66	65	64
+R Intermediate	70	65	70
−R Advanced	97	95	96
+R Advanced	84	84	79
Native speakers	96	97	95

their grammar between ungrammatical sentences with resumptives and grammatical sentences with gaps. In addition, factors such as animacy did not seem to have much effect on the judgments. The authors argued that their results do not support a representational deficit account. Findings on processing resumptives in English by Najdi Arabic speakers (Aldwayan, Fiorentino, and Gabriele 2010) also go against a representational deficit. Research on this topic is very much continuing. In the future, proponents on both sides of the debate will have to think of innovative research designs to tease apart underlying competence from superficially attained, or indirectly acquired, competence.

8.6 Conclusion

We started this chapter with an overview of the notion of linguistic parameter through the fifty-year-long history of the generative research enterprise. Changes in the theory inevitably affect the debate between Representational Deficit accounts and Full Functional Representation accounts. In a reconsideration of theories, Belikova and White (2009) argued that a great deal of the research findings on differential sensitivity to weak and strong *wh*-movement violations, which were previously argued to be acquired despite

---

However, the very same subjects that produced sentences like (i) and (ii) rejected them in the acceptability task. It has been long acknowledged that speakers of many languages have prescriptive attitudes towards resumptive pronouns. However, sentences with resumptives in English that do not violate Subjacency are still unacceptable:

(iii)   *I saw the boy that Mary loves him.

Poverty of the Stimulus, turned out to be based in universal grammatical constraints. The outcome of this process of reconceptualization of parameters is that it now appears to be impossible to distinguish between the effects of the L1 and of UG. The L2 acquisition process, however, remains UG-constrained as much as ever. All languages share a minimal UG accompanied by cognition-based functional hierarchies and processing efficiency constraints. However, the parametric differences between Chinese and English *wh*-questions that we discussed at the outset of Section 8.5 are still very much the same. Formal features reflected in the functional lexicon and their configurations are all that needs to be acquired. As Belikova and White point out, it is no longer even clear whether it is *possible* for the L1 and L2 acquisition processes to be fundamentally different (Belikova and White 2009: 219).

8.7 Exercises

Exercise 8.1. In this chapter, we discussed two studies on the L2 acquisition of resumptive pronouns, Tsimpli and Dimitrakopoulou (2007) and Leal Méndez and Slabakova (2014). Find and download the original articles from the respective journal sites. Here is your task:

1. Here is a subset of the test sentences given in the Appendix of Tsimpli and Dimitrakopoulou. On one day, go through the first list and record your judgments based on a Yes or No decision. On another day, go through the sentences again (see end of chapter) and record your judgments using the scale. Is there a difference in your performance? Discuss the methodological matter of using Likert scales versus categorical choices. Does the type of construction matter for this choice, in other words, are scales better for some constructions, and Yes–No answers for others?

Record your judgment of the acceptability of the following sentences. If you find the sentence acceptable, choose Yes. If you find the sentence sounds unacceptable, choose No.

1. What did you say that Maria forgot it when she was leaving home?   Yes   No
2. What do teachers insist that pupils should read before the exams?   Yes   No

3. Who does Peter think that Mary should meet?   Yes   No
4. What has John decided that he should buy for Christmas?   Yes   No
5. Who do you think that he met Katerina?   Yes   No
6. Who have you suggested that he should not resign?   Yes   No
7. What do you think that it makes the book very interesting? Yes   No
8. Who did the students think he would be the best president? Yes   No
9. Who do you think that Susan would marry him?   Yes   No
10. What do people think it makes American cinema popular?   Yes   No
11. Who did Mary say he wanted to study abroad?   Yes   No
12. Who does Kathryn think is a good painter?   Yes   No
13. Which politician did Jane say he is very honest?   Yes   No
14. Who did John say kissed Susan?   Yes   No
15. What did John suggest should be announced at the   Yes   No
    meeting?
16. What have you insisted that student should read it before No   Yes
    the exam?

Leal Méndez and Slabakova presented the same sentences (the list above is a subset), embedded under contexts such as this one below. Note that the *wh*-word is different from the ones above.

Gabriel and Maria were chatting at the Java House. Maria said that Peter liked that new book "Going Rogue" so much that he memorized every word. Gabriel corrected her and said that "Going Wild" was the book Peter had read so carefully. To resolve the argument, Maria called Peter's best friend Vladimir and asked him:

   Which book do you remember that Peter read it carefully?
Do you think that the context makes a difference for the acceptability of the questions? Why, or why not? Create several contexts of your own for some of the sentences in the list.

Exercise 8.2. The following series of questions will be based on Grüter (2006): "Another take on the L2 initial state: Evidence from comprehension in L2 German," Language Acquisition 13(4), 287–317. It is a study that addresses the Minimal Trees Hypothesis discussed in this chapter and brings evidence from comprehension of German questions.

   Answer the questions in sequence. This is a long exercise, but at this point in the textbook, you are prepared to tackle it.

Question 1. What does the Minimal Trees Hypothesis propose for the initial stages of L2A? What is the principled linguistic distinction that the researchers use?

Question 2. If lexical categories transfer from the native language and functional categories don't, what are some predictions for linguistic behavior at the very first stages? Will the learners at these stages be able to produce negative sentences? Sentences with past tense verbs? Will they be able to produce questions, considering that they only operate with one VP, and no functional category (or a very restricted one) above it?

Question 3. There is a growing skepticism as to whether production data are fully indicative of learners' knowledge. As pointed out by White (2003): "Indeed, to investigate the possibility that there might be a stage prior to the emergence of L2 speech in which functional categories are lacking, we need methodologies that do not rely on production data." Grüter (2005/6) is the answer to that skepticism. She set out to devise a comprehension experiment to address the L2 initial state. But before we discuss the study, what is the underlying assumption that makes it possible to use comprehension and production data to check knowledge of functional categories?

Question 4. The study takes advantage of the ambiguity of some German questions: with feminine or neuter nominals, the questions in (1) can be interpreted as either subject or object questions.

(1)   a. Was beisst die Katze?
          what bite-3SG the cat
          'What is biting the cat?'   (= subject question)
          OR 'What is the cat biting?'   (= object question)

      b. Was hat die Katze gebissen?
          what have-3SG the cat bitten
          'What has bitten the cat?'   (= subject question)
          OR 'What has the cat bitten?'   (= object question)

Here are the two possible analyses for the sentence in (1a). Discuss them and show how the ambiguity arises. Then provide the structures for the sentence in (1b). HINT: the tree structures will be roughly the same, copy them and try to fit the words in the slots. Note: Grüter's structure has two VPs to accommodate the auxiliary verb but you don't have to. Note also that the intermediate projections are not shown (c′, etc.).

(2)

a. Subject question
   What is biting the cat?

b. Object question
   What is the cat biting?

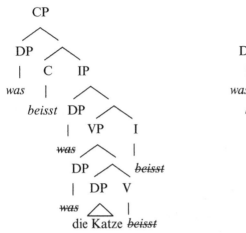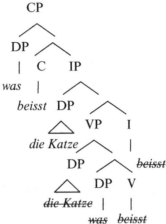

Question 5. We already discussed the basic structure of English and German sentences, see (10) and (11) above. If English learners of German transfer all the L1 functional categories into their initial L2 grammars, as the Full Transfer Full Access hypothesis (FTFA) would have it, draw their initial interlanguage sentence structure.

Question 6. If on the other hand, there are no functional categories in the initial stages, and the VP is transferred from the native language, draw these same learners' sentence structure.

Question 7. Grüter provides the tree showing how a string such as *Was beisst die Katze* would be analyzed according to the Minimal Trees Hypothesis (MT).

(3)

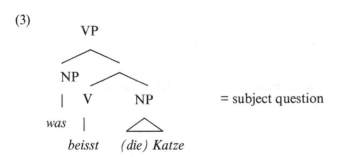

= subject question

Provide the tree for the FTFA analysis. Is a subject or an object interpretation possible? Is an ambiguous interpretation possible?

Question 8. The analysis of the sentence in (1b) *Was hat die Katze gebissen?* under FTFA assumptions is provided below:

(4)

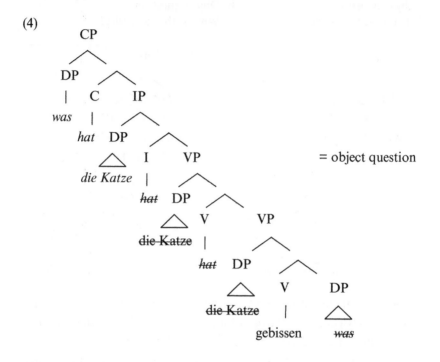

The verb-final structure is difficult to accommodate under the MT analysis of the initial state, see below.

(5)

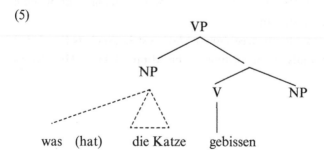

Based on those structures, formulate clear predictions about learner behavior. Fill in the blanks:

According to FTFA, the present tense structure will be interpreted as a
_____ question.

According to MT, the present tense structure will be interpreted as a
_____ question.

According to FTFA, the perfect tense structure will be interpreted as a
_____ question.

According to MT, the perfect tense structure will be interpreted as a
_____ question.

Question 9. Grüter made a special effort to ascertain that the learners were
at the absolute initial state of their German interlanguage. What kind of
data would give us certainty that they are?

Here is what the test participants had to do. They saw the picture in
Figure 8.1, followed by some questions like the one below it. They were
tested one at a time, face-to-face with the researcher.

(6)   Was jagt das Kamel?
       what chase-3SG the camel
       'What is chasing the camel?' / 'What is the camel chasing?'

Question 10. Figures 8.2 and 8.3 present the frequencies of the learner and
native choices. Since the options were two animals (corresponding to a
subject and an object interpretation), both or neither, the percentage choices
add up to 100. Do all the native speakers realize the ambiguity of the

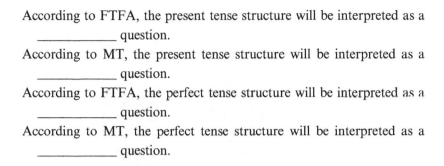

Figure 8.1   Visual stimuli for the interpretation task, from Grüter (2006)
Reproduced with permission from Taylor and Francis

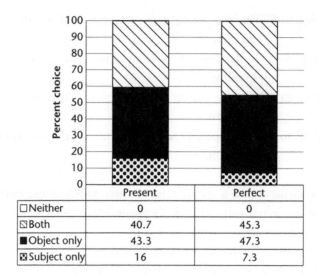

Figure 8.2   Interpretation choices of native speakers, from Grüter (2006)

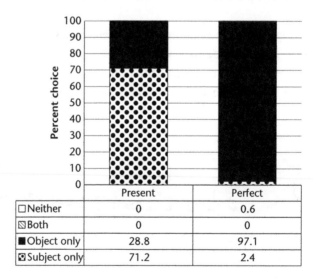

Figure 8.3   Interpretation choices of learners, from Grüter (2006)

questions? Is there a qualitative difference between the natives' choices for the present and the perfect questions?

How about the learners? Is there a qualitative difference between their choices on the two types of questions? Which is the most common interpretation of the present question? Which is the most common interpretation of the perfect question? Which model's predictions, FTFA's or MT's, are supported by these data? Why? Be specific.

Bonus points: What is going on in the mind of the learners (28.8%) who chose only the object interpretation of *Was beisst die Katze?* Which model can accommodate these answers?

Exercise 8.1 (reprise): On a different day, record your judgment of the acceptability of the following sentences. If you find the sentence fully acceptable, choose +2. If you find the sentence less than fully acceptable, choose +1. If, on the other hand, the sentence sounds unacceptable, choose −2. Slightly less unacceptable gets −1. If you cannot offer a judgment, circle "IDK" ("I don't know").

1. What did you say that Maria forgot it when she was leaving home?   −2 −1 1 2   IDK
2. What do teachers insist that pupils should read before the exams?   −2 −1 1 2   IDK
3. Who does Peter think that Mary should meet?   −2 −1 1 2   IDK
4. What has John decided that he should buy for Christmas?   −2 −1 1 2   IDK
5. Who do you think that he met Katerina?   −2 −1 1 2   IDK
6. Who have you suggested that he should not resign?   −2 −1 1 2   IDK
7. What do you think that it makes the book very interesting?   −2 −1 1 2   IDK
8. Who did the students think he would be the best president?   −2 −1 1 2   IDK
9. Who do you think that Susan would marry him?   −2 −1 1 2   IDK
10. What do people think it makes American cinema popular?   −2 −1 1 2   IDK
11. Who did Mary say he wanted to study abroad?   −2 −1 1 2   IDK

12. Who does Kathryn think is a good   −2 −1 1 2 IDK
    painter?
13. Which politician did Jane say he is very −2 −1 1 2 IDK
    honest?
14. Who did John say kissed Susan?   −2 −1 1 2 IDK
15. What did John suggest should be   −2 −1 1 2 IDK
    announced at the meeting?
16. What have you insisted that student   −2 −1 1 2 IDK
    should read it before the exam?

9

Acquisition of the mental lexicon

In Chapter 7 of this textbook, we focused on the functional lexicon (the functional morphology) of L2 learners, arguing that it is of central import-ance to linguistic competence and performance because it contains the features that regulate grammatical meanings and syntactic transformations. In Chapter 8, we went on to describe and explain how learners convert these grammatical features into targetlike syntactic structures and meanings. In this chapter, our attention will be on words more generally speaking. Words are the basic building blocks of sentences that need to be represented and accessed in the mental lexicon when a sentence is comprehended or pro-duced.[1] Word meanings are comprised of their own, idiosyncratic, lexical

---

[1] In discussing the mental lexicon, we talk about bilinguals. As a reminder, in the literature on the mental lexicon, "the term *bilingual* is used to refer to an individual with some competence in at least two languages without regard for the level of second language proficiency, regularity of second language use, or age or context of second

content (*door* is different from *gate*), but also of category features that organize them into classes of words with specific morphosyntactic behavior (both *door* and *gate* are concrete countable nouns, etc.). Words can be composed of several morphemes, some lexical and some functional, and lexical access may depend on that composition. Finally, some words may have literal as well as figurative meanings, which change the meaning of the whole sentence they participate in. In this chapter, I will attempt to provide a comprehensive outline of what we know when we know words and what aspects of that knowledge are easy or hard for L2 speakers.

9.1 Mental representation and access of lexical items

The study of the mental lexicon is one of the most vigorously developing areas of bilingualism. Several important discoveries have been made in the last 30 years that were unexpected from the point of view of our previous assumptions about the way words are organized and accessed in the bilingual and multilingual lexicon. We will see some earlier proposals for that organization, we will then review more recent behavioral data that seem to contradict the earlier models and to support one updated model. Following Dijkstra and van Heuven (2012), we will first discuss the facts about the bilingual lexicon on which most theoretical models agree, and which find support from recent neuroimaging (functional Magnetic Resonance Imaging, fMRI) and electrophysiological (event-related brain potential, ERP) studies. Next, we will discuss some issues on which researchers do not agree yet.

But before we go on to discuss the findings, let me introduce the tasks that are used in studying the mental lexicon. In a *lexical decision task*, participants are shown lexical items in isolation (usually on a computer screen) and asked to decide whether these are legitimate words in a language. In a *semantic task*, they are asked whether words are related in meaning. In a *naming task*, they are shown pictures and asked to come up with a name of an object as quickly and accurately as possible. Reaction times, ERP effects, and blood flow can be measured while research participants are performing

language acquisition" (Tokowicz 2014: 4). Very often in this literature, the term *bilingual* is used to refer to multilingual individuals as well, in the way we described the term in Chapter 5.

these tasks. In a *primed lexical decision*, words can be preceded for a very short time (say, 250 milliseconds) by a certain other word, or part of a word, before the actual lexical decision task is performed. This previous exposure is referred to as "priming." It has been shown that participants are faster to respond to words when they are primed with a semantically related word. For example, participants are faster to confirm that *nurse* is a word of English when primed with *doctor* than when primed with *butter*. In studies using the *visual world paradigm* in eye tracking, an array of objects is presented either physically or on a computer screen, and the individual's eye movements are tracked. These experimental tasks and the measurements they yield allow researchers to ascertain the relations of words and morphemes in the mental lexicon.

9.1.1 Bilingual lexicon representation models

Generally speaking, memory representation models try to describe the way that word forms and meanings are represented in memory, and how the words in the two languages and their meanings are related to each other. One class of models considers two levels of representation within the bilingual memory: that is why they are called "hierarchical." For example, the Revised Hierarchical Model (Kroll and Stewart 1984) postulates that the words of the two languages reside in separate memory systems, but that concepts are stored in a common memory system. The model also proposes that the interconnections between these representation systems, or stores, are asymmetric: L1 words have a stronger connection to the common meaning store than L2 words. Because of this asymmetry between the systems, the so-called *translation equivalents* (words with roughly the same meaning) are crucial in the beginning stages of acquisition. They mediate between the L1 and the L2 at the lexical level, until learners are skilled enough to access the L2 meanings directly.

Another class of models is called "interactive." Prominent among them is the Bilingual Interactive Activation Plus model (BIA+) (Dijkstra and van Heuven 2002), which postulates organization of the mental lexicon on three levels: one level of conceptual representation (the lemma level),[2] a lower

---

[2] Psycholinguists distinguish two separate aspects of the mental lexicon entries, named *lexeme* and *lemma*. The lexeme stores morphological and formal information about a word, such as the different versions of spelling and pronunciation of the word; the lemma

level containing the words, and the lowest level containing orthographic, grammatical, and phonological word features. In accessing a word, orthographic information (for example, if a word is read) activates the orthographic word representation, and activation then spreads to the higher levels of representation.[3] In an earlier instantiation of the model (BIA, van Heuven, Dijkstra, and Grainger 1998), there was a fourth level included, the language node. Since words are connected to the language node to which they belong, the model contains a way for making a language decision (which language am I speaking now?). Use of one word over another can raise the activation of one language while inhibiting the other. Using this mechanism, the model can account for the effects of relative second language proficiency. Later findings made the proponents of the BIA+ model adjust the language node as a task/decision component affected by extra-linguistic factors.

Both the hierarchical and the interactive models assume that the lexicon entries of the two languages are not located in separate parts of the brain but are instead functionally interconnected and have a common conceptual-semantic basis, as discussed below.

9.1.2 The bilingual lexicon is integrated across languages

After several decades of experimental research, it is widely accepted that the lexical items of the different languages in a multilingual individual's brain are integrated and stored together. It is not the case that the lexical items for the L1 and the L2 reside in different areas of the brain, or even in separate stores. This is true for orthographic, phonological, and semantic representations. The implication **from an integrated mental lexicon** is that "lexical representations belonging to different languages affect each other in the same way as representations within a language" (Dijkstra and van Heuven 2012: 453). To use a spatial metaphor, representations are stored closer together the more similar they are, irrespective of the language they belong to. This is true for both phonological and orthographic representations.

---

stores semantic and syntactic information about a word, such as word category and the meaning of the word. Research has shown that the lemma develops first when a word is acquired into a child's vocabulary, the lexeme develops later with repeated exposure.

[3] The model is based on the interactive activation model of McLelland and Rumelhart (1981).

This brain organization has been supported with consistent findings from brain imaging studies. When the degree of L2 proficiency among speakers has been high, and comparable to the L1, the same brain areas have been activated in L1 and L2 processing.[4] The activations found for the L2 were similar, if not identical, with those utilized by the same individuals in L1 lexical item retrieval. Moreover, this happened irrespective of the degree of difference between languages in orthography, phonology, or syntax (Chee, Tan, and Thiel 1999). These findings are also consistent across various tasks: lexical decisions and semantic judgments. As we saw before, at lower proficiency levels, L2 users were utilizing wider areas in the cortex to compensate for the less efficient access. Factors affecting the location of activations, apart from proficiency, are age of acquisition of the second language and (type of) language exposure.

9.1.3 The bilingual lexicon is accessed in a language-independent way

The second important discovery coming from recent research on the mental lexicon has to do with the lexical search and access. To cite the engaging example from Tokowicz (2014: 1), imagine you speak Spanish and English, and your friend asks you in English to hand her one of a few items within your reach. The beginning sound of the word is /k/ and that sound is compatible with a cup and a spoon (*cuchara* in Spanish). What happens next? The question is whether, when we are confronted with a word, we first access the lexicon of one language and then the other, or there is a **parallel search through both/all languages,** words not being organized primarily on the basis of language, but in semantic and phonological fields on the basis of frequency.

The evidence comes on the side of the second option: alternatives in each language are activated when only one language is being read/heard or produced. For example, using the visual world paradigm, Spivey and Marian (1999) and Marian and Spivey (2003) have shown that bilingual listeners look more to the competitor item (the spoon in the example above) than to control items that start with other sounds in Spanish and English. In another example, presenting English words such as *blue* to a Dutch-English bilingual will activate not only other English words such as *clue* and *glue* but

---

[4] These are the left frontal and temporal-parietal areas. For a review, see Abutalebi and Della Rosa (2012).

also Dutch words like *blut* and *blus* (Dijkstra and van Heuven 2002: 454). Such findings suggest that all the available lexicons are briefly activated in the beginning of the lexical search. This view has been dubbed the "language-nonspecific access." The so-called neighborhood effect provides another set of evidence against selective access (van Heuven et al. 1998, Jared and Kroll 2001, Dijkstra 2003): if a word has many "neighbors," words that differ in one letter or sound as in the example above, it will take longer to recognize that word in a lexical decision task. Of course, if a bilingual could access words selectively in one of the two languages, such interference would not surface. It has been determined that neighbors from the second language do increase the reaction times for accessing L1 words, which shouldn't happen if the language stores were separate. These findings have been interpreted to support non-selective access, since lexical items of both languages obviously compete in the activation process.

Neuroimaging studies of interlingual homographs also offer support for language-nonselective access. Interlingual homographs are words that have the same orthography but are separate lexical items with different meaning in the L1 and the L2. One such word is *ramp*: the word has a few meanings in English but in Dutch it means "disaster." Behavioral studies often provide evidence for interference when processing such words. Van Heuven, Schriefers, Dijkstra, and Hagoort (2008) investigated the source of interlingual homograph conflicts with two fMRI experiments. In one experiment, brain responses of Dutch-English bilinguals were examined when performing an English lexical decision task (is this a word of English?). In the other experiment, they were given a generalized Dutch-English task (is this a word?) In both cases, co-activation was expected. However, a conflict should arise only in the English lexical decision task, because a Dutch word in that experiment should be rejected. As expected, imaging showed a response conflict only in the English lexical decision task. In both tasks, co-activation was also established. Evidence from studies using cognates, homophones, and cross-linguistic priming follow a similar logic as in the interlingual homograph studies, and the evidence for non-selective activation of lexical items is overwhelming.

9.1.4 Language exposure and use affects the activation of words in the lexicon

This assertion is hardly surprising. When words are used more often in daily life, hence are more frequent, they become established more strongly in long-term memory and are easier to access when we need them. This is true of words from the native language as well as any subsequent language. Based on that premise, it is logical that relative L2 proficiency, age of acquisition, and language use are all factors that affect accuracy of recognition and speed of access. However, consider that frequency is to some extent relative and individual-based. Even frequent words may be less frequent in the usage pattern of a non-proficient bilingual, and it is this personal frequency that matters in lexical access. Cognitive neuroscientific studies confirm that proficiency affects the activation pattern of the L2 lexical access (relative to the L1 access). We will cite here only one of many studies, Chee, Hon, Lee, and Soon (2001), which established that in making semantic judgments in their L2 English, Chinese participants showed a larger activation area (in the left prefrontal and parietal locations, as well as additional activation in the right inferior frontal gyrus). A general finding of such studies is that more extensive or greater levels of brain activation can be detected in the less proficient language of bilinguals. This is true not only of word processing but more generally of language processing. The more the language is practiced, the more efficient processing becomes.

9.1.5 Language context may not affect bilingual language activation

How do speakers choose the words that they are going to use in a sentence while producing speech? In other words, how does language selection occur? Kroll, Gullifer, and Rossi (2013) review cues for language selection, the most interesting and obvious being the surrounding linguistic context (which language is being spoken). If bilinguals are not very good at language selection when accessing words, we would expect to see pervasive errors in bilinguals' speech, in the form of using lexical items from the other language often and haphazardly. This does not happen on a regular basis, so bilinguals must have a mechanism for overcoming that influence.

However, there is little doubt that this influence exists. For example, Van Asche et al. (2009) reported cognate effects when reading sentences in the native Dutch of English-Dutch bilinguals. Although the sentences appeared only in their native language, there was a persistent effect of English, their L2, on their L1. Such results suggest that even when processing one language, the influence of the other language, or languages, that the bilinguals know remains very much in evidence, and in action. This discovery is particularly surprising when the second language knowledge influences the functioning of the native language. However, that discovery logically leads us to postulate that bilinguals must constantly inhibit one language when speaking the other. Another conclusion is that a great deal of cognitive control is necessary for the lexical performance of a bilingual to be accurate. This last claim leads us to the next section.

9.2 Inhibition of one language to speak another

The third discovery, which is true of language processing in general but was first formulated about and exemplified in the mental lexicon, is that **it is virtually impossible to switch off the language not in use.** The parallel activation of a bilingual's two languages can be observed in reading, listening, and in planning speech (Costa 2005, Dijkstra 2005, Kroll et al. 2006, Marian and Spivey 2003, Schwartz, Kroll, and Diaz, 2007). Thus the main challenge for bilinguals trying to access the vocabulary of one language is actually suppressing the vocabulary of the other language(s) she knows.

Let us look at this inhibition process in more detail. David Green's Inhibitory Control model (Green 1998) was designed to explain how bilinguals regulate and exercise control over which language they speak in. Within the area of the mental lexicon, Green and other researchers (Guo Liu, Misra, and Kroll 2011, Misra, Guo, Bobb, and Kroll 2012, among others) have proposed that there is competition for lexical selection, with candidates from both languages available, and subsequent inhibition of the language not in use. When this language happens to be the stronger or more dominant language, the processing costs of inhibition are greater. Interesting support for this claim comes from language switch costs.

Meuter and Allport (1999) used a task in which bilinguals had to read aloud numerals, and then switch to another language unpredictably, cued by a background color. The researchers established that bilinguals suffer larger switch costs when switching from the L2 to the L1 than in the opposite direction. Although this may seem counterintuitive at first, it is explained by a spillover effect. In order to name objects in the L2, the more available and activated L1 is should be suppressed, and that inhibition spills over into the subsequent naming trial, although the word to be named is in the L1.

Current experimental methods such as ERPs allow us to investigate the course of planning during actual or tacit naming. Compared to the brain imaging methods that monitor blood flow, ERPs are capable of tracking very fast processes, on the order of milliseconds. In this respect, they permit more time-sensitive analyses of ongoing cognitive processes. One such ERP component is the N2, (sometimes also referred to as the N200), which reaches its peak at approximately 300 milliseconds after stimulus onset. Although researchers are not yet in agreement on what the N2 exactly signifies (inhibition of a response or a response conflict), there is relative consensus on its being an index of a control process. According to the Inhibitory Control model (Green 1998, Abutalebi 2008), bilinguals select the words of the language in use by inhibiting the activation of the other language. ERP studies using the switching experimental paradigm found a significant N2 effect for switch trials, hence supported the Inhibitory Control model. Gollan and Ferreira (2009) also supported the model with a voluntary switch paradigm in a naming task, comparing switch trials to single-language trials. The cost to naming times for the voluntary switching condition was greater for the dominant language. Gollan and Ferreira (2009) concluded that inhibition of the first language is a standard part of production in the second language, even for proficient bilinguals.

The competition that is hypothesized to be a result of selecting lexical candidates for production is regulated by a network of brain structures associated with executive function and inhibitory control (e.g., the left prefrontal cortex and the anterior cingulate cortex, ACC). It is precisely this constant inhibition (exercised through executive control) that Bialystok credits with giving bilinguals a cognitive advantage over monolinguals. This constant parallel activity produces changes in the bilingual brain. A recent study, Abutalebi et al (2012) showed that the ACC appears to be changed by bilingualism. When placed in a context where they are expected to monitor conflict, not only do bilinguals outperform monolinguals, but they also appear to need fewer cognitive resources to do it. Bilinguals have also been shown to outperform monolinguals on task switching and ignoring irrelevant information. It could be the case that components of the brain that enable constant monitoring and control of the bilingual functioning spill over more general cognitive functioning. If this is indeed the case, as evidence suggests, there is a big fat cognitive bonus of bilingualism.

Teaching relevance

In this section, we have been discussing lexical access and usage. The results of the studies we reviewed cannot be directly used in language classrooms. However, there is an interesting recent finding in this area that is a dramatic demonstration of the impact teaching a second language has on the brain of even very beginning learners. The seminal study of McLaughlin, Osterhout, and Kim (2004) provides evidence that the brain starts processing and learning at the very first exposure to the second language, and crucially, before any learning is detected in behavior changes. ERPs were recorded at 14, 53, and 138 mean hours of instruction of French to native English speakers. The control group was monolingual. The participants performed a primed lexical decision task. The prime target pairs were either semantically related words (*chien–chat* 'dog–cat'), semantically unrelated words (*chien–table* 'dog–table') or word–nonword pairs (*chien–nasier* 'dog–nasier'). Even after the earliest exposure, 14 hours of French lessons, learners showed a significant modulation of the N400 ERP component, which references lexical semantic processes, although their behavior was the same as that of the non-learners. Thus, this is a positive indication that learners' minds are indeed changing, even if it doesn't appear to be the case in behavior. Even at 14 hours' exposure, learners have already started to build a mental grammar!

In summary, the processes of lexical access seem to be largely similar in first and second language acquisition and use. The areas of the brain utilized in processing also seem to be largely overlapping, and those are the main language-processing areas. Proficiency seems to drive the crucial L1–L2 differences, in the sense that greater engagement of brain areas appear to be related with processing language that is not mastered to a nativelike level. That activity may reflect executive control over access to short-term or long-term memory representations such as grammatical, phonological, or lexical representations. The main idea is that a low-proficient second language will be processed through neural pathways related to controlled processing, that is, with the active engagement of the brain areas related to cognitive control. Such control is necessary to inhibit the stronger or native language when we are speaking a weaker language or a second language. On the other hand, a proficient second language is processed in a more nativelike manner, that is, with a higher degree of automaticity and efficiency.

9.3 Morphological decomposition in the lexicon

We turn to a different topic now, namely, what the processes are that go on within the L2 lexicon itself when we store words in the mental lexicon. At issue is whether words are stored whole, or decomposed into morphemes in storage and assembled online when needed. True to the main focus of this book, we will be mostly interested in the processing of functional morphology. Michael Ullman's Declarative/Procedural model is the one relevant here.[5] The model argues that processing a language, even one's native language, involves two different brain systems: the *declarative and procedural memory systems*. The former is a lexical store of memorized words that depends on our declarative memory, the part of the brain that we use to recall and recite memorized information such as the state and country capitals. The latter is a combinatorial mental grammar that uses productive rules, working with memorized units such as words and morphemes to produce novel but legitimate combinations of these.

The two memory systems are not only functionally separate but also rooted in different brain structures. Given these assumptions, Ullman (2001, 2004) argues that maturational changes occurring during childhood/adolescence lead to the weakening of the procedural and a boost of the declarative system. Thus L2 learning and processing in adulthood are much more dependent on the lexical memory system and not so much on the procedural system, compared to L1 processing. Of course, these claims are not to be taken as categorical. If adult L2 learners could *only* use their declarative memory, they would not be able to produce a single sentence that they had not heard before. (Almost) everything is a matter of degree.

What would Ullman's model predict with respect to how adult L2 learners process functional morphology? Keep in mind that if words are stored in the mental lexicon decomposed into affix and stem, then they have to be composed on the fly, as needed in production or comprehension. Thus morphological decomposition engages the procedural memory system while whole-word lexical storage can be serviced better by the declarative memory system.

---

[5] Michel Paradis's neurolinguistic account of SLA is largely in agreement with Ullman's model (Paradis 2004, 2009).

Whether bilinguals decompose regularly inflected words or not can be studied with a lexical decision and lexical priming tasks. In morphological (not semantic) priming, the prime is morphologically related to the target word and it flashes on the screen for a very short time (e.g., 60ms). If the past participle *work-ed* is primed with the stem *work* and access is facilitated (that is, *faster* as compared to a foil such as *play*), then this is considered evidence for morphological decomposition in the mental lexicon: a part of the word primes the whole. The most popular version of this task uses "masked" priming, where the prime is masked by symbols such as ###### before and after it appears, to diminish the prime's visibility and make its effect over the lexical decision even more automatic and unconscious.

In a series of experiments, Neubauer and Clahsen (2009) investigated lexical access to German participles ending in –*t* (regular) and –*n* (irregular) by German native speakers and very highly proficient Polish learners of German. The lexical decision task uncovered an effect of frequency in both groups: more frequent grammatical forms were recognized more quickly. However, this frequency effect was only attested for the irregular participles but not for the regular participles in the natives. In contrast, learners showed frequency effects for both regular and irregular participles. This outcome suggests that L2 processing relies more on memory storage than L1 processing, supporting Ullman's model. Natives store regular participles in decomposed form (stem and affix), so frequency is not so important for fast lexical access. In contrast, learners presumably store participles whole, without decomposing them into stem and affix. In accessing them, they use declarative memory, and so word frequency is the most important factor for the speed of that access. In the priming tasks of the same study, Neubauer and Clahsen found that the full stem primed the regular participles in natives, but not in learners, in support of the lexical decision findings. Similar findings come from another experiment by Silva and Clahsen (2008), this time from the access of derivationally composed words. In the priming tasks, *bitter* did not prime *BITTER-NESS* in the learners, indicating that they store each word whole and do not decompose.

However, morphological decomposition in bilinguals has been experimentally attested as well. The first study to document decomposition is Diependaele, Duñabeitia, Morris, and Keuleers (2011). It explored morphological processing in a native and nonnative language using derivational relationships (e.g., *walker-WALK*) in a masked priming lexical decision task with semantically transparent and opaque derivational relationships, as well as form-related items. For example, in *walker-WALK*, the derivational relation is transparent, in *corner-CORN* the derivational relationship is opaque; while *freeze-FREE* are only related in form. A group of native English speakers and two groups of Spanish-English bilinguals of varying levels of proficiency participated. Interestingly, results showed similar priming patterns for the native participants and the two groups of bilinguals (i.e., no significant differences in the magnitude of the morphological priming effects). Derived words from a nonnative language were decomposed early and accessed through the constituent morphemes in a fashion similar to that from a native language. In addition, this experimental study suggested that morphological decomposition of polymorphemic words may be an automatic process that does not depend on the proficiency of the reader in the language at stake.

Similar conclusions were reached by other recent studies.[6] Gor and Jackson (2013) set out to challenge the view that L2 learners do not decompose morphology in their mental lexicon. The also used masked priming tasks; their participants were learners of Russian as an L2 at three levels of proficiency. Russian is a morphologically rich language, so it is common for words to contain a root, derivational and inflectional morphemes, in a Russian doll fashion. The example in (1) illustrates the root and the derivational suffix that make up the stem, to which the inflectional morpheme is added.

(1) rabot   – aj   – u   'I work'
     root   suffix inflection

Using regular, semi-regular, and irregular verb forms, the researchers found that morphological decomposition is pervasive and automatic at all three proficiency levels, at least for the outside inflection morphemes. Secondly, bilinguals access the stem representation either directly or by further decomposing the stem into root and suffix. This second stage of lexical processing is gradually acquired by late learners, from productive and less complex stem allomorphs to unproductive and more complex stem allomorphs.

---

[6] De Diego Balaguer et al. (2005), Duñabeitia, Dimitropoulou, Morris and Diependaele (2013), Gor and Jackson (2013), Feldman et al. (2010). See the special issue on recent advances in morphological processing, *Language and Cognitive Processes*, 28, 7, 2013.

Together with the results of the studies mentioned above, Gor and Jackson's findings suggest that L2 speakers do decompose polymorphemic words. Frequency, regularity, morphological richness of the native language, and L2 proficiency are all important factors in this decomposition process. At the same time, there is no doubt that the arc of development is as described by the declarative/procedural model. Learners start from storing whole words, but as proficiency increases, they are capable of using their procedural system more and more. Gor and Jackson (2013:1066) make a very valid point: for some highly inflected languages such as Russian, using only declarative memory to store enough low-frequency inflected words undecomposed may be impractical. Almost immediately after the beginning stage, when L2 learning relies on memorizing whole words and chunks, learners have to start decomposing many inflected words for which they might not yet have whole-word stored representations. The bottom line of this discussion is that, as with almost all linguistic processes, morphological decomposition in the mental lexicon is available to L2 speakers, but it could also depend on the language being acquired.

9.4 Argument structure

In this section, I turn to explorations of lexical semantics acquisition, both from the point of view of generative grammar and of cognitive semantics. The focus will be on cases where there is a lexical semantics mismatch between the native and target language in argument structure. To remind the reader, the array of arguments that is necessary for the expression of a verb meaning is considered its argument structure. Generative studies of lexical semantics explore the relationship between argument structure, lexical meaning, and overt syntax. The theoretical foundation for much of this work is the semantic decomposition of lexical items into primitives or conceptual categories such as Thing, Event, State, Path, Place, Property, Manner, etc. (Jackendoff 1990, Pinker 1989, Grimshaw 1990). For example, the meaning of the verbs *kill* and *break* can be represented as made up of the following semantic primitive concepts (in caps) that are seen as making part of the meaning of other verbs as well:

(2)   kill = CAUSE [BECOME [NOT [alive]]
       break = CAUSE [BECOME [NOT [whole]]

Other theoretical proposals establish concrete linking rules between syntactic positions and thematic roles (Levin and Rappaport Hovav 1995, 2005). Verbs can appear in different configurations with their arguments, and when they do, we call this a syntactic alternation. The sentences in (3) exemplify the so-called *causative–inchoative alternation*.

(3) a. John broke the vase.   (causative)
     b. The vase broke.   (inchoative)

Is the meaning of the verb *break* the same in the two sentences, or does it change slightly? In (3a) the verb appears with an Agent as subject and a Theme as object. However, in (3b) the Theme is linked to subject position. To take another example from the English dative alternation, it may seem that the two syntactic frames that alternate, the double object and the dative, are completely semantically equivalent, but it is not really so.

(4) a. Mary sent John the package.   (Double object syntactic frame)
     b. *Mary sent Chicago the package.
     c. Mary sent the package to John.   (Dative syntactic frame)
     d. Mary sent the package to Chicago.

In the double-object frame exemplified in (4a) and (4b), it is necessary that at the end of the event of sending, the Goal is actually in possession of the Theme, the package. While this is possible in the case of a Goal such as John, it is not possible for a Goal such as the city of Chicago. A city cannot possess a package.

Note that the dative syntactic frame exemplified in (4c) and (4d) might actually confuse the learner of this alternation. Why is Chicago an acceptable Goal in (4d) but not in (4b)? This is because, as linguists have argued, the dative alternation does not have the requirement (constraint) that the Goal should be in possession of the Theme: the latter could have just been sent in the direction of Chicago. In other words, the difference between the two constructions is a matter of the entailment of possession in the double object construction, and lack of such entailment, in the dative construction. The clincher in this line of argument comes from a slight change of meaning. If you imagine that two office workers are talking about a package that has to be sent to the head office of their company, which happens to be in

Chicago, then sentence (4b) becomes acceptable. In that new construal, Chicago stands for the head office, not the city, and presumably there are people in the main office who can be in possession of the package.

Before going forward, discuss the following examples. What is going on here?

(i)   The noise gave Terry a headache.
(ii) * The noise gave a headache to Terry.

Furthermore, it is not the case that every verb that can take a dative argument alternates with a double object construction. For example, the sentence in (5) is unacceptable.

(5)   *Sam pushed Molly the package.

Why is the double object frame available for *send* but not for *push*? Why is the possession entailment available only for the double object construction? To address learnability challenges such as these, Juffs (1996) and Montrul (2001a) have argued that in the mapping from the lexicon to syntax, there is a logical problem for L2 acquisition: L2 learners have to discover the possible mappings between meaning and form in the absence of abundant evidence. Both the patterns exemplified in (4) and in (5) constitute a Poverty of the Stimulus learning situation: superficial analogy between two constructions leads to wrong assumptions about acceptability. There is rarely a one-to-one relationship between syntactic frames and available meanings. Though some mappings may be universal, there is a lot of cross-linguistic variation in this respect. It is very easy to overgeneralize lexical alternations that appear in the native language (thus assume that (5) is acceptable), and it is not obvious how learners can retract from such overgeneralizations. Such research questions inspired a lot of experimental studies in the 1980s and through the early 2000s. Mazurkewich (1984), White (1987), Bley-Vroman and Yoshinaga (1992), and Whong-Barr and Schwartz (2002) studied the dative–double object alternations. Findings of these studies are largely consistent with the claim that L2 learners initially adopt L1 argument structures.

Cross-linguistic differences in conflation patterns (i.e., what primitives of meaning are conflated in a verb) as illustrated by the Chinese and English examples in (6) and (7) were taken up by Juffs (1996) and Inagaki (2001). In English, verbs that express psychological states can appear with a Theme subject and an Experiencer object, as in (6) while in Chinese this usage is not possible, as (7) illustrates.

(6) The book disappointed Mary.

(7) *Nei ben shu shiwang le   Zhang San
     that CL book disappoint PERF Zhang San
     'That book disappointed Zhang San.'

Of course, Chinese can express a similar meaning, but with another, periphrastic, construction (Juffs 1996). However, this gap in argument structures presents difficulties for L2 acquisition: in learning English, Chinese speakers have to learn the availability of constructions such as (6); in learning Chinese, English speakers have to unlearn, preempt, or acquire the fact that (7) is unavailable. Juffs tested Chinese native speakers learning English in China on acceptance and production of psychological, causative, and locative verbs that do not have an equivalent in Chinese. He related these three types of verbs to a lexical conflation parameter: English verbs allow the semantic primitives CAUSE and STATE to be conflated in the same verbal root, while Chinese does not. Results suggest that learners at low to advanced levels of proficiency are sensitive to the conflation pattern of English, having acquired structures unavailable in their native language.

Another study examining conflation differences, Inagaki (2001), is a bidirectional (English to Japanese and Japanese to English) study of motion verbs with Goal PPs. Using the same test in both learning directions, a picture followed by sentences to be judged for appropriateness, Inagaki found that there is evidence for directional differences in acquiring L2 conflation patterns. English learners of Japanese overgeneralize their native pattern, which is unavailable in Japanese, but Japanese learners of English have no trouble learning the new pattern on the basis of positive evidence. While supporting L1 transfer in learning lexical form–meaning mappings, such results also highlight the issue of the availability of negative evidence in L2 acquisition. See Exercise 9.2 for more details of this study.

Unaccusativity presents another subtle semantic difference between classes of verbs that relies on argument structure mapping. Intransitive verbs are verbs that allow only one argument. However, not all intransitive verbs are created equal. Linguistic tests distinguish two classes of intransitive verbs, with different syntactic behavior and subtle differences in meaning. Unaccusative verbs are intransitive verbs whose only argument is a Theme, or underlying object (e.g., *fall, arrive*), while unergative verbs are intransitives with an Agent argument (e.g., *dance, laugh, sneeze*).[7]

(8)   a. John danced.
     b. John danced a jig/a polka/a little dance.

(9)   a. John fell.
     b. *John fell a fall/a nasty fall.

The subject of the unergative verb *dance* is an Agent, that is, in control of the event and causing it. Although the verb is intransitive in (8a), it can also appear with a cognate object, or with names of certain dances, as (8b) illustrates. On the other hand, the only argument of the verb *fall* is a Theme: John undergoes an action that he did not cause. Falling happens *to* you precisely because you are not in control. This analysis is supported by the impossibility of adding more Theme arguments as objects in (9b). The unaccusative–unergative distinction is a universal distinction in the sense that all languages have the two classes of verbs. Moreover, this distinction can be related to verb meaning: unaccusatives express processes that can happen autonomously, spontaneously, without external influence, while unergative verbs express changes which have some (possibly unexpressed) external causer.

Unaccusativity can be syntactically manifested in different ways in different languages. For example, some languages such as German distinguish between these verbs through auxiliary selection: unergatives take the equivalent of *have* and unaccusatives take the equivalent of *be,* when they are used in complex tenses such as the perfect or the *passé composé.* In addition, in French only the participles of unaccusative verbs agree with the subject in gender (13–14).

(10)   Sie **hat** gearbeitet/telefoniert/gekocht/geraucht.   [German]
       she has worked/telephoned/cooked/smoked

---

[7] These names are terms that come from the linguistic literature and may not be meaningful to the reader. They should be remembered as terms.

(11)   Sie **ist** gestorben/alt geworden/runtergefallen/aufgewacht.
       she 'is' died/become old/fallen down/woken up

(12)   Elle **est** mort-**e**   hier.   [French]
       she is   died-FEM yesterday
       'She died yesterday.'

(13)   Elle **a** écrit pendant toute la journée.
       she has written during the whole day
       'She wrote the whole day.'

Hirakawa (1999) tested knowledge of the unaccusativity verb distinction in the interlanguage of Chinese and English native speakers learning Japanese. One of the properties she investigated was whether learners were aware of the fact that combined with different classes of verbs, the adverb *takusan* 'a lot' refers to different arguments. The number sign (#) signals that the interpretation expressed in the sentence is not available.

(14)   Takusan yon-da.   [Japanese]
       a lot   read-PAST
       'Somebody read a lot of things.'
       #'A lot of people read something.'

(15)   Takusan   ason-da.
       a lot   play-PAST
       'Somebody played a lot.'

(16)   Takusan tui-ta.
       a lot   arrive-PAST
       'A lot of people arrived.'

Hirakawa took advantage of a particular property of Japanese: that the overt subject and object can be dropped (if recoverable from context). The reading of (14), a sentence with a transitive verb but no overt argument, is that somebody read a lot of things but not that a lot of people read one thing. This is how we know that *takusan* modifies the underlying object, or Theme argument. The reading of (15) with an unergative verb is along the same lines. However, the meaning of (16) with an unaccusative verb is that a lot of people arrived, not that someone did a lot of arriving. Thus *takusan* modification distinguishes unaccusative and unergative verbs in Japanese. However, recall that the verb distinction itself is universal, only its markers vary across languages (see examples (8)–(16) above). Hirakawa used a Truth Value Judgment Task with pictures to probe underlying linguistic knowledge. Again as in Juffs' and Inagaki's studies, the findings indicated successful acquisition. Those learners who had acquired the meaning of (14) were also accurate on the distinction between (15) and (16). Hirakawa argued that her participants displayed knowledge of deep unaccusativity.

Finally, in a series of studies, Montrul (2000, 2001b) studied acquisition of the causative–inchoative alternation and its relation to inflectional morphology, in L2 Spanish, L2 Turkish, and L2 English. We exemplified the causative–inchoative alternation for English in (3): the verb forms are the same, no matter whether they are in a causative or an inchoative frame. As can be seen from the examples below, in Spanish (17) the inchoative member of the alternation is morphologically marked with a reflexive particle *se*. On the other hand, in Turkish, both members of the alternation can be marked, but with different morphology: causative in (18) and passive in (19). The examples are from Montrul (2000).

(17)   a. El enemigo hundió el barco.
           the enemy   sank   the ship
           'The enemy sank the ship.'

       b. El barco **se**   hundió.
           the ship REFL sank
           'The ship sank.'

(18)   a. Düşman gemi-yi bat-**ır**-mış.
           enemy ship-ACC sink-CAUS-PAST
           'The enemy sank the ship."

       b. Gemi bat-mış.
           ship sink-PAST
           'The ship sank.'

(19)   a. Hırsız pencere-yi   kır-dı.
          thief   window-ACC break-PAST
          'The thief broke the window.'

       b. Pencere kır-ıl-dı.
          window break-PASS-PAST
          'The window broke.'

The gist of Montrul's findings is that acquisition of argument structure alternations crucially depends on the argument-change-signaling morphology. Learners who speak a language where alternations are overtly marked in the morphology (a suffix signaling the causative in Turkish, a clitic signaling the inchoative Spanish) are more sensitive to these alternations in a second language than learners whose native language has no overt morphological reflex of the alternation (English). Such outcomes suggest that overt morphology actually facilitates the acquisition of argument structure alternations, highlighting the logical problem of lexical meaning acquisition in some languages that are poor in such morphology. (And another confirmation that functional morphology is crucial in acquisition.)

Very similar learnability issues have also been studied within the framework of cognitive semantics, that is why we will discuss some of those results, too. Within cognitive semantics, the influential work of Talmy (1991, 2000) has provided inspiration for much L2 acquisition research. Talmy (1991) suggests that languages can be divided into two typological groups depending on how Path of motion is lexicalized: in the verb (verb-framed) or outside the verb (satellite-framed).

(20)   Tama-ga   saka-o   kudaru
       ball-NOM hill-ACC descend
       'The ball descends the slope'

(21)   The ball rolls down the hill.

In (20), a prototypical example from Japanese, the event Path is lexicalized in the verb *kudaru* 'descend.' In (21), a corresponding prototypical example from English, Path is lexicalized in the so-called satellite, the verb particle *down*. The reader should be reminded of a very similar property tested by Inagaki (2001). It is important to note a methodological difference: while generative studies on lexical meaning typically employ experimental methods for assessing comprehension, cognitive semantics studies typically scrutinize language production, either elicited or from corpora. In a series of studies, Cadierno and colleagues[8] investigated this type of lexicalization pattern in L2 English and L2 Spanish by learners speaking typologically similar and typologically different languages. Findings indicate that even though intermediate and advanced L2 learners are generally able to develop the appropriate L2 lexicalization patterns, they still seem to exhibit some L1 transfer effects. In particular, in Cadierno and Robinson (2009), the two groups of learners (Danish-to-English and Japanese-to-English) demonstrated possible successful acquisition, L1 effects, as well as some effects of task complexity. Brown and Gullberg (2010) argue that learning a second language affects the lexicalization pattern employed in the native language, so language transfer is not only unidirectional.

In a corpus-based study, Lemmens and Perez (2010) investigate the use of Dutch posture verbs (equivalents of *stand, lie*, and *sit*) by French learners of Dutch. The authors come to the conclusion that the interlanguage system should be treated as a linguistic system in its own right, and that it shows both errors due to L1 transfer, in this case underuse of posture verbs, as well as errors due to overextension of the pattern that learners have acquired in the target language. Looking at the usage of similar verbs (*put* versus *set/lay*) in speech analysis as well as in gesture, Gullberg (2009) employed an elicited production task of describing placing events that English native learners of Dutch have just seen on video. Their production was video-recorded. Along the lines of Lemmens and Perez, Gullberg also argues that her subjects show some sensitivity to the target semantic patterns of the L2, although they are not targetlike.

In sum, research within cognitive linguistics more often scrutinizes production rather than measures comprehension as generative lexical semantic research does. Nevertheless, both research traditions come to very similar conclusions: lexical semantics presents significant difficulties to L2 learners. This is particularly evident when learners have to restructure their lexical knowledge in such a way as to acquire new markers of verb alternations or new argument structure mappings. However, these difficulties are not insurmountable and successful acquisition is attested in the majority of studies.

---

[8] Cadierno (2004, 2008), Cadierno and Ruiz (2006), Cadierno and Robinson (2009).

9.5 Transfer of reference

At the end of this chapter, I would like to highlight another area of lexical acquisition that has garnered even less research attention than argument structure alternations, but nevertheless may present substantial difficulties to learners. It goes by many names: metonymy,[9] polysemy, figurative language, enriched composition,[10] and transfer of reference.[11] What is involved is a type of implicature, but on a lexical level: what is said is different from what is actually meant. Let's take a classic example from this literature (Jackendoff 1992, Nunberg 1979, 1995).

(22) The ham sandwich wants another coffee.
      [*meaning:* the person contextually associated with a ham sandwich]

Now, this sentence is plainly nonsensical if uttered out of the blue and in just any situation. But if it happens in a diner, and if this is a conversation between two waiters, the sentence suddenly makes sense: they are referring to the person contextually associated with a ham sandwich, maybe because s/he ordered one, or is eating one. Let's consider two more examples:

(23) Ringo was hit in the fender by a truck when he was momentarily
      distracted by a motorcycle.
                        (Nunberg 1995, modified from Jackendoff 1992)
      [*meaning*: the car Ringo was driving]

(24) [One flight attendant to another]:
      Ask seat 19 whether he wants to swap.
                  (Markert and Nissim 2006: 159, British National Corpus)
      [*meaning*: the person sitting in seat 19]

The literal meaning of the underlined phrase, determined by the meanings of the constituent words, is enriched to a pragmatically determined additional meaning given in square brackets under the examples.

Of course, metonymy is a well-established mental process, whereby naming some entity (activity, person, thing, time period, etc.) is interpreted to stand for a related entity. Typical sense substitutions of this sort include the

---

[9] E.g., Lakoff (1987).   [10] Jackendoff (1997).   [11] Nunberg (1979, 1995).

capital for the country's government as in (25), a place name for an event as in (26), and a place name for a typical product (27).

(25)   But it was unclear whether Beijing would meet past UN demands for unrestricted access to [...].

(cited from Markert and Nissim
2006: 159, British National Corpus)

(26)   At the time of Vietnam, increased spending led to inflation and a trade deficit.

(*ibid.* p. 158)

(27)   We drank a nice Bordeaux last night.

The associations underlying such metonymies are lexicalized, and they may feature in the lexicon as co-existing senses of a word meaning—Bordeaux: 1) region of France; 2) type of wine. These are cases of "regular metonymy" because they reflect recurrent, entrenched conceptual mappings such as part for whole, cause for effect, person for role, place for event, etc.

However, metonymies such as the ones illustrated in (22)–(24) cannot be considered lexicalized, although they use the same mental processes. Many of them are produced and comprehended online; that is, they are novel and their interpretation depends on the concrete context of the utterance together with linguistic and pragmatic principles of interpretation. These utterances can be deemed unacceptable if the context in which they are produced is not taken into account, such as in the case of (22). We could consider them "novel" or "productive" metonymy, being mindful of the fact that regular and novel metonymy are not mutually exclusive, but rather two opposites on a cline of metonymy lexicalization.[12]

---

[12] Comprehension of metaphor is an even more productive process. The boundaries between metaphor and metonymy may be blurred; they may also be combined, as the following example suggests. "Sacred cow" is a metaphor, while "the streets of Stockholm" is a metonymy.

(i) The streets of Stockholm are awash with the blood of sacred cows. (The Economist) This sentence refers to the time when the Swedish government decided to privatize and outsource education, health care, and care for the elderly. Note how much cultural and circumstantial knowledge is necessary to interpret the sentence correctly.

What happens when acquiring this lexical process in a second language? Different linguistic approaches agree that metonymy calculation is a universally available mechanism, although it is dependent on conceptual structures, cultural knowledge, and pragmatic routines. We are in familiar territory again: the mechanism is universal, so comprehending metonymic transfer of meaning should be easy for second language learners (once they know the words involved). However, comprehension involves computation over and above mere lexical access, including consideration of the context (sometimes cultural context), so one might expect to see some higher processing costs incurred. Existing research (Rundblad and Annaz 2010) suggests that metonymy comprehension in L1 English develops over time and reaches ceiling around the age of 12. This age of acquisition is considerably later than the ages when functional morphology or syntax are acquired. In an eyetracking study, Frisson and Pickering (2007) looked at the effect of familiarity on the processing of the producer for product regular metonymic pattern. They found that familiar metonyms (e.g., 'read Dickens') were straightforward to process, but unfamiliar metonyms (e.g., 'read Needham') caused processing difficulty unless context made it clear that the metonymic interpretation would be appropriate.

If children do not comprehend metonymy at ceiling until 12, it is a safe bet that L2 learners will also have a steep hill to climb. Among the notable recent studies are Chen and Lai (2011), which looks at Chinese native speakers' awareness of figurative language in L2 English, and Littlemore, Trautman Chen, Koester, and Barnden (2011), looking at nonnative undergraduates at British universities and their comprehension of academic texts. The latter authors analyzed the sources of difficulty and found that, among the expressions composed of words known to the participants, around 40% were metaphoric expressions. Slabakova, Cabrelli Amaro, and Kang (2014) investigated knowledge of regular and novel metonymy by Spanish and Korean learners of English. They discovered that the learners were influenced by their native patterns but the advanced participants were extremely proficient with metonymy calculation, having overcome native biases. Research on metonymy and more generally figurative language comprehension and use in the second language is still scarce, but very needed.

> **Teaching relevance**
>
> Research on figurative language computation suggests that non-compositional meaning enrichment increases the cognitive load of L2 speakers and leads to errors of understanding. It is very possible that these breakdowns of communication remain undetected in language classrooms and even university lecture halls. Furthermore, although the mechanism is universal, different languages use metonymy to different extents and with different frequency. Thirdly, the novel metonymy cases in the Slabakova at al. study were not highly rated by the native speakers, implying that such examples may be rare in the input to learners. All of these factors make it indispensable for teachers to understand the process of transfer of reference/metonymy/figurative language and to be able to expose learners to it.

9.6 Conclusion

The acquisition of the lexicon is under-investigated, from a pedagogical perspective. While we know a lot about how lexical items are stored in the mental lexicon of bilinguals and how they are accessed (sections 9.1 and 9.2), we do not seem to know enough to make the acquisition of a second language lexicon an easier, or at least a more manageable task. Exercise 9.2 contains one example of unnatural sounding learner speech but other examples abound. The research discussed in Section 9.3 goes some way towards addressing the difficulty of the acquisition task, thus making the work of language teachers more effective. This type of research promotes the idea that lexical meanings are composed of smaller semantic primitives, and that there are regular mappings between some of these semantic primitives, theta roles, and syntactic categories (subject, object). If verbs are learned in classes, instead of as chaotic assemblies of unstructured lists, acquisition will be more manageable and more successful. Similarly, exposing learners to regular as well as novel, productive metonymy and figurative language will enrich their linguistic repertoire profitably.

9.7 Exercises

Exercise 9.1. Take a lexical decision task in English. The link below provides three tasks, and you can try them all.

http://www.intro2psycholing.net/experiments/visual/vis_expt_index.php
Here is another type of lexical decision task:
http://psytoolkit.gla.ac.uk/library/ldt/

Exercise 9.2. *Everything is Illuminated* by Jonathan Safran Foer (2002).

Jonathan Safran Foer's debut novel tells the story of a young writer named Jonathan Safran Foer, who travels to Ukraine. The narrative alternates between his voice and that of his Ukrainian translator Alexander Perchov, a young man with a creative use of the English language. In this opening section, Alex introduces himself and prepares to meet his American visitor.

My legal name is Alexander Perchov. But all of my friends dub me Alex, because that is a more flaccid-to-utter version of my legal name. Mother dubs me Alexi-stop-spleening-me!, because I am always spleening her. If you want to know why I am always spleening her, it is because I am always elsewhere with friends, and disseminating so much currency, and performing so many things that can spleen a mother. Father used to dub me Shapka, for the fur hat I would don even in the summer month. He ceased dubbing me that because I ordered him to cease dubbing me that. It sounded boyish to me, and I have always thought of myself as very potent and generative. I have many many girls, believe me, and they all have a different name for me. One dubs me Baby, not because I am a baby, but because she attends to me. Another dubs me All Night. Do you want to know why? I have a girl who dubs me Currency, because I disseminate so much currency around her. She licks my chops for it. I have a miniature brother who dubs me Alli. I do not dig this name very much, but I dig him very much, so OK, I permit him to dub me Alli. As for his name, it is Little Igor, but Father dubs him Clumsy One, because he is always promenading into things. It was only four days previous that he made his eye blue from a mismanagement with a brick wall.

   . . .

   When we found each other, I was very flabbergasted by his appearance. This is an American? I thought. And also, This is a Jew? He was severely short. He wore spectacles and had diminutive hairs which were not split anywhere, but rested on his head like a Shapka. (If I were like Father, I might even have dubbed him Shapka.) He did not appear like either the Americans I had witnessed in magazines, with yellow hairs and muscles, or the Jews from history books, with no hairs and prominent bones. He was wearing nor blue jeans nor the uniform. In truth, he did not look like anything special at all. I was underwhelmed to the maximum.

Extracted from Jonathan Safran Foer's "Everything is Illuminated," published in the US by Penguin and in the UK by Harper Perennial.

Question 1: Why does this monologue sound unnatural in English? Is it because the construction of sentences is unacceptable, or is it that the lexical

items are used in unacceptable combinations? Do you have trouble understanding what the intended message is?

   See an excerpt of the movie (directed by Liev Schreiber) where Jonathan
and Alex meet: https://www.youtube.com/watch?v=id15tjDK3K0.

Question 2: Go through the excerpt and make lists of unacceptable choices
of words and grammatical errors. Which list is longer?

Exercise 9.3. Re-read the discussion of unaccusative and unergative verbs in
the chapter. Then consider the following adjectival uses of perfect participles:

   (i) fallen leaves, sunken ships, wilted lettuce, increased prices, escaped convicts
  (ii) *worked people, *sung children, *dined people, *thought philosophers
 (iii) murdered people, stolen books, destroyed buildings, rebuilt houses

Question 1: Explain informally what the above data may tell us about
adjectival participles. How do the verbs in (i), (ii), and (iii) differ? What
theta role (Agent or Theme) do adjectival participles modify? Do these
examples support what we discussed in the chapter?
Question 2: Make a prediction for the L2 acquisition of these particles.

Exercise 9.4. Consider the three possible learning situations (illustrated
below) in which the L2 input partially fits the L1 grammar.

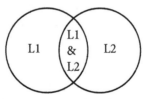

Case A: *Partial overlap between L1 and L2*

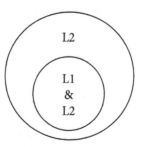

Case B: *Subset L1–superset L2*

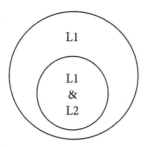

Case C: *Superset L1–subset L2*

Give examples of all three learning situations, numbering and explaining them clearly. (You can use studies discussed in previous chapters and exercises.) You may decide to give examples from argument structure, from syntactic properties, or from morphological properties. A learning principle has been proposed to describe Case B and Case C, it is called the Subset Principle. It states that learning in Case B (expanding the grammar) is easier than in Case C (shrinking the grammar). Use the unavailability of negative evidence in L2 acquisition to explain the Subset Principle. Why doesn't it apply to Case A? In which case is initial L1 transfer expected and why? What would you predict will happen in the later interlanguage development for each situation? Be sure to discuss negative and positive evidence, undergeneralization and overgeneralization.

Exercise 9.5 (do after Exercise 9.4). This exercise is based on the Inagaki (2001) study mentioned in the chapter. Try not to read the study before you tackle all the questions below. We will consider motion verbs with locational/directional PPs in English and Japanese. *Walk* and *run* are considered examples of manner-of-motion verbs while *go* and *come* are directed motion verbs.

(1) a. *John walked to school.*
     b. *John ran into the house.*
     c. *John went to school walking.*
     d. *John went/came into the house running.*

(2) a. ?**John-ga*   *gakkoo-ni*   *aruita.*
        John-NOM   school-at   walked
        'John walked to school.'

b. ?*_John-ga_   _ie-no_   _naka-ni_   _hasitta._
   John-NOM   house-GEN   inside-at   ran
   'John ran into the house.'

c. _John-ga_   _arui-te_   _gakkoo-ni_   _itta._
   John-NOM   walk-GER   school-at   went
   'John went to school walking.'

d. _John-ga_   _hasit-te_   _ie-no_   _naka-ni_   _itta/haitta._
   John-NOM   run-GER   house-GEN   inside-at   went/entered
   'John went into/entered the house running.'

(NOTE: The Japanese examples contain one PP, where both the NP (subject) and the PP are case-marked.)

Question 1: In which of the three cases illustrated in Exercise 9.3 above (A, B, or C) does this argument structure property fall? Which language allows a broader range of motion verbs to appear with a goal PP? Draw a figure similar to the three above to illustrate the learning situation.

There is another contrast between English and Japanese in this domain: In English, manner-of-motion verbs with PPs involving such Ps as _under_, _behind_, and _in_ allow either a locational or a directional reading (3), whereas their Japanese counterparts allow only a locational reading (4).

(3) a. _John swam under the bridge._   (directional/locational)
     b. _John ran behind the wall._   (directional/locational)
     c. _John jumped in the water._   (directional/locational)

(4) a. _John-ga_   _hasi-no_   _sita-de_   _oyoida._   (locational only)
        John-NOM   bridge-GEN   under-at   swam
        'John swam under the bridge.'

     b. _John-ga_   _kabe-no_   _usiro-de_   _hasitta._   (locational only)
        John-NOM   wall-GEN   back-at   ran
        'John ran behind the wall.'

     c. _John-ga_   _puuru-no_   _naka-de_   _tonda._   (locational only)
        John-NOM   pool-GEN   inside-at   jumped
        'John jumped in the pool.'

Question 2: Is there a subset–superset relationship here? Explain and illustrate.

Hypotheses for the study

Question 3: Formulate working hypotheses about the L2 acquisition of these properties by Japanese speakers learning English and English speakers learning Japanese. Explain where your hypotheses stem from. You are asked to use the relevant generative SLA theories and learning principles to formulate the hypotheses.

Participants

A bidirectional study was designed involving two sub-studies, one on Japanese speakers' acquisition of English as a second language (the ESL study) and the other on English speakers' acquisition of Japanese as a second language (the JSL study). Since each participant completed both English and Japanese versions of the experimental tasks, the Japanese participants in the ESL study served as a control group in the JSL study and the English participants in the JSL study served as a control group in the ESL study.

The ESL study compared a group of Japanese-speaking learners of English to a group of English controls. The learner group consisted of 47 first-year university students at Osaka Prefecture University who were majoring in engineering. They were divided into different proficiency levels (low and high intermediate), based on their scores on two sections (grammar and vocabulary) of the Michigan test. The control group consisted of 48 native speakers of English who were undergraduate or graduate students at the University of Hawaii.

The JSL study compared a group of English-speaking learners of Japanese to a group of Japanese controls. The learner group was the same as the control group of 48 English speakers in the ESL study. They were divided into three different proficiency levels (low intermediate, high intermediate, advanced) based on their scores on a proficiency test that was adapted from the Japanese Language Proficiency Test, Level 3. The control group consisted of 47 native speakers of Japanese, who constituted the learner group in the ESL study.

Test Instruments

A written picture-matching task was used for the ESL study. (See Figure 9.1, Inagaki's Appendix A for an example test item. The appendices can be found at the very end of this exercise.) Each test item consisted of an English sentence containing a manner-of-motion verb with a PP that was ambiguous between locational and directional readings. A pair of pictures, one of which showed a directional context and the other a locational context, followed the test sentence. In each picture, there were two objects—an object that moves, or a "figure," and an object with respect to which the figure moves, or the "ground". For example, in Appendix A (Figure 9.1), *Tom* was the figure and *bridge* was the ground. Both the figure and the ground were named in English to make sure that participants were familiar with the vocabulary. Participants were told that all pictures showed situations that took place in the past, and thus that all sentences would be in the past tense. Below each sentence were three options, *1 only*, *2 only*, and *either 1 or 2*. Participants were asked to circle *1 only* if the sentence matched the first picture only, *2 only* if it matched the second picture only, and *either 1 or 2* if it matched either the first or the second picture.

There were eight target items consisting of five manner-of-motion verbs (*walk, run, swim, crawl, jump*) and four prepositions *(in, on, under, behind)*. There were also seven distractors including both ambiguous and unambiguous sentences. To control for possible ordering effects, the test items and distractors were presented in two random orders, with about half of the participants taking one version and the rest the other version. The two pictures within each item were also randomly ordered for the same purpose.

A similar type of picture-matching task was developed for the JSL study. (See Appendix C, Figure 9.3, for an example test item.) Japanese was written in standard Japanese script, a mixture of *kanji* (characters of Chinese origin) and *kana* (the Japanese syllabary). *Kanji* characters were accompanied by *furigana* (a transliteration of *kanji* into *kana*) in order to ensure that participants had no difficulties comprehending the orthographic form of the sentences. Each test item consisted of a Japanese sentence containing a manner-of-motion verb with a PP headed by *de* 'at,' which is unambiguously locational, unlike its English counterpart, which is either locational or directional. In Figure 9.2, Inagaki's Appendix C, the test sentence *Tom-wa hasi-no sita-de aruita* 'Tom walked under the bridge' is followed by directional and locational pictures. Again, the test items and distractors were presented in two random orders, with about half of the participants taking one version and half the other. The two pictures within each item were also randomly ordered.

Question 4: Comment on the study design. In particular, do you find the task appropriate and why? What about the use of distractors and the two orders of the test? Have a look at the test sentences and comment on their number and naturalness. Is there anything in these test instruments that you would do differently? Be critical, and remember that all studies can be improved: no study is perfect.

Results

The ESL Study

Table 9.1 Mean responses by Japanese and English speakers in percentages (Standard Deviations in parentheses)

	Loc. only	Dir. only	Loc./Dir.
Low intermediate	69.92 (21.73)	7.42 (12.24)	22.66 (21.17)
High intermediate	76.67 (19.97)	5.83 (9.29)	17.50 (18.18)
English	25.52 (23.34)	8.33 (16.58)	66.15 (26.16)

Question 5: Illustrate the same results with a figure, using Excel or any other graph-creating software. Do not include the standard deviations in the figure.

A one-way ANOVA (analysis of variance) revealed that within responses of *locational only*, there was a significant effect of proficiency levels, $F(2, 92)=52.11$, $p=.0001$. Scheffé tests revealed that both the low- and high-intermediate Japanese groups differed significantly from the English group ($p = .0001$), but that they did not differ from each other. Furthermore, another one-way ANOVA showed that within responses of *either locational or directional*, there was a significant effect of proficiency levels, $F(2, 92)=44.15$, $p=.0001$, with Scheffé tests revealing significant differences between the English group and both of the two Japanese groups, which did not differ from each other.

Question 6: What do these results indicate with respect to your hypotheses?

Table 9.2 Number of Japanese and English participants answering either directional only or either locational or directional

Frequency of either Dir. only or Loc./Dir. responses (k=8)	Low intermediate (n=32)	High intermediate (n=15)	English (n=48)
0 – 3	24	14	5
4 – 6	8	1	22
7 or 8	0	0	21

We now turn to individual results to see if the group results above indeed reflect how participants of each group performed individually. Table 9.2 presents the number of participants in each group who answered *directional only* or *either locational or directional* a certain number of times. Responses of these two options are combined because what is crucial here is whether or not the participants recognized the directional reading of the target sentences.

Question 7: Describe what we see in Table 9.3. Do these individual results support the group results and why, or why not? Is your hypothesis for the ESL study confirmed or refuted?

The JSL Study

Table 9.3 Mean responses by English and Japanese speakers in percentages (Standard Deviations in parentheses)

	Loc. only	Dir. only	Loc./Dir.
Low intermediate	54.12 (35.19)	23.53 (24.73)	22.35 (22.23)
High intermediate	65.26 (32.55)	15.79 (17.10)	18.95 (28.65)
Advanced	68.33 (39.51)	13.33 (19.70)	18.33 (30.10)
Japanese	92.77 (12.11)	2.55 (7.93)	4.68 (9.52)

Question 8: Illustrate the same results with a figure. Do not include the standard deviations in the figure.

A one-way ANOVA shows that within responses of *locational only*, there was a significant effect of proficiency levels, $F(3, 91)=11.64$, $p=.0001$. Scheffé tests revealed that the control group was significantly different from all the learner groups ($p < .05$), which did not differ from each other. Within responses of *either locational or directional*, there was a significant effect of proficiency levels, $F(3, 91)=4.71$, $p=.0042$, with Scheffé tests revealing that the only significant difference existed between the low intermediate and the control groups ($p < .05$). Within responses of *directional only*, there was a significant effect of proficiency levels, $F(3, 91)=8.85$, $p=.0001$, with Scheffé tests revealing that the low- and high-intermediate groups were significantly different the control group, which did not differ from the advanced group.

Question 9: What do these results indicate with respect to your hypothesis?

Table 9.4 Number of English and Japanese participants answering either directional only or either locational or directional

Frequency of either *Dir. only* or *Loc./Dir.* responses ($k=5$)	Low intermediate ($n=17$)	High intermediate ($n=19$)	Advanced ($n=12$)	Japanese ($n=47$)
0	3	5	6	33
1 or 2	8	8	2	14
3 or 4	3	5	2	0
5	3	1	2	0

Table 9.4 presents the number of participants in each group who answered either *directional only* or *either locational or directional* a certain number of times. Responses of these two options are combined.

Question 10: Describe what we see in Table 9.4. Do these individual results support the group results? Why or why not? Is your hypothesis for the JSL study confirmed or refuted? Explain how, and refer to the data in the tables and figures.

Discussion

Question 11: Discuss the results of the two studies together. What do these results tell us about the learning principle called the Subset Principle and the nature of the input in second language acquisition? Is one of the two learning directions investigated in this study more successful than the other, and why might that be? Conclude by stating the central finding of this study.

Question 12: Discuss what the results of this study tell us about L1 transfer in L2 acquisition. If you think that there is evidence of L1 transfer in the data, discuss how it affects the pace of L2 acquisition (refer to the different proficiency groups).

Question 13: What are the implications of this study for the contemporary theories of adult second language acquisition?

Inagaki's (2006) picture-matching tasks

Appendix A

Example Test Item in the ESL Study

Tom walked under the bridge.

1 only   2 only   either 1 or 2

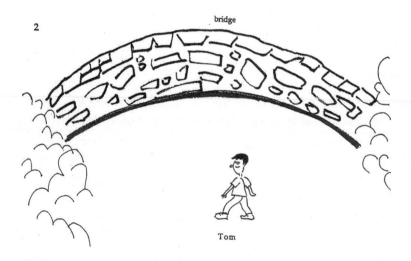

Figure 9.1   Appendix A, from Inagaki (2006)

Reproduced with permission from John Benjamins

Appendix B

Sentences Included in the ESL
Picture-Matching Task

A: Test sentences

1. Jim walked behind the house.
2. Tom walked under the bridge.
3. Ted ran behind the wall.
4. Mary ran on the stage.
5. Peter swam in the cave.
6. The baby crawled under the table.
7. The mouse crawled on the table.
8. Fred jumped in the pool.

B: Distractors

Directional only

1. Sam walked to the beach.
2. John ran into the gym.
3. Paul jumped onto the bed.

Locational only

4. Jim was in the park.
5. John ran at the racetrack.

Ambiguous

6. Tom watched the man with binoculars.
7. John saw fat cats and dogs.

Appendix C

Example Test Item in the JSL Study

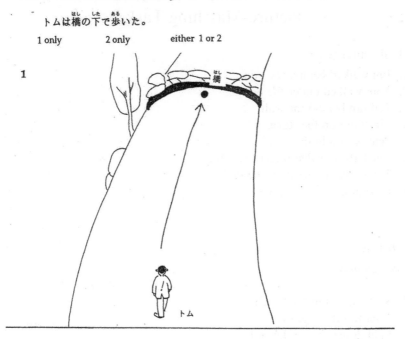

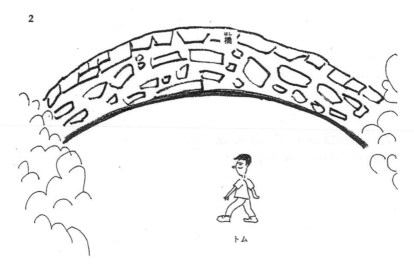

Figure 9.2   Appendix C, from Inagaki (2006)

Reproduced with permission from John Benjamins

Appendix D

Sentences Included in the JSL
Picture-Matching Task

A: Test sentences

1. *Tom-wa   hasi-no   sita-de   aruita.*
   Tom-TOP   bridge-GEN   under-at   walked
   'Tom walked under the bridge.'

2. *John-wa   taiikukan-no   naka-de   hasitta.*
   John-TOP   gym-GEN   in-at   walked
   'John ran in the gym.'

3. *Akachan-wa   ie-no   ura-de   hatta.*
   baby-TOP   house-GEN   behind-at   crawled
   'The baby crawled behind the house.'

4. *Paul-wa   beddo-no   ue-de   tonda.*
   Paul-TOP   bed-GEN   on-at   jumped
   'Paul jumped on the bed.'

5. *Hikoosen-wa   sima-no   ue-de   tonda.*
   blimp-TOP   island-GEN   over-at   flew
   'The blimp flew over the island.'

B: Distractors

Directional only

1. *Sam-wa   hamabe-ni   aruite   itta.*
   Sam-TOP   beach-at   walking   went
   'Sam went to the beach walking.'

2. *Mary-wa   steezi-no   ue-ni   hasitte   agatta.*
   Mary-TOP   stage-GEN   on-at   running   went-up
   'Mary went onto the stage running.'

3. *Peter-wa   dookutu-no   naka-ni   oyoide   haitta.*
   Peter-TOP   cave-GEN   in-ni   swimming   entered
   'Peter entered the cave swimming.'

Ambiguous

4. *Mary-wa   Paul to   Tom-no   otoosan-ni   atta.*
   Mary-TOP   Paul and   Tom-GEN   father-DAT   met
   'Mary met Paul and Mary's father.'

5. *John-wa   Mary-ga   sukidatta.*
   John-TOP   Mary-NOM   loved
   'John loved Mary' or 'John, Mary loved.'

10

Acquisition of the syntax–semantics interface

10.1 Types of meaning

Few people start learning a second language for the exotic sounds, or for the elegant sentence structure that they detect in it. *Meaning* is what we are all after. We would all like to understand and to be able to convey thoughts and feelings and observations in another language the way we do in our native language. Ever since Aristotle, linguists have considered language to be the pairing of form (sound or written strings) and meaning. In this chapter, we examine the road to meaning, that is, how we come to understand and convey meaning in a second language, and where the pitfalls to that may lie.

We will begin by distinguishing between several types of meanings that go in a linguistic message (although some of this will be reinforcement of material from previous chapters):

- lexical
- (phrasal) semantic
- grammatical
- discourse-related
- pragmatic.

For many people, when they think of learning a foreign language, semantics describes predominantly what meanings are encoded in the foreign words. These are lexical meanings. For example, the English *cat* is *gatto* in Italian; both words denote "a small furry animal." The term "denotation" stands for the literal, or primary meaning of a word. It is common to think of these meanings as stored in our mental lexicon and being accessed whenever we need them to use in a sentence we want to produce.

Phrasal, or sentential, semantics is compositional, that is, it is calculated by combining the meanings of all the words in a sentence and taking their order and other rules into account. Take for example the English sentence in (1).

(1)   Cats were exterminated in a cataclysm.

Think about the word "cats" in this sentence as if you hear this sentence as part of a story. What does the word mean? Depending on the context, it may mean that *a number of cats* were exterminated in a specific tragic event in the past, but it can also mean (untruthfully) that *all cats* were affected by a cataclysm and are now extinct like dinosaurs. You can think of stories that would make the two different meanings plausible. Of these two meaning of *cats*, only the first one is available for the equivalent Italian sentence while the second is not (Longobardi 2001).

(2)   Gatti sono stati sterminati da un cataclisma.
      cats   were   exterminated in a cataclysm.
      First meaning: Some (unspecified) number of cats
      Second meaning: Cats in general, all cats
                      (not available in Italian, available in English)

Although *cats* and *gatti* have the same lexical meaning in both languages, when used in a sentence, they give rise to two different meanings in English (*some cats, all cats*), only one meaning in Italian (*some cats*). This difference is captured and explained by the rules for calculating sentence meaning in the two languages, combined with some syntactic rules, and is the research focus of (phrasal) semantics.

Grammatical meaning also comes into consideration in calculating sentential meaning. Consider the two sentences below:

(3)   Jane eats sushi.

(4)   Jane ate sushi.

They contain two identical lexical items (*Jane, sushi*) and the third, the verbal form, encodes a grammatical difference in tense and aspect. We understand that a present habitual (but not an ongoing) event is meant by the utterance in (3) while a past habitual event or a past completed event is a possible reading of (4). As we saw in Chapter 7, grammatical meanings are mostly encoded in inflectional morphology, for example *-ed* for past simple, *-s* for 3rd person singular present simple, etc.

A fourth type of meaning depends on context consideration. It is well known that the neutral English word order is Subject–Verb–Object, as for example in (3). So what are the fronted objects in a sentence like (5) signifying?

(5)   Question: Does Jane like sushi?
      Answer: Sushi, she eats; but sashimi, she adores.

When the object is already mentioned in the discourse, English can front it (move the object before the verb) in a context-dependent operation called "topicalization." The meaning of this fronting is something along the lines of: "If we're talking about sushi, Jane eats it, . . . " The sentence is rendered even more natural by the mentioning of another fronted object, sashimi, in a contrast between the two. Note that the meaning of topic depends on the previous sentence, so it is discourse-related.

Finally, there are sentences in which what a speaker says can fail to be fully meaningful without considering an additional implication: pragmatic meaning. The latter is the object of investigation of linguistic pragmatics. Scalar implicatures are a good example of the dissociation between semantic (or logical) and pragmatic meaning. Consider the following example of a well-known pragmatic inference. When we hear the sentence in (6a) we actually understand that the speaker wants to say something stronger along the lines of (6b).

(6) a. Bonnie ate some of the strawberries.
     b. Bonnie did not eat all of the strawberries.

Notice that the meaning *not all* is not encoded by the speaker's utterance, nor is it part of what the speaker has said. Rather, that interpretation is an assumption inferentially derived by the hearer on the basis of what the speaker has said. Logically speaking, *some* means *some and possibly all*. For pragmatic felicity, however, *some* means *some but not all*. The rationale goes like this: If the speaker wanted to say that *some and possibly all* strawberries are gone, she would have uttered *Bonnie ate (all) the straw-berries*, being maximally informative. Since she did not, she must really mean that there are some strawberries left. Understatements of this sort in human speech are regulated by Gricean maxims, and more specifically, the Maxim of Quantity: Make your contribution as informative as is required; do not make your contribution more informative than is required (Grice 1989). Lexical items that induce such calculations are arranged on a scale: *<some, most, all>*, *<start, finish>*, and so on, where uttering the lower placed item implies that the higher placed item is not true.

Indexical lexical items such as *today, this month*, etc. provide another example of pragmatic meaning. It is common knowledge that the denota-tion of the word *today* changes every day, and so the sentence in (7) will be true if uttered on a Tuesday but false if uttered the next day. Such pragmatic knowledge is truly universal.

(7) Today is Tuesday.

The boundaries between semantic and pragmatic meaning are notori-ously fluid, and debated by many linguists. A rule of thumb is that semantic, compositional meaning is calculated disregarding the context and general knowledge of the world. For example, let us consider the cat example one more time. An English speaker who is able to calculate the two compos-itional meanings in (1) and compare them will also be able to discard the second one as untrue if this person knows that cats do exist in the present day. Thus, the first meaning will be preferred, unless some special context is invoked (such as a fairy tale, or science fiction). That second process (checking the plausibility of an available interpretation against knowledge of the world and the discourse situation) is a pragmatic calculation. Semantics proposes, pragmatics disposes.[1]

Let us further illustrate the various linguistic meanings with the different types of information that is brought from the lexicon, syntax, semantics, and pragmatics and that lead to the calculation of meaning of the sentence in (8).

(8)   Mona likes tea.

An important characteristic of the verb *like* is that its subject is someone (a sentient being) who experiences a feeling, let's call it the Experiencer. Its object is the person, event, or thing that gives rise to the feeling of liking, or a Theme. The noun *tea* in the lexicon is ambiguous between a drink and the dried tea leaves from which the drink is made (think of these two meanings available in the sentence Where is the tea?).[2] However, the sentence in (8) is not really ambiguous, since most hearers would interpret *tea* as the drink. That is, out of the two possible lexical meanings, one is brought forward by the sentence in (8). The agreement marker *-s* carries the grammatical meanings of present tense and habitual aspect (among others). Thus, we know that the feeling of liking is characteristic of Mona in a time period including the present moment. The word order in (8) is neutral. This fact in itself carries information about the type of discourse where the sentence is felicitous, especially when we compare it to the topicalized sentence *Tea, Mona likes* or the focused *TEA Mona likes, not coffee*. Finally, knowledge of pragmatics tells us that the full meaning of the sentence *Mona likes tea* is most likely *Mona likes to drink tea*, as opposed to watching it or driving it. The latter would be unusual or inappropriate actions one does with a drink.

---

[1] The following example, borrowed from David Lodge's *Paradise News,* reinforces the latter point:

'I just met the old Irishman and his son, coming out of the toilet.'
'I wouldn't have thought there was room for the two of them.'
'No silly, I mean *I* was coming out of the toilet. They were waiting.' (1992: 65).

[2] In some parts of the United Kingdom, "tea" can also have a third meaning: "an evening meal."

> **Practice:** Before going any further, try to distinguish the various meanings (lexical, grammatical, semantic, discourse-related, and pragmatic) in the following sentences:
>
> 1. The writer began the book.
> 2. The goat began the book.

10.2 Mismatches at the syntax–semantics interface

All meanings can be conveyed in all languages. This is a notion worth repeating because it is the cornerstone of our approach to second language meaning. All languages can convey all meanings. A concept such as *liking* with its participants the Experiencer and the Theme, grammatical meanings such as present time and habitual action, pragmatic meanings such as topic and focus, and implied meaning are all universal. However, languages may have different rules for encoding these meanings and for putting them together in various morphemes, words, phrases, and word orders. When universal grammatical meanings are captured by different grammatical morphemes, as we shall see in the examples below, it is not enough to just learn the new words and put together the L2 sentences. L2 learners have to do some special restructuring in their grammar.

In this section, we will go through several examples of syntax–semantics mismatches and the studies that investigated the L2 acquisition of these properties. While the content of meaning is the same (concepts and relations between them), different linguistic forms map different natural groupings of meanings. Let us start by illustrating a mismatch at this interface with Spanish and English aspectual tenses. While the English past progressive tense signifies an ongoing event in the past, Spanish Imperfect can have both an ongoing and a habitual interpretation. The English simple past tense, on the other hand, has a one-time completed event interpretation and a habitual interpretation while the Spanish Preterit has only the former.

(9)   a. *Habitual event*
         Guillermo robaba en la calle.
         Guillermo rob-IMP in the street
         'Guillermo habitually robbed (people) in the street.'

b. *One-time completed event*
Guillermo robó   en la calle.
Guillermo rob-PRET in the street
'Guillermo robbed (someone) in the street.'

c. *Ongoing event*
Guillermo robaba a alquien en la calle (cuando llegó la policía)
Guillermo rob-IMP someone in the street (when arrived the police)
'Guillermo was robbing someone in the street when the police arrived.'

(10) a. *Habitual event*
Felix robbed (people) in the street.

b. *One-time completed event*
Felix robbed a person in the street.

c. *Ongoing event*
Felix was robbing a person in the street (when the police arrived).

Thus, the same semantic primitive meanings (ongoing, habitual, and one-time finished event), arguably part of universal conceptual structure, are distributed over different pieces of functional morphology in English and in Spanish. Table 10.1 illustrates the mismatch.

Another example comes from the marking of politeness in languages like German, Bulgarian, and Russian, as opposed to English. German uses the second person plural pronoun *Sie* in situations when the addressee is singular, but the speaker wants to be polite, and employs *du* (you-SG) for all other cases. Bulgarian uses *Vie* 'you-PL' and *ti* 'you-SG' in exactly the same way. English does not reflect this distinction in the morphology of personal pronouns. Again, that does not mean that English speakers have no concept of politeness. They just express it with other means, for example the polite *Sir, Madam,* or *Miss*.

Table 10.1 Mapping between forms and meanings in Spanish and English aspectual tenses

	One-time completed event	Habitual event	Ongoing event
English	past simple		past progressive
Spanish	Preterit	Imperfect	

When learning a second language, speakers are faced with four different acquisition tasks regarding meaning: they have to learn the lexical items of the target language, that is, map linguistic form and lexical meaning one by one. This is certainly a laborious task. Learning the functional morphology is qualitatively different: abstracting away from irregular morphology, once a speaker learns that *-ed* in English encodes a past habit or a past completed event, she can apply this knowledge to all English regular verbs. Sentential and pragmatic meanings are calculated using universal mechanisms of human language. Once the lexical and grammatical meanings are learned, sentential and pragmatic meanings come for free and do not constitute a barrier for acquisition. However, the hardest acquisition situation is when there is a mismatch between which meanings are mapped onto which forms in the native and the second language. In what follows, we will look at some studies investigating such learning situations.

10.3 L2 acquisition of syntax–semantics mismatches

The linguistic properties whose acquisition Slabakova (2003) investigates have to do with grammatical aspect: meanings like ongoing or completed event exemplified in the section above. English differs from German, Romance, and Slavic with respect to the semantics of the present tense. It is well known that the English bare infinitive denotes not only the process part of an event but includes the completion of that event. When talking about *crossing the street,* for example, there is a part of the event which is a process, the walking, and another part which is the completion, taking the last step having crossed the street.

(11)   a. I saw Mary cross the street.   (completion entailed)
      b. I saw Mary crossing the street.   (no completion entailed)

In trying to explain the facts illustrated in (11), many researchers have noticed that English verbal morphology is impoverished. The experimental study adopts Giorgi and Pianesi's (1997) proposal. English verbs such as *cross*, they argue, are "naked" forms that can express several verbal values, such as the bare infinitive, the first and second person singular, and the first, second, and third person plural. Some verbal forms are indistinguishable from nouns. Giorgi and Pianesi (1997) propose that verbs are distinguished in English by being marked in the lexicon with the aspectual feature [+perfective], standing for 'completed.' Thus, children acquiring English can differentiate verbal forms from nouns, since the latter will not have the feature [+perfective].

In Romance, Slavic, and other Germanic languages, on the other hand, all verbal forms have to be inflected for person, number, and tense. Thus, nouns and verbs cannot have identical forms, unlike in English. The Bulgarian verb, for example, is associated with typical verbal inflections, such as person and number, and it is recognizable and learnable as a verb because of these inflections. Bulgarian verbs are therefore not associated with a [+perfective] feature. Consequently, Bulgarian equivalents to bare infinitives do not denote a complete event, as (12) illustrates.

(12)   Ivan vidja Maria da presiča ulicata.   (no completion entailed)
       Ivan saw   Maria to cross   street-DET
       'John saw Mary crossing the street.'

In the acquisition of English by Bulgarian native speakers, then, the learning task is to notice the fact that English inflectional morphology is highly impoverished, lacking many person–number–tense verb endings.

However, this is not all. The attachment of the feature [+perfective] to English eventive verbs would bring along, if Giorgi and Pianesi are correct, knowledge of four different interpretive facts: 1) bare verb forms denote a completed event (as in 11a); 2) present tense has only habitual interpretation (*Jane goes to school in the morning*); 3) the progressive affix is needed for ongoing interpretation of eventive verbs (*Jane is going to school right now*); 4) states in the progressive denote temporary states (*Jane is being stupid*). In contrast, Bulgarian has no progressive tense, and the present simple tense is ambiguous between habitual and ongoing events, characteristic or temporary states.

Practice: Before going any further, discuss these four meanings with other students. You can use these examples or give some others:

1. I heard Mary sing a German aria.
2. Monty repairs cars.
3. Mary is repairing her car.
4. Marilyn is being lazy.
5. Marilyn is lazy.

Which sentences do you predict will be the same in Bulgarian?

All the properties above follow from (or are related to) the presence of the feature [+perfective] on the English verb. Thus the syntax-semantics mismatch is really much wider: a minimal difference between languages—the presence or absence of a feature in the lexicon—leads to various and superficially unconnected interpretive mismatches. All of the meanings that have to be learned are not attested in the native language of the learners. Even more importantly, of the four meanings enumerated above, the second, third, and fourth are introduced, discussed, and drilled in language classrooms. The first one, however, is not explicitly taught.

Let us consider the experimental study now. A hundred and twelve Bulgarian learners of English took part in the experiment, as well as 24 native speaker controls. The learners were divided into groups of low, high-intermediate, and advanced proficiency in English. They were typical classroom-instructed learners. All participants took a production task to make sure they had knowledge of inflectional morphology and a Truth Value Judgment Task with a story in their native language and a test sentence in English. (13) offers an example of a set of four test items. Each story was followed by a single sentence, each story–sentence pair appeared in different places in the test, but I collapse a quadruple here for lack of space. Think about how you would answer if you were taking this test.

(13)   A quadruple testing completed interpretation of English bare verb forms (the construction is known as "perceptual reports": X observed/watched/heard Y Verb)

Matt had an enormous appetite. He was one of those people who could eat a whole cake at one sitting. But these days he is much more careful what he eats. For example, yesterday he bought a chocolate and vanilla ice cream cake, but ate only half of it after dinner. I know, because I was there with him.

      I observed Matt eat a cake.   True   False
      I observed Matt eating a cake. True   False

Alicia is a thin person, but she has an astounding capacity for eating big quantities of food. Once when I was at her house, she took a whole ice cream cake out of the freezer and ate it all. I almost got sick just watching her.

I watched Alicia eat a cake.   True   False
I watched Alicia eating a cake.   True   False

Results on the acquisition of all four semantic properties pattern the same way. On the three instructed properties (habitual interpretation of the present, progressive needed for ongoing interpretation, states in the progressive denote temporary states), the advanced learners are highly accurate. Intermediate learners are more accurate on the habitual presents than on ongoing progressives. Thus, initial L1 transfer and subsequent morphological acquisition are clearly attested in the data.

Figure 10.1 presents the mean accuracy on the untaught construction, perceptual reports. As we can see in the figure, advanced learners are even more accurate (but not significantly so) than native speakers in their knowledge that an English bare verb denotes a complete event, and consequently is incompatible with an incomplete event story (look at first group of columns). This is a meaning that cannot transfer from the L1, as example (12) indicates.

After establishing that it is *possible* to acquire semantic properties in the second language that are not manifested in the native language, let us now turn to the impact of the instruction variable. Slabakova (2003) reports that

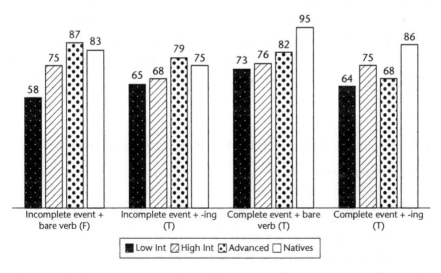

Figure 10.1   Mean accuracy on bare verb versus *-ing* form on perceptual reports in combination with incomplete event or complete event contexts (percent), from Slabakova (2003)

extensive scrutiny of the instruction materials and discussions with the instructors ascertained that the present simple and progressive tense meanings are explicitly taught and drilled from the beginning of classroom instruction. On the other hand, the fact that the bare verb expresses a complete event is not taught, and the Bulgarian teachers are not consciously aware of it. Is it the case that instruction is a significant variable and learners were more accurate on the taught than on untaught properties? The short answer is "no." Statistical analysis on the data for each group, with condition as the sole factor, indicated that all groups perform equally well on all conditions. The theoretical implication of this finding is that all semantic effects of learning the observable trigger (English verbs are morphologically impoverished) and the related property ([+perfective] feature attached to verbs in the lexicon) appear to be engaged at the same time. Even untaught syntax–semantics mismatches are learnable to a nativelike level.

Another learning situation that exemplifies a syntax–semantics mismatch comes from the work of Ionin, Montrul, and colleagues. In a series of studies, they investigated knowledge of genericity and its expressions in English, Spanish, and Brazilian Portuguese. A noun phrase has generic meaning if it refers to the whole class of individuals denoted by the noun (e.g., *Lions are dangerous animals*). A noun phrase has specific meaning if it refers to something or someone that is known to the speaker, and that is noteworthy in some way in the context (e.g., *A student in Semantics cheated on the exam. His name is David.*) (We shall see specificity contrasted with definiteness later on in this chapter, so you will become experts in identifying specific readings.) Take for example the English and Spanish sentences in (14) through (17), all examples following Ionin, Montrul, and Crivos (2013: 485).

(14)   Tigers eat meat.   [√generic reading, ∗specific reading]

(15)   The tigers eat meat.   [∗generic reading, √specific reading]

(16)   ∗Tigres comen carne.
       tigers   eat   meat

(17)   Los   tigres comen carne.   [√generic reading, √specific reading]
       the-PL   tigers eat   meat
       'The tigers eat meat.'

The sentence in (14) describes a characteristic of all tigers (the generic meaning) while the equivalent Spanish sentence in (16) is ungrammatical.

Table 10.2 Mapping between forms and meanings in Spanish and English plural NPs in subject position

	Generic meaning	Specific meaning
English	bare plurals	definite plurals
Spanish	definite plurals	definite plurals

The two superficially similar phrases in (15) and (17) also have different meanings: while the Spanish sentence can refer to all tigers in general as well as tigers made specific by a concrete discourse, the English sentence only has the second meaning. Note that this is a complex syntax–semantics mismatch, in which some of the equivalent NPs are unattested, but others are possible with different meanings. Table 10.2 summarizes the form mismatch within the generic meaning. The fact that there is no mismatch within the specific meaning is potentially misleading, because it can lead to overgeneralizations.

Ionin and Montrul (2010) and Ionin, Montrul, and Crivos (2013) studied this contrast in the acquisition of Spanish and English, using a meaning-focused Truth Value Judgment Task and a more metalinguistic acceptability judgment task. Figure 10.2 provides an example from the TVJT with pictures.

Results of this bidirectional study (Spanish to English and English to Spanish) suggest that acquisition can be quite successful, in the sense that learners were influenced by native language transfer but were also able to retreat from it to attain targetlike interpretations. In addition, learning which types of NPs are ungrammatical in the L2 (such as (16)) proved to be easier than learning all the possible NP interpretations, since accuracy with ungrammaticality was documented at earlier levels of proficiency. In this sense, the authors documented a dissociation between narrow syntax and semantic properties, implying that these two types of knowledge may be developmentally uncoupled. Comparing their own results with findings from Serratrice, Sorace, Filiaci, and Baldo (2009), a study using a different methodology,[3] the researchers note a similarity between the way bilingual

---

[3] Serratrice et al. (2009) used a form-focused, metalinguistic task, in which the children were asked to make judgments about the grammatical acceptability of the sentences (presented in the context of pictures).

Context :
In our zoo, we have two very
unusual tigers. Most tigers eat meat
all the time. But our two tigers are
vegetarian: they love to eat carrots,
and they hate meat.

Test sentence:
The tigers like carrots.   TRUE

Test sentence:
Tigers like carrots.   FALSE

Figure 10.2   Picture and example test items from the Truth Value Judgment Task,
with a bare plural and a definite plural test item, from Ionin and Montrul (2010)
Reproduced with permission from John Wiley & Sons

and monolingual children acquire this semantic paradigm and the way
adults acquire it. Specifically, all three populations have difficulty deciding
which contexts in English are compatible with definite plurals and which
with bare plurals, although targetlike behavior comes with increased age
and proficiency. However, children and adults have to be tested with the
same methods and the same test instrument before any definite conclusions
can be drawn about the causes of the learning difficulty.

Working with very advanced learners and looking at the same definite
and bare plural noun phrases in subject positions, Cuza, Guijarro-Fuentes,
Pires, and Rothman (2013) also document successful L2 Spanish acquisition. Their learners had expanded their grammars to allow definite plurals
to have a generic interpretation, but only half of the learners successfully
uncoupled bare plurals (ungrammatical in subject position in Spanish)

from the generic interpretation. These two studies point to challenging, although ultimately successful, acquisition of this particular mismatch. Future studies of this and similar complex mismatches could involve fresh language combinations and new form–meaning mappings.

10.4 Poverty of the Stimulus learning situations in semantics

Very close in difficulty to syntax–semantics mismatches are Poverty of the Stimulus (POS) situations. These are learning situations in which the linguistic input to learners is purportedly insufficient for language acquisition to take place. These situations exist in child language acquisition as well, but in L2 acquisition they take on additional significance. In most cases, we are dealing with a learning situation as illustrated in Table 10.3, where two related and minimally different sentences differ in available interpretations as shown. Sentence 1 has two meanings, while one of the meanings is not attested for Sentence 2. However, learners have no way of knowing about the absence of one of the meanings in Sentence 2, without negative evidence. Negative evidence refers to explicit instruction on what is ungrammatical in a language, e.g., a teacher saying to the student, "This is not a good way to say X in language Y." Since negative evidence of this sort is almost never offered to learners, the assumption is that the innate language faculty aids the learners through constraining their hypothesis space (the hypotheses they entertain about the meaning of a string). This type of research at the syntax–semantics interface was pioneered by Laurent Dekydtspotter and Rex Sprouse (e.g., Dekydtspotter and Sprouse 2001). We will discuss two such studies with variations of the learning tasks in what follows.

A perfect illustration of the learning situation in Table 10.3 is provided by the experimental studies reported in Slabakova and Montrul (2002, 2003) and Montrul and Slabakova (2002, 2003). These studies investigated knowledge of viewpoint aspectual contrasts in Spanish-English interlanguage. One of the conditions in the Truth Value Judgment Task was related to a

Table 10.3 Mapping of sentence strings and meanings in a POS learning situation

	Meaning 1	Meaning 2
Test sentence 1	✓	✓
Test sentence 2	✓	✗ !

POS property: the two interpretations of impersonal subjects as illustrated in (18) and (19) below.

(18) *Se   comía   bien en casa de la abuela.*
      se   eat-IMP   well in house of the grandmother
      'One/We would eat well at grandma's.'
                        se = la gente en general 'people in general' (generic)
                        se = nosotros 'we' (specific)

(19) *Se   comió   bien en casa de la abuela.*
      se   eat-PRET   well in house of the grandmother
      'We ate well at grandma's.'
                        se = #la gente en general 'people' (#generic)
                        se = nosotros 'we' (specific)

Notice how similar these sentences are: they differ just in the verbal tense. While the impersonal subject *se* in sentences with the imperfect tense can be interpreted both generically and specifically, the impersonal subject in preterit sentences has only the latter interpretation. Since impersonal subject meanings are not taught in language classrooms, and since knowledge of the absence of one interpretation (out of a possible two) has to be acquired, the authors argued that this is indeed a POS learning situation. They found that advanced learners were over 85% accurate in judging these interpretations, including the lack of one interpretation. The correct knowledge started to emerge even among intermediate learners.

The second study exemplifying a semantic POS, Marsden (2009), looks at the acquisition of distributive quantifiers in L2 Japanese by English and Korean native speakers. Sentences with quantifiers such as *some(one)* and *every(one)* provide the clearest evidence for the fact that some meanings are calculated with movement of the arguments but covert movement, movement that is not visible to the eye. Let's start with English. The sentence in (20) has two possible interpretations.

(20) Someone read every book.

One interpretation is that there is *some person, call her X, who read every book.* In this construal, we have one person and many books. On the other interpretation, which you may have to work harder to get, there are many books and many people: *for each book Y, there was some person or other who read that book Y*. Notice that in the paraphrasing of the latter construal, the object has moved (linguists say, taken scope) over the subject. But this movement of the object happens only in our heads, for the purposes of interpretation, while the original sentence stays the same. It just has two possible meanings.

Now, recall the linguistic transformation called "scrambling," we saw some German scrambled sentences in Chapter 8 (and they reminded us of scrambled eggs). English is averse to scrambling while Japanese and Korean, exemplified below, allow it.

(21) a. Japanese: Dareka-ga   dono hon-mo   yonda.   (SOV)
          Korean: Nwukwunka-ka enu chayk-ina   ilkessta.
                    someone-NOM every book   read
                    'Someone read every book.'

Interpretation: There is some person X, such that X read every book.

      b. Japanese: Dono hon-mo dareka-ga   yonda.   (OSV)
          Korean: Enu chayk-ina nwukwunka-ka ilkessta.
                    every book someone-NOM   read
                    'Someone read every book. (scrambled)'

Interpretations: There is some person X, such that X read every book.
                For each book Y, some person or other read Y.

In (21a), we have the nonscrambled SOV sentences in Japanese and Korean, and you can notice that they have only one of the two English interpretations. In (21b), the scrambled OSV sentence has both interpretations. Note how this learning situation is very close to the form–meaning mapping illustrated in Table 10.3: two very close strings, produced through a common transformation, scrambling, do not have the same interpretations. The missing interpretation will never be exemplified in input to learners (because it is missing), so how can they learn that the string in (21a) has only one interpretation? This is the Poverty of the Stimulus learning situation that Marsden investigated. In her design, the two learner groups are predicted to behave differently. Korean learners of Japanese should have smooth sailing, since their native language works the same way as the target language. The

English native speakers, on the other hand, will have the hard task of rejecting one interpretation to the canonical word order sentence that their native language makes available. It is a bonus that three native speaker groups (Japanese, Korean, and English) were included in this experimental study, which confirmed the semantics literature claims about these languages' quantifier interactions.

During the experiment, two pictures (as in Figure 10.3) were shown to the participants one after the other for 10 seconds. Then the written sentence was revealed, and at the same time, an audio recording of the sentence was played. "Presenting the picture (that is to say, the interpretation) before the sentence was intended to reduce the possibility of participants determining their own interpretation of each sentence, then rejecting any picture–sentence pairings—possible or not—that did not match their preconceived idea" (Marsden 2009: 144–5).

In the picture on the left in Figure 10.3, one person is stroking every cat, while in the picture on the right, each cat is enjoying the attention of its own stroking person.

The results from the Korean learners confirmed the hypothesis of L1 transfer in the realm of semantics. The judgments of the English native speakers and the English native learners of Japanese were of most interest. Confirming previous findings (Kurtzman and MacDonald 1993), the English native speakers accepted the object wide scope sentences, the second construal of (20), less readily than the first construal, with 67.5% versus

S>O scope picture   O>S scope picture

Figure 10.3 Two pictures illustrating TVJT meanings, from Marsden (2009)

98%, a statistically significant difference. With such high variability in native judgments, Marsden looked carefully at individual results to identify speakers with consistent evaluations. The most significant finding was that half of the advanced English learners consistently rejected the object high scope of Japanese sentences as in (21a), as expected. Since POS by definition entails that there is no overt evidence for the knowledge acquired (unavailability of some interpretation), these learners' knowledge must arise from internal mechanisms, namely, Universal Grammar. The careful design of this study provides convincing evidence that UG is accessible in second language acquisition, even in investigating interpretations that are shaky and prone to individual variation in the learners' native language.

> **Practice:** Before going any further, discuss the differences between syntax–semantics mismatches and POS learning situations. Is there any indication of which one is more difficult to acquire?

10.5 Meaning of novel constructions

This section will present another learning situation studied in second language acquisition, mainly in the work of Laurent Dekydtspotter, Rex Sprouse, and their students at Indiana University. When the second language makes available a syntactic construction whose equivalent does not exist in the native language, learners' first task is to acquire the syntax of the new construction. However, after the construction is learned, all the semantic effects that follow from it will be part of the learners' grammar. As an example, we shall examine interpretations of discontinuous interrogatives, as studied by Dekydtspotter and Sprouse (2001). Consider the examples in (22) and (23) and compare the *wh*-phrases in them. In (22), the whole *wh*-phrase has moved to the beginning of the clause, but the one in (23) has split: the qualifying PP *de célèbre* is left in the verb phrase and you see it below the verb. This one is the discontinuous interrogative.

(22) *Qui de célèbre fumait au bistro dans les années 70?*
       Who of famous smoked in the bar in the 70s?
       'Which famous person smoked in bars in the 70s?'

(23)   *Qui fumait **de célèbre** au bistro dans les années 70?*
         Who smoked of famous in the bar in the 70s?
         'Which famous person smoked in bars in the 70s?'

Both of these sentences are possible sentences in French; however, their meaning is not exactly identical. A possible answer to the question in (22) may involve a person who is currently famous but was not famous in the 70s, say, the US media celebrity Oprah Winfrey, or a person who was a celebrity in the 70s, say, the soul and blues singer Al Green.[4] On the other hand, it is impossible to answer the discontinuous interrogative as in (23) with a present celebrity. Only someone who was a celebrity in the past is the appropriate answer.

Without going into the details of the syntactic analysis, the two interpretations depend on where the adjectival phrase *de célèbre* is interpreted in the structure: below or above the tense morpheme. In (22) the adjective is above the tense morpheme on the verb, so a past or present celebrity would fit the bill. In (23) the adjective is below the past tense marker in the structure (in its power, so to say), and only someone who was famous in the past would be the appropriate answer.

What kind of knowledge must an L2 learner have in order to be aware of both interpretations in the case of continuous *wh*-phrases but only one interpretation in the case of discontinuous ones? First, knowledge of overt *wh*-movement is required. It relies on properties of *wh*-words encoded in the functional lexicon, but such knowledge can be transferred from the native language in English-French interlanguage, since both English and French exhibit *wh*-movement. Second, knowledge that discontinuous interrogatives are allowed in French is necessary. This property is not taught in French classrooms (Dekydtspotter and Sprouse 2001) but was given to the participants of the experiment in the form of the test sentences (assuming they did not believe that the researchers had tricked them into judging ungrammatical sentences). Third, the (not taught) language-specific knowledge that French allows the *wh*-word *qui* 'who' to have an adjectival restriction at

---

[4] I am aware that this example depends on time-sensitive cultural knowledge. For the purposes of this example, assume that Oprah Winfrey was not famous in the 70s but is now famous as an actor as well as a media personality; Al Green was a famous soul and blues star in the 70s although young people may not have heard of him today. Both are amazing artists, as viewing their performances on YouTube can ascertain.

all is necessary, while English *who famous* and *who of famous* are not legitimate phrases. Most importantly, however, what Dekydtspotter and Sprouse labeled *the universal deductive procedure* is indispensable for reaching the interpretive knowledge. The authors make a convincing case for the interpretations not being learnable on the basis of input alone and not transferable from English, making this another POS situation.

The task of the participants was to read a paragraph-length context in English (the native language of the learners) matched with a test question-and-answer pair in French, the target language. After each story and Q–A pair, the participants had to indicate whether that was the correct answer to the question in the context of the story. They were not asked to judge the acceptability of the question strings, just the appropriateness of the answer. Dekydtspotter and Sprouse were the pioneers this type of design. I have changed the example story a little to accord with my examples of famous people.

(24)   Example context and test quadruple, after Dekydtspotter and Sprouse (2001)

Attitudes toward smoking have changed drastically since the 1970s. In the 70s, many people would go to bars and smoke every night. For example, Al Green was a famous star in those days and was often seen at bars smoking with Oprah Winfrey, who was then totally unknown. How times have changed! Now it is Oprah Winfrey who is famous, and neither of them smokes anymore!

Continuous interrogative with past time answer:
    Mme Goyette: *Qui de célèbre fumait – dans le bistro – pendant les années 70?*
    Élève: *Al Green.*

Continuous interrogative with speech time answer:
    Mme Goyette: *Qui de célèbre fumait – dans le bistro – pendant les années 70?*
    Élève: *Oprah Winfrey.*

Discontinuous interrogative with past time answer:
    Mme Goyette: *Qui fumait de célèbre – dans le bistro – pendant les années 70?*
    Élève: *Al Green.*

Discontinuous interrogative with speech time answer:

> Mme Goyette: *Qui fumait de célèbre – dans le bistro – pendant les*
> *années 70?*
> Élève: *Oprah Winfrey.*

Question for respondents on all items:
Is this a correct answer to the question?

The results reveal that past-time readings were preferred for continuous and discontinuous interrogatives by natives and learners alike. In this respect, learners followed the native pattern. It is knowledge of the unavailable interpretation, namely, the speech-time reading (in example (23), someone who is a celebrity at present) with discontinuous interrogatives that is crucial in answering the research question of this study. Both intermediate and advanced learners demonstrated a statistically significant difference in their acceptance of the available and the unavailable interpretations, in the expected direction. In other words, they reliably treated the two constructions differently.

Learners were capable of successfully combining the properties related to the French functional lexicon—the availability of *wh*-movement and discontinuous interrogatives—with the universal meaning-calculating algorithm. Even not very proficient L2 learners, in this case learners with as little as three semesters of exposure to French, manifested knowledge depending on this universal algorithm. It is no small achievement on the part of the learners that even with infrequent strings or subtle interpretations and under severe POS, they manage to exhibit the contrasts we expect based on the respective syntactic structures and the universal meaning computation procedure. Let me reiterate that meanings that obtain as a result of two possible derivations of the syntactic construction, such as present and past readings of the adjectival restriction (a present celebrity and a past celebrity) follow from the normal compositional-semantic calculation of the two available structures. Once learners are aware of the syntactic structures, the two meanings come for free. The case will be made in this book that in such learning situations, it is the syntax that has to come first while the semantics will inevitably follow, hence there is no need to teach it (see Chapter 13).

10.6 Conjuring up something from nothing

A special type of learning situation concerning meaning is the case when a grammatical conceptual meaning such as definiteness is captured by dedicated morphemes in the L2 but presented by a variety of means, including lexical items, aspectual prefixes, word order, and context in the native language. This particularly difficult task will be illustrated with the work of Ionin, Ko, and Wexler (2004) on Russian and Korean native speakers acquiring definite articles in English. These authors argue that the acquisition of articles is regulated by a semantic parameter, and that the patterns of learner accuracy in definite and specific contexts support the conclusion that learners are setting a parameter value. Another way of conceptualizing the learning task in Russian-English interlanguage is to think of one-to-many mapping: there is one way of signaling definiteness in English but many ways in Russian, including fixing definiteness values through the context.

It is well known that speakers of a language without articles (e.g., Japanese, Chinese, Korean, Russian) have a hard time using articles correctly in English. A number of experimental studies[5] have identified two types of errors these learners make: they either omit articles altogether or use them in inappropriate contexts. While these studies identified the error pattern in definite article use and linked it to the specificity of the nominal phrase in the target language, they offered no principled explanation as to why L2 learners' choices should be affected by specificity. A series of recent studies, starting from Ionin (2003) and Ionin, Ko, and Wexler (2004), provide a principled, parameter-based explanation of learner article interpretation and use. Before looking at the learning task and the syntax–semantics mismatch, let us go over some informal definitions of definiteness and specificity, following Ionin, Ko, and Wexler (2004).

Definiteness and specificity are semantic features; both are part of the conceptual arsenal of language. They are also discourse-related since they rely on the knowledge of the speaker and the hearer in a communication situation. By using a definite nominal phrase, a speaker refers to a uniquely identified individual in the mind of the speaker and the hearer. Definiteness is morphologically encoded by *the*; indefiniteness is encoded by *a(n)* for

---

[5] E.g., Huebner (1983), Robertson (2000), Thomas (1989).

singular count nouns and by the zero article for plural nouns (e.g., *a car–cars*). Uniqueness can be established either by prior mention, or by shared knowledge. Take (25) for example.

(25)   Julie saw <u>a car</u> in the driveway. <u>The car</u> was red and shiny.

Since the first mention of the object (the car) does not satisfy the presupposition of uniqueness in the mind of the speaker and the hearer, it is indefinite and marked with *a*. At the second mention, the object is already established in the discourse as known to the speaker and the hearer, hence it is definite and marked with *the*. An object need not be mentioned in the discourse immediately preceding the definite noun phrase if it is known to both the speaker and the hearer. The example in (26) is an out-of-the-blue statement between a husband and wife who have ordered a computer repair person to visit their home:

(26)   <u>The computer guy</u> is coming at 10. Can you stay at home to meet him?

Specificity also reflects the property of uniqueness, an object or person being activated in the mind, but only of the speaker, not of the hearer. A specific nominal phrase has to be noteworthy in some discourse-related way. Specificity is not marked morphologically in standard English; that is, both indefinite and definite nominal phrases can be specific or not, as the examples in (27) illustrate. Examples (27c,d) are from Ionin, Ko, and Wexler (2004), their (9a,b).

(27)   a. Jill wants to marry <u>a Canadian</u>. She is going to present <u>him</u> to her family at Christmas. (indefinite specific)
       b. Jill wants to marry <u>a Canadian</u>, but she has not met one yet. (indefinite nonspecific)
       c. I want to speak to <u>the winner</u> of today's race—she is my best friend! (definite specific)
       d. I want to speak to <u>the winner</u> of today's race—whoever that is; I'm writing a story about this race for the newspaper. (definite nonspecific)

Colloquial English does have a marker of specificity, the demonstrative *this*, but its usage is optional and colloquial, see (28).

(28) I saw a/this kitty in the pet shop, and I want to buy her for my
      daughter.

When speakers of a language without articles have to acquire articles in
English, their learning task is to map the semantic feature definiteness onto
its morphological expression *the*, and the lack of it to *a(n)* in singulars or
zero article in plurals. Note that in article-less languages definiteness is
established through context and other linguistic means such as demonstrative pronouns but does not have dedicated morphology. Thus, the semantic
feature definiteness is not new to the learners, but its morphological expression is new. The two semantic features, specificity and definiteness, are
somewhat close in meaning, having to do with establishing uniqueness of
an object in the discourse. It is not inconceivable, then, for learners to use
both features in semantically bootstrapping themselves into the morphology. However, Ionin (2003) and Ionin, Ko, and Wexler (2004) go one
step further and propose the Article Choice Parameter as in (29), a principled explanation of how languages choose which feature their articles
reflect.

(29) A language that has two articles distinguishes them as follows:
      The definiteness setting: Articles are distinguished on the basis of
      definiteness (exemplified in English)
      The specificity setting: Articles are distinguished on the basis of
      specificity (exemplified in Samoan)

Cross-linguistic evidence for this semantic parameter comes mainly from
Samoan, a language that purportedly uses the article *le* with specific nominal phrases and the article *se* with nonspecific ones, regardless of definiteness. Based on the Article Choice Parameter, Ionin, Ko, and Wexler (2004)
predicted that learners of English from article-less languages would fluctu-
ate between the different settings of the UG-supplied semantic parameter
until the input leads them to the target value (definiteness). Their native
language would not aid them in this choice since it distinguishes both
features, but none of them morphologically. Table 10.4 summarizes these
predictions.
    Ionin, Ko, and Wexler tested beginning, intermediate, and advanced
learners of English with Russian or Korean as their native languages.
They employed a forced-choice elicitation task and a production task. The

Table 10.4 Predictions for article choice in L2 English by learners whose L1 lacks articles

	Definite NP (Target *the*)	**Indefinite NP (Target *a*)**
Specific NP	Correct use of *the*	Overuse of *the*
Nonspecific NP	Overuse of *a*	Correct use of *a*

forced-choice elicitation task included short dialogs for context, the test sentences were part of the dialogs as in (30).

(30)   Definite nonspecific context:
  Conversation between a police officer and a reporter:
  Reporter: *Several days ago, Mr. James Peterson, a famous politician, was murdered! Are you investigating his murder?*
  Police officer: *Yes, we are trying to find (a, the, ___) murderer of Mr. Peterson, but we still don't know who he is.*

We will look at the results of the elicitation task from the intermediate and advanced Russian learners only. The Korean learners were much more accurate than the Russian learners and did not exhibit the expected fluctuation pattern as clearly as the Russians, since they were performing at ceiling. Table 10.5, adapted from Ionin, Ko, and Wexler's Table 12, indicates the Russian group results. The percentages in the cells do not add to 100 because article omissions are excluded. Compare Tables 10.4 and 10.5. As the group results in Table 10.5 show, the predictions of the Article Choice Parameter were supported indeed. Learners' behavior was not random, their choice of article was significantly affected by the specificity of the nominal phrase. Compare the choices of articles when the target is definite: the learners choose the definite article more often when the noun phrase is specific. The opposite is true when the target is indefinite.

The Article Choice Parameter and the related fluctuation prediction turn out to be a principled explanation of learners' ostensibly erratic, but actually predictable article choice. In addition, it is an eminently testable hypothesis. Moreover, as more English L2 groups are being tested from different languages without articles, some interesting variation is uncovered. For example, the presence of classifiers in Chinese may be aiding the learners in acquiring English articles, while the presence of demonstrative pronouns (which are specificity and deixis markers) is not aiding Polish and Russian

Table 10.5 Percentage use of articles in different contexts by Russian L2 learners of English

	Definite NP (Target *the*)	**Indefinite NP (Target *a*)**
Specific NP	79% *the*, 8% *a*	**36% *the*, 54% *a***
Nonspecific NP	**57% *the*, 33% *a***	7% *the*, 84% *a*

learners in a similar way. However, the main conclusion remains that, even though the learners cannot transfer any morphology knowledge from their native languages, the universal semantics helps them to bootstrap themselves into language-specific morphological expressions of definiteness. I have to add that there are other accounts (e.g., Trenkic 2008) of L2 article difficulty, but the Article Choice Parameter has gained currency and support from replications.[6]

10.7 Conclusions

We saw several learning situations in this chapter related to the acquisition of some meaning coupled with some form. In the POS situation, two sentences in the target language seem very similar in form; however, one of them is ambiguous while the other is not. By definition, this configuration of form–meaning mappings cannot be acquired without negative evidence. In a syntax–semantics mismatch, similar forms and meanings exist in both the L1 and the L2; however, they are misaligned (see Table 10.1). In principle, positive evidence should be sufficient for acquiring such mismatches, but in practice they create difficulty for learners because the native form–

[6] Ionin, Zubizarreta, and Philippov (2009) modified the original Fluctuation Hypothesis proposed in Ionin et al. (2004). New linguistic research (Fuli 2007, Tryzna 2009) has showed that instead of distinguishing between articles based on specificity and not on definiteness, Samoan distinguishes specificity, but within indefinites only. Since the universal specificity distinction is only demonstrated within a part of the article space, children and adult L2 learners are expected to be overusing *the* with specific indefinites, but not overuse *a* with nonspecific definites. Ionin et al. (2009) argue that only specificity-related errors with indefinites, not specificity-related errors with definites, reflect L2-learners' access to the semantic universal of specificity. Their revised proposal was anticipated in some of the results from Ionin et al. (2004) and receives support from further findings with L1-Russian children acquiring English.

meaning mapping is securely entrenched. Thirdly, in situations where the syntax maps onto interpretations in a regular fashion (while both are unavailable in the L1), the universal semantic computation mechanism can be employed and acquisition does not seem problematic. Finally, functional elements such as articles that can potentially encode two meanings cross-linguistically (definiteness and specificity) are a big challenge. If the native language does not encode either of these meanings with overt and dedicated morphology, then choosing between the two meanings for L2 articles may take considerable exposure to input and practice. I should add that article meaning is acknowledged as an extremely difficult area of L2 acquisition, possibly because article-less languages have other means of expressing specificity and definiteness (such as topic and focus, word order, demonstratives, etc.). If we look at the learning task in this way, acquiring article semantics turns into a syntax–semantics mismatch and involves (semantic) feature reassembly.[7]

10.8 Exercises

Exercise 10.1. Describe the differences represented in the examples below as syntax–semantics mismatches:

Temporal morphology in Italian and Portuguese (Giorgi and Pianesi 1997: 50)

(i)   a. *Ho mangiato alle quattro.*   Italian
           have.SG eaten at four
           'I have eaten at four (e.g., once before/all my life).'

      b. *Mangiai alle quattro.*
           ate.SG at four
           'I ate at four.'

(ii)   a. *Comi as quatro.*   Portuguese
           ate.SG at four
           'I have eaten at four (e.g., once before/all my life) / I ate at four.'

---

[7] See Cho and Slabakova (2014) for discussion.

b. *Tenho comido as quatro.*
    have.SG eaten at four
    'I took the habit of eating at four'

How would you describe this mismatch? Pay attention to the forms of the main verb and the auxiliary *have* on the second line of the examples, the gloss, and then compare the meanings given in the translations on the third line of each example.
Tense in Mandarin Chinese and English:

(iii) *Zhang San zhù zài zhèr.*
       Zhang San live at here
       'Zhang San lives here.'

(iv) *Zhang San 1989 nián zhù zài zhèr.*
       Zhang San 1989 year live at here
       'Zhang San lived here in 1989.'

Now examine another mismatch as in (iii) and (iv) and compare the Mandarin verb form with the English verb form in the translations of the Chinese examples. How do we know which Chinese sentence describes a past event, if we see/hear these sentences out of context?

Finally, compare the Italian–Portuguese mismatch and the Mandarin–English mismatch. Which one do you think would present more difficulty for second language learners, and in which learning direction?

Exercise 10.2. Examine the last two groups of columns in Figure 10.1. They reflect the mean ratings of participants on sentences such as *I observed Matt eat a cake* and *I observed Matt eating a cake* in the context of a complete story (Matt finished the cake). In principle, both sentences should be judged as plausible, since to observe an event in its completion includes the observation of the process as well as the end of the event. Compare the ratings of the native speakers for the two test sentences in the complete context. What do they show? Is the pattern repeated in any other group of participants?

Now, recall that the native language of the learners has only one form for *eat* and *eating* in this type of sentence; that is, Bulgarian does not distinguish between the bare verb and the present participle in perceptual reports. How would you evaluate the learners' performance on the English contrast, keeping in mind the native language? Discuss the performance of all learner groups. Remember that chance is 50% in this experimental design.

Exercise 10.3. Look at the Ionin, Ko, and Wexler (2004) experimental setup again. Below is another context and test sentence (forced choice) from that test.

Indefinite specific context:

Phone conversation:

    Jeweler: *Hello, this is Robertson's Jewelry. What can I do for you, ma'am? Are you looking for some new jewelry?*

    Client: *Not quite. I heard that you also buy back people's old jewelry.*

    Jeweler: *That is correct.*

    Client: *In that case, I would like to sell you (a, the, ___) beautiful silver necklace. It is very valuable, it has been in my family for 100 years!*

Come up with two other context–sentence pairs: a definite specific context and an indefinite nonspecific context. Make them plausible and easy to understand by nonnative speakers.

In Ionin, Zubizarreta, and Philipov (2009), the authors use a very similar design but they make one important change in the elicitation task: they do not provide articles to choose from in the test sentence *(a, the, ___)* but leave the space blank and ask the participants to provide the appropriate word, including absence of any word. The test sentence would look like that:

Client: *In that case, I would like to sell you ( ) beautiful silver necklace. It is very valuable, it has been in my family for 100 years!*

Which task is harder and why? The elicitation task has been criticized as possibly tapping extralinguistic, or learned, knowledge of grammar, especially with classroom learners. What other task can be used for the elicitation of articles that would avoid this criticism?

Exercise 10.4. Still staying within the article choice parameter, in another study, Ionin, Zubizarreta, and Maldonado (2008) compared Russian learners of English and Spanish learners of English on the same task. What is the motivation for such an experimental design, if Spanish and English both have overt articles while Russian does not? Tables 10.6 and 10.7 below give the main results. Comment on what these results show.

Table 10.6 Elicitation test results: L1-Russian speakers (n = 19), Ionin et al. (2008: 564)

	Definite NP (Target *the*)	Indefinite NP (Target *a*)
Specific NP	**93% *the***	23.7% *the*
	5.3% *a*	**74.6% *a***
	0% __	0% __
	0.9% other	1.8% other
Nonspecific NP	**86% *the***	3.5% *the*
	14% *a*	**95.6% *a***
	0% __	0% __
	0% other	0.9% other

Table 10.7 Elicitation test results: L1-Spanish speakers (n = 20), Ionin et al. (2008: 565)

	Definite NP (Target *the*)	Indefinite NP (Target *a*)
Specific NP	**87.5% *the***	1.7% *the*
	0.8% *a*	**92.5% *a***
	8.3% __	0% __
	2.5% other	5% other
Nonspecific NP	**96.7% *the***	4.1% *the*
	0.8% *a*	**91.7% *a***
	1.7% __	0.8% __
	0.8% other	3.3% other

*Note that the unexpected lower accuracy on this category of items was traced to only one example that was a direct transfer from the native language, since Spanish requires article omission in this context (*Fui a casa*, lit. 'I went to house').

Do you think these findings offer evidence for the Article Choice Parameter and why/why not?

Exercise 10.5. We shall look at a complete study, Gabriele (2005), which tests a Japanese–English contrast within aspectual tenses. I shall describe the syntax–semantics mismatch to be acquired, the research questions and the study, and ask some questions along the way. At the end, you will be asked to interpret the results and draw conclusions.

On the surface, it looks like the Japanese inflectional morpheme *te-iru* and the English progressive form *be V-ing* are a perfect match. With most event verbs (ii-a) and all incomplete activities (ii-b), *te-iru* has an ongoing interpretation, as does *be V-ing* (i-a,b). The mismatch is manifested only with instantaneous event verbs: while *be V-ing* is unnatural with some such verbs (iii-a), with some others it highlights the process immediately preceding the change of state (iii-b). Crucially, *te-iru* cannot have an ongoing interpretation but only a completion, that is, a perfective interpretation (iv). The Japanese examples are from Gabriele (2005).

(i) a. *Samantha is making a cake.*
     b. *Samantha is running.*

(ii) a. *Ken-wa*   *isu-o*   *tukut-te i-ru*
         Ken-TOP   chair-ACC   make-ASP-NONPAST
         'Ken is making a chair.'

      b. *Ken-ga*   *utat-te i-ru*
         Ken-NOM   sing-ASP-NONPAST
         'Ken is singing.'

(iii) a. **I am losing my wallet.*
      b. *The plane is arriving at the airport.*

(iv) *Hikōki-ga*   *kūkō-ni*   *tui-te i-ru*
      plane-NOM   airport at   arrive-ASP-NONPAST
      The plane has arrived at the airport.
      DOES NOT MEAN 'The plane is arriving at the airport.'

The meaning of Japanese *te-iru* interacts with aspectual verb class, in the sense that one meaning (ongoing) is available for some verbs (events and activities) but another meaning (perfective) surfaces with other verbs (instantaneous events). Does this meaning difference between Japanese and English constitute a syntax–semantics mismatch and why, or why not?

Gabriele (2005) presents two studies of this syntax–semantics mismatch, one of Japanese as a second language and one of English as a second language. She had somewhat different research questions and employed complex tests with many conditions, but here we will only concentrate on the results relevant to the acquisition of the present progressive *be V-ing* and present *te-iru* (the past form is *te-ita*). In order to test sentence interpretation, she used a modified Truth Value Judgment Task with pictures. In the two studies, the stories were presented aurally in the target language, not in the native language. Learners listened to recorded stories and saw two pictures. They were then presented with a sentence both visually and aurally and asked to judge on a scale from 1 (worst) to 5 (best) whether the sentence made sense as a description of the story. For each verb, a complete context and an incomplete context were provided. Here are some examples:

(v) a. Complete event context for *paint a portrait*, an event VP
   Picture 1: Ken is an artist. At 12:00 he begins to paint a portrait of his family.
   Picture 2: At 8:00 he gives the portrait to his mother for her birthday.
   Ken is painting a portrait of his family.
                                    (Expected answer 1 in Japanese and English)

   b. Incomplete event context for *paint a portrait*, an event VP
   Picture 1: Ken is an artist. At 12:00 he begins to paint a portrait of his family.
   Picture 2: At 12:30 he paints his mother and father.
   Ken is painting a portrait of his family.
                                    (Expected answer 5 in Japanese and English)

(vi) a. Complete event context for *arrive*, an instantaneous event VP
   Picture 1: This is the plane to Tokyo. At 4:00 the plane is near the airport.
   Picture 2: At 5:00 the passengers are at the airport.
   The plane is arriving at the airport.
                                    (Expected answer 1 in English, 5 in Japanese)

   b. Incomplete event context for *arrive*, an instantaneous event VP
   Picture 1: This is the plane to Tokyo. At 4:00 the plane is near the airport.
   Picture 2: There is a lot of wind. At 4:30 the plane is still in the air.
   The plane is arriving at the airport.
                                    (Expected answer 5 in English, 1 in Japanese)

In study 1, Gabriele tested 101 native speakers of Japanese learning English in Japan and 9 near-native Japanese individuals living in New York City, as well as 23 native Japanese as controls. In study 2, she tested 33 native English speakers learning Japanese in the US, as well as 31 native speaker controls. Proficiency tests were used to divide the participants into groups. One thing to note is that the Japanese L2 low group is of lower proficiency than the English L2 lowest group.

Turning to results, we shall look at the Japanese → English direction first (Table 10.8).

Compare the two ratings within groups, starting with the native speakers. If a group has a sufficient distance in its ratings of the acceptable and

Table 10.8 Mean scores on instantaneous events in the English present progressive (range between 1 and 5)

	Low (n=46)	Interm (n=39)	High (n=16)	Near-native (n=9)	Native (n=23)
is arriving refers to incomplete event	3.08	2.89	4	4.25	4.1
is arriving refers to complete event	3.64	3.45	2.56	3.25	1.5

Table 10.9 Mean scores on instantaneous events with *te-iru* (range between 1 and 5)

	Low (n=16)	High (n=17)	Native (n=31)
tui-te i-ru 'is arriving' refers to incomplete event	3.28	2.04	1.35
tui-te i-ru 'is arriving' refers to complete event	4.39	3.93	4.84

unacceptable meanings, this suggests that the group accepts the appropriate meaning and also rejects the unavailable one. Answer the following questions on the results. Have the four groups of Japanese learners of English acquired the incomplete event interpretation? Have they acquired the fact that *The plane is arriving* does not mean *The plane has arrived*? Which of the four groups seems to be doing the best? (Statistical analysis is necessary to answer this question, but estimate the answer by just eyeballing the ratings.)

Next, look at the results of the English → Japanese direction (Table 10.9). What can we say about this learning direction? Have the English learners of Japanese acquired the complete event interpretation of *te-iru*? Have all levels acquired it? Is there a difference between the two learning directions, English → Japanese and Japanese → English? Describe the difference, using comparisons between equivalent levels of proficiency in the L2. Can you speculate on why this would be the case?

Now compare the accuracy on the constructions that are the same in the native language and the accuracy on constructions that have to be added to the L2 grammar, the ones that cannot be transferred from the native grammar. Is there a pattern of (successful or unsuccessful) acquisition that you see? Describe the patterns in this way: Acquiring an L2 construction or meaning that also exists in the native language is.... Acquiring an L2 construction or meaning that also is new in the second language is....

11

Acquisition of the syntax–discourse and semantics–pragmatics interfaces

11.1 Where is the syntax–discourse interface?

In our journey through SLA, we have discussed the acquisition of morphology, syntax, lexicon, and the syntax–semantics interface. A common aspect of these properties is that they are considered to be language-internal, that is, regulated by rules intrinsic to the language faculty. As the diagram (Figure 11.1) based on White (2009) visualizes, the central box containing the core grammar modules: lexicon, phonology, morphology, syntax, and semantics, interfaces with meanings and sounds through dedicated interfaces (Logical Form and Phonetic Form). In this chapter, we will be thinking about properties of the grammar that touch and are contingent on the extralinguistic context, the life situation surrounding the language expressions. The

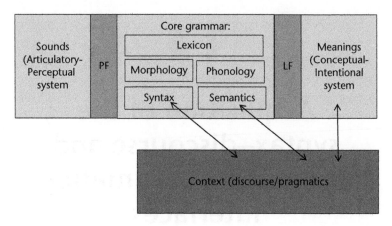

Figure 11.1   A working language faculty representation, based on White (2009)

meanings that we will encounter cannot be successfully computed, or appreciated, if context is not taken into account. Consequently, they are considered harder to figure out than other meanings and forms. As Figure 11.1 shows, context can be thought of as being outside of the box of the linguistic modules proper but certainly interacting with meanings; context has an effect on syntactic expressions as well.

To elucidate the terminology and combat confusion, we should start from the basics. Interpretation in language arises from the interaction of semantics and pragmatics. Sentences are built up in the morphosyntax, or the core syntax, module. Next, their propositional content is calculated in the semantics module; at the end of that process they are assigned truth conditions. The usage of the propositional content (i.e., truth conditions) in concrete communication is governed by pragmatic norms. In uttering a sentence, not only do we care about its truth conditional content, but we also aim at being appropriate, relevant, and cooperative, as the philosopher of language Paul Grice proposed in his famous lectures (Grice 1989). Therefore, meaning scholars often repeat the adage: Semantics proposes, pragmatics disposes. To understand exactly how semantics and pragmatics interact in the computation of the final meaning (what is said but also what is meant), semantics and pragmatics scholars battle it out with concrete proposals. The division of labor seems to be different for different constructions.

There has been a general confusion as to what linguistic properties belong to the semantics–pragmatics interface and which belong to the syntax–discourse interface. Furthermore, many linguists use these terms interchangeably, which can be confusing. I shall try to straighten out the terms

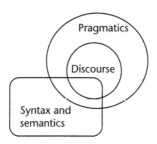

Figure 11.2   Relationship between syntax, discourse, and pragmatics

as much as I can. Although both can be considered external interfaces, the syntax–discourse interface properties represent the set while the semantics–pragmatics properties represent the superset (see Figure 11.2). The former include all constructions whose meaning computation and acceptability depend on information coming from the previous discourse: for example, what entity was mentioned in the previous sentence as given information (Topic) and information about what entity was required (Focus).[1] As we shall see below, properties that are calculated at this interface include preverbal and postverbal subjects in languages like Spanish and Italian, the use of overt subjects in Topic shift contexts, binding of pronouns, doubling of topicalized objects with clitics in, for example, Spanish and Bulgarian, contrastive focus, discourse-related word order optionality (scrambling) in German, etc. When definiteness is based on previous mention of a referent, its calculation is also discourse-based.

The level of linguistic pragmatics is much larger in scope than discourse-pragmatics. The *Handbook of Pragmatics* edited by Horn and Ward (2004) lists conversational implicature, presupposition, reference, deixis, definiteness, and speech acts as the principal domains of pragmatics. Of these six large areas, only reference and partially definiteness are contingent on the discourse context, while properties in the other areas are interpreted depending on knowledge of the world, Gricean maxims of co-operation, and other universal pragmatic principles. Speech acts are both culture- and education-dependent. When talking about the semantics–pragmatics interface (not including discourse-based constructions), linguists usually have in mind

---

[1] Semantics is not bypassed by this interface, as its name might suggest. A more appropriate name would be syntax–semantics–discourse interface, as the linguistic structures produced in the core syntax are checked for their truth conditions as well as their appropriateness to the discourse context.

scalar implicatures, presuppositions, deictic expressions, aspectual and other types of coercion, transfer of reference, and so on. Roughly, this interface regulates the difference between what is said (literally) and what is actually meant and understood. Universal pragmatic principles as well as knowledge of the world are crucial for comprehending language and can be transferred from the native language. Thus the semantics–pragmatics interface is not very likely to present much difficulty to nonnative speakers, unless some computations with added cognitive complexity are involved. Figure 11.2 represents this view of the relationship between syntax, semantics, pragmatics, and discourse.

It would be more *precise* if we used "syntax–discourse" for the interface where we calculate meaning based on our knowledge of the discourse context while reserving "semantics–pragmatics" for the interface where we recalculate meaning coming from the semantics (propositional content of sentences) based on knowledge of the world and universal pragmatic principles. Furthermore, since the two terms are in a set–superset relation, it is not a contradiction to use the wider term standing for the narrow term. When we use the narrow term (syntax–discourse), we imply that the wider term (semantics–pragmatics) is not applicable. This usage itself is a scalar implicature, as we shall see later in the chapter. Of course, we should always keep in mind that for calculation of the complete meaning, all modules and interfaces have to work in consort.

11.2 Marking of Topic and Focus across second languages

The most prominent and frequent use of discourse information in language is the marking of Topic and Focus, known as Information Structure. This structure regulates the information available to the speaker and hearer when they encode and decode a sentence in context. If a constituent has already been mentioned (activated) in the discourse or is well known to speaker and hearer, it acts as Topic. If a constituent encodes new information not previously known or mentioned, it is Focus. Questions open the possibility to answer with new information (e.g., *When did she arrive? Last night.*) Languages employ very different means of signaling this all-important discourse information, that is, marking Topic and Focus. The main means are permutations on neutral word order (left and right dislocations), doubling of dislocated elements, other word order changes, and specific intonation. The L2A challenge is when learners have to acquire a different way of marking Topic and Focus from their native system marking.

In this section, I will start by presenting studies investigating clitic-doubling as a means of signaling topicalization. Recall that a clitic is a special type of pronoun which is phonologically dependent on a host and may double (refer to) an argument already present in the sentence. There has been quite a lot of work recently on this particular property of clitic doubling. For starters, let me note that topicalization, that is, moving an object to sentence-initial position to mark it as old information, is common across languages. However, languages differ in whether the topicalized constituent is doubled with a clitic referring to it. Note the two examples below from English (1) and Bulgarian (2).

(1)   A: Did Jane like the wine?
       B: Oh, the wine she didn't drink (*it). She stuck to lemon ices.

(2)   A: Maria haresa   li vinoto?
           Maria like-PAST Q wine-DET
           'Did Maria like the wine?'

       B: Vinoto   tja   ne *(go) pi.   Boleshe ja glavata.
           wine-DET   she not it   drink-PAST   hurt her head
           'The wine she didn't drink. She had a headache.'

Note that in the same context, both English and Bulgarian can (option-ally) dislocate the object *the wine* because it is mentioned in the question and thus old information. However, in the English sentence in (1B), the pronoun *it* referring to the wine is ungrammatical, which is marked by the star inside the parentheses (*it* cannot be in that position). On the other hand, the Bulgarian sentence in (2B) sounds strange without the clitic *go* referring to and agreeing in gender with *vinoto* 'the wine', which is marked by the star outside the parentheses (meaning that *go* is not optional). Note that SVO is the neutral word order in both English and Bulgarian and the object dislocation cannot be uttered out of the blue, without appropriate context. In acquiring the construction, English-native learners of Bulgarian have to add the clitic to their mental representation; in the opposite direction, learners have to acquire the ungrammaticality of the pronoun. We shall see examples of both types of studies below.

One of the first studies investigating the acceptance of topicalization, known as clitic left dislocation in Spanish, was Valenzuela (2005, 2006). Valenzuela capitalized on the observation that in Spanish, only specific objects as in (3ab) are successfully doubled with a clitic, while generic objects as in (4ab) are not. The examples below are from her sentence selection task. In this task, near-native learners of Spanish heard a short context story in Spanish where the discourse antecedents were introduced. They then heard two possible concluding sentences for the story in Spanish and were asked to select the most appropriate answer. They could also choose 'neither a nor b' as well as 'both a and b', as shown:

(3) Ayer por la mañana, Eva se fue a la universidad y vio a su amigo Pedro
     y a su amiga Inés, pero como tenía muchas cosas que hacer...
     'Yesterday morning, Eva went to the university and saw her friend
     Pedro and her friend Inés, but since she had many things to do...'

    a. A Pedro,   no   lo saludó.   ← expected response
       Acc. Pedro,   not   CL greeted
       'Pedro, I didn't greet.'

    b. A Pedro,   no   saludó.
       Acc. Pedro,   not   greeted
       'Pedro, I didn't greet.'

    c. Ni a ni b
       'Neither a nor b'

    d. Ambas a y b
       'Both a and b'

(4) El médico de Paco le dijo que tenía que tomar mucha agua. También le
     dijo que tenía que comer más fruta y verdura. Pero Paco es muy
     cabezón y...
     'Paco's doctor told him that he has to drink a lot of water. He also told
     him that he needs to eat fruit and vegetables. But Paco is very stubborn
     and...'

    a. Agua,   no   toma   nunca.   ← expected response
       water,   not   drinks   never
       'Water, he never drinks.'

b. Agua, no   la   toma nunca.
   water, not CL   drinks never
   'Water, he never drinks.'

c. Ni a ni b
   'Neither a nor b'

d. Ambas a y b
   'Both a and b'

Valenzuela's near-native participants were 100% accurate on the sentences as in (3), even more accurate than the native speakers. On the other hand, with generic dislocated objects, the Spanish native speakers gave the expected response (4a) only 53% of the time. They also chose the clitic-doubled option 14% of the time, and the "both constructions are possible" option 19% of the time. For the near-native speakers the respective answers were 40%, 37%, and 20%, which was significantly different from the natives. Valenzuela argued that the learners' knowledge of this construction is deficient.

Ivanov (2009, 2012) is another study that looked at the same property, but in the acquisition of Bulgarian. For the purposes of our comparison here, we have to know that Spanish and Bulgarian work similarly. The only difference is that Bulgarian topicalized objects have to be doubled with a clitic no matter whether they are dislocated or in their usual position after the verb. This possibility is observable in the examples from the test items. Ivanov tested native speakers of English who were advanced and intermediate learners of L2 Bulgarian. First of all, just as Valenzuela did, Ivanov ascertained that the research participants knew the syntactic properties of clitics. There is no need to search for knowledge of clitic doubling at the syntax–discourse interface if the learners have not acquired clitics in the first place. Secondly, he used an acceptability judgment task where the test items were presented aurally as well as in writing. Intonation is very important for the marking of Focus and Topic and test sentences should not be evaluated without the required intonation. A test sentence with the choices that had to be evaluated on a scale of 1 (unacceptable) to 5 (perfect) is given in (5). The number sign (#) means that the sentence is unacceptable in this context.

(5) Q: Poluči?   li koleta ot Peter
        receive-2.SG.PAST Q package from Peter
        'Did you receive the package from Peter?'

A: a. Koleta **go** polučih minalata sedmica. [+Object fronting][+Clitic doubling]
        package Cl.ACC receive-1.SG.PAST last week
        'I received that package last week'

    b. Minalata sedmica **go** polučih koleta. [–Object fronting][–Clitic doubling]

    c. #Koleta polučih minalata sedmica. [+Object fronting][–Clitic doubling]

    d. #Minalata sedmica polučih koleta. [–Object fronting][–Clitic doubling]

Ivanov tested both accusative and dative objects in Topic as well as Focus contexts. The exact same sentences are acceptable with clitic doubling in Topic contexts and without clitic doubling in Focus contexts as in (6). As I mentioned above, questions create a Focus context because the answer is new information.

(6)   Q: Kakvo zagub-i   dokato   bjaga-še   tazi sutrin?
         what lose-2SG.PAST   while   run-2SG.PAST   this morning
         'What did you lose when you were running this morning?'

      A: a. #Ključovete za kolata   gi zagubix. [+Object fronting][+clitic doubling]
             keys-DET   for car-DET CL.ACC lost-1SG
             'I lost the car keys.'
         b. #Zagubix gi ključovete za kolata   [–Object fronting][+clitic doubling]
         c. Zagubix ključovete za kolata.   [–Object fronting][–clitic doubling]
         d. Ključovete za kolata zagubix.   [+Object fronting][–clitic doubling]

While Ivanov's intermediate learners had not acquired the acceptability of these sentences in context, the advanced group ratings demonstrated a significant difference between the acceptable and unacceptable sentences. In addition, their ratings were not significantly different from the Bulgarian native speakers' ratings. Thus, it seems that the results of Valenzuela's and Ivanov's experiments point to different outcomes. In order to resolve this apparent contradiction, Slabakova and Ivanov (2011) reanalyzed Valenzuela's data on generic sentences as in (4). Conspicuously, the behavior of the native speakers on these sentences was far from categorical, with the expected answer being chosen only about half of the time. This suggests a variability in the input that the learners are exposed to, which may well have affected their own choices.

A second experimental study on Spanish clitic left dislocation, Slabakova, Kempchinsky, and Rothman (2012), attested successful acquisition of an additional semantic constraint on the dislocation: the clitic-doubled and dislocated object (the chairs) was just a subset of the object mentioned in the context (furniture).

(7) [context: What did the movers do with the furniture?]
Las sillas las dejaron en el pasillo, pero no sé dónde están las mesas.
the chairs CL left.3PL in the hallway, but NEG know.1SG where are the tables
'The chairs, they left them in the hallway, but I don't know what they did with the tables.'

Donaldson (2011a,b, 2012) examined clitic right dislocation and clitic left dislocation, among other properties, in near-native L2 French. French is a language that uses these constructions a lot. His study followed the natural conversations of ten native speaker–near-native speaker dyads. He demonstrated that the behavior of the near-native speakers was not qualitatively and quantitatively different from the native behavior.

Finally, Slabakova and García Mayo (2015) tested topicalizations as in (1), repeated here, contrastive fronted focus as in (8), and the so-called left dislocations as in (9), in English as a second and a third language.

(1) A: Did Jane like the wine?
B: Oh, the wine she didn't drink (*it). She stuck to lemon ices.

(8) Customer: Can I get something for breakfast? Maybe a bagel?
Mark: No, sorry. We're out of bagels. A bran muffin I can give you/*it to you.

(9) My wonderful Felix, everyone likes *(him).

While topicalizations and fronted focus constructions depend on context and do not allow a pronoun that refers to the moved constituent (called a "resumptive" pronoun), the left dislocation can be uttered out of the blue, and the pronoun in object position refers to the sentence-initial phrase. That's because that phrase did not move from object position but was adjoined to the sentence. The format of this experiment was very similar to those of Ivanov and Slabakova et al's experiments, with a rating scale from 1 to 7. However, the findings were very surprising. Neither the second language learners nor the third language learners[2] showed any knowledge of topicalization, although they were better on focus and left dislocations. The measure of success in this study, as above, was whether the ratings of the unacceptable construction were significantly different from the ratings of the acceptable constructions. On topicalization, the ratings of all learner groups converged on essentially the same value, in the middle of the scale (3.5). That is, they were not sure about the acceptability of both the sentences with the pronouns and those without.

In summary, we see mixed results in the acquisition of dislocations, with some clear successes (Ivanov, Donaldson, Slabakova et al.) and some disasters (Slabakova and García Mayo). It is very tempting to use the Interface Hypothesis as an explanation of these findings. The Interface Hypothesis, proposed by Antonella Sorace and her associates, operational-ized the idea that learners will show much more variability and optional behaviors at interfaces in general. This variable behavior can be due to limitations in working memory, processing capacity or processing efficiency that are experienced by bilinguals and multilinguals. In addition, inefficient resource allocation that obtains as a byproduct of bilingualism has been suggested as another possible reason for underperformance at interfaces (Sorace 2011). In essence, the idea is that when too much information has to be used in the calculation of some meaning or some word order, the bilingual or multilingual mind experiences strain of capacity. This strain is manifested in acceptance (or indiscriminate ratings) of two opposing con-structions, for example, left dislocations with and without a clitic/pronoun doubling, as described in the Slabakova and García Mayo experiment above. This optionality is often reflected in significantly different ratings of native and nonnative experimental participants. However, see Exercise 11.1 on the significance of those differences.

Over time, the Interface hypothesis was extended to virtually all contexts and consequences of bilingualism (e.g., adult L2 acquisition, child 2L1, child L2, and L1 attrition, see Sorace, 2011, Tsimpli et al. 2004). In part based on the recent emergence of quality data sets, examining multiple languages and multiple interface-conditioned domains of grammar, the

---

[2] Who were Basque–Spanish and Spanish–Basque bilinguals learning English as a third language.

Interface Hypothesis has been revised (or clarified, see Sorace, 2011) to no longer make claims about vulnerability for all interfaces. At present, the IH targets (emerging) optionality at the external interfaces only and at the level of near-native ultimate attainment or first language attrition (i.e., it is not part of development). However, other researchers (e.g., Lardiere 2011 and White 2011) argue that a linguistic issue manifested at near-native levels of proficiency should also be noticeable when learners are less proficient. After all, progression in L2 proficiency entails better grammar knowledge and better computational efficiency at the later stages than at the earlier stages.

But why would syntax–discourse interface properties be more vulnerable than other interface properties? The problem is hypothesized to stem from the very limitations in cognitive resources in bilinguals, but it is noticeable in child language comprehension as well. When faced with a decision about meaning that depends on juggling several sources of information (the syntax, the extralinguistic information, and frequently intonation as well), children and inexperienced L2 learners might suffer a breakdown in meaning calculation, at which point they resort to guessing. Reinhart (2006) specifically argues for such a scenario in scalar implicature and pronoun comprehension by children, but it is easy to see how this explanation can be extended to second language learners. In such learning situations, experimental results frequently hover around 50% accuracy. Children of ages 4 to 6 may still be developing the brain capacity to manage several sources of information. That same capacity may be taxed by the costs of inhibition needed to deactivate the multiple grammars present in a multilingual's mind.

While the Interface Hypothesis is rigorously argued, based on a principled distinction within the language faculty and supported by a number of studies, there are also other studies whose results point against it. In this section, we only looked at object fronting to mark Topic, and we reviewed more studies that documented success than studies that attested failure of learning. For example, in acquiring clitic left dislocations in Spanish, advanced learners were indistinguishable from native speakers (Slabakova et al. 2012). In the opposite learning direction, from Spanish to English, even very advanced learners were at a complete loss with the same construction (Slabakova and García Mayo 2015). Obviously, this discrepancy cannot be due to the uniform difficulty of the syntax–discourse interface. There must be some other factor, or factors, involved. Slabakova (2015c) attributes the difference in success rates in the two learning directions to the frequency of the two constructions in the target languages. In English, topicalization is very rare while clitic left dislocation in Spanish is about 1000 times more frequent, according to corpus data (Slabakova 2015c).[3] In addition, English does have a construction such as left dislocation (see example (9) above), which not only allows but requires a resumptive pronoun. As we have seen previously in this textbook, quantity and quality of input may provide the best explanation again: it is only rarely that English learners experience topicalization, and the competition from left dislocation may make the learning task even more confusing. After all, the meanings of the two constructions overlap even if their distribution does not.

While the Interface Hypothesis is falsified by such results, it still points to a valid source of difficulty, as we will see in the next sections. It is still the case that constructions at the syntax–discourse interface are difficult, it is just not the case that they are uniformly difficult, and also not the case that such difficulty is insurmountable.

11.3 Word order: constraints and strategies

In this section, we will look at some studies that investigate the order of subject and verb in discourse-dependent contexts. As you will see in the examples below, in (neutral SVO) languages that allow this, the subject can follow the verb if it is new information, or focus. In fact, this construction is part of the cluster of constructions that rely on the Null Subject Parameter. In other words, the possibility of null subjects and Verb–Subject order are related (Rizzi 1982, Belletti 2000, 2003). But first, let us distinguish between contrastive and presentational focus. Although both present new information, contrastive focus necessarily compares two propositions as in (10), where caps stand for emphatic intonation.

(10) Q: Do you like my new jacket?
      A: I like your new SHIRT; the jacket not so much.

---

[3] The data for this comparison come from the Switchboard Telephone Speech Corpus in English, described by Gregory and Michaelis (2001), and from the NOCANDO corpus in Spanish, Brunetti, Bott, Costa, and Vallduví (2011).

Presentational focus, on the other hand, does not evaluate options but simply introduces new information (11). It is marked *in situ*, which means that nothing has moved about in the sentence (É. Kiss 1998, Rochemont 1998, Domínguez 2004).

(11)   Q: Who came late last night?
       A: Linda came late.

A third term we shall make use of here is "thetic sentences": these are produced out of the blue, with no previous mention, or they are answers to the question "What happened?" as in (12).

(12)   Q: What happened at the party last night?
       A: The police came. We were making too much noise.

Observe that the word order in English is Subject–Verb in all of the answers above. It is possible for English to invert the subject and the verb, but this happens rarely and only under very special conditions; it is the (first) auxiliary that moves over the subject:

(13)   Never have I heard such an amazing proposal.

But of course, English is not a null-subject language. Spanish, a null-subject language, allows the subject to follow the verb. Inversion is possible even in unfocused (out of the blue) contexts. However, native speakers invert the subject much more with unaccusative than with unergative verbs.

Notice: this is a way in which the discourse, the lexicon, and the syntax interact in complex ways! Can you think of other cases of such interactions?

Recall from Chapter 9 that in unaccusative verbs such as *arrive*, the subject has the semantic role of Patient, or Theme, while in unergative verbs such as *shout*, the subject is an Agent. We reviewed proposals to the effect that the two types of subjects start from different underlying positions in the verb phrase, which is reflected in the inversion preferences. Examples are from Lozano (2006). In (14) and (15), the lead question, which asks about the whole event, makes the answer all new, and therefore thetic.

(14)   Q: ¿Qué pasó anoche en la fiesta?
          'What happened last night at the party?'
          A: Vino la policía.   unaccusative: preference for VS
          'The police arrived.'

(15)   Q: ¿Qué pasó anoche en la calle?
          'What happened last night in the street?'
          A: Una mujer gritó.   unergative: preference for SV
          'A woman shouted.'

However, when the lead question asks about a specific person and the answer involves presentational focus, the judgments are different: both unergative and unaccusative verbs sound better with the inverted VS order. In other words, presentational focus neutralizes the unaccusative–unergative distinction.

(16)   Q: ¿Quién gritó anoche en la calle?
          'Who shouted last night in the street?'
          A: Gritó una mujer.   unergative verb: VS
          'A woman shouted.'

(17)   Q: ¿Quién vino anoche a la fiesta?
          ' Who arrived last night at the party?'
          A: Vino la polícia.   unaccusative: VS
          'The police arrived.'

In order to master the complete data set in (14)–(17) above, a learner of Spanish has to be aware of the possibility and preference for VS structures with unaccusative verbs but not with unergative verbs. This is lexical knowledge reflected at the lexicon–syntax interface (we saw some studies on this issue in Chapter 9). In addition, sensitivity to the discourse status of the answer sentence (out of the blue/thetic or presentational focus) should be acquired. That sensitivity is arguably reflected at the syntax–discourse interface. Since this is an attractive paradigm to investigate, it has provoked considerable research interest. I shall mention a few studies here. Hertel's (2003) study investigated the production of presentational focus VS order in L2 Spanish by American English natives at four proficiency levels (beginner, low intermediate, high intermediate, advanced). She found that her learners did favor SV with unergatives but VS with unaccusatives and, therefore, were sensitive to the syntactic effects of the lexicon even at advanced stages of acquisition. Unexpectedly, she also found that her participants were producing presentational focus at even lower proficiency levels than advanced.

Lozano (2006) created an experimental study where learners of Spanish with English and Greek as native languages evaluated the acceptability of answers such as those in (14) to (17) in unfocused and presentational focus contexts. Greek as a native language is investigated in this study because Greek presentational focus only allows SV sentences (just as English) while similar to Spanish, it inverts unaccusative VS orders. Thus, Greek learners have a possible transfer advantage, but only for the word orders in unfocused contexts. In the experiment, even the English learners of Spanish were accurate with the lexical property. Greek and English learners demonstrated significant preference for SV with unergative verbs and VS with unaccusative verbs. However, the two learner groups, which were at advanced proficiency, allowed both word orders (SV/VS) in presentational focus contexts equally. In other words, they did not feel that VS was more appropriate in such contexts. Learners were not sensitive to the discursive constraint although they were able to observe the lexical distinction. Lozano argued that his findings support the Interface Hypothesis, as they clearly do.

Later work by Lozano and Mendikoetxea (2010) looked at the production of VS structures in a L1 Spanish–L2 English learner corpus and a comparable English native corpus. They classified the productions as obeying the interface principles: inversions are allowed when the verb is unaccusative, when the subject is heavy (contains many words) and when it is focused. Learners and native speakers obeyed all these principles equally well. The errors that learners made were in the syntactic form of the sentences with inversion. They used the expletive *it* or nothing instead of *there* in the preverbal position:

(18) a. *In the name of religion **it** had occurred many important events ...

   b. *It is difficult that Ø exist volunteers with such a feeling against it.

Focus can be marked by subject–verb inversion, but it can also be marked by the appropriate emphatic intonation (*I want to see YOU*) or by a cleft construction (*It is you that I want to see*). Belletti (2013) calls these various ways of encoding Focus "different answering strategies" because they are all legitimate in Italian and in many other languages. However, native speakers and L2 learners exhibit striking differences in the preference for these answering strategies, with most learners maintaining their native answering strategies in the L2 (Belletti and Leonini 2004, Belletti, Bennati, and Sorace 2007, Lozano 2006). For example, French learners of Italian employ mostly clefts, while English learners of Italian employ intonation marking by stressing the subject. Studies in the other learning direction, Italian to English (Belletti 2013), suggest that learners respect grammatical necessities and only employ native answering preferences when the grammar allows it. Even when demonstrating that the null subject property of the target L2 language has been properly (re)set, the free VS inversion option is accessed only to a limited extent. Belletti argues that the choice of a particular strategy is only partly conditioned by grammatical factors.

Arguments and findings such as Belletti's bring up the question of the representational versus processing source of difficulties and optionality at the syntax–discourse interface. They suggest that even if nativelike grammatical representations are in place, and especially when the grammar allows choices, even near-native learners will reach for the native answering strategies under the burden of communication and bilingualism pressures. Of course, I am talking of preferences for options that are allowed by the target grammar, and the near-native learners discussed by Belletti are not choosing anything unacceptable. On the other hand, utilizing nonnative strategies does not exclude having grammatical problems, too, for the less experienced learners.

11.4 Pronoun reference

In the previous section, we discussed how the inversion of the subject and the verb, VS word order, can signal the presentation of new information in some languages. A similar interaction of grammar and discourse–pragmatics is found in pronoun reference calculation. Postverbal subjects are part of the Null Subject Parameter cluster, and thus are related to another interesting manifestation of discourse sensitivity: a division of labor between null and overt pronominal subjects for different communication situations. In a nutshell, native speakers of Spanish and Italian prefer to use null subjects when the subject of the main clause is maintained as the subject of the embedded clause. This is known as Topic maintenance. On the other hand, they prefer to use overt pronominal subjects when the embedded subject refers to another argument in the main clause, but not the subject. This is known as Topic shift.[4] Let me illustrate with a couple of sentences from Italian (from Belletti, Bennati, and Sorace 2007).

(19)   La vecchietta saluta la ragazza quando Ø attraversa la strada.
       the old.lady   greets the girl   when   crosses the street
       'The old lady greets the girl when she crosses the street.'

                                                    she=the old lady

(20)   La vecchietta saluta la ragazza quando *lei* attraversa la strada.
       the old lady   greets the girl   when   she crosses the street
       'The old lady greets the girl when she crosses the street.'

                                                    she=the girl

In processing sentences such as (19) and (20), (Belletti et al. 2007) found that Italian near-native speakers interpreted the overt pronominal subject of the embedded clause as referring to the lexical subject of the main clause 30% of the time, while the natives only interpreted it in this way 5% of the time; a significant difference. At the same time, 65% of near-native answers and 85% of native answers converged on the correct interpretation (embedded subject refers to matrix complement). Thus, the Italian near-natives in this study were less sensitive than the native speakers to Topic shift discourse situations. In addition to being statistically significant, this lower sensitivity is considered an important competence distinction, because the near-native speakers of Italian were very proficient in all other respects. See Exercise 11.1 for another interpretation of these findings.

Since this division of labor of null and overt pronouns may be a processing strategy, Keating, VanPatten, and Jegerski (2011) tested three groups of speakers in a processing experiment. One group contained monolingually raised native speakers of Spanish, the second group contained heritage speakers of Spanish, and the third group, adult L2 learners. They saw sentences like (21) on a computer screen and had to choose one of the two answers (a forced choice task).

---

[4] Carminatti (2002) postulated a division of labor between overt and null pronouns in the embedded clause. She called it the Position of Antecedent strategy and argued that it is a processing constraint.

(21) Daniel ya no ve a Miguel desde que Ø se casó.
      'Daniel no longer sees Miguel ever since he got married.'
      ¿Quién se casó ?
      'Who got married?'
            A. Daniel   B. Miguel

    Although the results of the Keating et al. (2011) study demonstrate a statistically significant bias in antecedent assignment, they did not reveal a neat division of labor between null and overt pronouns overall. The mono-lingually raised Spanish speakers did prefer the main subject as the ante-cedent of the null pronoun in the embedded subject position (so they answered *Daniel* in (21)), but their preferences for the overt pronoun were rather more individually varied and noncategorical as a group. The heritage and the L2 learner groups did not demonstrate significant preferences for one or the other pronoun reference. The authors argued that there are significant distinctions between Spanish and Italian with respect to the antecedent strategy (i.e., the null pronoun refers to main clause subject, *Daniel* in this example; overt pronoun refers to main clause object, *Miguel* in this example). While in Italian this strategy is obeyed much more categor-ically, in Spanish it is not. As a result, the learners may not have had sufficient input to acquire the preference, while the heritage speakers may have lost it under the influence of their English. The lack of clear antecedent biases for either overt or null pronoun suggests that the L2 learners are still sorting out the pragmatic constraints on pronominal subject distribution, and for them the null and overt pronouns are in completely free variation. However, another possibility arises with respect to the heritage speakers. Shin and Cairns (2009) found that sensitivity to Topic shift contexts emerges in Mexican children between the ages of 7 and 9 years. Since the heritage speakers in this study (and generally in the US) are exposed to English and become bilingual before the age of 7, it could be that they never acquired the strategy.[5] In any event, the results of Keating et al., both for heritage speakers and for L2 learners, are in line with explanations of problems at the syntax–discourse interface.

    Finally, Zhao's (2012) study provides a very different perspective on the same issue at this interface. Chinese is a null-subject language, but it also

---

[5] This would be a case of incomplete native language acquisition, as discussed in Chapter 5, see Montrul (2008).

allows null objects. It is interesting that, in contrast to Romance languages, both the embedded null subject and the embedded overt subject can refer to either a local antecedent (such as the main clause subject *John* in (22)) or an external antecedent (someone mentioned in the discourse but not in the same sentence). This is what the subscript "i/j" stands for: "i" is the subscript of *John* and *he,* while the referent of "j" is not explicitly mentioned but known from the discourse. The following examples will help you understand the Chinese facts:

(22)   John$_i$ says that he$_{i/j}$ likes Tom.

(23)   Xiao Zhang$_i$ shuo Ø$_{i/j}$/ta$_{i/j}$ xihuan Lao Wang.
       Xiao Zhang   say   he   like   Lao Wang
       'Xiao Zhang says that he likes Lao Wang.'

Now compare the two sentences in (24) and (25). In the English sentence, the object pronoun *him* can refer to John and to a third person unmentioned in this particular sentence, but known to the interlocutors. In the Chinese sentence, the overt pronoun *ta* has the same interpretation as the English *him*. However, the null object pronoun Ø$_{*i/j}$ can only refer to the third person familiar from the discourse, not to Xiao Zhang.

(24)   John says that Tom likes him$_{i/j}$.

(25)   Xiao Zhang$_i$ shuo Lao Wang xihuan Ø$_{*i/j}$/ta$_{i/j}$.
       Xiao Zhang say   Lao Wang like   him
       'Xiao Zhang says that Lao Wang likes him.'

   As you can appreciate, this is quite a complex set of data for the learners of Chinese to acquire, given that their native English allows no null pronouns, either as subject or as objects. Following up on Yuan (1993), which had established that learners of Chinese accept null subjects and null objects from very early stages of acquisition, Zhao's study asked if learners actually had the correct interpretation for the null pronouns they accepted. She used a picture selection task with two types of pictures. In one type of picture, a speaker was talking about a third person; in the second type of picture, the speaker was referring to himself. These two types of pictures try to capture the two possible interpretations of *John$_i$ says that he$_{i/j}$ likes watching* *football*. Learners had to rate four sentences with respect to each picture. The prediction was that, even if they had null elements in their L2 grammar, learners of Chinese might not be able to make the interpretive distinction between the null embedded subject and the null embedded object. To be fully competent, they should rate the sentences low where the embedded object is null but the picture shows it refers to the matrix subject (see example (25)). This is exactly the state of knowledge that Zhao uncovered, at least with the advanced learners. Their ratings patterned with the native speakers'. The intermediate learners' ratings were somewhat shakier, but still largely in line with the natives. All in all, these results are a success story.

   Why should the Chinese syntax–discourse interface be different from the Romance syntax–discourse interface? While we need more studies with various language pairs, it is already clear from the research summarized in this section that the syntax–discourse interface is not monolithic, and that even very similar properties across various languages may create great difficulties for learners, or not so much difficulty. This situation calls for the scrutinizing of other factors that can impact behavior at this interface, such as frequency of the constructions in the input, processing strategies, and the relationship of discourse properties with other parts of the grammar.

11.5 Intonation at the syntax–discourse interface

Since intonation is one of the basic means of signaling information structure, this chapter would be remiss if it did not touch on this issue, although not much work has been done to date, at least in L2 acquisition. Please look at Figure 11.1 again. This research would be investigating the missing arrow between the discourse–pragmatics box and phonology, within the core grammar. But first of all let us recall the definition of prosody. "Prosody refers to the way in which words are grouped in speech, the relative acoustic prominence of words, and the overall tune of an utterance" (Breen et al. 2010: 1047). Prosody involves acoustic features such as fundamental frequency (F0), duration, and loudness of the speech unit. The combinations of these acoustic features give rise to psychological perceptions such as phrasing (grouping of words), stress (prominence), and tonal movement (intonation). In every sentence, there is one word in particular that receives main prominence relative to its neighbors. Such rhythmic prominence is known as Nuclear Stress (NS). In many languages, NS serves the important function of identifying the focus domain of a sentence.[6]

In a series of experiments, Breen et al. (2010) asked their English-speaking research participants to produce sentences with focus, having manipulated the Information Structure by providing preceding context. They analyzed the recordings and found that speakers systematically provided prosodic cues as to which part of the sentence is focused material. They also provided clues as to whether the whole sentence (wide focus in thetic sentences) or only parts of the sentence was new information (narrow or presentational focus). This would be the difference between *What happened this morning?* versus *What did Joe fry this morning?* Finally, they established that speakers *can* distinguish between contrastive and presentational focus, but don't do it all the time. English native speakers signal contrastive focus only when they perceive syntactic ambiguity and want to disambiguate the message (*JOE fried an omelet, not Stan.*)

The acquisition study we examine here is by Nava and Zubizarreta (2009, 2010). It is based on the important theoretical treatment for Spanish by Zubizarreta (1998). The authors start by noting that while in English the primary mode of signaling information structure (Topic and Focus) is prosody, Spanish uses word order flexibility for the same purpose.[7] More specifically, the distinction between English and Spanish is the variable placement of the nuclear stress (NS). In English each constituent can be emphatically stressed, and hence the NS can be on any constituent, while in Spanish only the last constituent can be emphatically stressed, that is, the NS is always last in the sentence. Underlining in the following examples marks NS.

When a sentence is an answer to a *What happened?* question, or it is uttered out of the blue, the NS rule is the unmarked stress pattern. The last word of the sentence gets the accent.

(26) a. What happened?   b. A boy broke his <u>leg</u>.   (wide focus)
      c. Barbara drew pictures on the <u>covers</u>.

---

[6] Chomsky and Halle (1968), Chomsky (1971), Jackendoff (1972), Ladd (1996), Zubizarreta (1998).

[7] See also Ladd (1996).

English may also generate NS on the subject or NS on the verb. This variable NS is exploited to distinguish the wide focus statements as in (26) from narrow focus statements as in (27).

(27)   a. Who broke his leg?   b. A <u>boy</u> broke his leg.   (narrow focus)

Another important prosodic rule of English is Anaphoric Deaccenting. This is the rule postulating that already known material loses prominence and the NS shifts to its sister node. In (28), since stamps have already been mentioned, the stress shifts to the verb *collect*. Pronounce the sentence with the emphasis on *stamps*, and appreciate that it sounds subtly wrong. Compare that with the Spanish equivalent in (29). If you speak Spanish, try to appreciate the prosodic distinction between (28) and (29).

(28)   Q: Why are you buying that old stamp? A: Because I <u>collect</u> *stamps*.

(29)   Q: ¿Por qué compras ese sello tan viejo?   A: Porque colecciono <u>sellos</u>.
       why are-you-buying this stamp so old   because I-collect stamps
       'Why are you buying this old stamp?'   'Because I collect stamps.'

Deaccenting is a rule that applies after the NS rule: they have to come in a sequence. Nava and Zubizarreta predicted that learners of English would acquire the deaccenting rule before the NS rule, because Spanish does not have deaccenting. Thus, this rule is completely new to the learners and without an equivalent in their native grammar. The native NS rule, on the other hand, has to be restructured in the L2. In a sense, they predicted it would be easier to learn a new rule than to change a previously existing native rule.

In their experimental study, Nava and Zubizarreta tested the NS assignment rule and the deaccenting rule. They found that quite a big proportion of their intermediate and even advanced learners did not obey the English prosodic rules. However, they also found learners who had acquired both rules. Looking at individual performances, they established that the deaccenting rule came in the grammar more easily than restructuring the NS rule. Ten learners had the former rule only, and none had the latter rule only. Thus their prediction was supported on the individual level.

Zubizarreta and Nava (2011) compared their results above with the results of Lozano (2006), which we already discussed. The comparison of the two learning directions (Spanish-to-English and English-to-Spanish) shows that the difficulty lies not only in learning the way of marking focus in the respective target language, but also generating the grammatical structures that are necessary to accomplish this marking. In other words, prosody always works in consort with grammar, and clearly complicates the acquisition picture.

11.6 Scalar implicatures

In this section, we tackle an issue that is arguably at the interface of semantics and pragmatics: scalar implicatures. Recall that very few properties at the semantics–pragmatics interface have been investigated in L2 acquisition. There is a reason for this: pragmatics is arguably largely universal. While some differences do exist, they are notably in the speech act area of pragmatics: the way we make a compliment or ask for a favor is not the same across cultures. Since this work is not done within the generative framework, we will not review it here, but see other recent surveys.[8] To exemplify the universality of pragmatics, let's consider space and temporal deixis. Deixis refers to the phenomenon wherein understanding the meaning of certain words and phrases in an utterance requires contextual information. Words that have a fixed semantic meaning but have a denotational meaning that constantly changes depending on time and/or place, are deictic. Classical examples involve the meaning of personal pronouns and adverbs such as *tomorrow* and *here*.

(30)   a. We went to the cinema last night.
        b. We live longer than men.

If she knows the meaning of the pronoun *we*, the L2 speaker of English certainly understands that the group of people referred to in (30b) is "all women," while the referents of *we* in (30a) are contextually determined (family, friends, partners, etc.).[9]

---

[8] See Bardovi-Harlig (2011, 2013) for two evaluative surveys of interlanguage pragmatics.

[9] For a review of work on all areas of linguistic pragmatics, see Slabakova (2013).

This type of implied meaning, in this case reference, is part of almost any communication. Remember, we are looking at the difference between what is said and what is meant. Consider the following example of a well-known pragmatic inference:

(31)   Some professors are smart.

Most people would agree that, in hearing the utterance in (31), they understand that the speaker has conveyed the assumption in (32).

(32)   Not all professors are smart.

Notice that (32) is not encoded by the speaker's utterance, nor is it part of what the speaker has *said*. Rather, (32) is an assumption inferentially derived by the hearer on the basis of what the speaker has said. Logically speaking, *some* means *some and possibly all*. But if the speaker of (32) had meant *all professors are smart*, she would have uttered (33) or (34), being maximally informative, and not (31). Since she didn't, then we can safely assume she means (32).

(33)   Professors are smart.

(34)   All professors are smart.

The first systematic attempt to explain how the inference in (31) is derived is due to the philosopher of language Paul Grice. In a series of lectures presented at Harvard in 1967, published later as Grice (1989), he offered a comprehensive framework of the mechanisms of inferential communication. More specifically, he suggested that communication is essentially governed by certain rational expectations about how a conversational exchange should be conducted, which he called "maxims." According to Grice's five maxims, interlocutors are normally expected to offer contributions that are truthful, informative, relevant to the goals of the conversation, and appropriately phrased. These expectations about rational conversational conduct constrain the range of interpretations hearers are entitled to entertain in interpreting utterances. Furthermore, these expectations can be violated (or exploited) to create a variety of effects. According to Grice's maxims, in producing (31) and meaning (32), the speaker has used part of the following maxim:

(35) Quantity Maxim
      i. make your contribution as informative as is required,
      ii do not make your contribution more informative than is required.
         (Grice 1989: 26)

The speaker has chosen a relatively weak term among a range of words ordered in terms of informational strength: *some... most... all*. Assuming that the speaker is trying to be cooperative and will say as much as she truthfully can, the fact that she chose the weaker term *some* gives the listener reason to think that she is not prepared to make the stronger statements in (33) and (34). This leads to the inference that the stronger statement does not hold, that is, to (32). The assumption in (32) is called a conversational implicature, and more specifically, a scalar implicature, since the quantifiers *some... most... all* (and the propositions they give rise to) are ordered on a scale (Horn 1972, Gazdar 1979). Implicatures are studied from the perspective of Relevance Theory (Sperber and Wilson 1986) and from a neo-Gricean perspective (Levinson 2000, Chierchia 2004).

Note that conversational implicature is universal, it is purportedly part of human language, and all languages should exhibit a similar process of implied meaning inferencing. Therefore, the issue of transfer from the native language plays out in an interesting way in this area of linguistic pragmatics. The mechanisms of scalar implicature computation, whatever they are, can readily be transfered from the native language of the learner. On the other hand, implicature in certain situations certainly depends on the lexical knowledge of set expressions, or chunks.

A pioneering series of studies on knowledge of conventional implicature was Bouton (1992, 1994). Initially based on a cross-sectional picture, Bouton followed the development of several types of conversational implicature such as relevance and implied criticism. He tested two groups of students after 17 months and after 54 months of residence in the US. The general conclusion from his findings was that the learners were capable of computing implicature after a period of study in the US. The only area of uncertainty and difficulty remained "specific points of American culture and not the type of implicature involved" (Bouton 1994: 163). Bouton's findings confirmed that implicature is a cognitive process distinct from cultural knowledge and that its acquisition does benefit from instruction and longer exposure to the target language.

There is an extensive literature on scalar implicature computation demonstrating that children can answer experimental questions in a pragmatic way, but not until the ages of 5 to 7 (e.g., Guasti et al. 2005, Papafragou and Musolino 2003). A central question of the child acquisition literature is whether scalar implicature computation development depends on the maturation of some cognitive capacity or on processing abilities. If scalar implicature calculation depends on the maturation of some cognitive capacity in children, we expect adult learners to be much better at it than children learning their mother tongue. Not only are they cognitively mature individuals but their native language is in a position to assist them in inference calculation. If, on the other hand, scalar implicature computation depends on processing capacity because it involves choice of an optimal competitor within a narrow set of options (a sentence with *some* versus a sentence with *not all*, as proposed by Reinhart 2006), we could expect adult L2 learners to have difficulty similar to that of young native speakers. To anticipate the upcoming discussion, since adult L2ers were also revealed to experience difficulty with scalar implicatures, the implication for L1 acquisition is that children's less-than-perfect implicature computation does depend on processing resources.

These two predictions were tested in Slabakova (2010), Snape and Hosoi (to appear), and Lieberman (2009). Slabakova investigated the L2 acquisition of scalar implicatures by Korean-native learners of English. In one experiment the participants had to judge the felicity of underinformative sentences without context and had to say whether they agree with the statement as in (36).

(36)   Some elephants have trunks.

A positive answer represents the logical option since *some* and indeed *all* elephants have trunks. However, the sentence is pragmatically infelicitous in that it is not maximally informative; the negative answer is the pragmatic answer. The test sentences were translated in Korean and administered to Korean native speakers, as well as to English natives in English. Slabakova found differences in the Korean speakers' performance in their native and in their second language. They gave around 40% pragmatic answers in their native language (not significantly different from the English native group) and about 60% pragmatic answers in their second language. The results suggest that L2 learners have no problem computing scalar implicatures;

indeed they did so more often than native speakers. In the second experiment with added context, the learners gave pragmatic answers over 90% of the time. Slabakova (2010) argued that the difference between native and second language speakers was due to scalar computations being taxing on the processing resources. Since the logical responses were arguably due to conjuring up alternative contexts in order to agree with the logical use of *some* (e.g., only some elephants have trunks because some others may have been injured or born without trunks[10]), speakers had a harder time coming up with these alternative contexts in their second language.

Lieberman (2009) continued the investigation of scalar implicature computation, focusing on the issue of processing resources. He tested the acceptance of computationally demanding implicatures as in (37) and compared them to less demanding sentences as in (38).

(37)   Max didn't read all of the books.

(38)   Max read some of the books.

A sentence such as (37) involves an indirect implicature because of a scale reversal and is harder to process than the direct implicature in (38), even for native speakers (Gillingham 2007). Lieberman tested Japanese-native learners of English on the scales *<sometimes, always>*, *<partly, completely>*, as well as *every* in the scope of negation. Participants had to evaluate the felicity of sentences in short contexts. When forced to judge the acceptability of single test sentences, both native speakers and learners had difficulty computing the indirect implicatures as compared to the direct ones. The nonnative speakers were even less accurate than the natives, suggesting that in these cases there is indeed a processing problem and the native–nonnative differences are a matter of degree. When the processing load was reduced by presenting the participants with two alternatives to choose from, one felicitous and one infelicitous, the nonnative speakers had no trouble with the task and performed similarly to the native speakers. It is interesting to note that neither in Slabakova (2010) nor in Lieberman (2009) was proficiency a factor in the learners' performance.

A very interesting dimension of child–adult comparisons and processing resources is highlighted by studying bilingual children. There is a well-

---

[10] As proposed in Guasti et al. (2005).

established effect of bilingualism on executive functioning (involving attention, inhibition, and focusing) in children and adults that we have already discussed on several occasions. Bialystok (2001), Bialystok and Senman (2004), Bialystok and Martin (2004) and others have shown that bilinguals often exhibit significantly superior executive functioning and attentional abilities that are associated with better responses on metacognitive and metalinguistic tasks. Thus, it is possible that the bilingual advantage is a factor in pragmatic development.

This research question was examined by Siegal, Iozzi, and Surian (2009), which compared pragmatic competence in bilingual and monolingual children. Children participating in this study were bilingual in Italian and Slovenian, or monolingual in either language. The researchers tested children aged 3–6 on a conversational violations test to find out whether they would obey Gricean maxims. Results of two experiments in Siegal et al. (2009) show that the bilingual children have a definite advantage over the monolingual ones on four Gricean maxims: Quantity II, Quality, Relation, and Politeness. Bilingual children were more accurate in choosing nonredundant answers, true answers over false ones, answers that were relevant to the questions, and polite answers over rude ones. The only maxim on which all the children performed equally well and hovered at around 60% pragmatic responses was the Maxim of Quantity I. Here is a test item:

(39)   Question: "What did you get for your birthday?"
        Logical but underinformative answer: "A present."
        Pragmatically appropriate answer: "A bicycle."

                                                    (Siegal et al. 2009: 116)

Results of 60% pragmatic answers for children before the age of 6 are largely in line with other studies in the literature on scalar implicature computation in children. More importantly, however, Siegal et al. (2009) did not establish an advantage for bilingual children comprehending underinformative sentences. Thus it is possible that comprehending underinformative sentences involves different semantic–pragmatic calculations than detecting relevance and rudeness.

In this section, studies were summarized investigating conversational implicature knowledge and scalar implicature knowledge in L2 speakers. Findings suggest that when universal computation mechanisms are at play, learners have no trouble comprehending them; when culturally specific knowledge or formulaic expressions are involved, learners are less accurate. In addition, the bilingual advantage may only be afforded with respect to the latter but not the former.

11.7 Conclusion

In this chapter, we examined findings from the L2 acquisition of the syntax–discourse and the semantics–pragmatics interfaces. As in other areas of the grammar, there is much that is universal at these interfaces, but there are also distinctions between languages that can be viewed as parametrically opposed. The hypothesis that the interface between syntax and discourse is especially difficult was entertained, as proposed by Sorace's Interface Hypothesis. However, findings of the studies we reviewed suggested that the syntax–discourse interface is not monolithic in terms of difficulty. In this respect, the syntax–discourse interface resembles other areas of the grammar such as morphosyntax and the lexicon–syntax interface. We saw that even very similar properties across various languages (such as clitic left dislocation in Spanish/Bulgarian and topicalization in English) may create differential problems for learners. Why would this be the case? And does this interface really create difficulties across the board? There are clearly other factors impacting behavior at this interface, such as frequency of the constructions in the input and processing strategies. In addition, even though the semantics–pragmatics interface is largely universal, whether speakers have to expend a lot of mental energy or not for calculating a meaning at this interface is another important factor.

11.8 Exercises

Exercise 11.1. This is a question on a methodological issue. In our discussion of second language acquisition, we can in principle compare the accurate comprehension or production of native and nonnative, or even near-native speakers of some language L. Imagine that we have created an experiment on some construction X, and we have tested native and nonnative speakers. We have included acceptable and unacceptable sentences in our test. Figures 11.3 and 11.4 are hypothetical, but such results are all too often attested in real experiments.

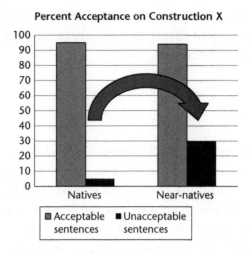

Figure 11.3 Hypothetical research result situation. The arrow indicates the group means that are not informative to compare: whether or not native speakers and learners reject an unacceptable construction with equal accuracy.

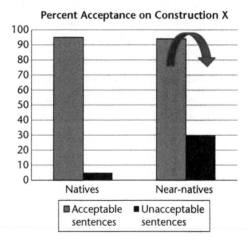

Figure 11.4 Hypothetical research result situation. The arrow indicates the group means that are informative to compare: whether or not the learners distinguish reliably between unacceptable and acceptable test items within the same construction.

What should we compare in such a situation, when the acceptance rates are very similar but the rejection rates differ? Should we compare the acceptance rates of the two constructions across speaker groups, natives and near-natives? Or should we be asking ourselves if the near-natives distinguish reliably between these two types of sentences? What is more important: that learners are indistinguishable from native speakers, or that learners acquire the contrasts in the target grammar? This choice refers to the Comparative Fallacy, proposed by Bley-Vroman (1983) and discussed in Chapter 10. Find the publication and discuss its main point. Then answer the questions I asked with respect to the two graphs above.

Exercise 11.2. Create experimental items. Here are two examples of sentence-story combinations from Slabakova and García Mayo (2015). The idea is to check whether learners of English know that focus fronting and topicalization involve moving an object to the beginning of the clause without a resumptive pronoun in the object position. In order to check on that knowledge, the experimental design offers a general context and an immediate context. Sentences are recorded to ensure the correct intonation. Participants are asked to evaluate the acceptability of the last sentence in the light of the story and the immediate context.

Task: Create three experimental items of each sort. Make sure to provide two dialogs for each, one with a resumptive pronoun and one without. The order of presentation of the acceptable and unacceptable sentence under each context has to be randomized.

(i) Fronted Focus
     Context: Mark works in a bakery in San Francisco. Their bagels are so famous that they often run out of them by the middle of the morning. This has happened again today.

     Dialog 1
     Customer: Can I get something for breakfast? Maybe a bagel?
     Mark: No, sorry. We're out of bagels. A bran muffin I can give you.

     Dialog 2
     Customer: Can I get something for breakfast? Maybe a bagel?
     Mark: No, sorry. We're out of bagels. A bran muffin I can give it to you.

(ii) Topicalization
     Context: John and his sister Sophie are in a Japanese restaurant. John has never eaten in this restaurant before, so he is not sure about what to order. He decides to ask Sophie.

     Dialog 1
     John: Have you tried the fish here?
     Sophie: Last week I had the sole. It was delicious. The salmon I haven't tried it yet.

Dialog 2
John: Have you tried the fish here?
Sophie: Last week I had the sole. It was delicious. The salmon I haven't tried yet.

Question: It is also possible to present each general context followed by one dialog, and then the same context followed by the other dialog, but in another place in the test.[11] Discuss the advantages and disadvantages of the two presentation modes. (Hint: One is better but the test takes more time.)

Exercise 11.3. Likert scales. The experiment mentioned in the previous exercise uses a Likert scale from 1 to 7 as shown below, where 1 stands for "the test sentence does not sound natural in this context," while 7 stands for "the test sentence sounds perfectly natural in this context." There is a separate point for IDK ("I don't know".)

1----- 2----- 3----- 4----- 5----- 6------ 7   I don't know
Not   Perfectly
natural   natural

What is a Likert scale? And how do we pronounce the name Likert? Is the first syllable "like" or "lick"? While both pronunciations are attested, Americans seem to prefer Like-ert, while Europeans tend towards Lick-ert. The correct pronunciation is with a short [ɪ] in the first syllable. Rensis Likert (1903–81) was an American administrator and organizational psychologist. His most famous creation is the eponymously named scale, a psychometric scale commonly involved in research using questionnaires. He proposed it in his dissertation and published the paper in 1932 (Likert 1932). It is used for measuring attitudes and is argued to capture more information than competing methods. The traditional Likert scale asks people the extent to which they agree or disagree with a statement on a 5-point scale. The scale ranges from 1=strongly agree, 2=agree, 3=undecided/neutral,

[11] Randomization is done, for example, by generating random numbers and entering each one of them in front of every story, then sorting. It is also a good idea to do pseudo-randomization, mixing the sentences up by blocks, so that similar conditions do not end up close together. Another option is to use survey services such as SurveyGizmo, Qualtrics, or Survey Monkey, which randomize the test item presentation for each participant.

4=disagree, 5=strongly disagree. Using a 5-point scale allowed Likert to rank people's attitudes with fewer questions and greater exactness. Notice that there is no true zero in this scale.

In applied linguistics, we use the Likert scale when we expect participants' judgments to be subtle and have nuances. Otherwise, we use a binary acceptability choice: Yes or No. Why do you think Slabakova and Garcia Mayo used a scale with 7 points? What would they have lost if the choices were simply Yes or No? Find the article and read the methodological discussion of the scale.

Why is it important that there is a separate answer point for IDK? Research the classical Likert scale and compare it with the usage in applied linguistics.

Read this publication by JD Brown, a well-known specialist on research methods and statistics in applied linguistics:

HTML: http://jalt.org/test/bro_34.htm
PDF: http://jalt.org/test/PDF/Brown34.pdf

Exercise 11.4. Roberts, Gullberg, and Indefrey (2008).
While this exercise is based on a published study, do not look at the original study before going through all the questions and attempting answers. After you are done with this exercise, allow yourself the pleasure to look at the study and compare your interpretations. First, let's look at the linguistic facts.

(1) a. English:
        Peter and Hans are in the office. While Peter is working, he is eating a sandwich.

    b. Dutch: Unstressed pronoun
        Peter en Hans zitten in het kantoor. Terwijl Peter$_1$ aan het werk is, eet hij$_1$ een boterham.

    c. Turkish: Zero pronoun
        Peter ve Hans$_2$ ofiste oturuyorlar. Peter$_1$ çalışırken, Ø$_{1/*2}$ sandeviç yiyor.

    d. Turkish: Overt subject pronoun
        Peter ve Hans$_2$ ofiste oturuyorlar. Peter$_1$ çalışırken, o$_{*1/2}$ sandeviç yiyor.

Question 1: Describe the linguistic facts as you see them in the English, Dutch, and Turkish examples in (1). First of all, who does *he* refer to in the English sentence? Is Peter the only possible antecedent, or the preferred antecedent? Note that the sentences involve the same constituents, although Turkish and Dutch are SOV languages. If a pronoun and a name share the same subscript (e.g., 1) they refer to the same individual, for example *Peter* and *hij* in (1b). Ø stands for the null pronoun while *o* is the Turkish equivalent of *he*. If a pronoun has two indexes 1/2, then it is ambiguous because it can refer to two possible antecedents. Which two languages of these three work similarly? Is there a reason for that?

Question 2: Roberts et al. (2008) tested three groups of participants: native speakers of Dutch and German and Turkish learners of Dutch at advanced proficiency. Can you explain the choice of these languages?

All participants undertook three experimental tasks, in which exactly the same experimental items appeared, to allow for a better comparison of the results across tasks. The session began with an eye-tracking experiment that was designed in such a way that the texts were read purely for meaning. Then an offline acceptability judgment task was administered, during which participants read each text and were asked to rate each one on a scale from 1 (least acceptable) to 6 (most acceptable). Finally, the participants completed a comprehension questionnaire. This was chosen as the last task because it specifically probed the participants' preferred referent for the subject pronoun, whereas the other two tasks did not.

Here are some sample test items, examine them all carefully. The first sentence introduces the context with an antecedent. It happens to be an antecedent external to the second, and all-important, test sentence. That sentence also introduces an antecedent, which we will call the local antecedent because it is in the same sentence as the pronoun in bold. Finally, the third sentence rounds off the context.

(2)   a. De werknemers zitten in het kantoor. Terwijl Peter aan het werk is, eet **hij** een boterham. Het is een rustige dag.
         'The workers are in the office. While Peter is working, he is eating a sandwich. It is a quiet day.'

      b. De werknemers zitten in het kantoor. Terwijl Peter aan het werk is, eten **zij** een boterham. Het is een rustige dag.
         'The workers are in the office. While Peter is working, they are eating a sandwich. It is a quiet day.'

c. Peter en Hans zitten in het kantoor. Terwijl Peter aan het werk is, eet **hij** een boterham. Het is een rustige dag.
'Peter and Hans are in the office. While Peter is working, he is eating a sandwich. It is a quiet day.'

Question 3: Identify the intended antecedent of the Dutch pronouns in bold, dependent on the context. Can you predict which of these sentences would be easiest to process, and why? Consider both the ambiguity of the pronoun and Topic shift.

We will summarize below some of the findings of the three experimental tasks. Let us call (2a) the *local* antecedent condition, (2b) the *external* antecedent condition, and (2c) the *ambiguous* condition because the two antecedents can be chosen optionally. Remember that all conditions were present in all three tasks.

In the **acceptability judgment** task, all groups performed similarly. Both natives and learners rated the external antecedent condition slightly lower than the other two, but found them largely acceptable.

The **comprehension** task actually asked for the speakers' preferred antecedent. The results are given in Table 11.1.

Question 4: Discuss these results. First of all, do you see any optionality in the behavior of the Dutch natives, in the "optional antecedent" condition? Which group seems to be choosing antecedents differently from the rest? Why do you think that is the case? Can we attribute it to L1 influence?

The results of the eye-tracking during reading task are quite complicated. The assumption underlying this task was that the time spent reading the region in which the pronoun antecedent is decided (also known as pronoun resolution) is a measure of how accessible the referent is and, thus, of the comparative difficulty of the pronoun resolution process. Simplistically put, the longer a reader gazes at a pronoun, the harder she is thinking about which is its possible antecedent. Both the Turkish and the German L2

Table 11.1 Mean (SDs) percentage of sentence internal referent (or local antecedent) chosen for the pronoun in the embedded clause of the second sentence

Group	Local antecedent (2a)	External antecedent (2b)	Optional antecedent (2c)
Dutch	100 (0)	7 (28)	100 (0)
German	98 (6)	8 (15)	91 (18)
Turkish	95 (14)	0 (0)	55 (33)

learners spent **more time** reading the critical region in the <u>optional</u> condition than in the local and external antecedent conditions. They also returned to gaze at the pronoun more times in that condition (compared to the other two).

Question 5: What can we make of these disparate results? How can we interpret the behavior of the bilinguals? You may want to assume, as the authors of the study do, that the acceptability judgment task is the most metalinguistic of the tasks, in the sense that the learners can think of rules they have been taught. The comprehension task is most reflective of under-lying competence with respect to pronoun antecedent choice in discourse, while the eye-tracking task reflects processing as well as competence. Keep in mind that German and Dutch work similarly while Turkish (being a null-subject language) is like the Spanish and Italian examples we saw in Section 11.3.

12

L2 processing

The literature on bilingual processing has veritably exploded in the last ten or fifteen years, as there is a lot of interest in finding new ways of addressing the fundamental issue of L2 acquisition: are the processes happening in the mind/brain of L2 speakers qualitatively different or qualitatively the same as the processes that native speakers engage in? A separate but related question is whether it is possible for adult L2 learners to acquire an L2 to nativelike levels. We have been interested in finding answers to these questions from the beginning of this textbook. In this chapter, we turn away from underlying grammatical representations and concentrate instead on how L2 speakers use these linguistic representations to parse language in real time. There is an interesting interplay between representation and processing, however. We have assumed in this book that linguistic representations are created in the course of language acquisition and they are subsequently accessed during language use. But we cannot "see" the linguistic representations themselves (yet), so we have to extrapolate what they might be, based on experimental findings of language use. If scholars find that L2 language processing employs the same eye-tracking signatures, shows the same ERP reflexes and patterns of processing over time as L1 language processing, it is possible to conclude that L1 and L2 representations are indeed similar. If, on the other hand, we uncover qualitative differences, they may be due to different representations, but also to similar representations accessed differently in processing. The answers to these questions are not settled yet, and they propel some cutting-edge current research. Before we go on to look at some findings, let us review the experimental methodologies we have been mentioning so far that are used to explore language processing.

12.1 Experimental techniques employed in bilingual processing studies

Behavioral measures of sentence processing frequently involve placing participants in front of a computer screen and presenting them with sentences that they read for comprehension or translation.[1] Sometimes, speakers are asked to perform other tasks on top of reading for comprehension, which are supposed to strain their working memory resources in order to see what effect this would have on performance. One commonly used experimental paradigm is the noncumulative moving window technique (also known as self-paced reading), as the reader will recall from Chapter 3. For example, in the experiment reported by Roberts and Felser (2011), sentences and comprehension questions were presented one word at a time, with participants bringing up each subsequent word by pushing a button on the button box. The final word of each sentence was indicated by a full stop. The authors created baseline and experimental items that differed minimally by one word. If there was a difference in the reading times of some region, it had to be due to the experimental manipulation.

(1) Experimental item: While the band played the song pleased all the customers.

(2) Baseline item: While the band played the beer pleased all the customers.

---

[1] For a recent review of bilingual processing using online behavioral measures, see Roberts (2013).

As the reader can appreciate, the initial words "while the band played the song" can immediately be integrated into a transitive structure where *the song* is the object of *played*. However, when the subsequent word *pleased* appears, it shows that the preceding analysis is wrong and a reanalysis is needed. Obviously, this reanalysis takes time, reflected in longer reaction times for incorporating that segment into the preceding sentence structure. Looking at example (2) now, as a band cannot play beer, it is immediately obvious that the verb *play* is used intransitively. Hence speakers do not spend so much time integrating the following words into the structure. The structures that can be studied with this and similar experimental techniques include subject and object relative clauses, high and low relative clause attachment, passive constructions, and others.

Another experimental technique that we introduced in Chapter 3 records the electric activity of the brain cortex collecting electroencephalography (EEG) data, and computing event-related brain potentials (ERPs) relative to the onset of the linguistic event, such as presentation of a phoneme, word, or morpheme. Activation is measured by placing a number of electrodes on a person's scalp. The biggest advantage of this method is that ERPs provide brain wave measures reflecting the neural activity without delay, with a temporal resolution of less than a millisecond, across the whole utterance (e.g., for each word, syllable, phoneme). Another advantage of ERPs is that they can distinguish between different cognitive processes without requiring metalinguistic tasks.[2]

One of the most remarkably consistent and replicable results over thirty years of cross-linguistic language-related ERP research is that lexico-semantic and morphosyntactic manipulations elicit qualitatively different brain responses. That, of course, is a nice confirmation of the fundamental linguistic division between lexical and functional morphemes. Now we know that the brain doesn't treat these two types of morphemes in the same way.

All content words elicit negative voltage with a peak at around 400 ms after presentation of the word, hence *the N400* name (see Figure 12.1).[3] The

---

[2] See Steinhauer (2014) for a review of this technique and findings from the perspective of the Critical Period Hypothesis.

[3] Negative values are plotted upwards on graphs (which does look strange). Note also that N400 can be elicited by nonlinguistic stimuli, such as different colors, or different images.

EEG → Event-related brain potentials (ERPs)

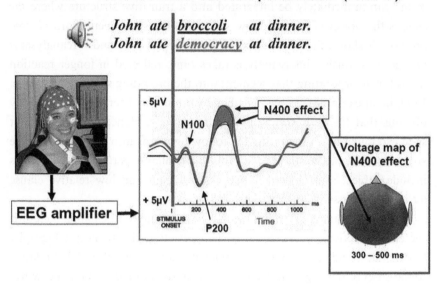

John ate *broccoli* *at dinner.*
John ate *democracy* *at dinner.*

Figure 12.1   EEG setup, N400 effect, and voltage map. EEG data collected from an electrode-cap during sentence processing are averaged time-locked to the target words (*broccoli* and *democracy*). The (schematic) ERP plot shows similar N100s and P200s in both conditions and an enhanced N400 for the semantic mismatch condition (negative polarity is plotted upwards). The voltage map illustrates the centro-parietal scalp distribution of this N400 effect between 300 and 500 ms (mismatch minus control, from Steinhauer (2014)

size of this peak depends on numerous factors, such as a word's semantic relatedness to a preceding context, its probability in the context, and frequency (Kutas and Federmeier 2011, Kutas and Hillyard 1980, Osterhout and Nicol 1999). In the original publication, Kutas and Hilliard (1980), sentences as in (3) were compared. The interesting reaction is to the final noun in bold:

(3) a. I shaved off my moustache and **beard**. (high probability word)
     b. I shaved off my moustache and **eyebrows**. (low probability word)
     c. I shaved of my moustache and **city.** (incongruent word)

On average, both unexpected final nouns (as in 3b,c) elicited an ERP waveform that was somehow different from the congruent control nouns (3a), but the negativity was larger and more robust for the incongruent word (3c). In later findings, it was argued that the N400 effect indexes not only semantic integration of the word into the previous sentence and discourse but also the reader/listener's expectations about the word, including those based on real-world knowledge.

Another very important language-related ERP effect is the P600, so called because it is a positive deflection in electrical brain activity starting at 500 milliseconds and peaking at 600 milliseconds after the onset of the triggering word. The P600 is elicited by hearing or reading morphological errors, syntactic reanalysis such as garden path sentences (as in (2)), and other syntactic anomalies (Hagoort et al. 1993). In particular, it has been related to ungrammatical continuations of the preceding material as in (4).

(4)   The spoiled child throw the toys on the floor.

As with the N400, it has recently been acknowledged that the P600 may be an umbrella effect for linguistically different processes triggered by ungrammaticality, garden paths, and long-distance *wh*-questions (Gouvea et al. 2010). The LAN (left anterior negativity) is another effect sensitive to morphosyntactic violations and grammatical processes that are at the phrase and clause level, so it comes earlier than the P600 (see Figure 12.2). It is generally considered that the P600 is more reliable while the LAN shows more variability. To reiterate, none of these components are unique to language processing: they have been attested in looking at pictures and listening to music.

The third technology that is used in contemporary psycholinguistic research on bilingualism is informally known as eye tracking.[4] This technique also measures real-time moment-by-moment processing. Its major advantage is that it captures processing decisions during natural, uninterrupted comprehension without the need to ask the participants for explicit linguistic judgments (Rayner 1998, 2009). The eye-movement tracking method comes in two main varieties. In one, the eyes of an individual are tracked while she is reading a written text. In the other, the eye movements are tracked over a visual scene during listening to sentences. The latter is called the "visual world paradigm." Research has shown that the eyes go to

---

[4] See the special issue of *SSLA* 2013 (2) edited by Paula Winke, Aline Godroid, and Susan Gass, especially the article by Roberts and Siyanova-Chanturia, for a review of the technique and findings.

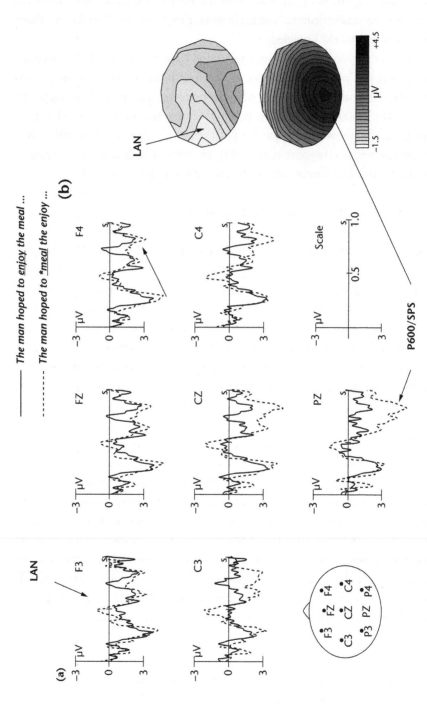

Figure 12.2 Biphasic LAN and P600 effects elicited by a syntactic word category violation in native English readers. (a) ERPs at seven electrodes show a LAN between 300–500 ms and a subsequent posterior P600 (600–1000 ms) for the ungrammatical target word (dotted line). (b) Voltage ... ... the scale distribution of both ERP effects. from Steinhauer (2014)

the image of the word on the screen within 200 ms of the word being pronounced as part of the linguistic signal.

In the former paradigm, eye tracking during reading, rapid eye movements are made from one fixation point to another. These movements are called "saccades" and they are so quick that researchers believe no new information is being input. Between saccades, there are "fixation points," and these fixation points and the time spent fixed on a word provide valuable information about processing decisions. Function words are not fixated on as long as content words. Although the direction of reading is forward, eye movements go back, too. About 15% of saccades are "regressions" of different duration: to the previous word or to the beginning of the sentence, or even to previous sentences. These regressions are interpreted as signs of processing difficulty. For example, ambiguous words, garden path sentences, or a more unusual integration of a word into a sentence meaning lead to longer regressions. We will discuss results of both types of studies in this chapter. Figure 12.3 from Roberts and Siyanova-Chanturia 2013 presents a hypothetical eye-movement record.

In addition to ERPs, eye-tracking, functional magnetic resonance imaging (fMRI) and magneto-encephalography (MEG) are used to study the neuronal underpinnings of language comprehension and production. The literature of this actively developing field of psycholinguistic inquiry is huge and growing every month. All these new techniques are most effective in elucidating human language processing when they are based on well-understood linguistic distinctions such as the distinction between lexical and functional morphemes or between nouns and verbs. Although there are significant disconnects between linguistic theory and the neurobiology of language (Poeppel and Embick 2005), there are also promising areas of

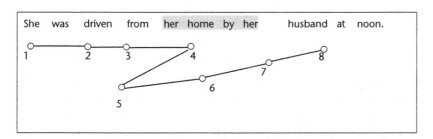

Figure 12.3 Hypothetical eye-movement record, with the gray area representing the region of interest, from Roberts and Siyanova-Chanturria (2013)

Notes: First fixation duration = 3, first pass reading time = 3+4, total reading time = 3+4+6, regression path duration = 3+4+5+6, rereading = 5+6, second pass reading time = 6, fixation count = 3+4+6 (3 fixations). First fixation duration and first pass reading time are considered early measures; the rest are considered late measures.

investigation where the neurosciences intersect with linguistic research more closely than before (Poeppel et al. 2012). Much of the integration between linguistics and neuroscience is in the future.

In the next sections, we will approach the processing of the different parts of the grammar: inflectional morphology, syntax, and lexical and context integration. Keep in mind that not all constructions that we covered in the previous chapters can be evaluated during processing, due to the various constraints of the experimental methodologies. However, there are enough constructions and properties representative of the three areas of the grammar that we can draw conclusions on how these areas are processed in real time and in natural comprehension. I will discuss some theoretical accounts of bilingual processing and what predictions they make for behavior. Then we will square these predictions with the findings we encounter.

12.2 Accounts and predictions

In considering bilingual processing, we will have to keep in mind the theoretical divide with respect to L1–L2 differences. Generally speaking, the two opposing groups of accounts mirror the competence accounts, arguing for fundamental difference or for fundamental similarity. As the reader will remember, among fundamental difference in competence accounts are Bley-Vroman's Fundamental Difference Hypothesis (1989, and especially 2009) and the Representational Deficit view of Tsimpli and Hawkins (Hawkins and Hattori 2006, Tsimpli and Dimitrakopoulou 2007). For processing, models with parallel predictions of difference are Clahsen and Felser's Shallow Structure Hypothesis (2006), and Ullman's declarative/procedural model (2005). These accounts are essentially in keeping with the Critical Period Hypothesis that we discussed in Chapter 4. The common underpinning of all these accounts is that once maturational constraints during early and late childhood have resulted in loss of plasticity in brain systems needed for native language acquisition, late learners have to allocate alternative brain systems for their L2 acquisition and have to approach the learning tasks with qualitative different mechanisms. Because learners' grammatical representations are different, their language processing routines and mechanisms are also qualitatively different from native ones. We shall see more concrete predictions as we go over the different areas of processing.

On the other side of the divide are models and proposals that consider L1 and L2 competence and processing mechanisms to be quantitatively, but not qualitatively different. Such models include the Full Transfer/Full Access/Full Parse model (Dekydtspotter, Schwartz, Sprouse 2006), Hopp's Fundamental Similarity Hypothesis (e.g., 2007) and Steinhauer et al.'s (2009) Convergence Hypothesis. Alan Juff's seminal work on L2 processing, although it does not provide a separate model, also supports this position (Juffs and Harrington 1996, Juffs 1998a,b). These models share the prediction that with increased levels of proficiency, the signatures of L2 processing of the various parts of the grammar will be approaching or converging with native processing signatures. L1 influence is not excluded by these accounts, but it is deemed possible to overcome at later levels of experience, since the processing mechanisms in L1 and L2 acquisition are essentially the same.

12.3 L2 processing of functional morphology

In Chapter 9, we discussed whether L2 speakers can decompose words into roots, stems, and affixes (derivational and inflectional). Recall that this decomposition works in the following way. Roots, stems, and morphemes are stored in the mental lexicon, together with the rules for their composition. For example *workers* is made up of the root *work*, the derivational affix *-er*, and the inflectional plural morpheme *-s*. *Work-er* is the stem for the addition of the plural morpheme. If a word is very frequent, it is likely that it will be stored whole by native as well as L2 speakers. If a word is less frequent, then composition of the constituent morphemes happens fast and online. At issue is whether L2 speakers are also capable of executing this process, as native speakers do. While results are mixed, we have enough experimental evidence from various highly inflected languages (Russian, Spanish, Serbian) showing that learners of these languages do indeed decompose. However, these studies investigated lexical access in isolation, usually through masked priming tasks.

In this section, we will look at how the inflectional morphology is processed in whole sentences and connected discourse. This is actually quite a different cognitive process compared to mental lexicon access, although the latter is certainly part of it. Functional morphemes have phonological realization; they also represent a bundle of grammatical meanings, or features that determine their syntactic behavior, i.e., their distribution within words and phrases relative to other morphemes and words in the sentence. In order to incorporate a functional morpheme in a sentence and evaluate its acceptability, it is commonly necessary to look at the whole sentence, not just the containing word. It is exactly this level in second language processing that we will review in this section. In the name of clarity, we will make a slightly artificial division between morpho-syntactic inflections and syntax proper, in the understanding that these two processes are completely integrated in language processing.

Neuroscientific data from the 1990s and early 2000s provided evidence in support of the view that the L2 morphosyntax presents insurmountable difficulties to bilinguals and that they are never up to scratch, compared to native speakers. The most influential study from that time is Weber-Fox and Neville (1996). The researchers replicated parts of the classic Johnson and Newport (1989) study, documenting a fundamental difference between late and early L2 learners, thus significantly boosting the Critical Period Hypothesis. Weber-Fox and Neville investigated various morphosyntactic and semantic violations read by adult Chinese and Korean learners of English. Two representative test items are given in (5) and (6). In the morphosyntactic violations as in (5) the preposition *of* and the noun head *proof* in the NP+PP item were switched. In the semantic violations as in (6), a similar structure with genitive nouns was sought. ERP components in reading acceptable and unacceptable sentences were compared for learners of various ages of arrival in the US, as well as native speakers.

(5)   *He criticized Max's of proof the theorem.

(6)   *John sailed Mary's cloud to Boston.

Only the very early learners (AoA before 2) showed an early LAN-like effect, as well as an appropriate P600. The adolescent arrivals exhibited a P600 but no LAN. Morphosyntactic violations did not elicit even P600s in the late arrivals. On the other hand, the semantic anomalies as in (6) elicited N400s in all groups, suggesting that grammar is processed differently from meaning. Later experiments (Hahne and Friederici 2001, Hahne 2001) extended these findings for auditory presentation of the stimuli. As Steinhauer (2014: 404) points out, by the year 2001, behavioral and ERP evidence seemed to strongly back up the Critical Period Hypothesis.

However, researchers in this area of psycholinguistics noticed a confound almost immediately. In studies that divide learners in groups according to age of arrival in the US, such as Johnson and Newport (1989) and Weber-Fox and Neville (1996), proficiency is confounded with age of arrival. Typically, a bilingual who arrived in an English-speaking country at the age of 2 is at a higher level of proficiency when tested than a bilingual who arrived in her or his twenties. This of course is a major problem for these studies, because it is not clear whether their results can be attributed to the later age of acquisition or to the lower proficiency of the bilinguals. We have previously discussed that the CPH should be falsified if we find even very few late learners to be capable of nativelike acquisition. This verification mechanism has another twist when processing is concerned. If the strong CPH claim is to be supported with neurophysiological findings, studies must show that successful learners use *different brain mechanisms* than native speakers. We are going to look at some later studies, which document similar brain mechanisms for L1 and L2 processing.

Another problem with the early studies, pointed out by Steinhauer (2014: 404–05) is their unbalanced experimental design. Since ERP effects are calculated only in comparison with the baseline, it is imperative that the baseline and the experimental sentences have exactly the same words before the violation. However, this is not the case for the experimental (5) and the baseline (7).[5] Can you see what the difference is?

(5)   *He criticized Max's **of** proof the theorem.

(7)   He criticized Max's proof **of** the theorem.

In general, many ERP researchers have argued that not all morphosyntactic violations reliably elicit LAN-like negativities in native speakers; sometimes native speakers show N400s followed by P600s (e.g., Tanner and van Hell 2014). In such cases, the lack of LANs cannot be considered as an indication of nonnative processing. In addition, ERP components can overlap in time, so that a positivity and a negativity, if they overlap even partially, can cancel themselves (at midline electrodes). Until these methodological issues with the technique are resolved to a general level of satisfaction, the lack of LAN effect in L2 learners should not be capitalized upon.

---

[5] Detailed criticism can be found in Steinhauer and Drury (2012).

A number of new studies have appeared, documenting similar ERP effects in natives and bilinguals, thereby casting doubt on the earlier findings (e.g., Rossi et al. 2006). These studies are careful not to confound age of acquisition and proficiency. For example, Rossi et al. (2006) tested Italians who were late learners of German and Germans who were late learners of Italian. This study documented that learners at high proficiency showed the native processing pattern of LAN plus P600 when detecting subject–verb agreement violations. The learners at lower levels of proficiency, matched with the other group on age of arrival, elicited a P600 only.

Gillon Dowens et al. (2010) showed that another interesting factor may be affecting nonnative processing: proximity of the agreeing elements. This study looked at number and gender agreement violations between determiner and noun within the NP, and between noun and adjective used predicatively, at a longer distance, in English–Spanish interlanguage. They found ERP patterns qualitatively similar to native ones, consisting of LAN, P600, and later negativities. However, those patterns were only elicited by the local agreement violations between determiner and noun. Violations of noun–adjective agreement did not elicit an early LAN. Thus, language proficiency alone cannot be responsible for all native–nonnative differences. The distance at which agreement is computed (local versus long-distance) also influences brain responses. L1 transfer of the various properties under investigation is also not ruled out, since behavioral measures show L2 learners of Spanish being less accurate on noun–adjective agreement than on determiner–noun agreement. The conclusion of L1 transfer is clinched by a later study by the same authors, Gillon Dowens et al. (2011), testing proficient Chinese learners of Spanish. Since Chinese has very little inflectional morphology, it was expected that the early processing signatures would not be attested. These expectations were confirmed: the Chinese learners showed P600 effects only.

It is instructive to compare findings on functional morphology from the two methodologies, ERPs and eye-tracking. Keating (2009) is an eye-tracking study that exploits the same property as Gillon Dowens et al. (2010). The critical constructions are as exemplified below in (8), (9), and (10), where the distance between the agreeing elements is manipulated.

(8) In the NP:
     Una casa pequeña cuesta mucho en San Francisco.
     'A small house costs a lot in San Francisco.'

(9)   In the matrix clause VP:
      La casa es bastante pequeña y necesita muchas reparaciones.
      'The house is quite small and needs a lot of repairs.'

(10) In the subordinate clause VP:
      Una casa cuesta menos si es pequeña y necesita reparaciones.
      'A house costs less if it is small and needs repairs.'

In the eye-tracking data, both longer fixation times on the critical elements (in this case the adjective *pequeña*), as well as regressions from the adjective back to the noun for (literally) checking the agreement indicate sensitivity to this grammatical property as well as processing difficulties. The learners' behavior showed an effect of proficiency as well as an effect of the distance between the noun head and the adjective. The native speakers displayed a response pattern including fixation and subsequent regression for all three noun–adjective distances. Only the highly advanced learners revealed the same nativelike pattern of behavior, and only for the most local configuration as in (8). However, if we consider the stimuli from the point of view of grammatical representations, the same formal features are involved in the noun–adjective agreement no matter the distance between head and modifier. Therefore, Keating argued that his eye-tracking data suggests successful acquisition but more labored processing. His learners had acquired the feature checking mechanism, but had a harder time applying it at a distance, in cases where they had to keep more words in working memory. Thus, the results of the eye tracking and the ERP studies of the same construction cohere completely.

Briefly comparing Keating (2009) to another eye tracking study, Foucart and Frenck-Mestre (2012), brings forward another reason for performance divergence. In the latter study, the agreeing noun and adjective are separated by the auxiliary *sont* 'are':

(11) Au printemps les pommes [Fem] sont vertes [Fem]/ *verts [Masc] sur
      cet arbre.
      'In spring, apples are green on this tree.'

While all Keating's subjects, even the native speakers, did not show longer fixation times for ungrammatical items, Foucart and Frenck-Mestre's natives and learners did spend a longer time fixated on the ungrammatical forms. Roberts and Siyanova-Chanturia (2013) attribute this difference to the task that participants had to perform. In Keatings's study, participants performed a meaning related task, while in the Foucart and Frenck-Mestre's study, participants' attention to grammar may have been heightened because they were asked to offer a grammaticality judgment. Thus, the different results could be due to different levels of attention to grammar. It is important, though, that in both experiments, learners patterned with the natives.

In conclusion, after the early ERP studies showing clear divergence between native and bilingual processing mechanisms of the inflectional morphology, later studies with improved designs attested to a higher level of convergence. It is not the case that the L2 learners, even at advanced proficiency, always perform as native speakers. However, factors such as more arduous processing and a lower degree of automaticity explain a lot of the differences. Importantly, acquisition of the inflectional morphology may require effort, and the knowledge may be hard to implement in real language processing, but neither nativelike acquisition nor nativelike processing are impossible.

12.4 Parsing and syntactic processing in the L2

We are going to look next at syntactic processing. Of course, processing of the inflectional morphology, discussed in the previous section, is truly syntactic processing, since all syntactic features are captured in inflectional morphology. In this section, we will pay attention to the visible reflexes of syntactic processes: movement of phrases at a distance and their interpretation.

But first, let me make abundantly clear what I assume to be the division of labor between the grammar and the parser (the language processing system), since this is a controversial but very important issue. The parser is a grammatical analyzer which quickly checks the words of the incoming sentence, considers their morphosyntactic information, and integrates them into syntactic structure in an incremental way (Crocker 1996, Fodor 1998). Based on the structure that the parser builds, a partial semantic interpretation is computed at each stage of syntactic derivation (see Chapter 2). Interpretation building takes into account the semantic information from the words, as well as pragmatic inferences and information from the context of the utterance. All this takes place in mere milliseconds, that is, as fast as lightning. Processing linguistic input in real time reveals information about the way representations of linguistic knowledge are structured and stored in the mind/brain of the hearer/reader. Without much argument, I have assumed here a view of linguistic processing which postulates that there is a *considerable overlap* between the grammar and the parser (following the seminal work of Janet Fodor, Lyn Frazier, and many others), and that the parser's operations are based on grammatical representations.[6] As we saw in Chapter 3, the grammar proposes (alternative construals), the parser disposes (which one should be selected as the correct one). There are ample research findings to support this assumption.

Teaching relevance

The teaching relevance of this assumption that the grammar and parsing go hand in hand is clear: the more practice learners have at comprehending and producing the second language, the more their underlying grammar will grow, hand in hand with their processing skills. An active parser can aid a developing grammar.

Let us take a more detailed look at some theoretical proposals for native syntactic processing. A model of native language processing called Late Assignment of Syntax Theory (LAST), Townsend and Bever (2001), proposes that all syntactic processing advances along two lines in parallel: a "pseudosyntactic" analysis based on canonical templates and semantic roles, which is immediately linked to semantic representations; and a true syntactic analysis that takes place independently of the semantics. The pseudosyntactic analysis is a "quick and dirty" parse dependent on associations and frequencies in the input. It moves the *wh*-words back to their original argument positions and then applies canonical template strategies (such as Agent–Verb–Theme)[7] to provide an initial meaning analysis. The

---

[6] For example, take this citation from Duffield (2006: 57). No one can say:

that a particular piece of linguistic performance—whether it comes from traditional behavioral methods such as response latencies, or from more modern techniques such as event-related potentials—is uniquely due to the grammar or to the processing system. [...] grammatical competence is always mediated by the processing system (in virtue of being part of it)....

[7] This is what the template does. If the parser assumes that every incoming sentence containing NP+VP+NP (e.g., *George offers help*) exemplifies the Agent–Verb–Theme

syntactic analysis proper goes through a cyclical derivation for the whole clause and offers a completely specified syntactic representation. At the end of the two parallel processes, their outputs are compared and if there is a match, the computed meaning is stored. If there is no match (due to garden path, reanalysis, etc.), the computation can start again at various points. The two lines of computation are argued to be independent up to the comparison point. Ferreira's Good Enough model for initial representations (Ferreira, Bailey, and Ferraro 2002) is reminiscent of the LAST model, although it may differ in the details.

Clahsen and Felser's (2006) Shallow Structure Hypothesis extends the insights from these two models to second language processing. The hypothesis postulates that the pseudosyntactic, or good-enough, way of parsing the incoming input is *the only way* bilinguals can parse language. According to the Shallow Structure Hypothesis, it is not just a processing issue: the L2 grammar does not provide the kind of information required to process complex syntax in nativelike ways, forcing L2 learners to fall back on "shallow" parsing strategies. L2 learners use lexical-semantic and pragmatic information as well as templates of predicate argument structure (Agent–Verb–Theme) to interpret incoming strings of words in a minimal (shallow) semantic representation, without mapping detailed and complete syntactic representations onto semantic representations. Several sentence-processing studies by Clahsen and associates have found that L2 learners indeed rely less on hierarchical phrase structure or on abstract syntactic elements such as movement traces, than native speakers during comprehension. Direct evidence for the SSH comes from the online processing of filler–gap dependencies. For example, as indicated by Marinis et al. (2005), learners do not process the intermediate copies of the moved *wh*-word *who* in examples like (12) as native speakers do.

(12)   [DP The nurse [RC [**who**] the doctor argued [CP [who2] that the rude patient had angered [who1]]]] ... is refusing to work late.

The relative pronoun *who* starts out as the object of the verb *to anger* and on its way to the top of the relative clause RC, it stops over in the

mapping between arguments and theta roles, it will be over 85% correct. Probabilistically speaking, that's a safe assumption. Sentences such as *The key opened the door*, not following the template, are rare in English.

intermediate CP position in front of *that*. In example (11), these two positions are marked ~~who~~₁ and ~~who~~₂. When the relative pronoun stops in the ~~who~~₂ position, it leaves a copy of itself and continues on its way. In the generative theory of *wh*-movement, copies of movement have psychological reality although they are not pronounced, and they are indicative of abstract structural representations of sentences. Since learners in the Marinis et al. (2005) study did not show sensitivity to this intermediate copy, as indicated by reading times, the researchers argued that second language speakers rely on lexical–semantic and predicate–argument relations between words, when they are processing such long-distance dependencies. In other words, their processing is meaning-based, not structure-based. Furthermore, Clahsen and Felser interpreted this to indicate that "L2 processing is different because of inadequacies of the L2 grammar" (Clahsen and Felser, 2006: 120). Felser and Roberts (2007) present more evidence for L2 speakers using quantitatively different processing routines from the native speakers.

Opponents of the Shallow Structure Hypothesis try to show that L2 speakers are indeed sensitive to such structural representations that are needed to calculate sentence meaning online. Among many recent studies, Omaki and Schultz (2011) demonstrate that both their English native speakers and Spanish learners of English obey relative clause island constraints. Aldwayan, Fiorentino, and Gabriele (2010) also show evidence that Najdi Arabic speakers process English *wh*-movement actively guided by syntactic constraints. Dekydtspotter and Miller (2013) study the activation of intermediate traces of *wh*-movement in a priming experiment and argue that their results are better explained by weak activation of semantic concepts, probably due to lexical access difficulties. They caution that research on the processing of *wh*-dependencies in sentence processing must give full consideration to lexical activation mechanisms. Dekydtspotter et al. (2012) report reading time asymmetries in L2 speakers that are consistent with observing constraints on binding. Within ERP studies, Reichle and Birdsong (2014) tested sensitivity to contrastive focus in French among advanced classroom learners. They observed a nativelike negativity in their more proficient learners.

Apart from findings inconsistent with it, one line of argumentation against the shallow processing idea for bilinguals, due to Indefrey (2006), counters that a number of native speakers also resort to using semantic-based processing most of the time. These happen to be low-educated, low-reading-span or nonproficient native speakers (Pakulak and Neville 2010).

The effect of lack of experience with a certain construction can be the same for monolingual native speakers and for bilinguals in their second language, as Dąbrowska's work on the passive has shown (although with a comprehension task). See more on this in the section on individual differences. The point that a lot of researchers make is that shallow processing is not exclusive to bilinguals.

Another interesting factor that may modulate shallow processing is learners' type of exposure: naturalistic (in the country where the L2 is spoken) versus in the classroom. In the typical case, naturalistic exposure, especially study abroad, would furnish richer and more varied language experience. Two recent experimental studies are relevant here. Pliatsikas and Marinis (2013a) tested Greek learners with either naturalistic and/or classroom exposure to English on the past tense rule. Both their highly proficient learners with an AoA (age of arrival) of 8–9 years performed similarly to natives, therefore suggesting that the type of exposure is not a factor in automatic processing of morphosyntax while age of acquisition and proficiency are. Pliatsikas and Marinis (2013b), however, examined the processing of two similar groups of Greek–English bilinguals with the same age of acquisition (8–9 years) and again with naturalistic or predominantly classroom exposure. Using the same stimuli from Marinis et al. (2005) exemplified in (11), they found that their naturalistic learners (but not the classroom learners) were indeed processing the intermediate traces like native speakers. These latter results suggest that linguistic immersion can indeed lead to nativelike abstract syntactic processing in the L2. They are also in line with the importance of experience for nativelike and efficient parsing.

On balance, the SSH appears to be falsified by numerous recent studies using self-paced reading, eye tracking, and ERP components. A lot of the studies reviewed here demonstrate that learners are sensitive to syntactic constrains in their second language. Apparent divergence may be due to linguistic experience with a specific construction, proficiency, and type of exposure.

12.5 Integration of meaning in syntactic processing

Most current models of language processing agree that, in online sentence processing, different types of constraints (lexical, morphological, syntactic and semantic) are very quickly taken into consideration during speaking and listening (or reading). Constraints on how words can be combined structurally operate alongside qualitatively distinct constraints on the combination of word meanings, on the grouping of words into phonological and intonational phrases, and on their integration into discourse. There is evidence that semantic, syntactic, and phonological unification processes (combinatory processes) all operate at the same time and influence each other to some extent. An example of semantic unification is the integration of word meaning into an unfolding discourse representation of the preceding context. For instance, the majority of common English words have more than one meaning. In the interaction with the preceding sentence and/or discourse context, the appropriate meaning is selected, so that a coherent interpretation results.

In this section, we will examine the evidence on incorporating lexical-semantic and subcategorization information into the online computation of meaning. To anticipate the findings, it turns out that L2 speakers are generally very good at integrating semantic information into the parse.

The crucial sentences where this is studied are garden path sentences. In the processing of garden paths, the subcategorization of the verbs involved is of utmost importance. But first, let's back off a little and revise what speakers know when they know a verb: quite a lot, actually. Each verb is learned with information about which thematic roles (theta roles) are needed for the sentence with this collocation to be acceptable (see Chapter 3, Section 3.4 and note 7). This information is known as verb valency (as in chemistry) or subcategorization: *give* takes an Agent, a Theme, and a Goal (*John gave a package to Mary*); *put* takes an Agent, a Theme, and a Location (*John put the apple on his head*), etc. Theta roles are mapped onto syntactic arguments (subject, direct object, indirect or prepositional object, etc.), not always in a uniform fashion. In a theory of incremental parsing based on theta roles and early satisfaction of grammatical principles (Pritchett 1992), the parser will use several sources of syntactic information. Let us look at what happens in the incremental processing of (13).

(13)   John gave a package to Mary.

After *John* appears in reading or in speech, the parser expects a verb. This verb, if finite, will satisfy the syntactic requirement of checking the case of the subject (Nominative). It will also assign the Agent theta role to *John*.

The verb *give* being tri-valent, that is, needing a Theme and a Goal in addition to the Agent, the parser will expect appropriate noun phrases or prepositional phrases to appear next. If these predictions are fulfilled, the parse can terminate successfully, producing an interpretation. Processing breakdown can occur if the words after the verb are not as expected by the parser for the immediate satisfaction of subcategorization and syntactic requirements. Furthermore, the parser can be fooled into positing one structure (temporarily): the appearance of subsequent words indicate that another structure is really warranted, so reanalysis is required. Take the garden path (GP) sentence in (14a).

(14)   a. After Bill drank the water proved to be poisonous.
       b. Sam warned the student cheated on the exam.
       c. After Sam arrived the guests began to eat.

Speakers know that the verb *drink* can appear with or without a Theme argument in object position. In the incremental appearance of the sentence words on the screen (in a self-paced reading task), *the water* satisfies grammatical and semantic requirements, so the temporary structure *After Bill drank the water* can be plausibly posited. After the appearance of the following verb, *proved*, it becomes clear that this new verb will also need a subject argument (although not an Agent). *The water* is reanalyzed as that argument. Note that on top of taking time and effort, reanalysis depends on the appropriate lexico-semantic and syntactic knowledge being available online.

The groundbreaking research on how L2 learners integrate this knowledge into the comprehension of a sentence is due to Juffs and Harrington (1996) and Juffs (1998a,b). The researchers examined the processing of sentences as in (14a,b,c) and found that Chinese–English bilinguals were slower to read the disambiguating verbs (*proved, cheated* in (14a,b)) in garden path sentences, as compared to non-GP sentences containing intransitive verbs (e.g., *arrive* in (14c)). This shows that learners were sensitive to the fact that *drink* and *warn* can be both transitive and intransitive, in English, but *arrive* is only intransitive. In a later experiment, Juffs (1998a) compared the processing of similar garden path structures by bilingual speakers with Chinese, Japanese, Korean, and Romance as native languages. As Figure 12.4 illustrates, the bilinguals are slower than the English native speakers, but their processing of garden paths is uniform: all groups are

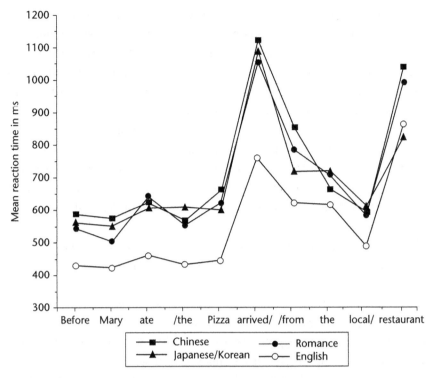

Figure 12.4 Meaning reading times for garden path sentences by four groups of speakers, from Juffs (1998a)

Reproduced with permission from Sage

surprised by the appearance of the verb *arrived*, and take time to reanalyze *the pizza.*[8]

In a similar vein, Dussias and Cramer Scaltz (2008) explored sensitivity to verb biases, the information on what type of argument (NP or complement clause) follows a verb most often. In a self-paced reading experiment, they found that Spanish–English bilinguals' reading times were longer when the continuation went against the verb biases in English.

(15)   a. The CIA director confirmed the rumor could mean a security risk.

   b. The ticket agent admitted the mistake when he got caught.

---

[8] See Juffs (1998a) for the findings on the non-GP sentences. It is on those sentences that the performance of the learners groups diverged, suggesting L1 influence.

Learners were sensitive to verb biases when they overlapped in the L1 and L2. When the Spanish verb biases were contrary to English, though, the learners transferred their native biases. Results of these and other experiments, taken together, demonstrate that bilinguals process the incoming linguistic signal incrementally and try to accommodate each word subcategorization information and bias, as long as they know it.

Roberts and Felser (2011) explored whether L2 speakers use plausibility information in their incremental processing. Even if a verb is known to be predominantly transitive, such as *read*, some objects following *read* are more plausible than others. The researchers used this to see how much plausibility will influence the ease of recovery after garden path sentences.

(16) a. The journalist wrote the book had amazed all the judges.
      b. The journalist wrote the girl had amazed all the judges.

Both sentences require reanalysis, but in (16a) the initial analysis is plausible (*the journalist wrote the book*) while in (16b) it is not (*the journalist wrote the girl*). The researchers hypothesized that readers will have a harder time recovering from the initial wrong analysis if it was plausible, that is, in cases such as (16a), which would be indexed by longer reading times at the disambiguating complement clause. That's exactly what they found, for natives and L2 speakers alike. They argued that the bilinguals' commitment to a plausible initial analysis is stronger than to an implausible one, and thus harder to abandon in the face of new evidence. However, this was not the case in constructions with fronted adjunct clauses, as in (17).

(17) a. While the band played the song pleased all the customers.
      b. While the band played the beer pleased all the customers.

The L2 readers continued to show elevated reanalysis reading times no matter whether the initial analysis was plausible or not. The authors argued that the more complex computation of the adjunct clause had affected the readers' ability to process incrementally. Still, L2 readers showed they could do lexico-semantic integration, even if processing complexity affected them negatively.

In sum, numerous analyses and comparative studies of bilingual processing acknowledge that lexico-semantic processing is not as challenging to learners as grammar processing. An indication of this is the fact that learners are quite accurate integrating lexico-semantic knowledge at lower levels of proficiency, in comparison to morphosyntactic knowledge. In contrast, the differences observed between native and L2 speakers lie in the area of grammar processing. For instance, L2 learners find it harder to recover from mis-analysis in some garden path sentences, and have trouble establishing grammatical relationships across clause boundaries, or when the material to be processed is structurally more complex. This state of affairs does not mean that morphosyntactic processing is not accessible, or that their linguistic representations are faulty; it just means that grammar processing is harder and nativelike behavior patterns are attained at later stages of development.

12.6 Individual differences in grammar processing

Language processing is a very complex process that involves a rapid application of lexico-semantic and morphosyntactic knowledge, the resulting parse being evaluated in the light of discourse pragmatic and world knowledge. In addition, during the structural analysis of the signal, predictions are generated as to what might be expected further along in the sentence string. Not surprisingly, researchers have established that there is a lot of variability among native speakers in all of these processes. Research so far has established that working memory, as tested by memory span tasks, shows some correlation with successful and fast processing of complex and/or long strings. It makes sense that individuals who can retain a larger number of words or numbers in short-term memory would also be able to use that memory to store and manipulate more complex linguistic structures. For example, King and Just (1991) found that participants with low scores on a test of verbal working memory ability produced longer reaction times on difficult regions of test sentences, compared to high-span participants. They were also less accurate on related comprehension questions. The idea was that taxing the lower memory resources with a complex computation led to more errors in comprehension.

However, Caplan and Waters (1999) argued against the existence of a single pool of working memory resources responsible for language comprehension and in favor of a multi-resource theory. Recent reviews of the available research (Farmer, Misiak, and Christianson 2012) suggest that verbal memory explains a rather small amount of variance among natives.

Instead, Farmer et al. (2012) propose an experience-based hypothesis: past linguistic experience substantially influences sentence processing. The more experience an individual has with a specific construction such as the passive, or in reading long and complicated sentences, the easier that processing becomes. (The teaching relevance of this thesis is quite clear, right?) In addition, differences in cognitive control, as measured by stroop tasks[9] and the like, may be affecting processing of ambiguous sentences (e.g., *Jane hit the man with the umbrella*) and garden paths, because one needs cognitive control in order to direct attention away from one analysis and contemplate another analysis (Novick et al. 2005).

In a recent review, Phillips and Ehrenhofer (in press) argue that the single substantial difference between native adult and native child processing is that children are not good at reanalysis (as needed in garden paths) or calculation of two meanings in ambiguous sentences. Children's first analysis is their last analysis, they argue, being their one and only analysis. We have already seen that in adult native speakers, this is not the case. Phillips and Ehrenhofer (in press: 7) plausibly attribute this child–adult difference to children's limitations in cognitive control abilities, and not to a growing of the grammar (Novick et al. 2005, Mazuka et al. 2009). For example, "children show broad difficulties in revising initial action plans, likely due to the delayed maturation of the frontal lobe, the primary home of executive function abilities (Davidson et al. 2006)." Language difficulties are part of a broader maturation picture.

Now, if this interpretation is on the right track and children have difficulties parsing some complex syntactic structures due to executive function limitations, could this explanation work for L2 learners? In principle, it should. Phillips and Ehrenhofer (in press) say no, but I disagree. Executive function in bilinguals is taxed by the constant inhibition of the language not in use and by the juggling of two lexical items for each concept, different grammatical rules, etc. Individual differences in cognitive abilities (e.g., executive function) should, again in principle, have a higher impact on processing in bilinguals than in monolinguals. What could the evidence be in support of such a processing explanation of L1–L2 differences?

---

[9] A stroop task is a demonstration of interference in task reaction. When the name of a color (e.g., "blue") is printed in a color different from the name (e.g., the word "red" printed in blue ink instead of red ink), naming the color of the word takes longer and is more prone to errors than when the color of the ink matches the name of the color.

We have established in the previous two sections that second language learners process the language in a similar, even if not in an identical, fashion with native speakers. They have more difficulty with complex structures (sentences such as (12) above), as well as structures where they have to keep a lot of material in short-term memory (sentences such as (17)). It is logical to expect, then, that at least some of the divergence between natives and bilinguals may be due to individual memory and cognitive differences. In addition, many researchers of second language acquisition suggest that native speakers also exhibit a range of processing capabilities, as do L2 learners, so we have to be careful in choosing comparison groups. In this section, we will briefly summarize what is currently known on this topic, provided that research on individual differences in bilingual processing is in its infancy.[10] However, it is an area of very vigorously developing research, and the reader can expect to hear much more about it in the future.

The most important factor impacting processing that L2 researchers test is L2 proficiency. Note that in this way they are applying Farmer et al.'s (2012) suggestion that linguistic experience may influence processing more than memory span. Intuitively it makes sense that L2 learners of higher proficiency are also those with more experience in that language. However, the findings are more complicated. Overall, it is attested that higher proficiency learners pattern as native speakers only when their attention is drawn to grammatical form (not meaning) in consideration of an additional experimental task. For example, Jackson and van Hell (2011) asked Dutch learners of English to process sentences such as those in (18).

(18) a. Who do you think _____ met the tourists in front of the museum? (subject *wh-* word extraction)
      b. Who do you think the tourists met ____ in front of the museum (object *wh-* word extraction)

Learners had to read as well as give grammaticality judgments on acceptable and unacceptable sentences of this sort. The less proficient learners experienced processing breakdown on the subject extraction sentences,[11]

---

[10] See Juffs and Harrington (2011) for an overview of the literature on working memory, and Roberts (2012) for a review of individual differences in L2A.

[11] Subject extractions are considered to be computationally more complex than object extractions, and they are dispreferred by children and adults alike.

while the more proficient learners patterned with the native speakers. Comparing the results of two self-paced reading studies makes this point abundantly clear. Jackson and Dussias (2009) asked English learners of German to read and to judge the grammaticality of sentences as in (19).

(19) a. Wer   denkst du, bewunderte den Sportler   nach den Spiel?
          Who.NOM think you admired   the.ACC athlete after the game
          'Who do you think admired the athlete after the game?'
      b. Wen   denkst du, bewunderte der Sportler   nach den Spiel?
          Who.ACC think you admired   the.NOM athlete after the game
          'Who do you think the athlete admired after the game?'

In that study, advanced learners showed nativelike processing of the questions. In subject extractions (19a), they tried to integrate the nominative-marked *wh*-word into the parsed sentence as soon as possible, that is, in matrix subject position. When they encountered *du* 'you' as the subject of the matrix clause, they experienced difficulty, reflected in longer reading times for that segment. This was not the case for object extraction sentences as in (19b). Upon reaching the complement clause, however, reading time preferences reversed for both the native and the L2 German speakers, with longer reading times on object extractions compared to subject extractions. This was attributed to the fact that the object extraction sentences were more difficult to process because the fronted object had to be kept in working memory for a longer time. In a continuation of the first study that had subjects read without grammatical evaluation (Jackson and Bobb 2009), no reading time differences were observed. There were no differences in the complement clauses of the two conditions (subject and object extraction). Crucially, no effects of proficiency or working memory capacity were attested.

The comparative findings of the two studies suggest that bilinguals process better when their attention to grammar is heightened. They often adopt processing strategies to fit the demands imposed by the task, especially when challenged by complex processing. The authors write that

these resulting strategies may not mirror the strategies employed by a majority of native speakers of the language in question, and they may be highly individualized, varying dramatically from L2 speaker to L2 speaker. Nevertheless, they highlight the ability of L2 speakers to make sophisticated use of the linguistic and cognitive resources they have at their disposal to successfully process and comprehend L2 input. (Jackson and Bobb, 2009: 631.)

I think the connection with executive function here is clear, although completely speculative: in a nutshell, when they put their mind to it, L2 speakers are successful even with the most complex structures. However, much more research on this idea is needed.

Another individual factor that can account for L1–L2 differences is processing efficiency. It is well known that L2 readers are slower than native readers, especially if they are reading in a script not their own.[12] However, as Roberts (2012) points out, the term "processing efficiency" is at this time not well defined.

It could relate to efficiency in a number of different processes undertaken during language comprehension, from decoding of orthography/speech sounds, to lexical access and selection, to integration of syntactic and other knowledge, as well as to prediction or anticipation of up-and-coming input. (Roberts 2012: 181.)

Roberts and Felser (2011) argue that being slower does appear to affect parsing procedures, particularly when the task involves reading for comprehension only. They also align reading speed with proficiency.

In a study particularly designed to test the effect of reading speed, Kaan, Ballantyne, and Wijnen (in press) used a self-paced reading task with English native speakers and Dutch learners. When they performed the statistical analysis of the grammatical manipulations (subject–verb agreement in object relative clauses) not controlling for reading speed, that is, including all of the participants, the L2 group performance appeared to differ from the native group in that the effect started later and was smaller than in native speakers. However, when the authors selected a group of L2 speakers who matched the natives in reading speed, differences in processing patterns disappeared. In other words, language background did not have any effect above and beyond reading speed.[13] In addition, the readers in this study had to perform an end-of-sentence verification task with True/False answers. Only the faster L2 readers but not the slower ones showed a nativelike pattern in this task. The researchers interpret the findings to suggest that L2 learners and native speakers have the same grammar and are able to build the same syntactic structures during online processing, but

---

[12] Some recent exceptions are Hopp (2015) and Kaan, Ballantyne, and Wijnen (in press), who found that some of their bilingual participants read faster than their native readers.

[13] Note that in this study, in order to create reading speed-matched groups, some of the fastest L2 readers had to be excluded, as they read faster than native speakers.

may differ in terms of allocation of processing resources (see also Hopp 2010, McDonald 2006). Even if some L2 speakers read at the same speed as the native speakers, they likely have more difficulty computing and maintaining the syntactic representations in short-term memory. This divergence may be due to slower lexical access, lower activation of the relevant information, or fewer available resources (e.g., because bilinguals need to inhibit competing native representations).

The interplay between processing efficiency and speed is addressed in Hopp (2010). It is generally assumed that when readers are forced to speed up their reading, their processing load increases. Hopp used a moving window word-by-word presentation, but varied the speed of presentation from 250 ms plus 17ms per each letter (Speed 1) to 155 ms (Speed 2), 105 ms (Speed 3), 88 ms (Speed 4), and 71 ms (Speed 5). Four groups of native speakers were tested on Speeds 2 to 5. The results showed that under conditions of speeded grammaticality judgments, the accuracy of native speakers deteriorated to the level of L2 learners at Speed 1. However, that happened only for gender violations, not for subject–verb agreement violations. The different treatment of gender and number violations fits in with behavioral findings determining that gender violations are particularly problematic for L2 learners, even if they have grammatical gender in their native language (e.g., Franceschina 2005). Thus, native speakers' performance under increased processing load and L2 speakers' performance converge on selected violations (e.g., for gender but not number). What is difficult for nonnatives is also difficult for natives under conditions of forced, less efficient processing. This finding suggests that even if natives and bilinguals share grammatical knowledge and processing architecture, bilinguals may not be able process the L2 as efficiently as natives.

Finally, Hopp's (2015) study brings forward another interesting dimension along which L2 learners may differ: individual allocation of resources, or attention, to either form or meaning. Hopp discusses L1 German–L2 English learners' use of morphosyntactic, semantic, and subcategorization information in the processing of temporarily ambiguous sentences as below.

(20)   a. When the girl was praying, the boy made some funny noises. (Control)
       b. When the girl was praying the boy made some funny noises. (Intransitive)
       c. When the girl was playing he made some funny noises. (Pronoun)

d. When the girl was playing the boy made some funny noises.
(Implausible)

e. When the girl was playing the piano made some funny noises.
(Plausible)

In order to gauge the individual factors of proficiency, reading speed, working memory span, and allocation of processing resources, Hopp tested the participants in a lexical decision task, a reading-span task, and a word-monitoring task. The main task was eye tracking during reading. While he confirmed previous findings of successful lexico-semantic integration, a plausibility effect, and morphosyntactic difficulties, the more interesting findings relate to individual processing profiles. The researcher divided the learners into low integration, mid integration, and high integration groups, depending on the syntactic integration ability they showed in the word-monitoring task. The low integration group was revealed as using plausibility and subcategorization information for recovery from garden paths but did not use morphosyntactic information. On the other hand, the high integration group showed a fully nativelike processing pattern in that it recruited morphosyntactic as well as subcategorization information incrementally in first-pass and second-pass measures of processing.

It seems then that individuals (bilingual learners as well as monolingual natives) might differ in the attention they pay to either form or meaning. This division is reminiscent of the dual pathway described by Townsend and Bever (2001) and Ferreira and colleagues (2002) for native processing (Section 12.4). Recall that according to these accounts, sentence processing can proceed along two routes: (a) a shallow analysis that relies on frequent and predictable surface patterns including lexical-semantic and plausibility information; and (b) a deep, syntactic parse that exploits grammatical structure. In natives, these routes are argued to work in parallel, but wide individual differences exist, too (Pakulak and Neville 2010). In the L2 learners participating in Hopp's study, accuracy did not seem to correlate with proficiency, lower working memory, or problems in lower level linguistic processing. The author suggests the different performance of individual learners on his tests stems from their need to allocate resources efficiently and to these resources being inherently limited in bilinguals.[14]

---

[14] See also Wilson, Sorace, and Keller (2009).

Furthermore, hitherto unexplained variation among speakers may also play a role here. The recent findings of Tanner and van Hell (2014),[15] an ERP study of monolingual native speakers detecting morphosyntactic violations, are illuminating. Recall that morphosyntactic violations are assumed to elicit a biphasic LAN–P600 effect, but not an N400 effect. The study did find such a biphasic pattern of responses in the group results. However, they did not find the expected biphasic LAN–P600 response for most of their individual participants. Instead, individuals' brain responses varied along a continuum between an N400 and a P600, with some biphasic patterns in between. The researchers explicitly argued that the individual patterns of responses to morphosyntactic violations were very similar to those uncovered in some bilingual speakers. In other words, we may be seeing variation among L2 learners because variation exists among ALL speakers of language, irrespective of nativeness, proficiency level, and education profiles. This is an area of research that will bring important new discoveries relevant to SLA in the future.

The studies we reviewed in this section all point to the conclusion that examination of individual differences should be an obligatory element of future psycholinguistic studies. L2 learners, just like native speakers are NOT a homogeneous group. Statements amounting to "L2 speakers do this or that" should not be acceptable if they do not differentiate between individual performances based on L2 proficiency, memory capacity, speed of reading, and processing efficiency.

12.7 Conclusion

Processing differences between monolingual native speakers and bilingual or multilingual L2 users, together with reliable and copious input, is emerging to be the most powerful explanation of L1–L2 competence differences. Researchers who would not agree on much else in L2A would nevertheless agree that bilingual processing is among the most important areas of L2A. Slower or more belabored processing in L2 learners should be distinguished from competence difference explanations such as the Fundamental Difference Hypothesis (Bley-Vroman 1989, 2009) and the Representational

---

[15] See also Tanner et al. (2013).

Deficit view (Hawkins and Hattori 2006, Tsimpli and Dimitrakopoulou 2007). In other words, an L2 user may appear to be different from a native language user for two reasons: either because their processing is different or because their competence (hence, linguistic representations) *and* processing are different. We reviewed accounts of L2 processing divided into two main positions, largely as follows. One position, exemplified in the work of Clahsen, Felser, Paradis, and Ullman, argues that the L2 processing mechanisms are qualitatively different. Furthermore, Clahsen and Felser attribute the processing divergence to an underlying competence divergence. The other position maintains that processing mechanisms in the second language are essentially the same as in the first language, but the pressures of bilingualism can lead to apparent L1–L2 differences. Processing preferences and routines can transfer from the native language, but can also be overcome. This position is exemplified in the work of Dekydtspotter, Dussias, Juffs, Gabriele, Omaki, Schulz, VanPatten, and many others. For recent reviews of this position, see Dekydtspotter (2009) and Belikova and White (2009). In the future, we can expect a lot of the answers to the fundamental questions of SLA to come from, or partially from, processing findings.

12.8 Exercises

Exercise 12.1. Do you agree with the logic that the CPH should be falsified if we find even one or two late L2 learners who are completely nativelike? In this chapter we mentioned that if the strong CPH claim is to be supported with neurophysiological findings, studies must show that successful learners use *different brain mechanisms* than native speakers. Discuss what that difference might mean in actual findings, keeping in mind the studies exemplified in the chapter. Is it enough to show that L2 and L1 speakers exhibit different behavioral measures (be that reaction times, eye movement saccades, ERP reflexes, etc.)? How about *different processing mechanisms*?

Exercise 12.2. Sato (2007) is a dissertation study, summarized in Clahsen et al. (2010), investigating L2 learners' sensitivity to subject–verb number agreement and pronominal case. In order to assess the possible influence of the presence versus absence of these grammatical categories in the learners' L1, Sato examined three groups of learners from typologically different L1 backgrounds (German, Japanese, and Chinese) in a series of speeded grammaticality judgment tasks. Note that German is similar to English in that it marks both case and S–V agreement, Japanese has a morphological case but lacks S–V agreement marking, whereas Chinese lacks both. All L2 learners scored 70% or above in the Oxford Placement Test, placing them within the intermediate to advanced proficiency range. They demonstrated close to ceiling knowledge on case and agreement in a separate offline task, confirming that they were aware of the relevant grammatical distinctions.

In the speeded judgment task, learners saw simple three-word sentences such as *We regularly sneezes* and *He admires she*. All sentences became ungrammatical at the final word. The experimental sentences were presented word-by-word at a rate of 350 ms per word to increase processing pressure. Participants were asked to judge whether a given sentence was well formed and meaningful immediately after reading the final word. Table 12.1 summarizes the results.

Question 1. Are learners more accurate on case or on agreement? How about the natives?

Question 2. Are learners faster on judging case or judging agreement? How about the natives?

Question 3. The results presented in Table 12.1 are based on the accuracy and speed of answers of ungrammatical sentences only. Why do you think the researcher made this decision?

Question 4. Is there L1 influence in these data? Why or why not? How does that square with the Failed Functional Features Hypothesis (Hawkins and Casillas 2008), according to which formal features are only accessible to adult L2 learners if they are instantiated in their L1, but not if they are not present in their L1?

Table 12.1 Summary of experimental findings on English case and agreement inflections: Error rate and RT differences between the ungrammatical Agreement and the ungrammatical Case conditions

	L1	German L2	Japanese L2	Chinese L2
Errors (Agreement–Case)	−0.7%	4.4% (*)	9.7%*	17.2%*
Response times (Agreement–Case)	3 ms	162 ms*	298 ms*	527 ms*

Note: Source data from Sato (2007).
* Significant at p < .05 by subjects and items.
(*) Significant at p < .05 by items.

Question 5. Here are some factors that could have affected the differential difficulty:

a. phonological salience (DeKeyser 2005)
b. slower processing speed (McDonald 2006)
c. computational resource limitations (McDonald 2006)
d. grammatical complexity in terms of number of formal features instantiated in the morphology
e. S–V agreement dependencies span the entire clause (and thus require comparatively complex structural scaffolding), whereas the object case is assigned locally within the verb phrase.

Discuss these factors in turn and decide which one could explain the findings.

Exercise 12.3. Find and download the following study: A. Foucart and C. Frenck-Mestre (2011). Can late L2 learners acquire new grammatical features? Evidence from ERPs and eye-tracking. *Journal of Memory and Language* 66, 226–248. Read it while thinking of the following questions. Then try to answer them without being influenced by the interpretation of the authors (where appropriate).

Question 1. From the introduction, make a list of the factors affecting acquisition of grammatical gender and its processing online.
Question 2. Are the research questions appropriate?
Question 3. In French, adjectives can be post-nominal, the more frequent option, and pre-nominal, the less frequent option. How is frequency used in this experiment? What other factor does it interact with?
Question 4. What is the rationale for the third ERP experiment?
Question 5. What does eye tracking in Experiment 4 add to the mix of experiments?
Question 6. What L2 processing theories are addressed in the general discussion? Which ones are the findings compatible with?
Question 7. Grammatical gender is a new feature for these learners, but out of the three possible placements of adjectives (pre-nominal, post-nominal and predicative) only the post-nominal placement is new for learners of French. How does this fact affect the accuracy of the learners? Which placement are they most accurate on?

Question 8. Which theoretical proposal does this finding support? Could there be other reasons for this accuracy, such as frequency of the collocation and instruction?

Exercise 12.4. Testing for individual differences. Imagine that you are in an ideal world and you can test everything and everyone you want with whatever techniques you deem appropriate. (Wouldn't that be great.) You are given the task to identify how individual differences affect L2 processing.

Question 1: What kind of research design would you use?

Question 2: What factors of difference between individuals would you include?

Question 3: What linguistic property or properties do you think are good to test in such a design? Will the properties be different in the L1 or L2, or the same? Why?

Question 4: Make a table of potential findings and identify what findings would suggest that individual differences among monolingual native speakers are smaller than, or similar to, those among L2 speakers.

13

The Bottleneck Hypothesis and its implications for the second language classroom

There is no doubt that second language acquisition is a complex process with many facets influenced by diverse factors. Learners have to become fluent and functional in a second language, and that may depend on their effort, perseverance, and learning motivation. They need to achieve the communicative competence to be able to function in an L2-based situation with native speakers of the L2 or in a lingua franca situation. Our focus in this book has been on learner interlanguage and its linguistic and psycholinguistic properties, because the creation of a system of grammatical representations and its efficient use is truly the *core* of second language acquisition.

The two absolutely indispensable elements of acquisition are the comprehensible linguistic input learners are exposed to and their language acquisition device (LAD). They already have a native language, which has engaged their language acquisition device, and are cognitively mature. They have a store of lexical-semantic concepts and grammatical meanings that is going to need expression in the second language, with the necessary adjustments. They are in possession of a universal parser that is going to guide them in attributing linguistic structure to the incoming string, even if some parsing strategies, routines, and preferences are different between the L1 and the L2. Like children acquiring L1, L2 learners may have more limited processing resources, which affects parsing, comprehension, and production in interesting ways. It could also be the case that linguistic processing masks, or underdetermines, linguistic representations in moment-by-moment performance. We will revisit and highlight these issues again in this chapter.

Our main focus is ultimately on classroom instruction. In the first section, I will summarize the motivation, and some empirical support, for the Bottleneck Hypothesis. I will argue that the hypothesis, and more generally the generative SLA findings, has direct implications for the second language classroom. At issue is how classroom instruction, language exposure, and interaction can aid and improve the L2 learning process. It may seem to the reader that in the rest of this textbook I have been describing learning tasks, situations, and processes where the input coupled with the LAD and the universal parser seem pretty sufficient to engender the L2 representations. It may be so, but there is solid evidence that SLA instruction does help acquisition (Norris and Ortega 2000, Spada and Tomita 2010). In the second part of the chapter, I articulate exactly how instruction and classroom interaction may help learners and teachers, within our approach. We will assume representational similarity between L1 and L2 systems (because, hopefully, this was demonstrated in the rest of this textbook). In other words, the linguistic representations of L2 learners and native speakers are NOT fundamentally different, and the ways L2 linguistic representations are established are fundamentally similar with the ways children acquire their native language.

But children don't need to be taught their native language while adult L2 learners benefit from instruction. Isn't this a contradiction? We will attribute initial and midway divergence from native patterns to a learning curve, to imperfect and insufficient input, and to possible differences between L1 and

L2 parsing and processing efficiency. We shall see that with experience and increased proficiency, L1–L2 convergence is a fact.

13.1 The Bottleneck Hypothesis again

13.1.1 What is special about the inflectional morphology?

We started out by arguing and demonstrating that generative linguistics attributes a special place to the functional morphology. Grammar-related parts of words (bound morphemes) and little words (free morphemes) carry grammatical meanings that change the meaning of a sentence radically. Building from the bottom up, if we want to combine *like, jazz, Peter* in a message to the effect that Peter is the experiencer of a feeling, and that feeling is being fond of a type of music, the production mechanism will start by putting *like + jazz* together into a verb phrase. Later on, the Experiencer argument will be added. However, *Peter like jazz* is not an acceptable sentence of English without the subject–verb agreement morpheme *-s*. It signals that the sentence reflects a habitual state that includes the present moment. The latter is temporal and aspectual information about the complete sentence *Peter likes jazz*. If we want to signal a past state, we have to add another morpheme, *-ed* as in *Peter liked jazz,* etc. I argued that most grammatical meanings are captured in functional morphology. There is a lot of important information packed into these little morphemes that has to do with the word order and the meaning of the sentence, therefore they are rightfully at the heart of language acquisition. One disregards them at one's peril.

The morpheme studies in the 70s (Bailey, Madden, and Krashen 1974) were truly groundbreaking for second language acquisition research. They brought forward the idea that if you are acquiring an L2 such as English, the inflectional morphemes come into the grammar in an ordered sequence that is the same no matter what your native language is. Most importantly, this sequence highlights the systematic nature of the internal interlanguage grammar. As Hawkins (2001) showed, this acquisitional sequence of functional morphemes is indicative of the building of a mental grammar, step by step. Ever since these early discoveries, second language researchers have tried to explain why normally developing children inevitably converge on the functional morphology of their native language, while second language learners show protracted periods of variability, during which they omit (more often) or substitute (less often) inflectional morphology.

There are principally two directions we can go in when we are searching for explanations of this variability. One direction is to invoke initially imperfect but developing representations; the other direction is imperfect processing. We will take these up in turn. But before doing that, let me say again what bears repeating: that functional morphology is difficult for second language learners. This is almost a truism in the L2 acquisition literature. De Keyser (2005: 5–6), for example, counts at least two dozen studies documenting problems with articles, classifiers, verbal aspect, and grammatical gender. The difficulties are more acute for learners whose native languages do not have these functional morphemes, but difficulties are certainly not reserved exclusively for them. This state of affairs is even more puzzling when we consider the fact that these inflectional morphemes are among the most frequent morphemes in any language. Learners are exposed to these morphemes multiple times from day one of any L2 exposure. Why can't they learn them quickly?

The most convincing and detailed explanation of the inherent difficulty of the functional morphology in recent years has come from the work of Donna Lardiere, as we discussed in Chapter 7. In a seminal article from 2009, she argued that what she calls "feature reassembly," and not so much parameter resetting, is what L2 learners need to accomplish in order to reach targetlike linguistic representations. Parameter resetting is too easy, as it were. If parameter values are provided by Universal Grammar, why isn't second language acquisition much more straightforward and breezy? Well, because the L2 acquisition process involves much more than parameter resetting, according to Lardiere (2009). The following is a citation from a later article.

The learner must acquire not only the knowledge of exactly which morpholexical forms and their allomorphic variants express which (combinations of) syntactic and semantic features, but also knowledge of potential conditioning factors that may be phonological, syntactic, lexical, semantic/pragmatic, and/or discourse-linked, including the conditions under which such forms are obligatory, optional, or prohibited. For adult L2 acquisition in particular, the constraining role of prior language knowledge (or first language transfer) should not be underestimated, especially at early stages of L2 acquisition; ... mature L2 learners bring to the L2 learning task an entrenched system of morphosyntactic features already assembled into lexical items; these are the morphemes associated with the functional categories of their native language(s). (Hwang and Lardiere 2013: 57–58.)

If any reader is left unconvinced that acquiring the L2 functional morphology is absolutely essential but difficult, I shall exemplify once again the feature reassembly task with a comparison between Korean and English plural marking.[1] A superficial look at Korean and English should establish that both languages have plural marking on nouns to mean "more than one." There is no parameter to reset since both parametric options should be set to the plus value. The actual situation is much more complex. Korean has two types of plural, intrinsic plural which seems closer to the English plural, and extrinsic plural which is rare in the input, marked EPL in the glosses below. However, the marker, -*tul* is used for both types, as in the examples below. Notice that the intrinsic plural marker is optional.

(1)   a. ai*(-tul)*-i   hakkyo-ey   ka-ss-ta.   (Intrinsic)
         child(-PL)-NOM   school-to   go-PAST-DECL
         With -*tul*: 'The/some specific children went to school.'
         Without -*tul*: 'A/the child or some unspecific children went to school.'
      b. haksayng-tul-i   yelsimhi*(-tul)* enehak-ul   kongpuha-n-ta.
         student-PL-NOM intently(-*EPL*) linguistics-ACC study-PRES-DECL
                                                                    (Extrinsic)
         'The students (every one of them) study linguistics intently.'

As Hwang and Lardiere explain, the intrinsic plural is similar to English in that it pluralizes nominal phrases, while the extrinsic plural pluralizes whole predicates, and can appear on adverbs as in (1b) and other categories. So it might seem at first glance that the extrinsic plural might create more problems. However, it turns out that the intrinsic plural is actually more complex, because its appearance is tightly constrained by various other features. In addition to marking the meaning [group], or "more than one," the intrinsic plural indicates nominal specificity, or the fact that the denotation of the noun is known to speaker and hearer, see (1a). Plural marking is almost obligatory when it co-occurs with demonstratives (which also make a noun specific). Plural marking is not allowed in constructions with numerals and classifiers (2a), unless the noun is human (2b), in which case it is allowed.

(2)   a. * chayk-*tul* twu   kwen-i   chayksang wiey iss-ta.
         book-*PL* two   CL-NOM   desk on exist-DECL
         'There are two books on the desk.'

---

[1] As described in Lardiere (2009) and Hwang and Lardiere (2013).

b. haksayng-*tul*   twu myeng-i   kyosil-ey   tulewa-ss-ta.
   student-*PL*   two CL-NOM   classroom-to   enter-PAST-DECL
   'Two students entered the classroom.'

However, numerals can appear without classifiers, as an exception, when the numeral is small and the noun is human. With nonnumeric quantifiers such as *many,* classifiers are not used and plural marking is optionally allowed, regardless of whether the noun is human or not. Finally, numeral–classifier constructions with or without plural marking can occur in either of two equally acceptable word orders: prenominal and postnominal. But when prenominal, the classifier has to appear with a genitive marker.[2]

So far, we have only described the conditions for the correct usage of the intrinsic plural -*tul* in Korean, the one that seemed close to English -*s*. As the reader can verify for himself/herself, it is anything but. It is far from sufficient for the English-native learner of Korean to map -*s* to -*tul*. Learners of L2 Korean will initially assume that the functional category of Number and its morpholexical expressions are organized in a manner similar to their native English, as per the Full Transfer Hypothesis. This initial impression will be supported by the existence of one plural marker in both languages and the fact that their uses do overlap to some extent. However, at later stages of acquisition and with more experience, learners will have to reconfigure the feature values and their expressions. Most importantly, they have to acquire the conditions under which the new features are realized.

Admittedly, this may seem like an extreme example of difficulty. The point is, however, that learning functional morphology may be more difficult than researchers and teachers suspect, if they assume a simple mapping of morphemes with roughly similar meanings. Using a comparative linguistic feature-based approach, in which the learning tasks are concrete and spelled out based on linguistic analysis, is our only hope of making testable predictions for acquisition sequences. Generally speaking, the predictions for ease or difficulty of acquisition are as follows: the more reassembly of features is required, the harder the acquisition process will be. In addition, less frequent features such as the extrinsic Korean plural will be hard to acquire because there will be insufficient evidence for them in the input.

---

[2] The interested reader is invited to see all the examples in the original article.

Let me summarize representation-related difficulties with the functional morphology. In order to acquire the morphological forms and to store them in their functional lexicon, learners have to

1) map forms to correct interpretations (grammatical meanings)
2) map forms to possibly different grammatical features (feature addition, subtraction, and general reassembly) and
3) identify the grammatical contexts for the morpheme occurrence.

This is a tall order indeed, but that is not all.

13.1.2 Lexical access and processing of functional morphology

There is another source of L2 morphology problems: imperfect lexical access and labored or slow processing. Even if learners' functional lexicon representations are completely nativelike, they still need to retrieve the correct inflectional morphology forms in the appropriate grammatical contexts. For example, in English -*s* is used only with 3rd person singular present tense verbs. Efficient lexical access would result in the correct production of these morphemes in speaking and writing. It also entails that learners attend to them in comprehension of text and speech. Furthermore, efficient lexical access is a prerequisite of efficient processing; both rely on adequate nativelike representations. In my own teaching experience, omitting functional morphology is a very common interlanguage error in oral or written production.

It may be useful to step aside here and to review the relationship between linguistic representations and processing in language acquisition research. As Omaki and Lidz (2014) remind us, following many other researchers before them, the external behavior that linguists observe, even one that is captured by the modern eye-tracking and ERP techniques, is one degree removed from linguistic representations. Linguistic behavior may not always be a good window into what occurs internally in the learner's mind, that is, linguistic representations. In other words, research can only scrutinize linguistic processing and, based on a processing–representation coupling, try to postulate what the representations look like.

Back to the lexical access and processing of the inflectional morphology. I discussed these issues in Chapter 9 but we shall see another recent example here. Clahsen et al. (2013) reports on two studies comparing whether very advanced learners and native speakers employ morphological decomposition of derivational and inflectional morphology and whether they are sensitive to morphological structure constraints. One study used a masked priming technique to investigate whether the past tense of a verb primed (accelerated access to) the verbal root. This morphological priming effect was attested in the natives, but not in the learners. As the researchers used two presentation speeds, and as they did not see priming even at the slower speed, they argued that the findings were not due solely to the (slow) speed of L2 processing. However, they compared the results of their masked priming study with results from overt priming designs, where facilitation with regular past tense forms was found to be nativelike (Basnight-Brown et al. 2007). It remains an open research question as to whether the discrepancy between these results can be informative about the timing of the decomposition. Masked priming[3] is supposed to be indicative of very early decomposition, and that is what the L2 learners do not seem able to do.

The second set of studies in Clahsen et al. (2013) investigated the prohibition of inflectional morphology appearing inside derivational morphology in English words. Thus, if some object is not infested with fleas plural, it is *flea-less*, not **flea-s-less*. The Dutch learners' eyes were tracked while they were reading sentences with such words. Although they were very accurate on an off-line task, bilinguals' eye movements revealed no reliable effect of the morphological structure constraint. In principle, such results are in a position to address the representation–processing divide. If the Dutch learners in this study were sensitive to morphological structure off-line, this behavior must come from somewhere. It is unlikely that these experimental participants were all influenced by some metalinguistic rule such as "Do not allow inflection inside derivation." that they were taught in a language classroom. Therefore, they must have this constraint represented in their internal grammar, they just cannot use it automatically and fast enough in online processing. Even more telling of a clash between representation and processing is the fact that the native language is ruled out as a potential factor in this particular case, because Dutch and English have similar constraints on inflection inside derivation. For the time being, Clahsen

---

[3] Masked priming, if you remember, exposes the regular past tense form for 60 ms, not enough time to notice it consciously but enough time to influence the following lexical retrieval. When native speakers are primed with *played*, they automatically decompose it into *play-ed,* and are subsequently faster on accessing *play*.

et al.'s conclusion "that the L2 comprehension system employs real-time grammatical analysis (in this case, morphological information) less than the L1 system" still holds.[4]

Some potential reasons for the less efficient usage of inflectional morphology structure in parsing may include the slower speed of processing. McDonald (2006) has proposed that the L2 processor makes use of the same mechanisms but that it operates more slowly than the L1 system.[5] Furthermore, as we saw in Chapter 12, speed and efficiency may go hand in hand. It is established that processing demands over and above the task requirements are reflected in a similar way by native and L2 speakers. McDonald (2006) compared the performance of native speakers to that of L2 speakers on a variety of linguistic structures. In a second experiment, the native speakers performed the same task under additional stress and their accuracy was compared to accuracy under no stress. Natives under stress and L2 speakers performed in a remarkably similar pattern, with articles, regular past tense and subject–verb agreement being affected the most, while SVO word order remained unaffected.

Furthermore, there appear to be correlations in emergence and error rates in the processing of functional morphology versus syntax across adult native speakers, children, and L2 speakers. For example, McDonald (2008a,b) looked at a wide range of grammatical constructions and general cognitive measures in the grammar of 7 to 11-year-old children and adult speakers. Half of the adult participants in McDonald (2008b) processed the test items under additional memory load (memorizing numbers), thereby reducing the processing resources they could allocate to linguistic processing. When relative construction difficulty for the children was compared to that of unstressed and stressed adults, it was found that children resembled adults under increased memory load. It may come as a shock, but the latest features to emerge and the hardest to process were subject–verb agreement and regular past tense. Not even the oldest group (11 years of age) had reached adult levels. McDonald concluded that later acquired and less resilient grammatical properties impose higher working memory and phonological demands on children as well as adults.

---

[4] Another researcher who has come to a similar conclusion is Jiang, see Jiang et al.'s (2011) Morphological Congruence Hypothesis.

[5] See also Hopp (2010).

Why would these particular functional morphemes (S–V agreement, past tense) pose the most problems? Relative salience and frequency of the morphemes, factors proposed by DeKeyser (2005), go only some way in explaining the discrepancy. From the perspective of linguistic theory discussed in this book, the grammatical information (expressed in the number of features and syntactic effects) that subject–verb agreement and past tense marking carry is much higher as compared to plural, for example, and affects the syntactic analysis of the whole sentence. If this is the case, then the fact that the same morphemes are hard for children, stressed adults, and L2 learners makes perfect sense.

Another possible reason for the less efficient usage of the functional morphology, language experience, is highlighted by the Weaker Links hypothesis of Gollan et al. (2008). Since bilinguals use words in each language less frequently than do monolinguals, lexical representations in both languages in the bilingual system will have accumulated less practice overall, relative to the lexical representations of the monolingual system. Over time, Gollan and associates propose, that would result in weaker links between semantics, phonology, and morphology, compared to monolinguals, because words that are produced more often are easier and faster to access. In addition, bilinguals get considerably less input in both languages, calculated purely in time of exposure, comprehension, and production, since the waking hours in a day are shared, and thus divided into two (in some proportion). If lexical access in a second language is weaker, this means that it is less automatic (more effortful), which entails that lexical access on its own taxes the learners' mental capacity more, relative to monolinguals (McDonald 2006, Hopp 2010). All of these explanations (slower, less automatic lexical access, slower processing overall, overloaded capabilities) probably conspire in accounting for why bilinguals have to devote more effort to integrating functional morphology in the appropriate grammatical contexts, resulting in more errors and variability, compared to monolinguals.

In summary, inflectional morphology contains the bulk of the grammatical information that has to be acquired in a second language. Very often, feature reassembly is required if, as is often the case, features and their morphophonological exponents are not perfectly aligned in the L1 and the L2. Finally, even with perfect linguistic representations, the strained processing of the inflectional morphology under the conditions of bilingualism[6] makes itself known as variable, frequently imperfect performance.

13.1.3 If the inflectional morphology is available, complex syntax is not a barrier to meaning

In this first section of Chapter 13, we are going through a list of arguments that together will spell out the Bottleneck Hypothesis. We have just seen why morphology presents problems to learners, and now we turn to areas of the grammar that are less onerous, since they come for free from the human language faculty and its meaning computation mechanisms.

The experimental study by Dekydtspotter and Sprouse (2001), reviewed in Chapter 10, exemplified several points. It had to do with the interpretation of sentences like these, where two possible interpretations are available for (3), a present and a past celebrity, while only one construal is available for (4), a past celebrity:

(3)   *Qui de célèbre fumait au bistro dans les années 70?*
      Who of famous smoked in the bar in the 70s?
      'Which famous person smoked in bars in the 70s?'

(4)   *Qui fumait de célèbre au bistro dans les années 70?*
      Who smoked of famous in the bar in the 70s?
      'Which famous person smoked in bars in the 70s?'

The study presented learners with a syntactically complex construction in French that they had not encountered in their native English. Based on this complex and unfamiliar syntax, learners were invited to read sentences for comprehension and interpret their meaning relative to a context given by a story. This experimental situation resembles natural communication. It is often the case that bilinguals are faced with the comprehension of sentences that they might have not encountered before or ones that they may have seen sporadically but not truly noticed. In such a situation, the universal parser and the universal meaning computation mechanism kick in. Furthermore, the context helps meaning integration, but does not change the

---

[6] As proposed by the Missing Surface Inflection Hypothesis (Prevost and White 2000).

interpretation that comes through parsing the syntactic structure. Notice that once the inflectional morphology is not at issue, that is, once it helps understanding the complex syntax, the correct attribution of meaning to structure (parsing) comes effortlessly and with high accuracy. This was indeed what the study found. Both learner groups showed a statistically significant difference between the available and the unavailable interpretations. In other words, they reliably treated the two constructions in (3) and (4) differently. Even the intermediate learners were accurate on the past construal of the discontinuous expressions, which suggests that they analyzed their syntactic form correctly. Their knowledge of the subtle interpretive contrast that comes not from the native grammar but through the universal meaning-computation mechanism was remarkable indeed.[7]

13.1.4 If the inflectional morphology is available, semantics and pragmatics are not a problem

In Chapters 10 and 11, we reviewed a lot of studies documenting learner success in acquiring meaning. I shall further exemplify the L2 acquisition of universal grammatical meanings with a recent Mandarin L2 experiment. At the heart of this experiment is the dissociation between cognitive grammatical categories and their linguistic expressions, or realizations. In this case, we will have to distinguish between the notion of time (temporality) and its grammatical expression, tense. It is well known that Mandarin Chinese does not have a dedicated inflection to mark past, present, or future. However, Chinese speakers can convey when an event happened: they do it through adverbials such as *yesterday*, *last week*, and the general monitoring of the discourse context.

Recently, Smith and Erbaugh (2005) and Lin (2003, 2006) have argued that the traditional explanation of temporal information being conveyed in Chinese by adverbials and discourse context is only partially correct. They propose that the main pattern of marking Mandarin temporality is the so-called deictic pattern: aspectual lexical class and viewpoint aspect convey information that allows speakers to locate the situation in time, in the absence of explicit tense marking. Bounded (complete) situations (e.g., *finish eating a sandwich*) are normally located in the past, unbounded (incomplete

---

[7] For review and further examples see Chapter 7 in Slabakova (2008).

and ongoing) situations (e.g., *eating a sandwich*) are typically interpreted as present, in the absence of temporal adverbials. Mandarin Chinese has an array of aspect-marking morphemes, which express complete, ongoing, resultative, and habitual situations. It is these functional morphemes that signal time as well as aspect, according to the deictic principle. Thus English and Mandarin differ in the ways they express past and present, something that Mandarin learners have to acquire.

Slabakova (2015) investigated whether English-native intermediate and advanced classroom learners of Mandarin Chinese are able to adequately comprehend the temporal reference of sentences in isolation and in context, in the absence of dedicated temporal morphology. The effect of the functional aspectual morphemes such as *le, zai, zhe*, and *guo*, on the interpretation of simple sentences was scrutinized. The experimental design involved processing Mandarin sentences without temporal adverbials for meaning and choosing from various interpretations that differed only in their value of temporality: past, present, or future. An example sentence is given in (5).

(5) Lǐsì chī-le   wǎnfàn (both Chinese characters and pinyin were provided)
     Lisi eat-Asp supper (gloss not provided to test participants)
     ☑ Lisi ate supper.
     ☒ Lisi is eating supper.
     ☒ Both meanings are possible.
     ☒ Neither meaning is possible

One line of reasoning about acquisition difficulty (DeKeyser 2005, Slabakova 2009, among others) predicts that this acquisition task would be complicated by the one-to-many relationship between the temporal meanings and their expressions. On the other hand, since learners are using universally available meaning computation mechanisms and have access to universal pragmatic principles, another line of reasoning, suggested by Dietrich, Klein, and Noyau (1985) and based on Smith and Erbaugh (2005), predicts that acquisition would be easy. The results were very clear: although diverging slightly from the native speakers, advanced learners of Mandarin were highly accurate in interpreting the temporal values of sentences. The intermediate learners deviated from native patterns considerably more, but they were still high above chance on all conditions, indicating that they were capable of interpreting temporal references perfectly adequately. Thus, these findings show that after the learners had acquired the aspectual morphology (as ascertained by a translation task), there was no difficulty in locating the action in time. The universal temporality calculation mechanism was fully functional in the grammar of the learners.

13.1.5 Putting it all together

In all the subsections of this section, I have given a couple of empirical research examples, but the studies were chosen because they were representative of a host of other studies. What message do these arguments spell out all together? So far, we have seen that:

- the functional morphology is the main locus of grammatical meanings and the locus of difference between languages;
- it is difficult to process and attend to for second language learners as well as native speakers without much experience with that morphology;
- since narrow syntax is universal, understanding complex structures is not a problem when all the grammatical features are in place or acquired; and finally,
- since meaning calculation is universal, meaning comes for free when the functional morphology is available.
- in order to acquire syntax and meaning in a second language, the learner cannot bypass the bottleneck of the functional morphology.

All of these arguments together point to the conclusion that the functional morphology is the bottleneck of second language acquisition. Imagine it as shown in Figure 13.1.

The upright bottle is our second language grammar. The different color beads stand for pieces of language knowledge. Note that they are finite in number. The dark-colored ones come from the native grammar, the white ones come from universal language learning systems, and the light gray ones are newly acquired pieces of knowledge from the target grammar. Some of these beads stand for lexical knowledge, some of them stand for grammatical rules and processing routines. When we are called upon to use our second language linguistic system, we turn the bottle upside down and try to squeeze what we need out of it. The tight place is the functional morphology. Without it, sentences would sound unacceptable to native speakers of the language. Without integrating functional morphology in comprehension, we will be reduced to shallow processing.

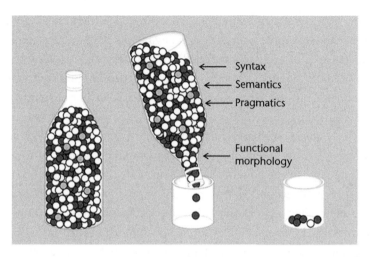

Figure 13.1 Illustration of the Bottleneck Hypothesis. The dark-colored beads stand for pieces of information coming from the native language; the white beads come from the target language grammar via comprehensible input; the light gray beads signify universal knowledge.

The good news is that the bottleneck is not solid, not rigid: it expands with practice. We have all heard that practice makes perfect. The legendary American football coach Vince Lombardi[8] said, "Practice does not make perfect. Perfect practice makes perfect." We should not be maximalist in arguing that we can come up with advice on the perfect language learning practice. The perfect practice for language learning probably differs from person to person. But at a minimum, practice should be smart. Teachers should know what is difficult to learn and therefore will take practice, and what is universal, hence so easy that it should come for free. Smart practice can make perfect sense in language classrooms.

13.2 Situating the Bottleneck Hypothesis in L2 learning and teaching

I said at the outset of this chapter that our focus will be on teaching. However, up to this point in the chapter, I have talked about linguistics,

---

[8] 1913–1970.

language acquisition, and language processing (as in the rest of the book). This is because I wanted to illustrate, yet again and with more examples, the logical sequence of arguments of the Bottleneck Hypothesis. Now that this is done (and the attentive reader could have skipped this first section, or just skimmed it), I turn to the message this hypothesis has for currently practicing or future language teachers.

It is fairly common to assert that the generative approach to L2 acquisition does not really have any predictions to make about how we should teach language. As a cognitive discipline with a theoretical perspective inherently not interested in the process of learning (as opposed to the process of implicit acquisition), this approach has frequently turned its attention to the L2 acquisition of subtle phenomena that are never discussed in language classrooms and that language teachers have no explicit knowledge of. Subjacency, the linguistic constraint that regulates how far a *wh*-phrase can move away from its original position and how many other phrases it may jump over, is one such example among many. Scrambling and its interpretive effects is another such property. Generative studies of L2 acquisition rarely incorporate classroom instruction as part of their design.[9]

It is also true that the stated goal of the generative SLA framework has never been to address pedagogical concerns.[10] From the outset, the goal of researchers working within this framework has been to determine what constitutes knowledge of language, how such knowledge is acquired, and how it is put to use in production and comprehension (Chomsky 1986, White 1989). Along with other theories and approaches which focus on this complex cognitive and social learning process, generative SLA is an approach assuming a specific theory of language, as well as a view of language acquisition and language usage based on that theory. We did not deal with sociolinguistic, sociocultural, or pragmalinguistic issues in this textbook, not because they are not interesting to study or because they do

[9] The White and colleagues studies investigating the Verb Movement Parameter are the notable exception (e.g., White 1991). Their general conclusion on the effect of targeted instruction was quite pessimistic.

[10] Generative SLA is not alone in its focus on acquisition, representation, and processing. Many other SLA research frameworks, approaches, and theories, such as Cognitive Grammar approaches, Processability theory, connectionist/emergentist approaches, general nativist approaches, functionalist approaches including the Aspect Hypothesis and Dynamic Systems Theory, among others, are similarly not directly concerned with their applicability to teaching.

not have an effect on SLA (they are, and they do), but because the creation of a system of grammatical representations and its efficient use is truly the *core* of SLA. Understanding grammatical representations is a necessary, although not sufficient, condition for understanding how their acquisition may be profitably influenced by explicit instruction and classroom inter-action. The premise is that one has to understand how a complex process works in order to guide and shape it.

Historically speaking, Chomskyan generative linguistics has had a sub-stantial influence on the wider field of SLA.[11] Its positive influence has also been widely debated. I will offer here an extended citation from Henry Widdowson (2000), which is quite eloquent on this point:

> [A] moment's reflection will reveal that Chomsky's linguistics was not useless at all. It had an enormous influence on how people concerned with pedagogy thought about language. His insights effectively led to a fundamental reconceptualization of the nature of the language learning process, and consequently of how language was to be defined as a subject. It was Chomsky who challenged the orthodox pedagogic view of the time that learning was a matter of habit formation to be induced by pattern practice and structural drill whereby learners were constrained into conformity. He made us conceive of learning in a totally different way, as an essentially cognitive and creative process. (Widdowson 2000: 29–30.)

Chomsky's ideas of language may have changed how we applied linguists think of language acquisition, but many practitioners remain unconvinced. It is still believed by many that the generative framework has nothing valuable to offer to language teachers. In a break with tradition, in the past decade generative applied linguists have started to point out clear pedagogical implications of their work (Slabakova 2008, 2009, Whong 2011, Whong, Gil, and Marsden, 2013). In this and the next sections, I will situate the Bottleneck Hypothesis message within current ideas of language teaching. I will not presume to tell teachers how to teach second language. I will only point out what might be useful to know, and what other applied linguistics approaches this message is congruent with.

In language classrooms, teaching techniques that emphasized communi-cative competence (Canale and Swain 1980, Hymes 1966, Savignon 1983) became popular in the 80s and are still quite prevalent (although see Kumaravadivelu 2006 for a critique). Such techniques encourage learners

---

[11] The earliest instantiation of SLA theory based on Chomsky's generative grammar is Stephen Krashen'S Monitor theory (Krashen 1981, 1982, 1985).

to use context, world knowledge, argument structure templates, and other pragmatic strategies to comprehend the message, capitalizing on the fact that learners almost certainly use their expectations of what is said to choose between alternative parses of a sentence. In fact, as we have seen, Clahsen and Felser's (2006) Shallow Structure Hypothesis proposes that context, pragmatic knowledge, and argument structure are the only processing strategies available to adult learners. However, many L2 researchers (e.g., Cook 1996: 76, Gass and Selinker 2001: 317) have questioned the direct connection between comprehending the L2 message and figuring out how the L2 syntax works. It is believed that some attention to, or focus on, *grammatical form* is beneficial and necessary for successful learning (Long 1996). In this respect, communicative competence approaches—with their exclusion of focus on grammatical form—may not be the best way to accomplish the ultimate goal of L2 learning: building a mental grammar of the target language.

Kumaravadivelu (2006) discussed two major shifts in language-teaching methods: (a) from communicative language teaching to task-based language teaching, and (b) from method-based pedagogy to postmethod pedagogy. The *Communicative approach* came to prominence in the 1980s, but lost ground to *Task-Based Language Teaching* (Bygate, Skehan, and Swain 2001, Crookes and Gass 1993, Ellis 2003) in the 1990s and the 2000s. Ellis (2003: 16) gives the following definition of task: "A task is a workplan that requires learners to process language pragmatically in order to achieve an outcome that can be evaluated in terms of whether the correct or appropriate propositional content has been conveyed." Skehan (1998: 121) refers to two extremes of task orientation: structure-oriented tasks and communicatively oriented tasks. He then stresses the need for a third approach in which "the central feature is a balance between form and meaning, and an alternation of attention between them." This third approach is Focus on Form (see next section).

Dörnyei (2009: 280) argues that "contemporary SLA researchers no longer believe in the existence or the desirability of pure teaching methods" and suggests that the question is not which method is best, but which combination of ingredients is best. This opinion reflects a wide consensus in the field of language teaching, captured best by Kumaravadivelu's (2006) macrostrategic framework. The ten macrostrategies include (a) maximize learning opportunities, (b) facilitate negotiated interaction, (c) minimize perceptual mismatches, among others. The strategies merely offer certain operating principles while any actual postmethod pedagogy has to be constructed by teachers themselves by taking into consideration linguistic, social, cultural, and political particularities. This situation places a lot of responsibility on teachers, but also makes them autonomous agents of instruction, free to choose the ingredients and emphases of instruction. In the next section, I will review some SLA approaches relevant to teaching that are in synch with the Bottleneck Hypothesis, in the sense that its theoretical conclusions support (some aspects of) these approaches.

13.3 Focus on form, interaction, practice, and input processing in the classroom

Although teachers in the postmethod condition are unencumbered by methodological prescriptions, research still needs to show what routines and practices work efficiently to enhance language learning. Michael Long (Long 1991, Long and Robinson 1998) has consistently argued that a focus on meaning alone is insufficient to achieve full nativelike competence. Instead, we need *focus on form*. Instruction can be improved upon, in terms of both rate and ultimate attainment, by occasionally turning to language as an object of attention. In language classrooms, this is best achieved not by explicit teaching or grammar rules, what he calls *focus on forms*, where classes spend most of their time in rote learning, drilling paradigms, and working through exercises on isolated linguistic structures. What is *focus on form* then? It is explicitly drawing the learners' focus to linguistic features if and when the classroom communicative activities and the negotiation of meaning demand these features. During an otherwise meaning-focused lesson, and using a variety of pedagogic procedures, learners' attention is briefly shifted to linguistic features. This is particularly memorable, hence helpful, when students experience problems as they work on communicative tasks, i.e., in a sequence determined by their own internal needs and current processing capacity. In other words, grammar instruction is in context, not isolated, and intrinsically related to communication. This is precisely the type of instruction that the Bottleneck Hypothesis would heartily endorse.

The *interaction approach* (Long 1996, Gass 1997, 2003, Mackey 2006, 2012) provides a wider perspective on the learning process, emphasizing the importance of communication. Studies within this approach focus on the role of input, interaction, output, and feedback in learning a language.

Although this approach is not directly applicable to language classrooms, it has served as the theoretical basis of teaching techniques such as focus on form and task-based language learning. The interaction approach considers the learner's exposure to language, production of language, and feedback on this production to be essential and indispensable elements of the learning process, each with its own specific contribution to the process. Language-related episodes are scrutinized, in which learners consciously reflect on their linguistic knowledge, either by realizing that they don't know a word or a construction, or by correcting themselves or others. As Gass (2003) points out, interaction research "takes as its starting point the assumption that language learning is stimulated by communicative pressure and examines the relationship between communication and acquisition and the mechanisms (e.g., noticing, attention) that mediate between them" (p. 224). The interaction approach and generative SLA completely agree on the crucial importance of comprehensible linguistic input, although their emphases on communication, output, and feedback diverge.

Within his Skill Acquisition Theory, DeKeyser (2007) brought forward the notion of *practice* in language learning. He defines practice as "[...] specific activities in the second language, engaged in systematically, deliberately, with the goal of developing knowledge of and skills in the second language" (p. 1). He argues for a reconsideration of the notion in the second language learning field, as issues of practice in this area are vastly underresearched. Although there is much to contend with in this fairly mechanistic view of language learning,[12] the emphasis on language as a skill in the cognitive psychology sense of the word (Anderson 2000, Carlson 2003) happens to dovetail with the approach taken in this book. Practicing of grammatical features, including the functional morphology, is viewed as a way to improve the automaticity of language processing. "Automatization" is regarded as the process of change from initial declarative, possibly instructed knowledge to procedural knowledge, where the functional morphology is accessed freely in the mental lexicon and integrated in production effectively. As DeKeyser (2007) correctly points out, automatization lowers the speed of processing and reduces the error rate.

Finally, VanPatten's Input Processing approach (VanPatten 1996, 2002a, b, 2004, VanPatten and Cadierno 1993) is interested in what kind of L2

---

[12] Learning language is nothing like/very much like learning to drive or learning to tie your shoelaces. Discuss.

input gets converted to intake and the rationale behind it. The intervention part of this theory is *Processing Instruction*, a specific approach to grammar instruction. VanPatten's research is powered by the question of how input processing can be manipulated to fuel the development of an implicit linguistic system, and in this sense, it is a developmental model largely assuming the generative approach we have taken here. Processing instruction proposes tasks such that learners have to show that they have attended to the meaning of specific target features when they are reading or hearing sentences in the target language. These tasks target features which a) appear to be slow to be acquired in production, b) differ from the learners' L1 features, and c) are likely to be "ignored" by learners when they normally hear or read the languages because the features are communicatively redundant (i.e., there are other clues in the input which communicate the same meaning, e.g., intonation, syntax, lexical items).

These four approaches (Focus on Form, Interaction, Practice, Processing Instruction) have established their usefulness in the classroom.[13] In their bigger message to language learners and teachers, namely, that grammar should not be neglected in language instruction, these approaches are germane and in synch with the message of the Bottleneck Hypothesis. The contribution of the latter is to demonstrate that the choice of *what to focus on, process or practice* should stem from consideration of linguistic structure. Language teachers should be aware of what is hard and what is easy to acquire, as well as appreciate the particular L1–L2 pairs of their students. This knowledge will make them more efficient teachers.

13.4 How to, and how not to, focus on the functional morphology in the classroom

The functional morphology in a language has some visible and some hidden characteristics. First, it may have phonetic form, and if it does, its distribution is in evidence and learnable. Second, it carries syntactic features that are responsible for the behavior of other, possibly displaced, elements and phrases in the sentence. Third, it carries one or more universal units of meaning. While the first trait of functional morphology may be observable

---

[13] The reader is invited to read more about these theories in VanPatten and Williams (2015), an excellent introduction to theories in SLA.

from the linguistic input, the second and third characteristics may not be so easy to detect. It is suggested here that practicing the functional morphology in language classrooms should take place in meaningful, plausible sentences where the syntactic effects and the semantic import of the morphology are absolutely transparent and unambiguous. In a sense, some drilling of the functional morphology is inevitable if the form has to move from the declarative to the procedural memory of the learner and then become sufficiently automatic for easy lexical access. However, drilling on its own is far from sufficient for the form–meaning mapping to be achieved. Practicing functional morphology in context should be very much like lexical learning (because it *is* lexical learning), and, as everybody who has tried to learn a second language as an adult (or even a teenager) knows, learning lexical items is painful but indispensable.

Now, is there a contradiction between my view and the position of linguists like Michel Paradis (e.g., Paradis 2004, 2009) and Bonnie D. Schwartz (e.g., Schwartz 1993) going back to Krashen's (1982) Monitor Model? Although for different reasons, Krashen, Schwartz, and Paradis have argued that declarative knowledge cannot be "transformed" into procedural knowledge because there is a barrier, like a firewall, between them. Krashen and Schwartz contend that mental representations are not amenable to manipulation from the outside. Instruction cannot directly cause mental representation to develop. Universal Grammar cannot operate on information *about* language but only on *comprehensible* data, that is, data for which the form–meaning connection is internally established. Such data are only derived implicitly from meaningful interaction with the second language and its speakers, but do not come from classroom instruction.

However, a view opposed to that of Schwartz and Paradis is gaining in importance within the generative SLA approach (Long and Rothman 2013, Rothman 2010, Slabakova 2008, Whong 2011, Whong, Gil and Marsden 2013, VanPatten and Rothman 2014). All the way back in 1991, Lydia White argued that explicit input may in fact contribute to underlying competence, particularly when the positive (implicit) input does not provide enough evidence, or provides misleading evidence, for a certain property to be acquired. Slabakova (2002) also contended that explicit instruction may shape grammar knowledge in some cases. A number of constructions in a parametric cluster had to be preempted by the learners in that study; that is, they had to learn that the whole cluster was unavailable. Ten of the 26 advanced subjects were able to successfully reset the whole parameter based on explicit instruction for only two of the four constructions in the cluster. This fact suggests that it is not impossible for negative evidence (in this case, explicit instruction on ungrammaticality) to be utilized in grammar reorganization.

The rationale of this latter view is that when a learner is instructed on and practices grammar, particularly functional morphology, in appropriate, varied, and unambiguous contexts in a classroom, she is implicitly acquiring all its underlying grammatical features. When she is prompted to notice some otherwise elusive property through explicit instruction, she may use this piece of knowledge consciously until it becomes procedural, then automatic, and enters grammatical competence. In such rare cases where positive input alone cannot do the job, instruction may be no more than a nudge in the right direction: the implicit (unconscious) grammar-building processes will do the rest. Although I put some emphasis in this textbook on learning paradigms and noticing grammatical morphemes, these are only shortcuts to internalization, processing, and building of mental representations.

Even though a focus on pedagogy has not been central to generative SLA research, our findings often offer new, sometimes unexpected pedagogical insights of benefit to teachers, curriculum designers, and textbook writers. Recent volumes such as Whong (2011) and Whong et al. (2013), as well as articles by Collentine, Rothman, and VanPatten in the journal *Hispania* (2010, issue i) illustrate the importance of detailed linguistic analysis for language teaching. For example, Stringer (2013) considers the pedagogical implications of new linguistic research on the order of modifiers (why *yellow lovely bird* is bad while *lovely yellow bird* is fine). He shows that instruction on modifiers needs to change, such that some aspects of the order should be taught (adjectives of opinion come before those of age), whereas others need not be taught because they are universal (gradable vs. nongradable adjectives). Hirakawa (2013) was motivated by the observation that some learners make overpassivization errors (they passivize intransitive verbs as in *the earthquake was happened*). In an intervention study, she demonstrated the importance of explicit instruction for learners to be able to overcome these errors. Bruhn de Garavito (2013) reviewed how properties of Spanish object clitics are taught in Spanish language textbooks. Armed with linguistic theory, she showed that in some cases textbooks present too much information at once, while the introduction of some other distinctions is unnecessary and may actually obstruct learning. Bruhn de Garavito also identified properties of clitics that should only be taught when learners are more advanced. The interested reader is invited to check out the whole collection.

Let us look at an actual example of a study that highlights the importance of classroom input, and how our perception of it may be wrong. VanPatten, Keating, and Leeser (2012) tested native speakers and intermediate-level (3rd-year university students) on three structures in Spanish. All were related to verb movement in some way: *wh*-question formation, adverb placement, and subject–verb agreement on simple present tense verbs. The participants were tested using the noncumulative self-paced reading technique, where the segments already read disappear from the screen and have to be kept in short term memory in order to answer a comprehension question at the end of the trial. Even though participants were reading for meaning, the expectation was that they would slow down a little on ungrammatical segments, as their internal processors detect something wrong. In this way, they would be demonstrating sensitivity to grammaticality.

The data revealed that the native speakers showed significant reading time differences between grammatical and ungrammatical sentences for all three structures. The L2 learners did slow down on the ungrammatical *wh*-questions and the wrong adverb placement sentences. However, they did not slow down on the wrong person and number agreement sentences. These results are reminiscent of the syntax-before-morphology view (see Chapter 7): Learners may know the syntactic consequences of the functional morphology before "knowing" the actual functional morphology. As the authors point out, question formation is taught inconsistently, adverb placement is never taught in language classrooms, while verb endings are perceived to be taught and drilled and practiced a lot. However, when they examined the linguistic input in typical classrooms and textbook materials, the researchers discovered that the input is relatively poor in terms of providing lots of examples of the various person–number verb endings. Third person singular (less so third person plural) tends to dominate the input overwhelmingly. Thus one clear implication of this and similar studies would be that full rather than partial verbal agreement paradigms have to be used in instruction.

In this section, we discussed two views on classroom instruction within the generative paradigm. One view, stemming from Krashen, argues that explicit instruction is in principle incapable of changing underlying competence. An opposing view contends that there are rare cases in which positive evidence is not sufficient, and explicit instruction may prove helpful. We reviewed the work of generative scholars who critically examine textbook presentation and classroom input, demonstrating some benefits of current linguistic research for second language pedagogy.

13.5 Final words: what is difficult and what is easy to acquire in a second language

The claim that functional morphology is "difficult" to acquire is certainly not new to the field of second language acquisition; in fact, the difficulty of morphology has spawned entire bodies of literature not only within the generative framework of SLA, but for example, within the processing instruction literature (VanPatten 2002; DeKeyser, Salaberry, Robinson, and Harrington, 2002). Much of the evidence for such a claim comes from production data, but there is also sufficient evidence that beginning and intermediate learners fail to recognize simple morphology that would help them to comprehend sentences (DeKeyser 2000, Johnson and Newport 1989, VanPatten 2004, Yeni-Komshian, Robbins, and Flege 2001).

We have grappled with this issue from the beginning of this book, and it is time to come to a conclusion. While the wider, nongenerative SLA literature has been preoccupied by this issue for a long time, it is only by taking linguistic description into account that one can hope to reach an adequate answer. This textbook, and the generative SLA theory that it represents, has hopefully made the issue of L2 difficulty much clearer. A representative view of what "difficulty" and "ease" of acquisition means in the wider SLA field is articulated in DeKeyser (2005). The three factors isolated by DeKeyser that make a linguistic property difficult—complexity of form, complexity of meaning, and complexity of form–meaning relationship—are not particularly illuminating as they stand, because they are not situated in a theory of language. Furthermore, it cannot be predicted, in a principled way, which of the three factors should create more difficulty than the others or whether they are equally potent.

The lack of language theory is particularly clear when we consider DeKeyser's second difficulty-increasing factor: *meaning*. He lists the following linguistic properties as constituting a source of difficulty due to novelty of meaning, abstractness of meaning, or both: articles, classifiers, grammatical gender, and verbal aspect. We have touched on the acquisition of all of these properties in this textbook. There is no doubt that these four are among the thorniest morphosyntactic properties in SLA, and substandard performance with them persists even in advanced learners. But "abstractness" of meaning is not the reason they are difficult. The idea that one grammatical meaning can be "novel" to another language is untenable because all languages can express every meaning. Languages differ in the way they mark those universal meanings: either through dedicated (sometimes polysemous) morphemes or by allowing the discourse context to fill in the relevant information.[14]

Reconsidering DeKeyser's (2005) three factors determining acquisition difficulty from the point of view of the different modules of the language faculty and assuming that semantic conceptual structure is universal, we can confidently divide the problematic L1–L2 mappings into:

(1) those that represent a *mismatch at the syntax–semantics interface*, in other words, a *form–meaning* mismatch, and
(2) those that represent *form–form mismatches* within a single module (morphology, syntax, etc.).

Opacity of form–meaning mapping would be an exacerbating factor for the first type of problem (which may be perceived as optionality). Redundancy, true optionality, and complex paradigms would be exacerbating factors for the second type of problem. In addition, as Lardiere points out, we cannot ignore the conditioning environments of the forms that are mismatched. It goes without saying that when both types of problems conspire in some L1–L2 contrast, acquisition will be even more difficult.

With the difficult linguistic properties that constitute mismatches at the syntax–semantics interface, the linguistic form is the bottleneck for the acquisition of meaning; hence, the meaning may not be acquired before the form is mastered to a certain reasonable level of recognition. This is true of learning situations where both languages have overt morphemes for marking the relevant properties, and maybe even for situations where one of the languages has no overt morphology to correspond to a meaning. Importantly, syntactic reflexes of the same functional category are acquired before the morphology is mastered and consistently supplied (White 2003).

---

[14] See Slabakova 2008, Chapter 8 for more detail.

Functional morphology is at the living center of the second language acquisition process: a hub for meaning and syntax, but at the same time a bottleneck. It makes a lot of sense then, to reiterate that practicing the inflectional morphology in language classrooms in ample unambiguous context, including all members of a paradigm, is a key to L2A success. SLA teaching techniques from Focus on Form to Processing Instruction have advocated for such an approach for a long time. The contribution of this book is to point to exactly why this is necessarily the case and to raise the consciousness of teachers and learners one more time.

Let us conclude on a high note. The message of this textbook is a positive one: Second language acquisition is possible. Additional languages are successfully acquired every day by millions of bilinguals and multilinguals. SLA does not involve a process fundamentally different from the natural process of native language development. Whatever the difficulties, they can be overcome with exposure to rich and diverse L2 input and language practice. Linguistic theory is our best tool for understanding the development process.

13.6 Exercises

Exercise 13.1. Interpretation of generic noun phrases in English and Spanish (based on the work of Ionin, Montrul, Santos, and Grolla on genericity, in English, Spanish, and Brazilian Portuguese). A star means that the sentence is ungrammatical while a number sign means that the sentence is not used with a generic meaning.

In English, bare plurals but not definite plurals can denote kinds at the NP level:
   ✓ Hummingbirds are rare in the United States.
   # The hummingbirds are rare in the United States.
For Spanish and most other Romance languages, it's just the opposite, in that definite but not bare plurals can denote kinds:
   * Picaflores son comunes en Argentina.
   ✓ Los picaflores son comunes en Argentina.
   'Hummingbirds are common in Argentina.'
But Brazilian Portuguese (BP) exceptionally allows both bare and definite plurals with kind readings (Schmitt and Munn 2002):

✓ Beija-flores são raros em São Paulo
✓ Os beija-flores são raros em São Paulo.
'Hummingbirds are rare in São Paulo.'

Based on these examples, answer the questions below:

Question 1. Make a table or a graph of meanings and morphemes. Any visual representation would do. Is this a morphosyntax–semantics mismatch?

Question 2. Describe the learning tasks in all learning directions.

Question 3. Assuming L1 transfer, what are your expectations for behavior of Spanish learners of English and BP, BP learners of Spanish and English, and English learners of Spanish and BP, at the initial state?

Question 4. What are your predictions for ultimate attainment?

Question 5. Discuss ways to teach this contrast, in a manner that draws the attention of potential learners to the form–meaning mismatches.

Exercise 13.2. Apply the Feature Reassembly Hypothesis to new data and language combinations. This exercise would be suitable for a final course project or even an MA thesis.

Step 1. Describe a learning situation for two languages that you are familiar with, where properties may seem the same but features are actually different, or expressed on different lexical items. This is a very hard task, but at least try to think about it. Differences may be lurking where you would not expect them.

Step 2. Using Hwang and Lardiere (2013) as an example, provide a description of the difference. If there is linguistic work on this issue, indicate the features involved.

Step 3. Try to spell out a concrete learning task: what has to be learned and what has to be reconfigured.

Step 4. Think about what experimental tasks would be able to test this L2 knowledge.

Step 5. Design an experiment, providing tasks and examples.

Exercise 13.3. **Processing Instruction**. Bill VanPatten's Input Processing (IP) theory specifies a number of "principles" that describe what learners tend to do on encountering new input. Learners' processing of the input is not necessarily correct and helpful, so processing instruction is an attempt to bring their attention to what might be helpful for successful acquisition. For example, when trying to understand a sentence, learners process content words before they process functional morphology, and then let the discourse context help them. One of the IP principles is *the first-noun principle*. It says that learners tend to process the first noun or pronoun they encounter in the sentence as the subject. (What does this observation remind you of? We have discussed similar proposals.)

Question 1. Assuming that input processing is universal, what are the predictions of this observation for languages with an OVS neutral word order? Are there such languages? What are the predictions for passive sentences in English? What are the predictions for languages that scramble the object to the front of the sentence, such as Spanish?

Question 2. What kind of processing instruction can you suggest to counter this tendency? In other words, how can you teach such sentences so that the learner cannot rely on context and has to rely on form, in order to get the meaning?

The French causative construction makes a good example (from VanPatten 2007):

(i) Jean fait   promener le chien   à Marie
     John makes to.walk   the dog   to Mary

Question 3: Assuming an Anglophone learner, what would be the first interpretation of this sentence?

Question 4: The sentence actually means: "John makes Mary walk the dog." It is a causative construction. Formulate a series of steps and activities to draw the attention of potential learners. The first step could be asking the question "Who walks the dog?"

Exercise 13.4. The questions in this exercise are based on David Stringer's chapter "Modifying the teaching of modifiers: A lesson from Universal Grammar," pp. 77–100 in *Universal Grammar and the Second Language Classroom*, edited by Melinda Whong, Kook-Hee Gil, and Heather Marsden. Find the chapter, download it, read it, and answer the questions.

Question 1. Why is the order of modifiers (**yellow lovely car* but ✓*lovely yellow car*) so important? What happens if we get it wrong in a second language.

Question 2. What is universal and what is L1-based in the order of modifiers in the noun phrase? Talk about the universal categories for each modifier.

Question 3. How do pedagogical materials deal with the order of modifiers, based on Stringer's survey of textbooks?

Question 4. What preliminary findings in the adjective order experiment (pp. 91–97) attests to knowledge of a linguistic universal? What knowledge does not come for free?

Question 5. What are the pedagogical implications of these findings?

Glossary

Age of acquisition: The age at which a learner is exposed to a second language in a linguistically rich environment. For children acquiring their native language this age is 0.

Argument structure alternations: Some verbs consistently appear in different syntactic frames, which map onto different meanings. The causative–inchoative alternation is a representative example: *John/the wind broke the window—The window broke*. The dative–double object and the locative alternations are also attested in English and other languages.

Argument structure: According to the type of event referred to, each verb combines with a number of arguments (including complements and the subject). Intransitive verbs include one argument, transitive verbs include two arguments, and di-transitive verbs include three arguments. For each verb, the information specified in the lexicon includes the thematic roles (Agent, Theme, Goal, etc.) that are assigned to its arguments and the hierarchy of the arguments (with the associated theta role).

Bilingual advantage: The cognitive advantage afforded to bilinguals and multilinguals through the constant parallel activation, selection, and inhibition of the language not in use, exercised through executive control brain structures.

Bilingual individual: An individual who is communicatively functional in two languages. Definitions vary widely.

C-command: Structural relationship between nodes on a syntactic tree. A and B are in a c-command relation if node A does not dominate node B, B does not dominate A, and the first branching node that dominates A also dominates B.

Child L2 acquisition: The process of acquiring a second language starting between the ages of 4 and 7.

Competence: Knowledge of language that allows the speaker to comprehend and produce all and only the acceptable phrases and sentences in a language in appropriate discourse.

Competition: In lexical access, candidates from both (or all) known languages are available and enter in competition with each other for lexical insertion in a sentence.

Compounding Parameter: A later parameter that unites productive compounds with a number of complex predicate constructions in a language.

Computational complexity: The complexity of a certain construction is measured not by string length but by the computational processes needed for its correct interpretation. Constructions that necessitate the examination of two possible analyses and choosing between them are more complex than constructions that do not need such examination, e.g., scalar implicatures.

Critical Period: An interval in biological development, during which exposure to some biological capacity is obligatory; otherwise, development is prevented. The CP hypothesis for language claims that there is an ideal time window to acquire language, after which further language acquisition becomes much more difficult and effortful.

Derivation: The formation of a new word from another word or stem. Derivation is not obligatory and typically produces a greater change of meaning from the original form, as compared to inflection. It is closer to the root than inflection, and often changes the word class (grammatical category) of the root.

Derivational complexity: The complexity of a certain construction is measured by how many times the operation Merge occurs, that is, how many words and phrases the sentence has. Movement (internal Merge) of phrases is also counted, as in *wh*-movement.

Discourse meaning: Meaning added to the sentential meaning by taking into account the discourse situation and the knowledge available to the speaker and hearer, e.g., topic and focus.

ERP: Event-related brain potentials, a technique for measuring the neural responses to linguistic stimuli, including syllables and morphemes to sentences and discourse. Normally, experimental materials are specially manipulated to check the brain wave responses to various violations: semantic, morphosyntactic, etc.

Eye tracking: The technique of recording the eye gaze of readers or listeners / comprehenders of language. Eye movements give us a lot of information on language processing, from lexical processing to sentences to discourse.

Feature Reassembly: Donna Lardiere's proposal that the most important task in L2A involves assembling and reassembling the formal features of the second language, on the new functional lexicon lexical items, as well as acquiring the new conditioning environments of those features.

Features: Properties, or elements, into which linguistic units can be broken down in order to be studied and described. They are objects in linguistic theory. A feature, [plural] for example, is used analogously to how chemists use H to designate hydrogen, a real chemical element that exists in the real world (Adger and Svenonius 2011). Features can be phonological (e.g., [voice]), semantic (e.g., [past]), and syntactic (e.g., [Nominative Case]).

Focus: The (marking of) new information in a sentence that is being sought by a question in the context or that is added as a comment onto a Topic.

Full Functional Representation: A group of positions on ultimate attainment, which argues that all properties of the L2 grammars, including those not present in the native grammar, are in principle attainable. Variation in L2A outcomes is due to the lack of comparable input and usage of the L2, the effects of bilingualism in processing language, and individual differences in processing capacity.

Functional morphology: Morphemes that carry the grammatical meanings in a language, such as tense, aspect, definiteness, person, number, gender, etc. It comprises inflectional morphemes, which are bound, and free morphemes, such as determiners and auxiliaries in English.

Garden path sentences: Temporarily ambiguous sentences that force the comprehender to go back and reconsider previously parsed structure.

Grammatical meaning: Meaning that pertains to classes of lexical items and captures (universal) cognitive concepts. It is expressed by an inflectional ending or some other grammatical device such as auxiliaries and word order. Like lexical meaning, grammatical meaning is usually operationalized as grammatical (functional) categories with values or features. Examples include the category *tense* with [past], [present], [future]; *number* with [singular], [plural]; aspect with [completed], [habitual], [ongoing], etc.

Head: The head of a phrase is the word that determines the syntactic category of the phrase. The noun is the head of the Noun Phrase, the verb is the head of the Verb Phrase, etc. Heads are the indispensable member of a phrase. The other elements in the phrase (complement, specifier) modify the head and are therefore the head's dependents. (See Exercise 2.2 for more on heads.)

Heritage language: The native language of infants, young children, or adolescents who are exposed to a majority language as a second language, usually in immigration. Heritage language displays a wide range of competence.

Implicature: The computation of not only what is said, but also what is implied by the speaker.

Inflection: Inflection is variation in the form of a word, typically by means of an affix, that expresses a grammatical meaning obligatory for the stem's word class in some given grammatical context. In contrast to derivation, inflection does not change the word category of the stem.

Inhibition: Bilinguals and multilinguals constantly inhibit the language(s) that they know but are not using at the moment.

Integrated mental lexicon: The proposal that the mental lexicons of the two or more languages of a multilingual individual are not separate but functionally integrated. They may have a common core of concepts.

Interface Hypothesis: a working hypothesis proposed by Antonella Sorace. It argues that properties at the interface between core linguistic modules and the extralinguistic environment, in other words, properties at the syntax–discourse interface, will constitute an insurmountable difficulty even for near-native learners.

Interfaces (between linguistic modules): Points of mapping between two modules, e.g., syntax and semantics, semantics and pragmatics.

Interlanguage: The dynamic linguistic system of the bilingual individual. It can contain elements from the native language as well as the target second language. It can contain hybrid grammatical rules as well as additional rules due to overgeneralization of specific target features. The term is attributed to Larry Selinker, based on ideas by Uriel Weinreich.

Interpretable formal features: features that remain in the derivation and pass on to the syntax–semantics interface where they are interpreted. They contribute to the overall meaning of the sentence, carrying grammatical information.

Islands: Clauses from which a *wh*-phrase cannot escape to a higher clause. Linguists distinguish *wh*-islands, relative clause islands, complex NP islands, adjunct and subject islands, etc.

L1 transfer: In second language acquisition, grammatical knowledge that can reasonably be traced back to the influence of the native language. Within the Principles and Parameters framework, principles transfer from UG or from the L1 (it is impossible to tease these apart), while parameter values transfer from the native language, at the initial stage of L2 acquisition (Schwartz and Sprouse 1994, 1996).

L3/Ln acquisition: The subsequent acquisition of a third or next language, after the first and the second have been acquired. Proficiency in the L2 of multi-linguals can vary widely, but when proficient, the L2 grammar can exert cross-linguistic influence.

LAN: A brain wave in the 300–500ms window, which is sometimes found in response to early morphosyntactic expectations, for example, phrase structure violations.

Language: A system of knowledge that humans use to construct and interpret linguistic signs: words, phrases, sentences, and larger units such as discourse.

Language attrition: The loss of one's native language. In most people, attrition comes through disuse and is mostly a processing effect ("rusty" language). In some extreme cases, the attrited native language can be substituted with the L2 grammar system.

Length of residence: In CP research, the length of time, usually measured in years, during which learners were exposed to the second language in a linguistically rich environment in the country where the L2 is a majority language.

Lexical meaning: The idiosyncratic meaning of each lexical item, e.g., *cat* = small domesticated feline. Sometimes lexical meaning is discussed in terms of lexical features which stand for properties or superordinates, such as [small], [domes-ticated], [feline], [animal].

Linguistic input: The comprehensible mapping between linguistic signs and mean-ing; the language production that learners are exposed to and which gives them information about the setting of parameters in the specific language.

Linguistic modules: Areas of linguistic computation that are relatively independ-ent of each other: sound, morphosyntax, meaning.

Metonymy: A figure of speech that replaces the name of a thing with the name of something else with which it is closely associated.

Minimalist Program: A conceptual program within generative grammar that guides the development of grammatical theory. Chomsky insists that it is a program, rather than a theory, and that there are Minimalist questions, but that the answers can be framed in any theory. Of all these questions, the one that plays the most crucial role is this: why language has the properties it has.

Missing Surface Inflection: The proposal that functional morphology errors in production are due to a breakdown of lexical access to the fully specified items, and their substitution with default items, or complete omission (Haznedar and Scwartz, Prévost and White). This breakdown is sporadic, dependent on com-munication pressures and does not affect underlying structural representations.

Monolingual individual: As opposed to a bilingual, an individual who is fluent only in her native language.

Morphological decomposition: The process whereby words are not stored whole but are decomposed into morphemes, and assembled online when needed.

N400: A brain wave in response to a lexico-semantic and probability/plausibility violation, in the 300–500ms window.

Nativelike linguistic performance: Linguistic performance statistically indistinguishable from native performance.

Near-native speaker: An individual who scores within the range of native speakers on some test of language skill, be that pronunciation, grammar, or meaning comprehension.

Null Subject Parameter: A classic parameter of Universal Grammar that regulates whether or not the null pronoun *pro* is allowed (including licensed and identified) in a language. This parameter is related to a cluster of constructions that are all dependent on the existence of *pro*.

P600: A consistent response to morphosyntactic violations, including syntactic reanalysis, found in the 600–1000ms window.

Parameter of UG: A point of variation among languages. Parameters have predetermined values, or settings, which also come supplied by UG.

Performance: The actual speech (writing, sign language) produced and comprehended at a specific time. It can be affected by errors, slips of the tongue, tiredness, time pressure, and other performance factors.

Phoneme: The smallest contrastive unit in the sound system of a language. A phoneme is manifested as one or more phones (phonetic sounds) in different environments. These phones are called allophones.

Phonotactic constraint: The rules of what are the allowed sound combinations in any given language.

Phrasal/sentential meaning: The meaning of a whole sentence, calculated by combining the lexical meanings of the constituent words and some additional rules such as word order.

Poverty of the Stimulus: Learning situations in which knowledge of the inavailability of some form or some interpretation cannot be obtained based on positive evidence in the input (just because the form does not appear in the speech signal or the interpretation is unavailable).

Pragmatic meaning: Meaning based on knowledge of the world, which can be added to the sentential meaning, e.g., the denotation of *today* changes every day, *he* refers to different individuals in different conversations, etc.

Principle of UG: A linguistic property or aspect of language design that is universal, thus manifested in all languages.

Principles and Parameters framework (also known as the Government and Binding theory): A framework, or an approach, practiced actively in the 1980s and early nineties 1990s which aimed to describe linguistic structure in terms of a finite system of universal principles and a succinctly delineated finite number of parameters. This framework preceded the Minimalist Program (Chomsky 1995).

Prosodic transfer: Goad and White's proposal that omission of functional morphology in production may be due to the different prosodification requirements of the L2 words, a factor external to underlying morphosyntactic competence.

Representational Deficit: A group of positions on ultimate attainment, which argues that properties not present in the native grammar cannot become part of the underlying L2 grammar. Apparent success with such properties is due to superficial imitation of the input.

Scalar implicature: A pragmatic meaning computation postulating that, if some quantifiers are arranged on a scale such as *<some, all>*, *<many, most>*, mentioning a lower (weaker) term implies that the higher (stronger) term is not true.

Scientific method in generative SLA: Experimental research questions test hypotheses about linguistic development. Theories of development must be falsifiable, in the sense that data should in principle exist that would lead to their rejection.

Scrambling: The movement of some phrase away from the position where it originally merged. Scrambling can be for the purposes of signaling Topic and Focus.

Shallow Structure Hypothesis: Clahsen and Felser's hypothesis to the effect that second language learners do not use full grammatical representations while processing language, and rely instead on verbal information, predicate argument templates, and world knowledge. Thus, according to this hypothesis, L1 and L2 processing are fundamentally different.

Stem: A stem is the root of a word plus any derivational affixes, to which inflection attaches. E.g., *work* is the root in *work-er*, *work-er* is the stem in *work-er-s*.

Structural complexity: The complexity of a certain construction is measured by the number of XP categories (S, VP, NP, etc.) between the original position of the moved element (subject, object) and the position it moved to at the top of the sentence.

Subjacency: A parameterized principle of Universal Grammar, which postulates that a *wh*-word (*who, what*) cannot jump over too many phrase structure nodes on its way to the top of the sentence. The measure is Bounding Nodes: one is fine, but two is too many.

Syntactic parser: Assigns structure to the incoming words of a sentence by taking into account the thematic relationships between the constituents and other factors. This is a fast and automatic process. When speech or written text is being parsed, each word in a sentence is accessed, examined, and then integrated into the structure built until that moment, such that it contributes to the overall meaning of the sentence.

Syntax–semantics mismatch: The linguistic situation where similar grammatical meanings are signaled by different means in different languages, e.g., definiteness in Russian and English.

Thematic roles: Thematic roles (often used interchangeably with theta roles) express the semantic relations that the entities denoted by the NPs or PPs bear towards the action or state denoted by the verb. Verbs (e.g., *send*) have theta grids such as this one: Agent–Verb–Theme–Goal. Only arguments, not adjuncts and not expletive pronouns, have theta roles.

Topic Maintenance and Topic Shift: A pragmatic calculation of pronoun ante-cedents in a bi-clausal sentence, where the language allows null subjects. If the embedded subject is null, it tends to refer to the main clause subject, so maintaining the Topic. If the embedded subject is overt, it tends to refer to another argument in the main clause, frequently object, thus shifting the Topic.

Topic: The (marking of) old information in a sentence that comes from the context or from knowledge of the situation.

Unaccusative: An intransitive verb where the single argument has a Theme theta role, e.g., *fall, arrive.*

Unergative: An intransitive verb where the single argument has an Agent theta role, e.g., *smile, dance.*

Uninterpretable formal features: Syntactic features that trigger agreement between phrases (e.g., subject and verb, adjective and noun) and movement of syntactic objects.

Universal Grammar (or the Language Acquisition Device (LAD), or the genetic endowment): The part of our knowledge of language that is innate, and hence comes to the language learner for free. It includes the common design features of all languages.

V2 Parameter: If a language has a positive value for this parameter, then the verb (main or auxiliary) has to be in second position in the sentence. It can be preceded by only one phrase (not one word), such as subject, object, or adverbial, etc. German and English are parametrically different in this way.

Verb Movement Parameter: The parameter that regulates whether the main verb moves out of the VP or not. On its way to TP and CP, it goes over VP-edge adverbs and negation. French and English are parametrically different in this way.

Wh-*movement Parameter*: The parameter that regulates whether the *wh*-phrase should obligatorily move to the beginning of the sentence, in the CP projection. Chinese and English are parametrically different in this way.

Word Order Parameter: The parameter that regulates the order of the verb and object in the VP. Japanese and English are parametrically different in this way.

References

ABRAHAMSSON, NICLAS and KENNETH HYLTENSTAM. 2009. "Age of onset and nativelikeness in a second language: Listener perception versus linguistic scrutiny," *Language Learning* 59, 2, 249–306.

ABRAHAMSSON, NICLAS. 2012. "Age of onset and nativelike l2 ultimate attainment of morphosyntactic and phonetic intuition," *Studies in Second Language Acquisition* 34, 2, 187–214.

ABUTALEBI, JUBIN. 2008. "Neural processing of second language representation and control," *Acta Psychologica* 128, 3, 466–478.

ABUTALEBI, JUBIN and DAVID W. GREEN. 2007. "Bilingual language production: The neurocognition of language representation and control," *Journal of Neurolinguistics* 20, 242–275.

ABUTALEBI, JUBIN, P. A. DELLA ROSA, D. W. GREEN, M. HERNANDEZ, P. SCIFO, R. KEIM, S. F. CAPPA, and A. COSTA. 2012. "Bilinguals tune the anterior cingulate cortex for conflict monitoring," *Cerebral Cortex* 22, 2076–2086.

ADGER, DAVID. 2003. *Core Syntax*. Oxford: Oxford University Press.

ADGER, DAVID and PETER SVENONIUS. 2011. "Features in Minimalist Syntax," in CEDRIC BOECKX (ed.), *The Oxford Handbook of Linguistic Minimalism,* pp. 27–51. Oxford: Oxford University Press.

ALBIRINI, ABDELKADER, ELABAS BENMAMOUN, and EMAN SAADAH. 2011. "Grammatical features of Egyptian and Palestinian Arabic heritage speakers oral production," *Studies in Second Language Acquisition* 33, 273–304.

ALDWAYAN, SAAD, ROBERT FIORENTINO, and ALISON GABRIELE. 2010. "Evidence of syntactic constraints in the processing of wh-movement: A study of Najdi Arabic learners of English," in BILL VANPATTEN and JILL JEGERSKI (eds.), *Research in Second Language Processing and Parsing*, pp. 65–86. Amsterdam: John Benjamins.

ALTMANN, G. and M. STEEDMAN. 1988. "Interaction with context during human sentence processing," *Cognition* 30, 191–238.

AMARAL, LUIS and TOM ROEPER. 2014. "Multiple Grammars and second language representation," *Second Language Research* 30, 1, 3–36.

ANDERSON, J. R. 2000. *Learning and Memory: An Integrated Approach*, 2nd edition, New York: John Wiley.

AU, T., L. KNIGHTLY, S-A. JUN, and J. OH. 2002. "Overhearing a language during childhood," *Psychological Science* 13, 238–243.

BADDELEY, A. D. 1999. *Essentials of Human Memory.* New York: Psychology Press.

BAILEY, NATALIE, CAROLYN MADDEN, and STEPHEN D. KRASHEN. 1974. "Is there a 'natural sequence' in adult second language learning?", *Language Learning*, 24, 235–243, doi:10.1111/j.1467-1770.1974. tb00505.x.

BAKER, MARK. 1996. *The Polysynthesis Parameter*, Oxford: Oxford University Press.

BAKER, MARK. 2007. "The creative aspect of language use and nonbiological nativism," in PETER CARRUTHERS, STEPHEN LAURENCE, and STEPHEN STICH (eds.), *The Innate Mind 3: Foundations and Future*, pp. 233–253. Oxford: Oxford University Press.

BAKER, MARK. 2008. "The macroparameter in a microparametric world," in THERESA BIBERAUER (ed.), *The Limits of Syntactic Variation*, pp. 351–373. Amsterdam: John Benjamins.

BARDEL, CAMILLA and YLVA FALK. 2007. "The role of the second language in third language acquisition: The case of Germanic syntax," *Second Language Research*, 23, 459–484.

BARDOVI-HARLIG, KATHLEEN. 2011. "Pragmatics in SLA," in S. M. GASS and A. MACKEY (eds.), *Handbook of Second Language Acquisition*. London: Routledge.

BARDOVI-HARLIG, KATHLEEN. 2013. "Developing L2 Pragmatics," *Language Learning*, 63, 1, 68–86.

D. BASNIGHT-BROWN, L. CHEN, A. HUA, A. KOSTIĆ, and L. FELDMAN. 2007. "Monolingual and bilingual recognition of regular and irregular English verbs: Sensitivity to form similarity varies with first language experience," *Journal of Memory and Language* 57, 65–80.

BECK, MARIA-LUISA. 1998. "L2 acquisition and obligatory head movement: English-speaking learners of German and the local impairment hypothesis," *Studies in Second Language Acquisition* 20, 311–348.

BELIKOVA, ALYONA and LYDIA WHITE. 2009. "Evidence for the Fundamental Difference Hypothesis or not? Island constraints revisited," *Studies in Second Language Acquisition* 31, 2, 199–223.

BELLETTI, ADRIANA. 2000. "'Inversion' as focalization," in A. HULK and J.-Y. POLLOCK (eds.), *Subject Inversion in Romance and the Theory of Universal Grammar*. Oxford: Oxford University Press.

BELLETTI, ADRIANA. 2003. "Aspects of the lower IP area," in L. RIZZI (ed.), *The Structure of CP and IP: The Cartography of Syntactic Structures*, volume 2. Oxford: Oxford University Press.

BELLETTI, ADRIANA. 2013. "Contributing to linguistic theory, language description and the characterization of language development through experimental studies," in MISHA BECKER, JOHN GRINSTEAD, and JASON ROTHMAN (eds.), *Generative Linguistics and Acquisition: Studies in Honor of Nina M. Hyams*, pp. 309–324. Amsterdam: John Benjamins.

BELLETTI, ADRIANA, ELISA BENNATI, and ANTONELLA SORACE. 2007. "Theoretical and developmental issues in the syntax of subjects: Evidence from near-native Italian," *Natural Language and Linguistic Theory* 25, 657–689.

BELLETTI, ADRIANA and C. LEONINI. 2004. "Subject inversion in L2 Italian," *Eurosla Yearbook* 4, 95–118.

BENMAMOUN, ELABAS, SILVINA MONTRUL, and MARIA PO-LINSKY. 2013a. "Heritage languages and their speakers: Opportunities and challenges for linguistics," keynote article in *Theoretical Linguistics* 39, 129–181.

BENMAMOUN, ELABAS, SILVINA MONTRUL, and MARIA PO-LINSKY. 2013b. "Defining an 'ideal' heritage speaker: Theoretical and methodological challenges, reply to peer commentaries," *Theoretical Linguistics* 39, 259–294.

BERENT, GERALD P. 2009. "The interlanguage development of deaf and hearing learners of L2 English: Parallelism via Minimalism," in WILLIAM C. RITCHIE and TEJ K. BHATIA (eds.), *The New Handbook of Second Language Acquisition*, pp. 523–543. Bingley, UK: Emerald Group.

BERENT, GERALD P., RONALD R. KELLY, and TANYA SCHUELER-CHOUKAIRI. 2012. "L2 and deaf learners' knowledge of numerically quantified sentences: Acquisitional parallels at the semantics/discourse-pragmatics interface," *Studies in Second Language Acquisition* 34, 1, 35–66. doi:10.1017/S0272263111000490.

BERKO, JEAN. 1958. "The child's learning of English morphology," *Word* 14, 150–177.

BIALYSTOK, ELLEN. 2001. *Bilingualism in Development: Language, Literacy, and Cognition.* New York: Cambridge University Press.

BIALYSTOK, ELLEN. 2009. "Bilingualism: The good, the bad, and the indifferent," *Bilingualism: Language and Cognition* 12, 1, 3–11. doi:10.1017/S1366728908003477.

BIALYSTOK, ELLEN and M. MARTIN. 2004. "Attention and inhibition in bilingual children: Evidence from the dimensional change card sort task," *Developmental Science* 7, 325–339.

BIALYSTOK, ELLEN and L. SENMAN. 2004. "Executive processes in appearance reality tasks: The role of inhibition of attention and symbolic representation," *Child Development* 75, 562–579.

BIBERAUER, THERESA (ed.). 2008. *The Limits of Syntactic Variation.* Amsterdam: John Benjamins.

BIRDSONG, DAVID. 2002. "Interpreting age effects in second language acquisition," in JUDITH F. KROLL and ANNETTE M. B. DE GROOT (eds.), *Handbook of Bilingualism: Psycholinguistic Approaches*, pp. 109–128. New York: Oxford University Press.

BIRDSONG, DAVID. 2005. "Interpreting age effects in second language acquisition," in JUDITH KROLL and ANETTE DE GROOT (eds.), *Handbook of Bilingualism: Psycholinguistic Perspectives*, pp. 109–127. Cambridge: Cambridge University Press.

BIRDSONG, DAVID. 2009. "Age and the end state of second language acquisition," in WILLIAM C. RITCHIE and TEJ K. BHATIA, (eds.), *The New Handbook of Second Language Acquisition.* Amsterdam: Elsevier.

BLEY-VROMAN, ROBERT. 1983. "The comparative fallacy in interlanguage studies: The case of systematicity," *Language Learning* 33, 1–17.

BLEY-VROMAN, ROBERT. 1989. "What is the logical problem of foreign language acquisition?", in SUSAN GASS and JACQUELINE SCHACHTER (eds.), *Linguistic Perspectives on Second Language Acquisition*, pp. 41–64. Cambridge, UK: Cambridge University Press.

BLEY-VROMAN, ROBERT. 1990. "The logical problem of foreign language learning", *Linguistic Analysis* 20, 3–49.

BLEY-VROMAN, ROBERT. 2009. "The evolving context of the Fundamental Difference Hypothesis," *Studies in Second Language Acquisition* 31, 2, 175–198. doi:10.1017/S0272263109090275.

BLEY-VROMAN, ROBERT and N. YOSHINAGA. 1992. "Broad and narrow constraints on the English dative alternation: Some fundamental differences between native speakers and foreign language learners," *University of Hawai'i Working Papers in ESL*, 11, 157–199.

BLOM, ELMA. 2008. "Testing the Domain-by-Age model: Inflection and placement of Dutch verbs," in BELMA HAZNEDAR and ELENA GAVRUSEVA (eds.), *Current Trends in Child Second Language Acquisition: A Generative Perspective*, pp. 271–300. Amsterdam: John Benjamins.

BLOOM, LOIS and M. LAHEY. 1978. *Language Development and Language Disorders*. New York: John Wiley & Sons.

BLOOM, PAUL. 2000. *How Children Learn the Meanings of Words*. Cambridge, MA: MIT Press.

BOBALJIK, JONATHAN. 2002. "A-chains and the PF interface: Copies and covert movement," *Natural Language and Linguistic Theory* 20, 197–267.

BOECKX, CEDRIC, and KLEANTHES K. GROHMANN. 2007. "The Biolinguistics manifesto." *Biolinguistics* 1, 1, 1–8.

BORER, HAGIT. 1984. *Parametric Syntax: Case Studies in Semitic and Romance Languages*. Dordrecht: Foris Publications.

BOŠKOVIĆ, ZELJKO. 2001. *On the Nature of the Syntax–Phonology Interface: Cliticization and Related Phenomena*. Amsterdam: Elsevier Science.

BOUTON, LAWRENCE. 1992. "The interpretation of implicature in English by NNS: Does it come automatically without being explicitly taught?," in LAWRENCE BOUTON (ed.), *Pragmatics and Language Learning Monograph Series*, vol. 3. DEIL, University of Illinois at Urbana-Champaign, pp. 64–77.

BOUTON, LAWRENCE. 1994. "Can NNS skill in interpreting implicature in American English be improved through explicit instruction? A pilot study," in L. BOUTON (ed.), *Pragmatics and Language Learning Monograph Series*, vol. 5. DEIL, University of Illinois at Urbana- Champaign, pp. 88–109.

BOWERMAN, MELISSA. 1974. "Learning the structure of causative verbs: A study in the relationship of cognitive, semantic, and syntactic development," *Papers and Reports on Child Language Development* 8, 142–178.

BREEN, MARA, EVELINA FEDORENKO, MICHAEL WAGNER, and EDWARD GIBSON. 2010. "Acoustic correlates of information structure," *Language and Cognitive Processes*, 25, 7–9, 1044–1098, doi:10.1080/01690965.2010.504378.

BROWN, AMANDA and MARIANNE GULLBERG. 2010. "Changes in encoding of path of motion in a first language during acquisition of a second language," *Cognitive Linguistics*, 21, 2, 263–286.

BROWN, R. 1973. *A First Language: The Early Years*. Cambridge, MA: Harvard University Press.

BRUHN DE GARAVITO, JOYCE. 2013. "What research can tell us about teaching: The case of pronouns and clitics," in MELINDA WHONG, KOOK-HEE GIL and HEATHER MARSDEN (eds.), *Universal Grammar and the Second Language Classroom*, pp. 17–34. Dordrecht: Springer.

BRUNETTI, LOUISE. 2009. "Discourse functions of fronted foci in Italian and Spanish," in A. DUFTER AND D. JACOB (eds.), *Focus and Background in Romance Languages*, pp. 43–81. Amsterdam: John Benjamins.

BRUNETTI, L., S. BOTT, J. COSTA, and E. VALLDUVÍ. 2011. "A multilingual annotated corpus for the study of information structure." Paper presented at the Grammar and Corpora 2009 Conference.

BYGATE, MARTIN, PETER SKEHAN, and MERRILL SWAIN. 2001. *Researching Pedagogic Tasks: Second Language Learning, Teaching, and Testing*. Harlow, UK: Pearson.

BYGATE, MARTIN, MERRILL SWAIN, and PETER SKEHAN (eds.). 2001. *Researching Pedagogic Tasks in Second Language Learning, Teaching, and Testing*. New York: Pearson Education.

BYLUND, EMANUEL, ABRAHAMSSON, NICLAS. and KENNETH HYLTENSTA. 2012. "Does L1 maintenance hamper L2 nativelikeness? A study of L2 ultimate attainment in early bilinguals," *Studies in Second Language Acquisition*, 34, 215–241.

BYLUND, EMANUEL, KENNETH HYLTENSTAM, and NIKLAS ABRAHAMSSON, N. 2013. "Age of acquisition effects or effects of bilingualism in second language ultimate attainment?," in GISELA GRAÑENA and MICHAEL LONG (eds.), *Sensitive Periods, Language Aptitude, and Ultimate L2 Attainment*, pp. 69–101. Amsterdam: John Benjamins.

CADIERNO, TERESA. 2004. "Expressing motion events in a second language: A cognitive typological perspective," in M. ACHARD and S. NIEMEIER (eds.), *Cognitive Linguistics, Second Language Acquisition and Foreign Language Teaching*, pp. 13–49. Berlin: Mouton de Gruyter.

CADIERNO, TERESA. 2008. "Learning to talk about motion in a foreign language," in P. ROBINSON and N. C. ELLIS (eds.), *Handbook of Cognitive Linguistics and Second Language Acquisition*, pp. 239–274. London: Routledge.

CADIERNO, TERESA and PETER ROBINSON. 2009. "Language typology, task complexity and the development of L2 lexicalization patterns for describing motion events," *Annual Review of Cognitive Linguistics* 7, 245–276.

CANALE, MICHAEL and MERRILL SWAIN. 1980. "Theoretical bases of communicative approaches to second language teaching and testing," *Applied Linguistics* 1, 1, 1–47. doi:10.1093/applin/I.1.1.

CAPLAN, DAVID and GLORIA S. WATERS. 1999. "Verbal working memory and sentence comprehension," *Behavioral and Brain Sciences* 22, 1, 77–94.

CARLSON, R. A. 2003. "Skill learning," in L. NADEL (ed.), *Encyclopedia of Cognitive Science*, vol. 4, pp. 36–42. London: Macmillan.

CARMINATTI, MARIA N. 2002. *The Processing of Italian Subject Pronouns*. Ph.D. dissertation. Amherst, MA University of Massachussets.

CARPENTER, PATRICIA, A. MIYAKE, and M. JUST. 1994. "Working memory constraints in comprehension: Evidence from individual differences, aphasia, and aging," in ANNE GERNSBACHER-MORTON (ed.), *Handbook of Psycholinguistics*, pp. 1075–1122. San Diego, CA: Academic Publishers.

CARREIRA, M. and O. KAGAN. 2011. "The results of the national heritage language survey: implications for teaching, curriculum design, and professional development," *Foreign Language Annals* 44, 40–64.

CHANG, C., E. HAYNES, R. RHODES, and Y. YAO. 2008. "A tale of two fricatives: Consonant contrast in heritage speakers of Mandarin," *University of Pennsylvania Working Papers in Linguistics* 15, 37–43.

CHEE M. W. L., N. HON, H. LING LEE, and C. S. SOON. 2001. "Relative language proficiency modulates BOLD signal change when bilinguals perform semantic judgments," *NeuroImage* 13, 1155–1163.

CHEE M. W. L., E. W. L. TAN, and T. THIEL. 1999. "Mandarin and English single word processing studies with fMRI," *Journal of Neuroscience* 19, 3050–3056.

CHEN, Y. and H. LAI. 2011. "EFL learners' awareness of metonymy–metaphor continuum in figurative expressions," *Language Awareness* 21, 3, 235–48.

CHIEN, Y.-C. and KENNETH WEXLER. 1990. "Children's knowledge of locality conditions on binding as evidence for the modularity of syntax and pragmatics," *Language Acquisition* 13, 225–295.

CHIERCHIA, GENNARO. 2004. "Scalar implicatures, polarity phenomena, and the syntax/pragmatics interface," in ADRIANA BELLETTI (ed.), *Structures and Beyond*. Oxford: Oxford University Press.

CHIPERE, NGONI. 2004. *Understanding Complex Sentences: Native Speaker Variation in Syntactic Competence*. Basingstoke, UK: Palgrave Macmillan.

CHO, JACEE and ROUMYANA SLABAKOVA. 2014. "Interpreting definiteness in a second language without articles: The case of L2 Russian," *Second Language Research* 30, 2, 159–190, doi:10.1177/0267658313509647.

CHOMSKY, NOAM. 1973. "Conditions on Transformations," in S. R. ANDERSON and P. KIPARSKY, *A Festschrift for Morris Halle*, pp. 232–286. New York: Holt, Rinehart & Winston.

CHOMSKY, NOAM. 1981. *Lectures on Government and Binding: The Pisa Lectures*. Dordrecht: Foris Publications.

CHOMSKY, NOAM. 1986. *Knowledge of Language: Its Nature, Origin, and Use*. New York: Praeger Publishers.

CHOMSKY, NOAM. 1988. *Language and Problems of Knowledge: The Managua Lectures.* Cambridge, MA: MIT Press.

CHOMSKY, NOAM. 1995. *The Minimalist Program.* Cambridge, MA: MIT Press.

CHOMSKY, NOAM. 1995. *The Minimalist Program.* Cambridge, MA: MIT Press.

CHOMSKY, NOAM. 2001."Derivation by Phase," in M. KENSTOWICZ (ed.), *Ken Hale: A Life in Language,* 1–52 Cambridge, MA: MIT Press.

CHOMSKY, NOAM. 2004. "Beyond explanatory adequacy," in BELLETTI ADRIANA (ed.), *Structures and Beyond: The Cartography of Syntactic Structure* Vol. 3., pp. 104–131. Oxford: Oxford University Press.

CHOMSKY, NOAM. 2005. "Three factors in Language Design." *Linguistic Inquiry* 36, 1, 1–22. doi:10.1162/0024389052993655.

CHOMSKY, NOAM. 2008. "On Phases," in ROBERT FREIDIN, CARLOS PEREGRÍN OTERO and MARÍA LUISA ZUBIZARRETA, (eds.), *Foundational Issues in Linguistic Theory: Essays in Honor of Jean-Roger Vergnaud,* pp. 133–166. Cambridge, MA: MIT Press.

CHOMSKY, NOAM. 2012. "Foreword," in A. GALLEGO (ed.), *Phases: Developing the Framework,* pp. 1–7. Berlin: Mouton de Gruyter.

CHOMSKY, NOAM and MORRIS HALLE. 1968. *The Sound Pattern of English.* New York: Harper Row.

CLAHSEN, HARALD. 1986. "Verbal inflection in German child language: acquisition of agreement markings and the functions they encode." *Linguistics* 24, 79–121.

CLAHSEN, HARALD, LOAY BALKHAIR, JOHN-SEBASTIAN SCHUTTER, and IAN CUNNINGS. 2013. "The time course of morphological processing in a second language," *Second Language Research* 29, 7–31.

CLAHSEN, HARALD and CLAUDIA FELSER. 2006. "Grammatical processing in first and second language learners," *Applied Psycholinguistics* 27, 1, 3–42. doi:10.1017/S0142716406060024.

CLAHSEN, HARALD, CLAUDIA FELSER, KATHLEEN NEUBAUER, MIKAKO SATO, and RENITA SILVA. 2010. "Morphological structure in native and nonnative language processing," *Language Learning* 60, 1, 21–43. doi:10.1111/j.1467-9922.2009.00550.x.

CLAHSEN, HARALD, MARTINA PENKE, and TERESA PARODI. 1993/4. "Functional categories in early child German," *Language Acquisition* 3, 395–429.

CLARK, EVE. 1993. *The Lexicon in Acquisition.* New York: Cambridge University Press.

CLARK, EVE. 2003. *First Language Acquisition.* New York: Cambridge University Press.

CLIFTON, CHARLES, M. TRAXLER, R. WILLIAMS, M. MOHAMMED, R. MORRIS, and K. RAYNER. 2003. "The use of thematic role information in parsing: Syntactic processing autonomy revisited," *Journal of Memory and Language* 49, 317–334.

COLE, PETER, DAVID GIL, GABRIELA HERMON, and URI TAD. 2001. "The acquisition of *in situ wh*-questions and *wh*-indefinites in Jakarta Indonesian." *BUCLD* 25.

COLOMÉ, ANGELS. 2001. "Lexical activation in bilinguals' speech production: Language-specific or language-independent?" *Journal of Memory and Language* 45, 4, 721–736.

CONRADIE, SIMONE. 2006. "Investigating the acquisition of the Split-IP parameter and the V2 parameter in second language Afrikaans," *Second Language Research* 22, 64–94.

COOK, V. 1996. *Second Language Learning and Language Teaching*, 2nd edition. London: Edward Arnold.

COSTA, ALBERT. 2005. "Lexical access in bilingual production," in JUDITH F. KROLL and ANETTE M. B. DE GROOT (eds.), *Handbook of Bilingualism: Psycholinguistic Approaches*, pp. 308–325. New York, NY: Oxford University Press.

COSTA, ALBERT, MICHELE MIOZZO, and ALFONSO CARAMAZZA. 1999. "Lexical selection in bilinguals: Do words in the bilinguals' two lexicons compete for selection?", *Journal of Memory and Language* 41, 365–397.

CROCKER, MATTHEW. 1996. *Computational psycholinguistics: An interdisciplinary approach to the study of language*, Dordrecht, NL: Kluwer.

CROOKES, GRAHAM and SUSAN GASS (eds.). 1993. *Tasks and Language Learning: Integrating Theory and Practice.* Clevedon, UK: Multilingual Matters.

CUMMINS, J. 2005. "A proposal for action: Strategies for recognizing heritage language competence as a learning resource within the mainstream classroom," *The Modern Language Journal* 89, 585–592.

CURTISS, S. 1977. *Genie: A Psycholinguistic Study of a Modern-Day "Wild Child."* New York: Academic Press.

CUZA, ALEJANDRO, PEDRO GUIJARRO-FUENTES, ACRISIO PIRES, and JASON ROTHMAN. 2013. "The syntax–semantics of bare and definite plural subjects in the L2 Spanish of English natives," *International Journal of Bilingualism* 17, 5, 632–652.

DĄBROWSKA, EWA and JAMES STREET. 2006. "Individual differences in language attainment: Comprehension of passive sentences by native and non-native English speakers," *Language Sciences* 28, 6, 604–615. doi:10.1016/j.langsci.2005.11.014.

DANEMAN, MEREDITH and PATRICIA A. CARPENTER. 1980. "Individual differences in working memory and reading," *Journal of Verbal Learning and Verbal Behavior* 19, 4, 450–466.

DAVIDSON, M. C., D. AMSO, L. C. ANDERSON, and A. DIAMOND. 2006. "Development of cognitive control and executive functions from 4 to 13 years: Evidence from manipulations of memory, inhibition, and task switching," *Neuropsychologia* 44, 2037–2078.

DE DIEGO BALAGUER, R., A. RODRÍGUEZ-FORNELLS, M. ROTTE, J. BAHLMANN, H.-J. HEINZE, and T. F. MÜNTE. 2006. "Neural circuits subserving the retrieval of stems and grammatical features in regular and irregular verbs," *Human Brain Mapping*, 27, 11, 874–888. doi:10.1002/hbm.20228.

DE HOUWER, ANNICK. 1990. *The Acquisition of Two Languages from Birth: A Case Study.* Cambridge: Cambridge University Press.

DE HOUWER, ANNICK. 2007. "Parental language input patterns and children's bilingual use," *Applied Psycholinguistics* 28, 3, 411–424.

DE VILLIERS, JILL and PETER DE VILLIERS. 1973. "Development of the use of word order in comprehension," *Journal of Psycholinguistic Research* 2, 331–41.

DEKEYSER, ROBERT. 1997. "Beyond explicit rule learning: Automatizing second language morphosyntax," *Studies in Second Language Acquisition* 19, 195–221.

DEKEYSER, ROBERT. 2000. "The robustness of Critical Period effects." SSLA, 22, 4, 499–533.

DEKEYSER, ROBERT. 2001. "Automaticity and automatization," in *Cognition and Second Language Instruction*, pp. 125–151. New York, NY: Cambridge University Press.

DEKEYSER, ROBERT. 2005. "What makes learning second-language grammar difficult? A review of issues," *Language Learning* 55, 1–25.

DEKEYSER, ROBERT. 2007. "Skill Acquisition Theory," in BILL VANPATTEN and JESSICA WILLIAMS (eds.), *Theories in Second Language Acquisition*, pp. 97–113. Mahwah, NJ: Erlbaum.

DEKEYSER, ROBERT and JENNIFER LARSON-HALL. 2005. "What does the Critical Period really mean?", in JUDITH F. KROLL, and ANNETTE M. B. DE GROOT (eds.), *Handbook of Bilingualism: Psycholinguistic Approaches*, pp. 88–108. New York: Oxford University Press.

DEKEYSER, ROBERT, RAFAEL SALABERRY, PETER ROBINSON, and MICHAEL HARRINGTON. 2002. "What gets processed in processing instruction? A commentary on Bill VanPatten's 'Processing Instruction: an update'," *Language Learning* 52, 805–823.

DEKEYSER, ROBERT, IRIS ALFI-SHABTAY, and DORIT RAVID. 2010. "Cross-linguistic evidence for the nature of age effects in second language acquisition," *Applied Psycholinguistics* 31, 3, 413–438.

DEKYDTSPOTTER, LAURENT. 2009. Second Language Epistemology, Take Two. *Studies in Second Language Acquisition* 31, 291–321.

DEKYDTSPOTTER, LAURENT and KATE MILLER. 2013. "Inhibitive and facilitative priming induced by traces in the processing of *wh*-dependencies in a second language," *Second Language Research*, 29, 3, 345–372.

DEKYDTSPOTTER, LAURENT, BONNIE D. SCHWARTZ, and REX SPROUSE. 2006. "The comparative fallacy in L2 processing research," in MEGAN G. O'BRIEN, CHRISTINE SHEA, and JOHN ARCHIBALD (eds.), *Proceedings of the 8th Generative Approaches to Second*

Language Acquisition Conference (GASLA 2006): The Banff Conference, pp. 33–40. Somerville, MA: Cascadilla Press.

DEKYDTSPOTTER, LAURENT and REX SPROUSE. 2001. "Mental design and (second) language epistemology: Adjectival restrictions of *wh*-quantifiers and tense in English-French interlanguage," *Second Language Research* 17, 1–35.

DEKYDTSPOTTER, LAURENT, YI-TING WANG, BORA KIM, HYUN-JIN KIM, HYE-KYUNG KIM, and JONG KUN LEE. 2012. "Anaphora under reconstruction during processing in English as a second language." *Studies in Second Language Acquisition,* 34, 561–590.

DIEPENDAELE, K., J. A. DUÑABEITIA, J. MORRIS, and E. KEULEERS. 2011. "Fast morphological effects in first and second language word recognition," *Journal of Memory and Language*, 64, 4, 344–358. doi:10.1016/j.jml.2011.01.003.

DIETRICH, RAINER, WOLFGANG KLEIN and COLETTE NOYAU (eds.). 1995. *The Acquisition of Temporality in a Second Language.* Philadelphia, PA: John Benjamins.

DIJKSTRA, TON. 2003. "Lexical storage and retrieval in bilinguals," in ROELAND VAN HOUT, AAFKE HULK, FOLKERT KUIKEN, and RICHARD J. TOWELL (eds.), *The Lexicon–Syntax Interface in Second Language Acquisition*, pp. 129–150. Amsterdam: John Benajmins.

DIJKSTRA, TON. 2005. "Bilingual visual word recognition and lexical access," in JUDITH F. KROLL and ANETTE M. B. DE GROOT (eds.), *Handbook of Bilingualism: Psycholinguistic Approaches*, pp. 179–201. New York, NY: Oxford University Press.

DIJKSTRA, TON and WALTER J. B. VAN HEUVEN. 1998. "The BIA model and bilingual word recognition," in J. GRAINGER and A. M. JACOBS (eds.), *Localist Connectionist Approaches to Human Cognition*, pp. 189–225. Mahwah, NJ: Lawrence Erlbaum Associates.

DIJKSTRA, TON and WALTER J. B. VAN HEUVEN. 2002. "The architecture of the bilingual word recognition system: From identification to decision," *Bilingualism: Language and Cognition*, 5, 175–197.

DIJKSTRA, TON and WALTER J. B. VAN HEUVEN. 2012. "Word recognition in the bilingual brain," in MIRIAM FAUST (ed.), *The Handbook of Neuropsychology of Language*, pp. 451–471. Blackwell.

DOMÍNGUEZ, LAURA. 2004. *Mapping Focus: The Syntax and Prosody of Focus in Spanish.* Ph.D. thesis, Boston University.

DOMÍNGUEZ, LAURA, MARIA J. ARCHE, and FLORENCE MYLES. 2011. "Testing the predictions of the feature-assembly hypothesis: evidence from the L2 acquisition of Spanish aspect morphology," in *BUCLD 35: Proceedings of the 35th Annual Boston University Conference on Language Development. 35th Annual Boston University Conference on Language Development.* Boston: Cascadilla Press.

DONALDSON, BRIAN. 2011. "Left-dislocation in near-native French," *Studies in Second Language Acquisition*, 33, 399–432.

DONALDSON, BRIAN. 2012. "Syntax and discourse in near-native French: Clefts and focus," *Language Learning*, 62, 902–930.

DÖRNYEI, ZOLTÁN. 2009. *The Psychology of Second Language Acquisition.* New York: Oxford University Press.

DRYER, MATTHEW S. 1992. "The Greenbergian word order correlations," *Language* 68, 1, 81–138.

DRYER, MATTHEW S. and MARTIN HASPELMATH (eds.). 2013. *The World Atlas of Language Structures Online.* Leipzig: Max Planck Institute for Evolutionary Anthropology. Available online at http://wals.info, accessed on 2014-01-30.

DUFFIELD, NIGEL. 2006. "How do you like your donuts? Commentary on Clahsen & Felser 'Grammatical Processing in Language Learners'," *Applied Psycholinguistics* 27, 1, 57–59.

DULAY, HEIDI C. and MARINA K. BURT. 1973. "Should we teach children syntax?", *Language Learning* 23, 245–258.

DULAY, HEIDI C. and MARINA K. BURT. 1974. "Natural sequences in child second language acquisition," *Language Learning* 24, 1, 37–53. doi:10.1111/j.1467-1770.1974.tb00234.x.

DUSSIAS, PAOLA. 2004. "Parsing a first language like a second: The erosion of L1 parsing strategies in Spanish–English bilinguals," *International Journal of Bilingualism*, 8, 355–371.

DUSSIAS, PAOLA and T. R. CRAMER SCALTZ. 2008. "Spanish-English L2 speakers' use of subcategorization bias information in the resolution of temporary ambiguity during second language reading," *Acta Psychologica* 128, 501–513.

É. KISS, KATALIN. 1998. "Identificational focus versus information focus," *Language* 74, 2, 245–273.

EIMAS, PETER, EINAR R. SIQUELAND, PETER JUSCZYK, and JAMES VIGORITO. 1971. "Speech perception in infants," *Science*, 171, 3968, 303–306.

ELLIS, ROD. 2003. *Task-based Language Learning and Teaching.* Oxford: Oxford University Press.

EPSTEIN, SAMUEL D., SUZANNE FLYNN, and GITA MARTO-HARDJONO. 1996. "Second language acquisition: Theoretical and experimental issues in contemporary research," *Behavioral and Brain Sciences* 19, 677–758.

ERBAUGH, MARY. 1992. "The acquisition of Mandarin," in D. SLOBIN (ed.), *The Cross-Linguistic Study of Language Acquisition*, vol. 3, pp. 373–455. Hillsdale, NJ: Lawrence Erlbaum.

EUBANK, LYNN. 1996. "Negation in early child German-English interlanguage: More valueless features in the L2 initial state," *Second Language Research* 12, 73–106.

FARMER, THOMAS A., JENNIFER B. MISYAK, and MORTEN H. CHRISTIANSEN. 2012. "Individual differences in sentence processing," in MICHAEL J. SPIVEY, MARC F. JOANNISSE, and KEN MCRAE (eds.), *Cambridge Handbook of Psycholinguistics*, pp. 353–364. Cambridge, UK: Cambridge University Press.

FELDMAN, L. B., A. KOSTIC, D. M. BASNIGHT-BROWN, D. FILIPOVIĆ ĐURĐEVIĆ, and M. J. PASTIZZO. 2010. "Morphological facilitation for regular and irregular verb formations in native and non-native speakers: Little evidence for two distinct mechanisms," *Bilingualism: Language and Cognition*, 13, 2, 119–135. doi:10.1017/S1366728909990459.

FELSER, CLAUDIA and LEAH ROBERTS. 2007. "Processing wh-dependencies in a second language: A cross-modal priming study," *Second Language Research*, 31, 9–36.

FERREIRA, FERNANDA and SWETS B. 2005. "The production and comprehension of resumptive pronouns in relative clause 'island' contexts," in ANNE CUTLER (ed.), *Twenty-First Century Psycholinguistics: Four Cornerstones*, pp. 263–278. Mahwah, NJ: Erlbaum.

FERREIRA, FERNANDA, KARL G. D. BAILEY, and VITTORIA FERRARO. 2002. "Good enough representations in language comprehension," *Current Directions in Psychological Science*, 11, 1, 11–15.

FISHMAN, JOSHUA A. 2006. 'Three-hundred plus years of heritage language education in the United States," in G. VALDÉS, J. FISHMAN, R. CHÁVEZ, and W. PÉREZ, *Developing Minority Language Resources: The Case of Spanish in California*, pp. 12–23. Clevedon: Multilingual Matters.

FLEGE, JAMES E. 1987. "The production of 'new' and 'similar' phones in a foreign language: Evidence for the effect of equivalence classification," *Journal of Phonetics*, 15, 47–65.

FLEGE, JAMES E. 1995. "Second-language speech learning: Theory, findings, and problems," in W. STRANGE (ed.), *Speech Perception and Linguistic Experience: Theoretical And Methodological Issues*, pp. 229–273. Timonium, MD: York Press.

FLEGE, JAMES E. 2009. "Give input a chance!", in THORSTEN PISKE and MARTHA YOUNG-SCHOLTEN (eds.), *Input Matters in SLA*, pp. 175–190. Clevedon, England: Multilingual Matters.

FLYNN, SUZANNE. 1987a. "Contrast and construction in a theory of second language acquisition," *Language Learning* 37, 1, 19–62.

FLYNN, SUZANNE. 1987b. *A Parameter-Setting Model of L2 Acquisition*. Dordrecht: Reidel.

FLYNN, SUZANNE and I. ESPINAL. 1985. "Head-Initial/Head-Final Parameter in adult L2 acquisition," *Second Language Research* 1, 2, 93–117.

FLYNN, SUSANNE, INNA VINNITSKAYA, and CLAIRE FOLEY. 2004. "The cumulative enhancement model for language acquisition: Comparing adults and children's patterns of development in first, second and third language acquisition of relative clauses," *International Journal of Multilingualism* 1, 3–16.

FODOR, JANET D. 1998. "Learning to parse?" *Journal of Psycholinguistic Research*, 27, 285–319.

FODOR, JERRY A. 1983. *Modularity of Mind: An Essay on Faculty Psychology*. Cambridge, MA: MIT Press.

FOUCART, ALICE and CHERYL FRENCK-MESTRE. 2011. "Can late L2 learners acquire new grammatical features? Evidence from ERPs and eye-tracking," *Journal of Memory and Language* 66, 226–248.

FRANCESCHINA, FLORENCIA. 2001. "Morphological or syntactic deficits in near-native speakers? An assessment of some current proposals," *Second Language Research* 17, 3, 213–247.

FRANCESCHINA, FLORENCIA. 2005. *Fossilized Second Language Grammars: The Acquisition of Grammatical Gender.* Amsterdam: John Benjamins.

FRAZIER, LYN. 1979. *On Comprehending Sentences: Syntactic Parsing Strategies.* Ph.D. thesis, University of Connecticut. West Bend, IN: Indiana University Linguistics Club.

FRAZIER, LYN. 1987. "Syntactic processing: Evidence from Dutch," *Natural Language and Linguistic Theory* 5, 4, 519–559. doi:10.1007/BF00138988.

FRAZIER, LYN and CHARLES CLIFTON, Jr. 1996. *Construal.* Cambridge, MA: MIT Press.

FRAZIER, LYN and KEITH RAYNER. 1982. "Making and correcting errors during sentence comprehension: Eye movements in the analysis of structurally ambiguous sentences," *Journal of Memory and Language* 37, 58–93.

FRISSON, STEVEN and MARTIN PICKERING. 2007. "The processing of familiar and novel senses of a word: Why reading Dickens is easy but reading Needham can be hard," *Language and Cognitive Processes* 22, 4, 595–613.

FULI, L. T. 2007. "Definiteness vs. specificity: An investigation into the terms used to describe articles in Gagana Samoa." Unpublished master's thesis, University of Auckland.

GABRIELE, ALISON. 2005. "The acquisition of aspect in a second language: A bidirectional study of learners of English and Japanese." Unpublished Ph.D. thesis, City University of New York.

GALLEGO, ANGEL. 2011. "Parameters," in CEDRIC BOECKX (ed.). *The Oxford Handbook of Linguistic Minimalism*, pp. 523–550. Oxford: Oxford University Press.

GASKELL, M. GARETH and WILLIAM D. MARSLEN-WILSON. 2002. "Representation and competition in the perception of spoken words," *Cognitive Psychology* 45, 2, 220–266.

GASS, SUSAN. 1997. *Input, Interaction and the Second Language Learner.* Mahwah, NJ: Lawrence Erlbaum.

GASS, SUSAN. 2003. "Input and interaction," in CATHY DOUGHTY and MICHAEL LONG (eds.), *Handbook of Second Language Acquisition*, pp. 224–255. Oxford, UK: Blackwell.

GASS, SUSAN and LARRY SELINKER. 2001. *Second Language Acquisition: An Introductory Course.* Mahwah, NJ: Lawrence Erlbaum.

GAVRUSEVA, ELENA and ROSALIND THORNTON. 2001. "Getting it right: Acquisition of whose questions in child English," *Language Acquisition* 9, 3, 229–267.

GAZDAR, GERALD A. 1979. *Pragmatics: Implicatures, Presuppositions and Logical Form.* New York, NY: Academic Press.

GENESEE, FRED. 1989. "Early bilingual development: One language or two?", *Journal of Child Language* 16, 1, 161–179.

GIBSON, EDWARD. 1998. "Linguistic complexity: locality of syntactic dependencies," *Cognition*, 68, 1–76.

GIBSON, EDWARD. 2000. "The dependency locality theory: A distance based theory of linguistic complexity," in Y. MIYASHITA, A. MARANTZ, and W. O'NEIL (eds.), *Image, Language, Brain*, pp. 95–126. Cambridge, MA: MIT Press.

GIL, KOOK-HEE and HEATHER MARSDEN. 2013. "Existential quantifiers in second language acquisition: A feature reassembly account," *Linguistic Approaches to Bilingualism*, 3, 2, 117–149.

GILLON DOWENS, M., M. VERGARA, H. BARBER, and M. CARREIRAS. 2010. "Morphosyntactic processing in late second language learners," *Journal of Cognitive Neuroscience* 22, 1870–1887.

GILLON DOWENS, M., T. GUO, J. GUO, H. BARBER, and M. CARREIRAS. 2011. "Gender and number processing in Chinese learners of Spanish: Evidence from event related potentials," *Neuropsychologia* 49, 1651–1659.

GIORGI, ALESSANDRA and FABIO PIANESI. 1997. *Tense and Aspect: From Semantics to Morphosyntax.* New York: Oxford University Press.

GOAD, HEATHER and LYDIA WHITE. 2004. "Ultimate attainment of L2 inflections: Effects of L1 prosodic structure," in SUSAN FOSTER-COHEN, MICHAEL SHARWOOD SMITH, ANTONELLA SORACE, and MITSUHIKO OTA (eds.), *EuroSLA Yearbook 4*, pp. 119–145. Amsterdam: John Benjamins.

GOAD, HEATHER and LYDIA WHITE. 2006. "Ultimate attainment in interlanguage grammars: A prosodic approach," *Second Language Research* 22, 3, 243–268. doi:10.1191/0267658306sr268oa.

GOAD, HEATHER and LYDIA WHITE. 2008. "Prosodic structure and the representation of L2 functional morphology: A nativist approach," *Lingua* 118, 577–594.

GOAD, HEATHER, LYDIA WHITE, and JEFFREY STEELE. 2003. "Missing inflection in L2 acquisition: Defective syntax or L1-constrained prosodic representations?" *Canadian Journal of Linguistics,* 48, 3/4, 243–263. doi:10.1353/cjl.2004.0027.

GOLLAN, TAMAR H., R. I. MONTOYA, C. M. CERA, and T. C. SANDOVAL. 2008. "More use almost always means smaller a frequency effect: Aging, bilingualism, and the weaker links hypothesis," *Journal of Memory and Language*, 58, 787–814.

GOLLAN, TAMAR H. and VICTOR S. FERREIRA. 2009. "Should I stay or should I switch? A cost–benefit analysis of voluntary language switching in young and aging bilinguals," *Journal of Experimental Psychology: Learning, Memory, and Cognition*, 35, 3, 640–665. doi:10.1037/a0014981.

GOR, KIRA and S. COOK. 2010. "Non-native processing of verbal morphology: In search of regularity," *Language Learning*, 60, 1, 88–126.

GOR, KIRA and SCOTT JACKSON. 2013. "Morphological decomposition and lexical access in a native and second language: A nesting doll effect," *Language and Cognitive Processes*, 28, 7, 1065–1091. doi:10.1080/01690965.2013.776696.

GOUVEA, ANA, COLIN PHILLIPS, NINA KAZANINA, and DAVID POEPPEL. 2010. "The linguistic processes underlying the P600," *Language and Cognitive Processes*, 25, 2, 149–188.

GRAÑENA, GISELA and MICHAEL LONG. 2013. *Sensitive Periods, Language Aptitude, and Ultimate L2 Attainment*. Amsterdam: John Benjamins.

GREEN, DAVID W. 1998. "Mental control of the bilingual lexico-semantic system," *Bilingualism: Language and Cognition* 1, 67–81.

GREEN, GEORGIA M. 1974. *Semantics and Syntactic Regularity*. Bloomington, IN: Indiana University Press.

GREENBERG, JOSEPH. 1963. "Some universals of grammar with particular reference to the order of meaningful elements," in J. GREENBERG (ed.), *Universals of Language*, pp. 73–113. Cambridge, MA: MIT Press.

GREGG, KEVIN R. 1989. "Second language acquisition theory: The case for a generative perspective," in SUSAN. M. GASS and JACQUELINE SCHACHTER (eds), *Linguistic Perspectives on Second Language Acquisition*, pp. 15–40. Cambridge: Cambridge University Press.

GREGG, KEVIN R. 2003. "SLA theory: Construction and assessment," in CATHERINE DOUGHTY and MICHAEL LONG (eds.), pp. 831–864, *The Handbook of Second Language Acquisition*. Oxford: Blackwell Publishing.

GREGORY, M. and L. MICHAELIS. 2001. "Topicalization and left dislocation: A functional opposition revisited," *Journal of Pragmatics*, 33, 1665–1706.

GRICE, HERBERT PAUL. 1968. "Utterer's meaning, sentence meaning, and word meaning," *Foundations of Language*, 4. Reprinted as Chapter 6 of Grice, 1989, *Studies in the Way of Words*, pp. 117–137. Cambridge, MA: Harvard University Press.

GRIMSHAW, JANE. 1990. *Argument Structure*. Cambridge, MA: MIT Press.

GROSJEAN, FRANCOIS. 1989. "Neurolinguists, beware! The bilingual is not two monolinguals in one person," *Brain and Language*, 36, 3–15.

GROSJEAN, FRANCOIS. 2001. The bilingual's language modes. In JANET NICOL (ed.), *One Mind, Two Languages: Bilingual Language Processing*, pp. 1–22. Oxford: Blackwell. Also in Li Wei (ed.). *The Bilingual Reader*, 2nd edition. London: Routledge, 2007.

GRÜTER, THERES. 2006. "Another take on the L2 initial state: Evidence from comprehension in L2 German," *Language Acquisition* 13, 287–317.

GUASTI, M. T., MARIA TERESA, GENNARO CHIERCHIA, STEPHEN CRAIN, F. FOPPOLO, A. GUALMINI, and L. MERONI. 2005. "Why children and adults sometimes (but not always) compute implicatures," *Language and Cognitive Processes* 20, 5, 667–696.

GUIJARRO-FUENTES, PEDRO. 2011. "Feature composition in Differential Object Marking," *EUROSLA Yearbook*, 11, 138–164.

GUIJARRO-FUENTES, PEDRO. 2012. "The acquisition of interpretable features in L2 Spanish: Personal *a*," *Bilingualism: Language and Cognition* 15, 4, 701–720.

GULLBERG, MARIANNE. 2009. "Reconstructing verb meaning in a second language: How English speakers of L2 Dutch talk and gesture about placement," *Annual Review of Cognitive Linguistics* 7, 221–244.

GUO, T., H. LIU, M. MISRA, and JUDITH KROLL. 2011. "Local and global inhibition in bilingual word production: fMRI evidence from Chinese-English bilinguals," *NeuroImage* 56, 2300–2309.

GUO, T., M. MISRA, J. W. TAM, and JUDITH F. KROLL. 2012. "On the time course of accessing meaning in a second language: An electrophysiological investigation of translation recognition," *Journal of Experimental Psychology: Learning, Memory, and Cognition*, 38, 1165–1186.

GÜREL, AYSE and G. YILMAZ. 2011. "Restructuring in the L1 Turkish grammar: Effects of L2 English and L2 Dutch," *Language, Interaction and Acquisition* 2, 2, 221–250.

HAGOORT, PETER, COLIN BROWN, and LEE OSTERHOUT. 1999. "The neural architecture of syntactic processing," in COLIN BROWN and PETER HAGOORT (eds.), *Neurocognition of Language*, pp. 273–316. Oxford: Oxford University Press.

HAHN, W. K. 1987. "Cerebral lateralization of function: From infancy through childhood," *Psychological Bulletin 101*, 396–392.

HAHNE, ANJA, JUTTA L. MUELLER, and HARALD CLAHSEN. 2006. "Morphological processing in a second language: Behavioral and event-related brain potential evidence for storage and decomposition," *Journal of Cognitive Neuroscience* 18, 1, 121–134. doi:10.1162/089892906775250067.

HÅKANSSON, GISELA. 1995. "Syntax and morphology in language attrition: A study of five bilingual expatriate Swedes," *International Journal of Applied Linguistics*, 5, 2, 153–169.

HALE, KENNETH. 1996."Can UG and L1 be distinguished in L2 acquisition?", *Behavioral and Brain Sciences* 19, 728–730.

HALL, D. GEOFFREY and SANDRA WAXMAN. 1993. "Assumptions about word meaning: Individuation and basic-level kinds," *Child Development* 64, 1550–1570.

HAN, ZHAOHONG and ELAINE TARONE (eds.). 2014. *Interlanguage: 40 Years Later*. Amsterdam: John Benjamins.

HARTSUIKER, R. J., M. J. PICKERING, and E. VELTKAMP. 2004. "Is syntax separate or shared between languages? Cross-linguistic syntactic priming in Spanish/English bilinguals," *Psychological Science*, 15, 6, 409–414.

HAWKINS, ROGER. 2001. *Second Language Syntax: A Generative Introduction*. Oxford: Blackwell.

HAWKINS, ROGER and GABRIELA CASILLAS. 2007. "Explaining frequency of verb morphology in early L2 speech," *Lingua*, 118, 595–612.

HAWKINS, ROGER and CECILIA CHAN. 1997. "The partial availability of Universal Grammar in second language acquisition: The 'failed functional features hypothesis'," *Second Language Research*, 13, 187–226.

HAWKINS, ROGER and FLORENCIA FRANCESCHINA. 2004. "Explaining the acquisition and non-acquisition of determiner noun gender concord in French and Spanish," in PHILIPPE PRÉVOST and JOHANNE PARADIS (eds.), *The Acquisition of French in Different Contexts*. Amsterdam/ Philadelphia: John Benjamins.

HAWKINS, ROGER and HAJIME HATTORI. 2006. "Interpretation of English multiple *wh*-questions by Japanese speakers: A missing uninterpretable feature account," *Second Language Research* 22, 3, 269–301. doi:10.1191/ 0267658306sr269oa.

HAWKINS, ROGER and SARAH LISZKA. 2003. "Locating the source of defective past tense marking in advanced L2 English speakers," in ROELAND VAN HOUT, AAFKE HULK, FOLKERT KUIKEN, and RICHARD TOWELL (eds.), *The Lexicon–Syntax Interface in Second Language Acquisition*, pp. 21–44. Amsterdam: John Benjamins.

HAZNEDAR, BELMA and BONNIE D. SCHWARTZ. 1997. "Are there optional infinitives in child L2 acquisition?", in ELIZABETH HUGHES, MARY HUGHES, and ANNABEL GREENHILL (eds.), *Proceedings of the 21st Annual Boston University Conference on Language Development (BUCLD)*, 257–268. Somerville, MA: Cascadilla Proceedings Project.

HAZNEDAR, BELMA. 2001. "The acquisition of the IP system in child L2 acquisition," *Studies in Second Language Acquisition* 23, 1–39.

HENSCH, TAKAO K. 2004. "Critical period regulation," *Annual Review of Neuroscience* 27, 549–579. doi:10.1146/annurev.neuro.27.070203.144327.

HERSCHENSOHN, JULIA. 2007. *Language Development and Age*. New York: Cambridge University Press.

HERSCHENSOHN, JULIA, JEFF STEVENSON, and JEREMY WALTMUNSON. 2005. "Children's acquisition of L2 Spanish morphosyntax in an immersion setting," *International Review of Applied Linguistics in Language Teaching (IRAL)* 43, 193–217. doi: 10.1515/iral.2005.43.3.193.

HERTEL, TAMMY J. 2003. "Lexical and discourse factors in the second language acquisition of Spanish word order," *Second Language Research* 19, 273–304.

HILDEBRAND, JOYCE. 1987. "The acquisition of preposition stranding," *Canadian Journal of Linguistics*, 32, 65–85.

HILLES, S. 1986. "Interlanguage and the pro-drop parameter," *Second Language Research* 2, 33–52.

HIRAKAWA, MAKIKO. 1999. "L2 acquisition of Japanese unaccusative verbs by speakers of English and Chinese," in KAZUE KANNO (ed.), *The Acquisition of Japanese as a Second Language*, pp. 89–113. Amsterdam: John Benjamins.

HIRAKAWA, MAKIKO. 2013. "Alternations and argument structure in second language English: Knowledge of two types of intransitive verbs," in MELINDA WHONG, KOOK-HEE GIL, and HEATHER MARSDEN (eds.), *Universal Grammar and the Second Language Classroom.* pp. 117–38. Dordrecht: Springer.

HOFF, ERIKA, CYNTHIS CORE, SILVIA PLACE, ROSARIO RUMICHE, MELISSA SEÑOR, and MARISOL PARRA. 2012. "Dual language exposure and early bilingual development," *Journal of Child Language* 39, 1–27. doi:10.1017/ S0305000910000759.

HOFMEISTER, PHILIP & IVAN A. SAG. 2010. "Cognitive constraints and island effects," *Language,* 86, 366–415.

HOLMBERG, ANDERS. 2010. "Parameters in minimalist theory: The case of Scandinavian," Linguistics 36, 1, 1–48.

HOPP, HOLGER. 2005. "Constraining second language word order optionality: Scrambling in advanced English-German and Japanese-German interlanguage," *Second Language Research* 21, 34–71.

HOPP, HOLGER. 2007. *Ultimate Attainment at the Interfaces in Second Language Acquisition: Grammar and Processing.* Ph.D. thesis, University of Groningen.

HOPP, HOLGER. 2010. "Ultimate attainment in L2 inflectional morphology: Performance similarities between non-native and native speakers," *Lingua* 120, 901–931.

HOPP, HOLGER. 2015. "Individual differences in the second language processing of object–subject ambiguities," *Applied Psycholinguistics* 36, 02, 129–173

HOPP, HOLGER and MONIKA SCHMID. 2013. "Perceived foreign accent in first language attrition and second language acquisition: The impact of age of acquisition and bilingualism," *Applied Psycholinguistics* 34, 361–394.

HORN, LAURENCE. 1972. *On the Semantic Properties of the Logical Operators in English.* Ph.D. dissertation, UCLA.

HORN, LAURENCE and GREGORY WARD (eds.). 2004. *The Handbook of Pragmatics.* Malden, MA: Blackwell Publishing.

HUANG, CHIUNG-CHIH. 2003. "Mandarin temporality inference in child, maternal and adult speech," *First Language,* 23, 147–169.

HUBEL, D. H. and T. N. WIESEL. 1970. "The period of susceptibility to the physiological effects of unilateral eye closure in kittens," *The Journal of Physiology* 206, 2, 419–436.

HUEBNER, THOM. 1983. *A Longitudinal Analysis of the Acquisition of English.* Ann Arbor, MI: Karoma.

HWANG, SUN HEE and DONNA LARDIERE. 2013. "Plural-marking in L2 Korean: A feature-based approach," *Second Language Research* 29, 1, 57–86.

HYAMS, NINA. 1986. *Language Acquisition and the Theory of Parameters.* Dordrecht, The Netherlands: D. Reidel Publishing Company.

HYAMS, NINA. 1994. "V2, null arguments and COMP projections," in TEUN HOEKSTRA and BONNIE D. SCHWARTZ (eds.), *Language Acquisition Studies in Generative Grammar*, pp. 21–55. Amsterdam: John Benjamins.

HYLTENSTAM KENNETH and NICLAS ABRAHAMSSON. 2003. "Maturational constraints in SLA," in CATHERINE J. DOUGHTY and MICHAEL II. LONG (eds.), *The Handbook of Second Language* Acquisition, pp. 539–587. Malden, MA: Blackwell.

HYMES, DELL H. 1966. "Two types of linguistic relativity," in BRIGHT, W. *Sociolinguistics*, pp. 114–158. The Hague: Mouton.

INAGAKI, SHUNJI. 2001. "Motion verbs with goal PPs in the L2 acquisition of English and Japanese," *Studies in Second Language Acquisition*, 23, 153–170.

INAGAKI, SHUNJI. 2006. "Manner of motion verbs with location/directional PPs in L2 English and Japanese," in ROUMYANA SLABAKOVA, SILVINA MONTRUL, and PHILIPPE PREVOST (eds.), *Inquiries in Linguistic Development*, pp. 41–66. Amsterdam: John Benjamins.

INDEFREY, PETER. 2006. "A meta-analysis of hemodynamic studies on first and second language processing: Which suggested differences can we trust and what do they mean?", *Language Learning* 56, 279–304.

IONIN, TANIA. 2003. *Article Semantics in Second Language Acquisition*. Ph.D. thesis, MIT.

IONIN, TANIA, HEEJEONG KO, and KENNETH WEXLER. 2004. "Article semantics in L2 acquisition: The role of specificity." *Language Acquisition* 12 (1): 3–69. doi:10.1207/s15327817la1201–2.

IONIN, TANIA and SILVINA MONTRUL. 2010. "The role of L1 transfer in the interpretation of articles with definite plurals in L2 english." *Language Learning* 60, 4, 877–925.

IONIN, TANIA, SILVINA MONTRUL, and MONICA CRIVOS. 2013. "A bidirectional study on the acquisition of plural noun phrase interpretation in English and Spanish," *Applied Psycholinguistics* 34, 483–518.

IONIN, TANIA, MARÍA LUISA ZUBIZARRETA, and VADIM PHILIPPOV. 2009. "Acquisition of article semantics by child and adult L2-English learners," *Bilingualism: Language and Cognition* 12, 3, 337–361.

IONIN, TANIA, MARÍA LUISA ZUBIZARRETA, and SALVADOR BAUTISTA MALDONADO. 2008. "Sources of linguistic knowledge in the second language acquisition of English articles," *Lingua* 118, 554–576.

IVANOV, IVAN. 2009. *Second Language Acquisition of Bulgarian Object Clitics: A Test Case for the Interface Hypothesis*. Unpublished doctoral dissertation, University of Iowa.

IVANOV, IVAN. 2012. "L2 acquisition of Bulgarian clitic-doubling: A test case for the interface hypothesis," *Second Language Research*, 28, 345–368.

IVERSON, MICHAEL. 2013. *Advanced Language Attrition of Spanish in Contact with Brazilian Portuguese*. Ph.D. thesis, University of Iowa.

JACKENDOFF, RAY. 1972. *Semantic Interpretation in Generative Grammar*. Cambridge, MA: MIT Press.

JACKENDOFF, RAY. 1990. *Semantic Structures*. Cambridge, MA: MIT Press.

JACKENDOFF, RAY. 1992. "Mme. Tussaud meets the Binding Theory," *Natural Language & Linguistic Theory* 10, 1, 1–31.

JACKENDOFF, RAY. 1997. *The Architecture of the Language Faculty*. Cambridge, MA: MIT Press.

JACKENDOFF, RAY. 2002. *Foundations of Language: Brain, Meaning, Grammar, Evolution.* New York: Oxford University Press.

JACKSON, CARRIE. N. and SUSAN C. BOBB. 2009. "The processing and comprehension of wh-questions among second language speakers of German," *Applied Psycholinguistics* 30, 603–636.

JACKSON, CARRIE N. and PAOLA DUSSIAS. 2009. "Cross-linguistic differences and their impact on L2 sentence processing," *Bilingualism: Language and Cognition* 12, 65–82.

JACKSON, CARRIE N. and JANET V. VAN HELL. 2011. "The effects of L2 proficiency on the processing of wh-questions among Dutch second language speakers of English," *International Review of Applied Linguistics and Language Teaching*, 49, 195–219.

JARED, DEBRA and JUDITH F. KROLL. 2001. "Do bilinguals activate phonological representations in one or both of their languages when naming words?", *Journal of Memory and Language* 44, 1, 2–31. doi:10.1006/jmla.2000.2747.

JEGERSKI, JILL, BILL VANPATTEN, and GREGORY KEATING. 2011. "The processing of ambiguous sentences by Spanish heritage speakers and by Spanish-dominant bilinguals," in A. ROCA, M. CARREIRA, and C. COLOMBÍ (eds.), *Global Spanish: Research on Bilingualism and Language Contact*. Somerville, MA: Cascadilla Press.

JOHNSON, JACQUELINE, K. SHENKMAN, E. NEWPORT, and D. MEDIN. 1996. "Indeterminacy in the grammar of adult language learners," *Journal of Memory and Language*, 35, 335–352.

JOHNSON, JACQUELINE S. and ELISSA NEWPORT. 1989. "Critical Period effects in second language learning: The influence of maturational state on the acquisition of English as a second language." *Cognitive Psychology* 21, 1, 60–99. doi:10.1016/0010-0285(89)90003-0.

JOHNSON, JACQUELINE S., and ELISSA NEWPORT. 1991. "Critical Period effects on universal properties of language: The Status of subjacency in the acquisition of a second language." *Cognition* 39, 3, 215–258. doi:10.1016/0010-0277(91)90054-8.

JUDITH F. KROLL, JASON W. GULLIFER, and ELEONORA ROSSI. 2013. "The multilingual lexicon: The cognitive and neural basis of lexical comprehension and production in two or more languages," *Annual Review of Applied Linguistics* 33, 102–127.

JUFFS, ALAN. 1996. *Learnability and the Lexicon: Theories and Second Language Acquisition Research*. Amsterdam: John Benjamins.

JUFFS, ALAN. 1998a. "Some effects of first language argument structure and syntax on second language processing," *Second Language Research* 14, 406–424.

JUFFS, ALAN. 1998b. "Main verb vs. reduced relative clause ambiguity resolution in second language sentence processing," *Language Learning* 48, 107–147.

JUFFS, ALAN and MICHAEL HARRINGTON. 1995. "Parsing effects in second language sentence processing: Subject and object asymmetries in wh-extraction," *Studies in Second Language Acquisition* 17, 483–516.

JUFFS, ALAN and MICHAEL HARRINGTON. 1996. "Garden path sentences and error data in second language sentence processing research," *Language Learning* 46, 286–324.

JUFFS, ALAN and GUILLERMO RODRÍGUEZ. 2015. *Second Language Sentence Processing*. New York: Routledge.

JUST, MARCEL A. and PATRICIA A. CARPENTER. 1980. "A theory of reading: From eye fixations to comprehension," *Psychological Review* 87, 329–354.

JUST, MARCEL A. and PATRICIA A. CARPENTER. 1992. "A capacity theory of comprehension: Individual differences in working memory," *Psychological Review* 99, 1, 122–149.

KAAN, EDITH, JOCELYN BALLANTYNE, and FRANK WIJNEN. 2015. "Effects of reading speed on second language sentence processing," *Applied Psycholinguistics* 36, 4, 799–830. http://dx.doi.org/10.1017/S0142716413000519.

KAYNE, RICHARD. 1994. *The Antisymmetry of Syntax*. Cambridge, MA: MIT Press.

KAYNE, RICHARD. 2005. "Some notes on comparative syntax, with special reference to English and French," in GUGLIELMO CINQUE and RICHARD KAYNE (eds.), *The Oxford Handbook of Comparative Syntax*, 3–69. New York: Oxford University Press.

KAZANINA, NINA and COLIN PHILLIPS. 2007. "A developmental perspective on the imperfective paradox," *Cognition* 105, 65–102.

KEATING, GREGORY D. 2009. "Sensitivity to violations of gender agreement in native and nonnative Spanish: An eye-movement investigation, *Language Learning* 59, 3, 503–535.

KEATING, GREGORY D., BILL VANPATTEN, and JILL JEGERSKY. 2011. "Who was walking on the beach? Anaphora resolution in Spanish heritage speakers and adult second language learners," *Studies in Second Language Acquisition* 33, 193–221.

KEIJZER, MEREL. 2007. *Last in First Out? An Investigation of the Regression Hypothesis in Dutch Emigrants in Anglophone Canada*. Ph.D. thesis, Vrije Universiteit, Amsterdam.

KELLERMAN, ERIC. 1983. "Now you see it, now you don't," in SUSAN GASS and LARRY SELINKER (eds.), *Language Transfer in Language Learning*, pp. 112–134. Rowley, MA: Newbury House.

KEMMERER, DAVID. 2012. "The cross-linguistic prevalence of SOV and SVO word orders reflects the sequential and hierarchical representation of action in Broca's area," *Language and Linguistics Compass* 6, 50–66.

KIM, JI-HEI, SILVINA MONTRUL, and JAMES YOON. 2009. "Binding interpretation of anaphors in Korean heritage speakers," *Language Acquisition* 16, 1, 3–35.

KING, J. and MARCEL A. JUST. 1991. "Individual differences in syntactic processing: The role of working memory," *Journal of Memory and Language*, 30, 580–602.

KLINE, MELISSA and KATHERINE DEMUTH. 2014. "Syntactic generalization with novel intransitive verbs," *Journal of Child Language*, 41, 543–574.

KLUENDER, ROBERT. 2004. "Are subject islands subject to a processing account?", *West Coast Conference on Formal Linguistics (WCCFL)* 23, 101–25.

KNIGHTLY, L., S. JUN, J. OH, and T. AU. 2003. "Production benefits of childhood overhearing," *Journal of the Acoustic Society of America* 114, 465–474.

KRASHEN, STEPHEN. 1981. *Second Language Acquisition and Second Language Learning*. Oxford, UK: Pergamon.

KRASHEN, STEPHEN. 1982. *Principles and Practice in Second Language Acquisition*. Oxford, UK: Pergamon.

KRASHEN, STEPHEN. 1985. *The Input Hypothesis: Issues and Implications*. London: Longman.

KRATZER, ANGELIKA. 1996. "Severing the external argument from its verb," in JOHANN ROORYCK and LAURIE ZARING (eds.), *Phrase Structure and the Lexicon*, pp. 109–137. Dordrecht, Kluwer.

KROLL, JUDITH F. and E. STEWART. 1994. "Category interference in translation and picture naming: Evidence for asymmetric connections between bilingual memory representations," *Journal of Memory and Language*, 33, 149–174.

KROLL, JUDITH F., S. BOBB, and Z. WODNIECKA. 2006. "Language selectivity is the exception, not the rule: Arguments against a fixed locus of language selection in bilingual speech," *Bilingualism: Language and Cognition*, 9, 119–135. doi:10.1017/S1366728906002483.

KROLL, JUDITH, CARI BOGULSKI, and RHONDA MCCLAIN. 2012. "Psycholinguistic perspectives on second language learning and bilingualism: The course and consequence of cross-language competition," *Linguistic Approaches to Bilingualism*, 2, 1, 1–24.

KUMARAVADIVELU, B. 2006. *Understanding Language Teaching: From Method to Postmethod.* Mahwah, NJ: Lawrence Erlbaum.

KUPISCH, TANJA. 2012. "Generic subjects in the Italian of early German-Italian bilinguals and German learners of Italian as a second language," *Bilingualism: Language and Cognition* 15, 4, 736–756.

KURTZMAN, HOWARD S. and MARYELLEN C. MACDONALD. 1993. "Resolution of quantifier scope ambiguities," *Cognition* 48, 243–279.

KUTAS, MARTA and S. A. HILLYARD. 1980. "Reading senseless sentences: Brain potentials reflect semantic incongruity," *Science* 207, 203–208.

KUTAS, MARTA and KARA D. FEDERMEIER. 2011. "Thirty years and counting: Finding meaning in the N400 component of the event-related brain potential (ERP)," *Annual Review of Psychology* 62, 621–647.

LAAHA, SABINE and STEVEN GILLIS (eds.). 2007. *Typological Perspectives on the Acquisition of Noun and Verb Morphology. Antwerp Papers in Linguistics* 112. Antwerp: Antwerp University.

LADD, D. ROBERT. 1996. *Intonational Phonology.* Cambridge: Cambridge University Press.

LADEFOGED, PETER. 2001. *Vowels and Consonants: An Introduction to the Sounds of Languages.* Oxford: Blackwell.

LAKOFF, GEORGE. 1987. *Women, Fire, and Dangerous Things: What Categories Reveal About the Mind.* Chicago: The University of Chicago Press.

LAKSHMANAN, USHA. 1995. "Child second language acquisition of syntax," *Studies in Second Language Acquisition* 17, 3, 301–329.

LARDIERE, DONNA. 1998a. "Case and tense in the 'fossilization' steady state," *Second Language Research* 14, 1–26.

LARDIERE, DONNA. 1998b. "Disassociating syntax from morphology in a divergent L2 end-state grammar," *Second Language Research* 14.4, 359–375.

LARDIERE, DONNA. 2000. "Mapping syntactic features to forms in second language acquisition," in JOHN ARCHIBALD (ed.) *Second Language Acquisition and Linguistic Theory.* Oxford: Blackwell, 102–129.

LARDIERE, DONNA. 2005. "On morphological competence," in *Proceedings of the 7th Generative Approaches to Second Language Acquisition Conference (GASLA 2004),* LAURENT DEKYDTSPOTTER et al. (eds.), 178–192. Somerville, MA: Cascadilla Proceedings Project.

LARDIERE, DONNA. 2007. *Ultimate Attainment in Second Language Acquisition: A Case Study.* Mahwah, NJ: Lawrence Erlbaum Associates.

LARDIERE, DONNA. 2008. "Feature assembly in second language acquisition," in JUANA LICERAS, HELMUT ZOBL, and HELEN GOODLUCK (eds.), *The Role of Features in Second Language Acquisition,* pp. 106–140. Mahwah, NJ: Lawrence Erlbaum Associates.

LARDIERE, DONNA. 2009a. "Some Thoughts on a Contrastive Analysis of Features in Second Language Acquisition." *Second Language Research* 25, 2, 173–227. doi:10.1177/0267658308100283.

LARDIERE, DONNA. 2009b. "Further thoughts on parameters and features in second language acquisition," *Second Language Research* 25, 3, 409–422.

LARDIERE, DONNA. 2011. "Who is the Interface Hypothesis about?", *Linguistic Approaches to Bilingualism* 1, 1, 48–53.

LEAL MÉNDEZ, TANIA and ROUMYANA SLABAKOVA. 2014. "The Interpretability Hypothesis again: A partial replication of Tsimpli and Dimitrakopoulou 2007," *International Journal of Bilingualism* 18, 6, 537–557. doi:10.1177/1367006912448125.

LECARME, JACQUELINE. 2003. "Nominal tense and evidentiality," in *Tense and Point of View,* JACQUELINE GUÉRON and LILIANE TAMOWSKI (eds.), 277–299. Presses de l'Université Paris X–Nanterre.

LECARME, JACQUELINE. 2004. "Tense in nominals," in JACQUELINE GUÉRON and JACQUELINE LECARME (eds.), *The Syntax of Time,* 441–476. Cambridge, MA: MIT Press.

LEMMENS, M and J. PEREZ. 2010. "On the use of posture verbs by French-speaking learners of Dutch: A corpus-based study," *Cognitive Linguistics* 20, 2, 315–347.

LENNEBERG, ERIC H. 1967. *Biological Foundations of Language.* Wiley.

LEUNG, YAN-KIT INGRID. 2006. "Full transfer versus partial transfer in L2 and L3 acquisition," in ROUMYANA SLABAKOVA, SILVINA MONTRUL, and PHILIPPE PREVOST (eds.), *Inquiries in Linguistic Development: In Honor of Lydia White,* pp. 157–188. Amsterdam: John Benjamins.

LEVIN, BETH and MALKA RAPPAPORT HOVAV. 1995. *Unaccusativity.* Cambridge, MA: MIT Press.

LEVIN, BETH and MALKA RAPPAPORT HOVAV. 2005. *Argument Realization.* Cambridge: Cambridge University Press.

LEVINSON, STEPHEN C. 2000. *Presumptive Meanings: The Theory of Generalized Conversational Implicature.* Cambridge, MA: MIT Press.

LI, MING-CHING. 2012. *The Acquisition of Tense and Agreement by Early Child Second Language Learners.* Unpublished Ph.D. thesis, University of Illinois at Urbana-Champaign.

LI, XIAOLI. 1998. "Adult L2 accessibility to UG: An issue revised," in SUZANNE FLYNN, GITA MARTOHARDJONO, and WAYNE A. O'NEIL (eds.), *The Generative Study of Second Language Acquisition,* pp. 89–110. Mahwah, NJ : Erlbaum.

LICERAS, JUANA M. 1988. "Syntax and stylistics: more on the pro-drop parameter," in JAMES PANKHURST, MICHAEL SHARWOOD-SMITH, and PAUL VAN BUREN (eds.), *Learnability and Second Languages,* Dordrecht: Foris.

LICERAS, JUANA M. 1989. "On some properties of the pro-drop parameter: Looking for missing subjects in non-native Spanish," in SUSAN GASS and JACQUELINE SCHACHTER (eds.), *Linguistic Perspectives in Second Language Acquisition.* Cambridge, MA: Cambridge University Press.

LIEBERMAN, MORDECAI. 2009. "Necessary interpretation at the syntax/pragmatics interface: L2 acquisition of scalar implicatures." Paper presented at the Workshop on the Mind–Context Divide: Language Acquisition and Interfaces of Cognitive Linguistic Modules. University of Iowa.

LIGHTFOOT, DAVID. 1993. *How to Set Parameters: Arguments from Language Change.* Cambridge, MA: MIT Press.

LIKERT, RENSIS. 1932. "A Technique for the measurement of attitudes," *Archives of Psychology* 140, 1–55.

LIN, JO–WANG. 2003. "Temporal reference in Mandarin Chinese," *Journal of East Asian Linguistics* 12, 259–311.

LIN, JO–WANG. 2006. "Time in a language without tense: The case of Chinese," *Journal of Semantics* 23, 1–53.

LITTLEMORE, JEANNETTE, P. TRAUTMAN CHEN, A. KOESTER, and J. BARNDEN. 2011. "Difficulties in metaphor comprehension faced by international students whose language is not English," *Applied Linguistics* 32, 4, 408–429.

LONG, DREW and JASON ROTHMAN. 2013. "Generative approaches and the Competing Systems Hypothesis: Formal acquisition to practical application," in JOHN SCHWEITER (ed.), *Theoretical and Pedagogical Innovations in SLA and Bilingualism*, pp. 63–83. Amsterdam/Philadelphia: John Benjamins.

LONG, MICHAEL H. 1981. "Input, Interaction, and Second Language Acquisition," *Annals of the New York Academy of Sciences* 379, 259–278. doi:10.1111/j.1749-6632.1981.tb42014.x.

LONG, MICHAEL H. 1991. "Focus on form: A design feature in language teaching methodology," in KEES DE BOT, RALPH B. GINSBERG, and CLAIRE KRAMSCH (eds.), *Foreign Language Research in Cross-Cultural Perspective*, pp. 39–52. Amsterdam: John Benjamins.

LONG, MICHAEL. 1996. "The role of the linguistic environment in second language acquisition," in *Handbook of Second Language Acquisition*, W. C. RITCHIE and T. K. BHATIA (eds.), 413–468. New York, NY: Academic Press.

LONG, MICHAEL H. 2005. "Problems with supposed counter-evidence to the Critical Period Hypothesis," *International Review of Applied Linguistics* 43, 4, 287–317. doi:10.1515/iral.2005.43.4.287.

LONG, MICHAEL H. and GRAHAM CROOKES. 1992. "Three approaches to task-based syllabus design," *TESOL Quarterly* 26, 1, 27–56. doi:10.2307/3587368.

LONG, MICHAEL H. and PETER ROBINSON. 1998. "Focus on form: Theory, research, and practice," in CATHERINE DOUGHTY and JESSICA WILLIAMS (eds.), *Focus on Form in Classroom Second Language Acquisition*, pp. 15–41. Cambridge: Cambridge University Press.

LONGOBARDI, GIUSEPPE. 2001. "How comparative is semantics? A unified parametric theory of bare nouns and proper names," *Natural Language Semantics* 9, 335–369.

LOZANO, CRISTÓBAL. 2006. "Focus and split-intransitivity: the acquisition of word order alternations in nonnative Spanish," *Second Language Research*, 22, 145–187.

LOZANO, CRISTÓBAL and AMAYA MENDIKOETXEA. 2010. "Interface conditions on postverbal subjects: A corpus study of L2 English," *Bilingualism: Language and Cognition* 13, 4, 2010, 475–497.

LUK, Z. P. and YASUHIRO SHIRAI. 2009. "Review article: Is the acquisition order of grammatical morphemes impervious to L1 knowledge? Evidence from the acquisition of plural *-s*, articles, and possessive *'s*," *Language Learning*, 59, 721–754.

LUKYANCHENKO, A. and KIRA GOR. 2011. "Perceptual correlates of phonological representations in heritage speakers and L2 learners," *Proceedings of the 35th Annual Boston University Conference on Language Development*, pp. 414–426. Somerville, MA: Cascadilla Press.

MACDONALD, MARYELLEN C., NEAL J. PEARLMUTTER, and MARK S. SEIDENBERG. 1994. "The lexical nature of syntactic ambiguity resolution," *Psychological Review* 101, 4, 676–703. doi:10.1037/0033-295X.101.4.676.

MACKEY, ALISON. 2006. "Feedback, noticing and instructed second language learning," *Applied Linguistics* 27, 405–430.

MACKEY, ALISON. 2012. *Input, Interaction and Corrective Feedback in L2 Learning*. Oxford, UK: Oxford University Press.

MARANTZ, ALEC. 1984. *On the Nature of Grammatical Relations*. Cambridge, MA: MIT Press.

MARCUS, GARY F., S. PINKER, M. ULLMAN, M. HOLLANDER, T. J. ROSEN, and F. XU. 1992. "Overregularization in language acquisition," *Monographs of the Society for Research in Child Development* 57, 4, 1–182.

MARIAN, VIORICA and MICHAEL SPIVEY. 2003. "Competing activation in bilingual language processing: Within- and between-language competition," *Bilingualism: Language and Cognition* 6, 2, 97–115. doi:10.1017/S1366728903001068.

MARINIS, THEODOROS, LEAH ROBERTS, CLAUDIA FELSER, and HARALD CLAHSEN. 2005. "Gaps in second language sentence processing," *Studies in Second Language Acquisition* 27, 53–78.

MARKERT, KATJA and MALVINA NISSIM. 2006. "Metonymic proper names: A corpus-based account," in A. STEFANOWITSCH and STEFAN GRIES (eds.), *Corpus-Based Approaches to Metaphor and Metonymy*, 158–174. Berlin: Mouton de Gruyter.

MARKMAN, ELLEN M. and J. E. HUTCHINSON. 1984. "Children's sensitivity to constraints on word meaning: Taxonomic vs thematic relations," *Cognitive Psychology* 16, 1–27.

MARKMAN, ELLEN M. and G. F. WACHTEL. 1988. "Children's use of mutual exclusivity to constrain the meanings of words," *Cognitive Psychology* 20, 121–157.

MARSDEN, HEATHER. 2009. "Distributive quantifier scope in English-Japanese and Korean-Japanese interlanguage," *Language Acquisition* 16, 135–177.

MARSLEN-WILSON, WILLIAM D. 1987. "Functional parallelism in spoken word-recognition," *Cognition* 25, 1, 71–102.

MARSLEN-WILSON, WILLIAM D. 2007. "Morphological processes in language comprehension," in G. GASKELL (ed.), *Oxford Handbook of Psycholinguistics*, pp. 175–193. Oxford: Oxford University Press.

MARSLEN-WILSON, WILLIAM D. and ALAN WELSH. 1978. "Processing interactions and lexical access during word recognition incontinuous speech," *Cognitive Psychology* 10, 1, 29–63.

MARTOHARDJONO, GITA. 1993. *Wh-Movement in the Acquisition of a Second Language: A Cross-Linguistic Study of Three Languages With and Without Movement*. Unpublished Ph.D. thesis, Cornell University.

MAZUKA, R., N. JINCHO, and H. OISHI. 2009. "Development of executive control and language processing," *Language and Linguistics Compass* 3, 59–89.

MAZURKEWICH, IRENE. 1984. "The acquisition of the dative alternation by second language learners and linguistic theory," *Language Learning* 34, 91–109.

MCCARTHY, CORRINE. 2008. "Morphological variability in the comprehension of agreement: An argument for representation over computation," *Second Language Research* 24, 459–486. doi:10.1177/0267658308095737.

MCCLELLAND, JAMES L. and JEFFREY L. ELMAN. 1986. "The TRACE model of speech perception," *Cognitive Psychology,* 18, 1, 1–86.

MCCLELLAND, JAMES L. and KARALYN PATTERSON. 2002. "Rules or connections in past-tense inflections: What does the evidence rule out?", *Trends in Cognitive Science* 6, 465–472; and "Reply to Pinker and Ullman," *Trends in Cognitive Science* 6, 464–465.

MCCLELLAND, JAMES L. and D. E. RUMELHART. 1981. "An interactive activation model of context effects in letter perception, Part 1: An account of basic findings." *Psychological Review* 88, 375–405.

MCCLELLAND, JAMES L. and DAVID E. RUMELHART. 1986. *Parallel Distributed Processing. Explorations in the Microstructure of Cognition. Volume 2: Psychological and Biological Models*. Cambridge, MA: MIT Press.

MCCLOSKEY, JAMES. 1979. *Transformational Syntax and Model-theoretic Semantics: A Case Study in Modern Irish*. Dordrecht: Reidel.

MCDONALD, JANET L. 2006. "Beyond the critical period: Processing-based explanations for poor grammaticality judgment performance by late second language learners," *Journal of Memory and Language*, 55, 381–401. doi:10.1016/j.jml.2006.06.006.

MCDONALD, JANET L. 2008a. "Grammaticality judgments in children: The role of age, working memory, and phonological ability," *Journal of Child Language* 35, 247–268.

MCDONALD, JANET L. 2008b. "Differences in the cognitive demands of word order, plurals, and subject–verb agreement constructions," *Psychonomic Bulletin & Review* 15, 980–984.

MCLAUGHLIN, J., L. OSTERHOUT, and A. KIM. 2004. "Neural correlates of second-language word learning: Minimal instruction produces rapid change," *Nature Neuroscience* 7, 703–704.

MCMURRAY, BOB. 2007. Defusing the childhood vocabulary explosion. *Science* 317(5838), 631.

MCRAE, KEN, MICHAEL J. SPIVEY-KNOWLTON, and MICHAEL K. TANENHAUS. 1998. "Modeling the influence of thematic fit (and other constraints) in on-line sentence comprehension," *Journal of Memory and Language* 38, 3, 283–312. doi:10.1006/jmla.1997.2543.

MEISEL, JÜRGEN M. 1989. "Early differentiation of languages in bilingual children," in KENNETH HYLTENSTAM and LORRAINE OBLER (eds.), *Bilingualism across the Lifespan: Aspects of Acquisition, Maturity and Loss*, pp. 13–40. Cambridge: Cambridge University Press.

MEISEL, JÜRGEN M. 2011. *First and Second Language Acquisition*. Cambridge: Cambridge University Press.

MEISEL, JÜRGEN M., HARALD CLAHSEN, and MANFRED PIENEMANN. 1981. "On determining developmental stages in natural second language acquisition," *Studies in Second Language Acquisition* 3, 109–35.

MEISEL, JÜRGEN M, MARTIN ELSIG, and MARTIN BONNESEN. 2011. "Delayed grammatical acquisition in first language development: Subject-verb inversion and subject clitics in French interrogatives," *Linguistic Approaches to Bilingualism* 1, 4, 347–390.

MEUTER, R. F. I. and A. ALLPORT. 1999. "Bilingual language switching in naming: Asymmetrical costs of language selection," *Journal of Memory and Language* 40, 25–40.

MILLER, KAREN and CRISTINA SCHMITT. 2010. "Effects of variable input in the acquisition of plural in two dialects of Spanish," *Lingua* 120, 1178–1193.

MISRA, M., T. GUO, S. C. BOBB, and J. F. KROLL, J. F. 2012. "When bilinguals choose a single word to speak: Electrophysiological evidence for inhibition of the native language," *Journal of Memory and Language* 67, 224–237.

MITHUN, M. and CHAFE, W. 1979. "Recapturing the Mohawk language," in *Languages and their Status*, T. SHOPEN (ed.), pp. 3–34, Winthrop Press.

MONTRUL, SILVINA. 2000. "Transitivity alternations in L2 acquisition: Toward a modular view of transfer," *Studies in Second Language Acquisition*, 22, 229–273.

MONTRUL, SILVINA. 2001a. "Introduction: Special issue on the lexicon in SLA," *Studies in Second Language Acquisition* 23, 145–151.

MONTRUL, SILVINA. 2001b. "Agentive verbs of manner of motion in Spanish and English as a second language," *Studies in Second Language Acquisition* 23, 171–206.

MONTRUL, SILVINA. 2008. *Incomplete Acquisition in Bilingualism: Re-examining the Age Factor*. Amsterdam: John Benjamins.

MONTRUL, SILVINA. 2009. "Re-examining the Fundamental Difference Hypothesis: What can early bilinguals tell us?" *Studies in Second Language Acquisition* 31, 2, 225–257. doi:10.1017/S0272263109090299.

MONTRUL, SILVINA. 2010. "How similar are L2 learners and heritage speakers? Spanish clitics and word order," *Applied Psycholinguistics* 31, 1, 167–207. doi:10.1017/S014271640999021X.

MONTRUL, SILVINA. 2011a. "Interfaces and incomplete acquisition," *Lingua* 212, 4, 591–604. doi:10.1016/j.lingua.2010.05.006.

MONTRUL, SILVINA. 2011b. "Morphological errors in Spanish second language learners and heritage speakers," *Studies in Second Language Acquisition* 33, 155–161.

MONTRUL, SILVINA. 2012. "Is the heritage language like a second language?", *EUROSLA Yearbook* 12, 1–29. doi 10.1075/eurosla.12.03mon.

MONTRUL, SILVINA. 2016. "Dominance and proficiency in early and late bilinguals," in C. SILVA-CORVALÁN and J. TREFFERS-DALLER (eds.), *Language Dominance in Bilinguals: Issues of Measurement and Operationalization.* pp. 15–35. Cambridge: Cambridge University Press.

MONTRUL, SILVINA, RAKESH BHATT, and ARCHNA BHATIA. 2012. "Erosion of case and agreement in Hindi heritage speakers," *Linguistic Approaches to Bilingualism* 2, 141–176.

MONTRUL, SILVINA, R. FOOTE, and S. PERPIÑÁN. 2008. "Gender agreement in adult second language learners and Spanish heritage speakers: The effects of age and context of acquisition," *Language Learning* 58: 503–553.

MONTRUL, SILVINA and T. IONIN. 2010. "Transfer effects in the interpretation of definite articles by Spanish heritage speakers," *Bilingualism: Language and Cognition* 13, 4, 449–473.

MONTRUL, SILVINA and JAMES YOON. 2009. "Putting parameters in their proper place: A response to Lardiere," *Second Language Research* 25, 2, 287–307.

MONTRUL, SILVINA and ROUMYANA SLABAKOVA. 2003a. "Acquiring morphosyntactic and semantic properties of preterit and imperfect tenses in L2 Spanish," in ANA-TEREZA PEREZ-LEROUX and JUANA LICERAS (eds.), *The Acquisition of Spanish Morphosyntax: The L1–L2 Connection*, pp. 113–149. Berlin: Springer.

MONTRUL, SILVINA and ROUMYANA SLABAKOVA. 2003b. "Competence similarities between native and near-native speakers: An investigation of the preterit/imperfect contrast in Spanish," *Studies in Second Language Acquisition 25*, 351–398. doi:10.1017/S0272263103000159.

MUELLER GATHERCOLE, C. VICTORIA, and ENLLI M. THOMAS. 2009. "Bilingual first-language development: Dominant language takeover, threatened minority language take-up," *Bilingualism: Language and Cognition* 12, 2, 213–237. doi:10.1017/S1366728909004015.

MÜLLER, NATASCHA and AAFKE HULK. 2001. "Crosslinguistic influence in bilingual language acquisition: Italian and French as recipient languages," *Bilingualism: Language and Cognition*, 4, 1, 1–21.

MUÑOZ, CARMEN and DAVID SINGLETON. 2011. "A critical review of age-related research on L2 ultimate attainment," *Language Teaching* 33 (1), 1–35. doi:10.1017/S0261444810000327.

MUÑOZ, CARMEN. 2014a. "Contrasting effects of starting age and input on the oral performance of foreign language learners," *Applied Linguistics* 35, 4, 463–482.

MUÑOZ, CARMEN. 2014b. Guest editor, special issue on "Complexities and interactions of age in second language learning: Broadening the research agenda," *Applied Linguistics*, volume 35, 4.

NAVA, EMILY and MARIA LUISA ZUBIZARRETA. 2009. "Order of L2 acquisition of prosodic prominence patterns: Evidence from L1Spanish/L2 English speech," in *Proceedings of Galana 3*, pp. 175–187. Somerville, MA: Cascadilla Press.

NAVA, EMILY and MARIA LUISA ZUBIZARRETA. 2010. "Deconstructing the Nuclear Stress Algorithm: evidence from second language Speech," in N. ERTESCHIK-SHIR and L. ROCHMAN (eds.), *The Sound Patterns of Syntax*, pp. 291–316. Oxford: Oxford University Press.

NEUBAUER, K. and HARALD CLAHSEN. 2009. "Decomposition of inflected words in a second language: An experimental study of German participles," *Studies in Second Language Acquisition* 31, 3, 403–435. doi:10.1017/S0272263109090354.

NORRIS, DENNIS. 1994. "Shortlist: A connectionist model of continuous speech recognition," *Cognition* 52, 189–234.

NORRIS, JOHN and LOURDES ORTEGA. 2000. "Effectiveness of L2 instruction: a research synthesis and quantitative meta-analysis," *Language Learning* 50, 3, 417–528.

NOVICK, J. M., J. C. TRUESWELL and S. L. THOMPSON-SCHILL, S. L. 2005. "Cognitive control and parsing: Reexamining the role of Broca's area in sentence comprehension," *Cognitive, Affective, & Behavioral Neuroscience* 5, 263–281.

NUNBERG, GEOFFREY. 1979. "The non-uniqueness of semantic solutions: Polysemy," *Linguistics and Philosophy* 3, 143–184.

NUNBERG, GEOFFREY. 1995. Transfers of meaning. *Journal of Semantics* 12, 143–184.

O'GRADY, WILLIAM. 1997. *Syntactic Development*. Chicago: University of Chicago Press.

O'GRADY, WILLIAM. 2005. *How Children Learn Language*. Cambridge, UK: Cambridge University Press.

O'GRADY, W., H. Y. KWAK, O.-S. LEE, and M. LEE. 2011. "An emergentist perspective on heritage language acquisition," *Studies in Second Language Acquisition* 33, 223–246.

O'GRADY, WILLIAM, MISEON LEE, and HYE-YOUNG KWAK. 2009. "Emergentism and second language acquisition," in W. C. RITCHIE and T. K. BHATIA (eds.), *The New Handbook of Second Language Acquisition*, 69–88. Bingley: Emerald.

OEHRLE, RICHARD T. 1976. *The Grammatical Status of the English Dative Alternation*. Ph.D. thesis, MIT.

OMAKI, AKIRA and JEFF LIDZ. 2014. "Linking parser development to acquisition of syntactic knowledge," *Language Acquisition*. Published online July 2014.

OMAKI, AKIRA and BARBARA SCHULZ. 2011. "Filler–gap dependencies and island constraints in second language sentence processing," *Studies in Second Language Acquisition* 33, 563–588.

ORTEGA, LOURDES. 2009. *Understanding Second Language Acquisition*. London: Hodder Education.

OSTERHOUT, LEE and J. NICOL. 1999. "On the distinctiveness, independence, and time course of the brain responses to syntactic and semantic anomalies," *Language & Cognitive Processes* 14, 283–317.

PAKULAK, ERIC and HELEN J. NEVILLE. 2010. "Proficiency differences in syntactic processing of monolingual native speakers," *Journal of Cognitive Neuroscience* 22, 12, 2728–2740.

PAPADOPOULOU, DESPINA, SPYRIDOULA VARLOKOSTA, VASSILIOS SPYROPOULOS, HASAN KAILI, SOPHIA PROKOU, and ANTHI REVITHIADOU. 2011. "Case morphology and word order in second language Turkish: Evidence from Greek learners," *Second Language research* 27, 2, 173–205. doi:10.1177/0267658310376348.

PAPAFRAGOU, ANNA and JULIEN MUSOLINO. 2003. "Scalar implicatures: Experiments at the semantics–pragmatics interface," *Cognition* 86, 253–282.

PARADIS, MICHEL. 2004. *A Neurolinguistic Theory of Bilingualism*. Amsterdam: John Benjamins.

PARADIS, MICHEL. 2009. *Declarative and Procedural Determinants of Second Languages*. Amsterdam: John Benjamins.

PASCUAL Y CABO, DIEGO and JASON ROTHMAN. 2012. "The (il) logical problem of heritage speaker bilingualism and incomplete acquisition," *Applied Linguistics* 33, 1–7.

PENFIELD, WILDER and L. ROBERTS. 1959. *Speech and Brain Mechanisms*. Princeton: Princeton University Press.

PHILLIPS, COLIN. 2013. "Parser-grammar relations: We don't understand everything twice," in M. SANZ, I. LAKA, and M. TANENHAUS (eds.), *Language Down the Garden Path: The Cognitive and Biological Basis for Linguistic Structure* pp. 294–315. Oxford University Press. doi:10.1093/acprof:oso/9780199677139.003.0017.

PHILLIPS, COLIN and LARA EHRENHOFER. 2015. "The role of language processing in language acquisition," *Linguistic Approaches to Bilingualism* 5, 4, 409–453.

PHINNEY, M. 1987. "The pro-drop parameter in second language acquisition," in THOMAS ROEPER and EDWIN WILLIAMS (eds.), *Parameter Setting*, pp. 221–38. Dordrecht: Reidel.

PICKERING, MARTIN and ROGER VAN GOMPEL. 2007. "Syntactic Parsing," in GARETH GASKELL (ed.), *The Oxford Handbook of Psycholinguistics*, pp. 289–307. Oxford: Oxford University Press.

PICKERING, MARTIN, M. J. TRAXLER, and M. W. CROCKER. 2000. "Ambiguity resolution in sentence processing: Evidence against frequency-based accounts," *Journal of Memory and Language* 43, 447–475.

PINKER, STEVEN. 1989. *Learnability and Cognition: The Acquisition of Argument Structure*. Cambridge, MA: MIT Press.

PINKER, STEVEN. 1994. *The Language Instinct: How the Mind Creates Language*. William Morrow and Company.

PINKER, STEVEN. 1998. "Roger Brown Obituary," *Cognition* 66, 199–213.

PINKER, STEVEN. 1999. *Words and Rules: The Ingredients of Language*. New York: HarperCollins.

PINKER, STEVEN and ALAN PRINCE. 1988. "On language and connectionism: Analysis of a distributed processing model of language acquisition," *Cognition* 28, 73–193.

PINKER, STEVEN and MICHAEL ULLMAN. 2002. "The past and future of the past tense," *Trends in Cognitive Science* 6, 11, 456–463.

PLIATSIKAS, CHRISTOS and THEO MARINIS. 2013a. "Processing of regular and irregular past tense morphology in highly proficient second language learners of English: A self-paced reading study," *Applied Psycholinguistics* 34, 5, 943–970.

PLIATSIKAS, CHRISTOS and THEO MARINIS. 2013b. "Processing empty categories in a second language: When naturalistic exposure fills the (intermediate) gap," *Bilingualism: Language and Cognition*, 16, 167–182.

PLUNKETT, K. and V. MARCHMAN. 1991. "U-shaped learning and frequency effects in a multi-layered perception: Implications for child language acquisition," *Cognition*, 38, 43–102.

PLUNKETT, K. and V. MARCHMAN. 1993. "From rote learning to system building: Acquiring verb morphology in children and connectionist nets," *Cognition*, 48, 21–69.

POEPPEL, DAVID and DAVID EMBICK. 2005. "Defining the relation between linguistics and neuroscience," in ANNE CUTLER (ed.) *Twenty-first Century Psycholinguistics: Four Cornerstones*. Lawrence Erlbaum.

POEPPEL, DAVID, KAREN EMMOREY, G. HICKOCK, and LIINA PYLKKÄNEN. 2012. "Towards a new neurobiology of language," *The Journal of Neuroscience*, 32, 41, 14125–14131; doi:10.1523/JNEUROSCI.3244-12.2012.

POEPPEL, DAVID and KEN WEXLER. 1993. "The Full Competence Hypothesis of clause structure in early German," *Language* 69, 1–33.

POLINSKY, MARIA. 2006. "Incomplete acquisition: American Russian," *Journal of Slavic Linguistics* 14, 2, 191–262.

POLINSKY, MARIA. 2011. "Reanalysis in adult heritage language: A case for attrition," *Studies in Second Language Acquisition* 33, 305–328.

POLK, THAD and SARAH FARRAH. 1998. "The neural development and organization of letter recognition: Evidence from functional neuroimaging, computational modeling, and behavioral studies," *Proceedings of the National Academy of Sciences of the US*, 95, 3, 847–852.

POLLOCK, JEAN-YVES. 1989. "Verb movement, Universal Grammar, and the structure of IP," *Linguistic Inquiry* 20, 3, 365–424.

PRÉVOST PHILIPPE. 1999. "The second language acquisition of the split CP structure," in E. C. KLEIN and GITA MARTOHARDJONO (eds.), *The Development of Second Language Grammars: A Generative Approach*. 45–79. Amsterdam: John Benjamins.

PRÉVOST, PHILIPPE and LYDIA WHITE. 2000a. "Accounting for morphological variability in second language acquisition: Truncation or missing inflection?", in: M.-A. FRIEDEMANN and LUIGI RIZZI (eds.), *The Acquisition of Syntax*, 202–235. London: Longman.

PRÉVOST, PHILIPPE and LYDIA WHITE. 2000b. "Missing Surface Inflection or Impairment in Second Language Acquisition? Evidence from Tense and Agreement," *Second Language Research* 16, 2, 103–134. doi:10.1191/026765800677556046.

PRITCHETT, BRADLEY L. 1988. Garden path phenomena and the grammatical basis of language processing. *Language* 64, 539–576.

PRITCHETT, BRADLEY L. 1992. *Grammatical Competence and Parsing Performance*. Chicago: University of Chicago Press.

QUINE, WILLARD VAN ORMAN. 1960. *Word and Object*, Cambridge, MA: MIT Press.

RADFORD, ANDREW. 1990. *Syntactic Theory and the Acquisition of English Syntax*. Oxford: Blackwell.

RAMCHAND, GILLIAN and PETER SVENONIUS. 2008. "Mapping a parochial lexicon onto a universal semantics," in THERESA BIBERBAUER (ed.), *Limits of Syntactic Variation*, pp. 219–245. Amsterdam: John Benjamins.

RAMCHAND, GILLIAN and PETER SVENONIUS. 2014. "Deriving the functional hierarchy," Language sciences 46, Part B, 152–174.

RAYNER, KEITH. 1998. "Eye movements in reading and information processing: 20 years of research," *Psychological Bulletin*, 124, 372–422.

RAYNER, KEITH. 2009. "Eye movements and attention in reading, scene perception and visual search," *Quarterly Journal of Experimental Psychology* 62, 1457–1506.

RAYNER, KEITH, MARCIA CARLSON, and LYN FRAZIER. 1983. "The interaction of syntax and semantics during sentence processing: Eye movements in the analysis of semantically biased sentences," *Journal of Verbal Learning and Verbal Behavior* 22, 3, 358–374. doi:10.1016/S0022-5371(83) 90236-0.

REICHLE, ROBERT and DAVID BIRDSONG. 2014. "Processing focus structure in L1 and L2 French," *Studies in Second Language Acquisition* 36, 03, 535–564.

REICHLE, ROBERT V., ANNIE TREMBLAY, and CAITLIN E. COUGHLIN. 2013. "Working-memory capacity effects in the processing of non-adjacent subject–verb agreement: An event-related brain potentials," ERIK VOSS et al. (eds.), in *Selected Proceedings of the 2011 Second Language Research Forum*, 54–69. Somerville, MA: Cascadilla Proceedings Project.

REINHART, TANYA. 2006. *Interface Strategies: Reference-set Computation.* Cambridge, MA: MIT Press.

RIZZI, LUIGI. 1982. *Issues in Italian Syntax.* Berlin: Walter de Gruyter.

ROBERTS, LEAH. 2012. "Individual differences in second language sentence processing," *Language Learning* 62, 2, 172–188.

ROBERTS, LEAH. 2013. "Sentence processing in bilinguals," in R. P. G. VAN GOMPEL (ed.), *Sentence Processing,* pp. 221–246. Hove: Psychology Press.

ROBERTS, LEAH and CLAUDIA FELSER. 2011. "Plausibility and recovery from garden paths in second language processing," *Applied Psycholinguistics* 32, 3, 299–331.

ROBERTS, LEAH, MARIANNE GULLBERT, and PETER INDEFREY. 2008. "Online pronoun resolution in L2 discourse: L1 influence and general learner effects," *Studies in Second Language Acquisition* 30, 3, 333–357. doi:10.1017/S0272263108080480.

ROBERTS, LEAH and ANNA SIYANOVA-CHANTURIA. 2013. "Using eye-tracking to investigate topics in L2 acquisition and L2 processing," *Studies in Second Language Acquisition* 35, 213–235.

ROBERTSON, DANIEL. 2000. "Variability in the use of the English article system by Chinese learners of English," *Second Language Research* 16, 135–172.

ROCHEMONT, MICHAEL. S. 1998. "Phonological focus and structural focus," in P. W. CULICOVER and L. MCNALLY (eds.), *The Limits of Syntax: Syntax and Semantics,* vol. 29, pp. 337–363. Academic Press.

ROEPER, TOM and JILL DE VILLIERS. 2011. "The acquisition path of wh-questions," in DE VILLIERS and Roeper (eds.), *Handbook of Generative Approaches to Language Acquisition,* pp. 189–246.

ROSS, JAMES R. 1967. *Constraints on Variables in Syntax.* Ph.D. dissertation, MIT, Cambridge, MA. (Published as *Infinite syntax!,* Norwood, NJ: Ablex, 1986.)

ROSSI, S., M. F. GUGLER, A. D. FRIEDERICI, and A. HAHNE. 2006. "The impact of proficiency on syntactic second-language processing of German and Italian: Evidence from event related potentials," *Journal of Cognitive Neuroscience* 18, 2030–2048.

ROTHMAN, JASON. 2007. "Heritage speaker competence differences, language change, and input type: Inflected infinitives in heritage Brazilian Portuguese," *The International Journal of Bilingualism* 11, 359–389.

ROTHMAN, JASON. 2008. "Why all counter-evidence to the Critical Period Hypothesis is not equal or problematic," *Language and Linguistics Compass* 2, 6, 1063–1088. doi:10.1111/j.1749-818X.2008.00098.x.

ROTHMAN, JASON. 2010. "Theoretical linguistics meets pedagogical practice: Pronominal subject use in Spanish as a second language (L2) as an example," *Hispania* 93, 1, 52–65.

ROTHMAN, JASON. 2015. "Linguistic and cognitive motivations for the Typological Primacy Model of third language transfer: Timing of acquisition and proficiency considered," *Bilingualism: Language and Cognition* 18, 2, 179–190.

ROTHMAN, JASON and JENNIFER CABRELLI AMARO. 2010. "What variables condition syntactic transfer? A look at the L3 initial state," *Second Language Research* 26, 189–218.

ROTHMAN, JASON and ROUMYANA SLABAKOVA. 2011. "The mind–context divide: On acquisition at the linguistic interfaces," *Lingua* 121, 568–576.

ROTHMAN, JASON and BILL VANPATTEN. 2014. "On multiplicity and mutual exclusivity: The Case For Different SLA theories," in GARCÍA-MAYO M. DEL PILAR, M. J. GUTIERREZ MANGADO, and M. MARTINEZ ADRIAN (eds.), *Contemporary Approaches to Second Language Acquisition*, pp. 243–256. Amsterdam/Philadelphia: John Benjamins Publishing.

RUNDBLAD, GABRIELLA and DAGMARA ANNAZ. 2010. "Development of metaphor and metonymy comprehension: Receptive vocabulary and conceptual knowledge," *British Journal of Developmental Psychology*, 28, 3, 547–63.

SAADAH, EMAN. 2011. *The Production of Arabic Vowels by English L2 Learners and Heritage Speakers of Arabic*. Unpublished Ph.D. thesis. University of Illinois at Urbana-Champaign.

SAG, IVAN A. and THOMAS WASOW. 2011. "Performance-compatible competence grammar," in R. BORSLEY and K. BORJARS (eds.), *Non-transformational Syntax: Formal and Explicit Models of Grammar*, pp. 359–377. Oxford: Wiley-Blackwell.

SATO, MIKAKO. 2007. *Sensitivity to Syntactic and Semantic Information in Second Language Sentence Processing*. Unpublished Ph.D. thesis, University of Essex.

SAVIGNON, SANDRA J. 1983. *Communicative Competence: Theory and Classroom Practice*. Reading, MA: Addison-Wesley.

SCHMID, MONIKA S. 2002. *First Language Attrition, Use and Maintenance: The Case of German Jews in Anglophone Countries*. Amsterdam: John Benjamins.

SCHMID, MONIKA S. 2007. "The role of L1 use for L1 attrition," in B. KÖPKE, M. S. SCHMID, M. KEIJZER and S. DOSTERT (eds.), *Language Attrition: Theoretical Perspectives* pp. 135–153. Amsterdam: John Benjamins.

SCHMID, MONIKA S. 2009. "On L1 attrition and the linguistic system." *EUROSLA Yearbook* 9, 1, 212–244. doi:10.1075/eurosla.9.11sch.

SCHMID, MONIKA S. 2011. *Language Attrition*. Cambridge: Cambridge University Press.

SCHMID, MONIKA S. 2013. "First language attrition," *Linguistic Approaches to Bilingualism* 3, 1, 96–117.

SCHMITT, CRISTINA and ALAN MUNN. 2002. "The syntax and semantics of bare arguments in Brazilian Portuguese," *Linguistic Variation Yearbook* 2, 185–216.

SCHWARTZ, A., J. F. KROLL, and M. DIAZ. 2007. "Reading words in Spanish and English: Mapping orthography to phonology in two languages," *Language and Cognitive Processes* 22, 106–129. doi:10.1080/01690960500463920.

SCHWARTZ, BONNIE D. 1992. "Testing between UG-based and problem-solving models of SLA: Developmental sequence data," *Language Acquisition*, 2, 1–19.

SCHWARTZ, BONNIE D. 1993. "On explicit and negative data effecting and affecting competence and linguistic behavior," *Studies in Second Language Acquisition* 15, 2, 147–163.

SCHWARTZ, BONNIE D. 2003. "Child L2 acquisition: Paving the way," in B. BEACHLEY, A. BROWN, and F. CONLIN (eds.), *Proceedings of the 27th Boston University Conference on Language Development*, 27, pp. 26–50. Somerville, MA: Cascadilla Press.

SCHWARTZ, BONNIE D. 2004. "Why child L2 acquisition?", in JACQUELINE VAN KAMPEN and SERGIO BAAUW (eds.), *Proceedings of GALA 2003*, vol. 1, 47–66. Utrecht: Netherlands Graduate School of Linguistics (LOT).

SCHWARTZ, BONNIE D. 2009. Unraveling inflection in child L2 development, *Acquisition et interaction en langue étrangère* 1, 63–88. URL: http://aile.revues.org/4509.

SCHWARTZ, BONNIE D. and REX A. SPROUSE. 1994. "Word order and nominative case in nonnative language acquisition: A longitudinal study of (L1 Turkish) German interlanguage," in *Language Acquisition Studies in Generative Grammar*, edited by TEUN HOEKSTRA and BONNIE D. SCHWARTZ, pp. 317–368. Amsterdam: John Benjamins.

SCHWARTZ, BONNIE D. and REX SPROUSE. 1996. "L2 cognitive states and the Full Transfer/Full Access Hypothesis," *Second Language Research* 12, 1, 40–72. doi:10.1177/026765839601200103.

SELINKER, LARRY. 1972. "Interlanguage," *International Review of Applied Linguistics* 10, 209–241.

SELKIRK, ELIZABETH O. 1996. "The prosodic structure of function words," in J. L. MORGAN and KATHERINE DEMUTH (eds.), *Signal to Syntax*, pp. 187–213. Mahwah, NJ: Lawrence Erlbaum.

SERRATRICE, LUDOVICA, ANTONELLA SORACE, FEDERICA FILIACI, and MICHELA BALDO. 2009. "Bilingual children's sensitivity to specificity and genericity: Evidence from metalinguistic awareness," *Bilingualism: Language and Cognition* 12, 239–257.

SHARWOOD SMITH, MICHAEL and JOHN TRUSCOTT. 2014. *The Multilingual Mind: A Modular Processing Perspective*. Cambridge: Cambridge University Press.

SHIMANSKAYA, ELENA. 2015. *Feature Reassembly of Semantic and Morphosyntactic Pronominal Features in L2 Acquisition*. Unpublished Ph.D. thesis, University of Iowa.

SHIMANSKAYA, ELENA and ROUMYANA SLABAKOVA. 2014. "Re-assembling Objects: A new look at the L2 acquisition of pronominal clitics," in WILL ORMAN and MATHEW J. VALLEAU (eds.) *BUCLD 38 Proceedings*, pp. 416–427. Cascadilla Proceedings Project.

SHIN, N. L. and HELEN S. CAIRNS. 2009. "Subject pronouns in child Spanish and continuity of reference," in *Selected Proceedings of the 11th Hispanic Linguistics Symposium*, ed. JOSEPH COLLENTINE et al., 155–164. Somerville, MA: Cascadilla Proceedings Project. Available at http://www.lingref.com/cpp/hls/11/paper2210.pdf.

SIEGAL, MICHAEL, LAURA IOZZI and LUCA SURIAN. 2009. "Bilingualism and conversational understanding in young children," *Cognition* 110, 115–122.

SILVA-CORVALÁN, CARMEN. 1994. *Language Contact and Change: Spanish in Los Angeles*. Oxford: Clarendon.

SILVA, RENITA and HARALD CLAHSEN. 2008. "Morphologically complex words in L1 and L2 processing: Evidence from masked priming experiments in English," *Bilingualism: Language and Cognition* 11, 2, 245–260. doi:10.1017/S1366728908003404.

SINGLETON, DAVID. 2003. "Critical Period or general age factor(s)?", in *Age and the Acquisition of English as a Foreign Language*, MARÍA DEL PILAR GARCÍA MAYO and MARÍA LUISA GARCÍA LECUMBERRI (eds.), pp. 3–22. Clevendon, UK: Multilingual Matters.

SINGLETON, DAVID. 2005. "The Critical Period Hypothesis: A coat of many colors," *International Review of Applied Linguistics* 43, 4, 269–285. doi:10.1515/iral.2005.43.4.269.

SKEHAN, PETER. 1998. *A Cognitive Approach to Language Learning*. Oxford: Oxford University Press.

SKINNER, BURRHUS FREDERIC. 1957. *Verbal Behavior*. New York: Appleton-Century-Crofts.

SLABAKOVA, ROUMYANA. 2002. "The Compounding Parameter in second language acquisition," *Studies in Second Language Acquisition* 24, 507–540.

SLABAKOVA, ROUMYANA. 2003. "Semantic evidence for functional categories in interlanguage grammars," *Second Language Research* 19, 42–75.

SLABAKOVA, ROUMYANA. 2006. "Is there a Critical Period for the acquisition of semantics?", *Second Language Research* 22, 3, 302–338. doi:10.1191/0267658306sr270oa.

SLABAKOVA, ROUMYANA. 2008. *Meaning in the Second Language*. New York/Berlin: Mouton de Gruyter.

SLABAKOVA, ROUMYANA. 2009. "What is easy and what is hard to acquire in a second language?", in *Proceedings of the 10th Generative Approaches to Second Language Acquisition Conference (GASLA 10)*, ed. MELISSA BOWLES, TANIA IONIN, SILVINA MONTRUL, and ANNIE TREMBLAY, pp. 280–294. Somerville, MA: Cascadilla Press.

SLABAKOVA, ROUMYANA. 2010. "Scalar implicatures in second language acquisition." *Lingua* 120, 10, pp. 2444–2462. doi:10.1016/j.lingua.2009.06.005.

SLABAKOVA, ROUMYANA. 2013. "Discourse and pragmatics," in JULIA HERSCHENSOHN and MARTHA YOUNG-SCHOLTEN (eds.), *The Cambridge Handbook of Second Language Acquisition*, pp. 482–504. Cambridge, UK: Cambridge University Press.

SLABAKOVA, ROUMYANA. 2015a. "Acquiring temporal meanings without tense morphology: The case of L2 Mandarin Chinese," *Modern Language Journal.* 99, 2, 283–307.

SLABAKOVA, ROUMYANA. 2015b. "The Scalpel model of L3 acquisition," plenary talk at the Workshop on Multilingual Language Acquisition, Processing and Use, Tromsø, Norway, March 20–21, 2015.

SLABAKOVA, ROUMYANA. 2015c. "The effect of construction frequency and native transfer on second language knowledge of the syntax–discourse interface," *Applied Psycholinguistics* 36, 3, 671–699. doi:10.1017/S0142716413000386.

SLABAKOVA, ROUMYANA, JENNIFER CABRELLI AMARO, and SANG KYUN KANG. in press 2014. "Regular and novel metonymy: Can you curl up with a good Agatha Christie in your Second Language?", *Applied Linguistics*, doi:10.1093/applin/amu003.

SLABAKOVA, ROUMYANA and MARÍA DEL PILAR GARCÍA MAYO. 2015. "The L3 syntax–discourse interface," *Bilingualism: Language and Cognition* 18, 2, 208–226.

SLABAKOVA, ROUMYANA and IVAN IVANOV. 2011. "A more careful look at the syntax-discourse interface," *Lingua* 121, 4, 637–651. doi:10.1016/j.lingua. 2010.05.003.

SLABAKOVA, ROUMYANA, PAULA KEMPCHINSKY, and JASON ROTHMAN. 2012. "Clitic-doubled left dislocation and focus fronting in L2 Spanish: A case of successful acquisition at the syntax–discourse interface," *Second Language Research* 28, 3, 319–343. doi:10.1177/0267658312447612.

SLABAKOVA, ROUMYANA and SILVINA MONTRUL. 2002. "On viewpoint aspect and its L2 acquisition: A UG perspective," in RAFAEL SALABERRY and YASUHIRO SHIRAI (eds.), *Tense-Aspect Morphology in L2 Acquisition*, pp. 363–398. Amsterdam: John Benjamins.

SLABAKOVA, ROUMYANA and SILVINA MONTRUL. 2003. "Genericity and aspect in L2 acquisition," *Language Acquisition* 11, 165–196.

SMITH, CARLOTA. 1997. *The Parameter of Aspect*. Dordrecht: Kluwer.

SMITH, CARLOTA and MARY ERBAUGH. 2005. "Temporal interpretation in Mandarin Chinese," *Linguistics* 43, 4, 713–756.

SMITH, MEGAN and BILL VANPATTEN. 2014. "Instructed SLA as parameter setting: evidence from earliest-stage learners of Japanese as L2," in *The Grammar Dimension in Instructed Second Language Learning*, ALESSANDRO BENATI, CÉCILE LAVAL, and MARÍA J. ARCHE (eds.), pp. 127 146. Bloomsbury Academic.

SNAPE, NEAL and HIRONOBU HOSOI. To appear. "Acquisition of scalar implicatures: Evidence from adult Japanese L2 learners of English," *Linguistic Approaches to Bilingualism.*

SNYDER, WILLIAM. 1995. *Language Acquisition and Language Variation: The Role of Morphology.* Ph.D. thesis, MIT. Distributed by MIT Working Papers in Linguistics.

SNYDER, WILLIAM. 2001. "On the nature of syntactic variation: Evidence from complex predicates and complex word-formation," *Language* 77: 324–342.

SNYDER, WILLIAM. 2007. *Child Language: The Parametric Approach.* Oxford, UK: Oxford University Press.

SONG, HYANG S. and BONNIE D. SCHWARTZ. 2009. "Testing the Fundamental Difference Hypothesis: L2 adult, L2 child, and L1 Child Comparisons in the acquisition of Korean *wh*-constructions with negative polarity items," *Studies in Second Language Acquisition* 31, 2, 323–361. doi:10.1017/S0272263109090329.

SONG, M., WILLIAM O'GRADY, S. CHO, and M. LEE. 1997. "The learning and teaching of Korean in community schools,' in Y.-H. KIM (ed.), *Korean Language in America 2*, pp. 111–127. Honolulu, HI: American Association of Teachers of Korean.

SOPATA, ALDONA. 2010. "V2 phenomenon in child second language acquisition," in MATTHEW T. PRIOR et al. (eds.), *Selected Proceedings of the 2008 Second Language Research Forum*, pp. 211–228.

SORACE, ANTONELLA. 1993. "Incomplete and divergent representations of unaccusativity in non-native grammars of Italian," *Second Language Research* 9, 22–48.

SORACE, ANTONELLA. 2000. "Differential effects of attrition in the L1 syntax of near-native L2 speakers," in S. CATHERINE HOWELL, SARAH A. FISH, and THEA KEITH-LUCAS (eds.), *Proceedings of the 24th Boston University Conference on Language Development (BUCLD 24)*, pp. 719–725. Somerville, MA: Cascadilla Press.

SORACE, ANTONELLA. 2003. "Near-nativeness," in CATHERINE DOUGHTY and MICHAEL LONG (eds.), *Handbook of Second Language Acquisition*, pp. 130–151. Oxford: Blackwell.

SORACE, ANTONELLA. 2004. "Native language attrition and developmental instability at the syntax–discourse interface: Data, interpretations and methods," *Bilingualism: Language and Cognition* 7, 143–145.

SORACE, ANTONELLA. 2005. "Selective optionality in language development," in LEONIE CORNIPS and K. P. CORRIGAN (eds.), *Syntax and Variation: Reconciling the Biological and the Social*, pp. 55–80. Amsterdam: John Benjamins.

SORACE, ANTONELLA. 2011. "Pinning down the concept of 'interface' in bilingualism," *Linguistic Approaches to Bilingualism* 1, 1, 1–34. doi:10.1075/lab.1.1.01sor.

SORACE, ANTONELLA and FEDERICA FILIACI. 2006. "Anaphora resolution near-native speakers of Italian," *Second Language Research* 22, 339–368. doi:10.1191/0267658306sr271oa.

SORACE, ANTONELLA and LUDOVICA SERRATRICE. 2009. "Internal and external interfaces in bilingual language development: Beyond structural overlap," *International Journal of Bilingualism* 13, 2, 195–210. doi:10.1177/1367006909339810.

SPADA, NINA and YASUYO TOMITA. 2010. "Interactions between type of instruction and type of language feature: A meta-analysis," *Language Learning* 60, 2, 263–308.

SPERBER, DAN and DEIRDRE WILSON. 1986/1995. *Relevance: Communication and Cognition*. 2nd edition. Oxford: Blackwell.

SPIVEY-KNOWLTON, MICHAEL and JULIE SEDIVY. 1995. "Resolving attachment ambiguities with multiple constraints," *Cognition* 55, 227–267.

SPIVEY, MICHAEL and VIORICA MARIAN. 1999. "Cross talk between native and second languages: Partial activation of an irrelevant lexicon," *Psychological Science*, 10, 281–284.

SPROUSE, REX A. 2006. "Full transfer and relexification: Second language acquisition and creole genesis," in CLAIRE LEFEBVRE, LYDIA WHITE, and CHRISTINE JOURDAN (eds.), *L2 Acquisition and Creole Geneis: Dialogues (Language Acquisition & Language Disorders, 42)*, pp. 169–181. Philadelphia, PA: John Benjamins.

SPROUSE, REX A. 2011. "The Interface Hypothesis and Full Transfer/Full Access/Full Parse: A brief comparison," *Linguistic Approaches to Bilingualism* 1, 97–100.

SPROUSE, JON, MATT WAGERS, and COLIN PHILLIPS. 2012. "A test of the relation between working memory capacity and syntactic island effects," *Language* 88, 1, 82–123.

STAUBLE, ANNE–MARIE. 1984. "A comparison of a Spanish-English and a Japanese-English second language continuum: Negation and verb morphology," in ROGER W. ANDERSEN (ed.), *Second Languages: A Cross-Linguistic Perspective*, pp. 323–353. Rowley, MA: Newbury House.

STEINHAUER, KARSTEN. 2014. "Event-related potentials (ERPs) in second language research: A brief introduction to the technique, a selected review, and an invitation to reconsider Critical Periods in L2," *AL* 35, 4, 393–417, doi:10.1093/applin/amu028.

STEINHAUER, KARSTEN and J. E. DRURY. 2012. "On the early left-anterior negativity (ELAN) in syntax studies," *Brain and Language* 120, 2, 135–62.

STEINHAUER, KARSTEN and J. F. CONNOLLY. 2008. "Event-related potentials in the study of language," in B. STEMMER and H. A. WHITAKER (eds.), *Handbook of the Neuroscience of Language*, pp. 91 104. Elsevier.

STEINHAUER, KARSTEN, E. WHITE, and J. E. DRURY. 2009. "Temporal dynamics of late second language acquisition: Evidence from event-related brain potentials,' *Second Language Research* 25, 1, 13–41.

STREET, JAMES and EWA DABROWSKA. 2010. "More individual differences in language attainment: How much do adult native speakers of English know about passives and quantifiers?", *Lingua* 120, 2080–2094.

STREETER, L. A. 1976. "Language perception of two-month old infants shows effects of both innate mechanisms and experience," *Nature* 259, 39–41.

STRIK, NELLEKE and ANNA TERESA PÉREZ-LEROUX. 2011. "Jij doe wat girafe? Wh-movement and inversion in Dutch-French bilingual children," *Linguistics Approaches to Bilingualism* 1, 2, 175–205.

STRINGER, DAVID. 2013. "Modifying the teaching of modifiers: A lesson from Universal Grammar," in MELINDA WHONG, KOOK-HEE GIL, and HEATHER MARSDEN (eds.): *Universal Grammar and the Second Language Classroom*, pp. 77–100. Dordrecht: Springer.

STROMSWOLD, KARIN. 1995. "The acquisition of subject and object questions," *Language Acquisition* 4, 5–48.

STROMSWOLD, KARIN. 1996. "Analyzing children's spontaneous speech," in DANA MCDANIEL, CECILE MCKEE, and HELEN SMITH CAIRNS, *Methods for Assessing Children's Syntax*, pp. 22–53. Cambridge, MA: MIT Press.

SUNDARA, MEGHA, KATHERINE DEMUTH, and PATRICIA KUHL. 2011. "Sentence-position effects on children's perception and production of English third person singular -s," *Journal of Speech, Language, and Hearing Research* 54, 55–71.

TAFT, M and KENNETH FORSTER. 1975. "Lexical storage and retrieval for prefixed words," *Journal of Verbal Learning and Verbal Behavior*, 14, 638–647.

TALMY LEONARD. 1991. "Path to realization: A typology of event conflation," in *Proceedings of the 17th Annual Meeting of the Berkeley Linguistic Society*, pp. 480–519. Berkeley, CA: Berkeley Linguistic Society.

TALMY, LEONARD. 2000. *Toward a Cognitive Semantics*, two volumes. Cambridge, MA: MIT Press.

TANNER, DARREN and JANET G. VAN HELL. 2014. "ERPs reveal individual differences in morphosyntactic processing," *Neuropsychologia* 56, 289–301.

TANNER, DARREN, JUDITH MCLAUGHLIN, JULIA HERSCHENSOHN, and LEE OSTERHOUT. 2013. "Individual differences reveal stages of L2 grammatical acquisition: ERP evidence," *Bilingualism: Language and Cognition*, 16, 367–382.

THIERRY, GUILLAUME and EIRINI SANOUDAKI. 2012. "Activation syntaxique non-sélective à la langue chez le bilingue précoce," *Revue Française de Linguistique Appliquée*, http://www.cairn.info/resume.php?ID–ARTICLE= RFLA–172–0033.

THOMAS, MARGARET. 1989. "The acquisition of English articles by first- and second-language learners," *Applied Psycholinguistics* 10, 335–355.

THORDARDOTTIR, ELIN. 2015. "The relationship between bilingual exposure and morphosyntactic development," *International Journal of Speech-Language Pathology* 17, 2, 97–114. doi:10.3109/17549507.2014.923509.

THORNTON, ROSALIND. 1990. *Adventures in Long-Distance Moving: The Acquisition of Complex Wh-questions*. Ph.D. thesis, University of Connecticut.

TOKOWICZ, NATASHA. 2014. *Lexical Processing and Second Language Acquisition*. Routledge.

TRAHEY, MARTHA and LYDIA WHITE. 1993. "Positive evidence and preemption in the second language classroom," *Studies in Second Language Acquisition* 15, 181–204.

TRAN, JENNIE. 2005a. "Verb position and verb form in English-speaking children's L2 acquisition of German," *Proceedings of the Annual Boston University Conference on Language Development* 29, 592–603.

TRAN, JENNIE. 2005b. "Word order and verb inflection in English-speaking children's L2 acquisition of German V2," *University of Hawai'i Working Papers in Linguistics* 36, 1–33.

TRAVIS, LISA DE MENA. 1984. *Parameters and Effects of Word Order Variation*. Ph.D. thesis, MIT, Cambridge MA.

TRAXLER, MATTHEW. 2012. *Introduction to Psycholinguistics: Understanding Language Science*. Chichester, UK: Wiley-Blackwell.

TRENKIC, DANIJELA. 2008. "The representation of English articles in second language grammars: Determiners or adjectives?", *Bilingualism: Language and Cognition* 11, 1, 1–18.

TRUESWELL, JOHN C., MICHAEL K. TANENHAUS, and SUSAN M. GARNSEY. 1994. "Semantic Influences on parsing: use of thematic role information in syntactic ambiguity resolution," *Journal of Memory and Language* 33, 285–318. doi:10.1006/jmla.1994.1014.

TRUSCOTT, JOHN and MIKE SHARWOOD SMITH. 2004. "Acquisition by processing: A modular approach to language development," *Bilingualism: Language and Cognition* 7, 1–20.

TRYZNA, MARTHA. 2009. "Questioning the validity of the Article Choice Parameter and the Fluctuation Hypothesis: Evidence from L2 English article use by L1 Polish and L1 Mandarin Chinese speakers," in MARÍA DEL PILAR GARCÍA MAYO and ROGER HAWKINS (eds.), *Second*

Language Acquisition of Articles: Empirical Findings and Theoretical Implications, pp. 67–86. Amsterdam: John Benjamins.

TSIMPLI, IANTHI MARIA and M. DIMITRAKOPOULOU. 2007. "The Interpretability Hypothesis: Evidence from wh-interrogatives in second language acquisition," *Second Language Research* 23, 215–242. doi:10.1177/0267658307076546.

TSIMPLI, IANTHI MARIA and ANTONELLA SORACE. 2006. "Differentiating interfaces: L2 performance in syntax–semantics and syntax–discourse phenomena," in D. BAMMAN, T. MAGNITSKAIA and C. ZALLER (eds.), *Proceedings of the 30th Annual Boston University Conference on Language Development, BUCLD 30*, pp. 653–664. Somerville, MA: Cascadilla Press.

TSIMPLI, IANTHI MARIA, ANTONELLA SORACE, CAROLINE HEYCOCK, and FRANCESCA FILIACI, F. 2004. "First language attrition and syntactic subjects: A study of Greek and Italian near-native speakers of English," *International Journal of Bilingualism* 8, 257–277.

TUCKER, RICHARD. 1999. "A global perspective on bilingualism and bilingual education," in JAMES E. ALATIS and AI-HUI TAN (eds.), *Georgetown University Round Table on Languages and Linguistics (GURT 1999): Language in Our Time: Bilingual Education and Official English, Ebonics, and Standard English*, pp. 332–340. Washington, D.C.: Georgetown University Press. http://www.cal.org/resources/Digest/digestglobal.html.

ULLMAN, MICHAEL T. 2001. "The neural basis of lexicon and grammar in first and second language: The declarative/procedural model," *Bilingualism: Language and Cognition* 4, 2, 105–122.

ULLMAN, MICHAEL T. 2004. "Contributions of memory circuits to language: The declarative/procedural model," *Cognition* 92, 1, 231–270.

UNSWORTH, SHARON. 2005. *Child L2, Adult L2, Child L1: Differences and Similarities: A Study on the Acquisition of Direct Object Scrambling in Dutch*. Ph.D. thesis, Utrecht University. doi:10.1080/10489220701353891.

UNSWORTH, SHARON. 2008a. "Age and input in the acquisition of grammatical gender in Dutch," *Second Language Research* 24, 365–396.

UNSWORTH, SHARON. 2008b. "Comparing child L2 development with adult L2 development: How to measure L2 proficiency," in GAVRUSEVA, E. and B. HAZNEDAR (eds.), *Current Trends in Child Second Language Acquisition*, pp. 301–336. Amsterdam: John Benjamins.

URIAGEREKA, JUAN. 1999. "Multiple Spell-Out," in SAMUEL D. EPSTEIN, and NORBERT HORNSTEIN (eds.), *Working Minimalism*, pp. 251–282. Cambridge, MA: MIT Press.

URIAGEREKA, JUAN. 2012. *Spell-Out and the Minimalist Program*. Oxford: Oxford University Press.

VAINIKKA ANNE and MARTHA YOUNG-SCHOLTEN. 1994. "Direct access to X'-theory: Evidence from Korean and Turkish adults learning German." in TEUN HOEKSTRA and BONNIE D. SCHWARTZ (eds.), *Language Acquisition Studies in Generative Grammar*, pp. 265–316. Amsterdam: John Benjamins.

VAINIKKA, ANNE and MARTHA YOUNG-SCHOLTEN. 1996. "Gradual Development of L2 Phrase Structure." *Second Language Research* 12, 1, 7–39. doi:10.1177/026765839601200102.

VAINIKKA, ANNE and MARTHA YOUNG-SCHOLTEN. 2013. "Universal minimal structure," *Linguistic Approaches to Bilingualism* 3, 2, 180–212.

VALENZUELA, ELENA. 2005. *L2 Ultimate Attainment and the Syntax–Discourse Interface: The Acquisition of Topic Constructions in Non-native Spanish and English.* Ph.D. thesis, McGill University.

VALENZUELA, ELENA. 2006. "L2 end state grammars and incomplete acquisition of the Spanish CLLD constructions," in ROUMYANA SLABAKOVA, SILVINA MONTRUL and PHILIPPE PRÉVOST (eds.), *Inquiries in Linguistic Development: In Honor of Lydia White*, pp. 283–304. Amsterdam: John Benjamins.

VAN ASSCHE, E., W. DUYCK, R. J. HARTSUIKER, and K. DIEPENDAELE. 2009. "Does bilingualism change native-language reading? Cognate effects in a sentence context," *Psychological Science* 20, 923–927.

VAN DER LELY, HEATHER K. J., MELANIE JONES, CHLOE R. MARSHALL. 2011. "Who did Buzz see someone? Grammaticality judgement of wh-questions in typically developing children and children with Grammatical-SLI," *Lingua* 121, 408–422.

VAN GOMPEL, P. G. ROGER, MARTIN PICKERING, and MATTHEW TRAXLER. 2000. "Unrestricted race: A new model of syntactic ambiguity resolution," in A. KENNEDY (ed.), *Reading as a Perceptual Process*, pp. 621–648. Amsterdam: Elsevier.

VAN GOMPEL, P. G. ROGER, MARTIN PICKERING, J. PEARSON, and SIMON LIVERSEDGE. 2005. "Evidence against competition during syntactic ambiguity resolution," *Journal of Memory and Language* 52, 284–307.

VAN HEUVEN, J. B. WALTER, TON DIJKSTRA, and JONATHAN GRAINGER. 1998. "Orthographic neighborhood effects in bilingual word recognition," *Journal of Memory and Language* 39, 3, 458–483. doi:10.1006/jmla.1998.2584.

VAN HEUVEN, J. B. WALTER, H. SCHRIEFERS, TON DIJKSTRA, and PETER HAGOORT. 2008. "Language conflict in the bilingual brain," *Cerebral Cortex* 18, 2706–2716.

VAN HOUT, ANGELIEK. 2005. "Imperfect imperfectives: On the acquisition of aspect in Polish," in PAULA KEMPCHINSKY and ROUMYANA SLABAKOVA (eds.), *Aspectual Inquiries*. Dordrecht: Springer. 317–344.

VANPATTEN, BILL. 1996. *Input Processing and Grammar Instruction in Second Language Acquisition.* Norwood, NJ: Ablex.

VANPATTEN, BILL. 2002a. "Processing Instruction: An Update," *Language Learning* 52, 4, 755–803. doi:10.1111/1467-9922.00203.

VANPATTEN, BILL. 2002b. "Processing the content of input processing and processing instruction research: A response to DeKeyser, Salaberry, Robinson and Harrington," *Language Learning* 52, 825–831.

VANPATTEN, BILL (ed.). 2004. *Processing Instruction: Theory, Research, and Commentary*. Mahwah, New Jersey: Lawrence Erlbaum.

VANPATTEN, BILL. 2007. "Processing instruction," in CRISTINA SANZ (ed.), *Mind and Context in Adult Second Language Acquisition*, pp. 267–281. Washington DC: Georgetown University Press.

VANPATTEN, BILL and TERESA CADIERNO. 1993. "Explicit instruction and input processing," *Studies in Second Language Acquisition*, 15, 225–241. doi:10.1017/S0272263100011979.

VANPATTEN, BILL and JILL JEGERSKI. (eds.). 2010. *Research in Second Language Processing and Parsing*. Philadelphia, PA: John Benjamins.

VANPATTEN, BILL, GREGORY D. KEATING and MICHAEL J. LEESER. 2012. "Missing verbal inflections as a representational problem," *Linguistic Approaches to Bilingualism* 2, 1, 109–140.

VANPATTEN, BILL and JASON ROTHMAN. 2014. "Against 'rules'," in ALESSANDRO BENATI, C. LAVAL, and MARIA ARCHE (eds.), *The Grammar Dimension in Instructed SLA: Theory, Research, and Practice*, pp. 15–35. London: Bloomsbury Press.

VANPATTEN, BILL and JESSICA WILLIAMS (eds.). 2015. *Theories in Second Language Acquisition: An Introduction*. New York and London: Routledge.

WAGNER-GOUGH, J. and E. HATCH. 1975. "The importance of input data in second language acquisition studies," *Language Learning*, 25, 297–308.

WAHLSTROM MCKAY, LOUISE. 2001. *The Acquisition and Use of Verb-second Structures by Second Language Learners of German*. Unpublished Ph.D. dissertation, University of Iowa.

WAKABAYASHI, SHIGENORI. 2002. "The acquisition of non-null subjects in English: A Minimalist account." *Second Language Research* 18, 1, 28–71. doi:10.1191/0267658302sr197oa.

WARTENBURGER, ISABELL, HAUKE R. HEEKEREN, JUBIN ABUTALEBI, STEPHANO F. CAPPA, ARNO VILLRINGER, and DANIELA PERANI. 2003. "Early Setting of Grammatical Processing in the Bilingual Brain," *Neuron* 37, 1, 159–170. doi:10.1016/S0896-6273(02)01150-9.

WEBER-FOX, CARA M. and HELEN J. NEVILLE. 1996. "Maturational constraints on functional specializations for language processing: ERP and behavioral evidence in bilingual speakers," *Journal of Cognitive Neuroscience* 8, 231–56.

WEBER, ANDREA and ODETTE SCHARENBORG. 2012. "Models of spoken-word recognition," *WIREs Cognitive Science* 3, 387–401. doi:10.1002/wcs.1178.

WEERMAN, FRED. 2002. *Dynamiek in Taal en de Explosie van de Neerlandistiek [Dynamics in Language and the Explosion of Dutch]*. Booklet for inaugural professorial lecture. Amsterdam: University of Amsterdam. English translation by Sharon Unsworth, cited in Schwartz (2009).

WELLS, J. B., M. H. CHRISTIANSEN, D. S. RACE, D. J. ACHESON, and M. C. MACDONALD. 2009. "Experience and sentence processing: Statistical learning and relative clause comprehension," *Cognitive Psychology*, 58, 250–271. doi:10.1016/j.cogpsych.2008.08.002.

WERKER, JANET F. and RICHARD C. TEES. 1984. "Cross-language speech perception: Evidence for perceptual reorganization in the first year of life," *Infant Behavior and Development* 7, 49–63.

WHITE, LYDIA. 1985. "The pro-drop parameter in adult second language acquisition," *Language Learning* 35, 47–62.

WHITE, LYDIA. 1987. "Markedness and second language acquisition: The question of transfer," *Studies in Second Language Acquisition* 9, 261–286.

WHITE, LYDIA. 1989. *Universal Grammar and Second Language Acquisition.* Amsterdam: John Benjamins.

WHITE, LYDIA. 1990. "The Verb Movement Parameter in second language acquisition," *Language Acquisition* 1, 2, 337–360. doi:10.1207/s15327817la0104–2.

WHITE, LYDIA. 1991. "Adverb placement in second language acquisition: Some effects of positive and negative evidence in the classroom," *Second Language Research* 7, 133–161.

WHITE, LYDIA. 1992. "Long and short verb movement in second language acquisition," *Canadian Journal of Linguistics* 37, 273–286.

WHITE, LYDIA. 2003. *Second Language Acquisition and Universal Grammar.* Cambridge: Cambridge University Press.

WHITE, LYDIA. 2009. "Grammatical theory: Interfaces and L2 knowledge," in W. C. RITCHIE, T. K. BHATIA (eds.), *The New Handbook of Second Language Acquisition*, pp. 49–65. Bingley: Emerald Group Publishing, Ltd.

WHITE, LYDIA. 2011. "The interface hypothesis: how far does it extend?", *Linguistic Approaches to Bilingualism* 1, 108–110.

WHITE, LYDIA and ALAN JUFFS. 1998. "Constraints on *wh*-movement in two different contexts of non-native language acquisition: Competence and processing," in SUZANNE FLYNN, GITA MARTOHARDJONO and WAYNE O'NEILL (eds.), *The Generative Study of Second Language Acquisition,* pp. 111–129. Mahwah, NJ: Erlbaum.

WHITE, LYDIA, NINA SPADA, PATSY M. LIGHTBOWN, and LEILA RANTA. 1991. "Input enhancement and L2 question formation," *Applied Linguistics* 12, 416–432.

WHONG, MELINDA. 2011. *Language Teaching: Linguistic Theory in Practice.* Edinburgh University Press.

WHONG MELINDA, KOOK-HEE GIL, and HEATHER MARSDEN (eds.). 2013. *Universal Grammar and the Second Language Classroom.* Dordrecht: Springer.

WHONG-BARR, MELINDA and BONNIE D. SCHWARTZ. 2002. "Morphological and syntactic transfer in child L2 acquisition of the English dative alternation," *Studies in Second Language Acquisition*, 24, 579–616.

WIDDOWSON, HENRY. 2000. "Object language and the language subject: On the mediating role of applied linguistics," *Annual Review of Applied Linguistics* 20, 21–33.

WILHELM, ANDREA and KEN HANNA. 1992. "On the acquisition of wh-questions," *Calgary Working Papers in Linguistics* 15, 89–98.

WILSON, FRANCIS, ANTONELLA SORACE, and FRANK KELLER. 2009. "Simulating L2 learners' deficits at the syntax–discourse interface in native speakers." Talk presented at the International Symposium on Bilingualism 7, Utrecht.

WILTSCHKO, MARTINA. 2014. *The Universal Structure of Categories: Towards a Formal Typology.* Cambridge: Cambridge University Press.

YANG, CHARLES. 2002. *Knowledge and Learning in Natural Language.* Oxford University Press.

YANG, CHARLES. 2003. *Knowledge and Learning in Natural Language.* Oxford: Oxford University Press.

YANG, CHARLES. 2004. "Universal Grammar, statistics, or both?", *Trends in Cognitive Sciences* 8, 10, 451–456. doi:10.1016/j.tics.2004.08.006.

YANG, CHARLES. 2006. *The Infinite Gift: How Children Learn and Unlearn the Languages of the World.* New York, NY: Scribner.

YANG, CHARLES. 2010. "Three factors in language variation," *Lingua* 120 (5), 1160–1177. doi:10.1016/j.lingua.2008.09.015.

YENI-KOMSHIAN, GRACE, JAMES FLEGE, and SERENA LIU. 2000. "Pronunciation proficiency in the first and second languages of Korean-English bilinguals," *Bilingualism: Language and Cognition* 3, 2, 131–149.

YENI-KOMSHIAN, GRACE, MEDINA ROBBINS, and JAMES FLEGE. 2001. "Effects of word class differences on L2 pronunciation accuracy," *Applied Psycholinguistics* 22, 03, 283–299.

YOSHINAGA, NAOKO. 1996. *Wh-questions: A Comparative Study of their Form and Acquisition in Japanese.* Unpublished Ph.D. thesis, University of Hawaii at Manoa.

YUAN, BOPING. 1993. *Directionality of Difficulty in Second Language Acquisition of Chinese and English.* Unpublished Ph.D. thesis, University of Edinburgh, UK.

ZHAO, LUCY XIA. 2012. "English-speaking learners Interpretation of Chinese overt and null embedded arguments by English-speaking learners," *Second Language Research* 28, 2, 169–190.

ZUBIZARRETA, MARÍA LUISA. 1998. *Focus, Prosody, and Word Order.* MIT Press: Cambridge, MA.

ZUBIZARRETA, MARÍA LUISA, and EMILY NAVA. 2011. "Encoding discourse-based meaning: Prosody vs. Syntax: Implications for second language acquisition," *Lingua* 121, 4, 652–669. doi:10.1016/j.lingua.2010.06.013.

Index